Other Books by Tom Lea

THE BRAVE BULLS

THE WONDERFUL COUNTRY

THE KING RANCH

VOLUME TWO

THE KING RANCH

BY

TOM LEA, 1907-

MAP AND DRAWINGS BY THE AUTHOR

RESEARCH

HOLLAND McCOMBS

ANNOTATION

FRANCIS L. FUGATE

BOSTON : LITTLE, BROWN AND COMPANY : TORONTO

Published simultaneously in Canada
by Little, Brown & Company (Canada) Limited

PRINTED IN THE UNITED STATES OF AMERICA

CHAPTERS

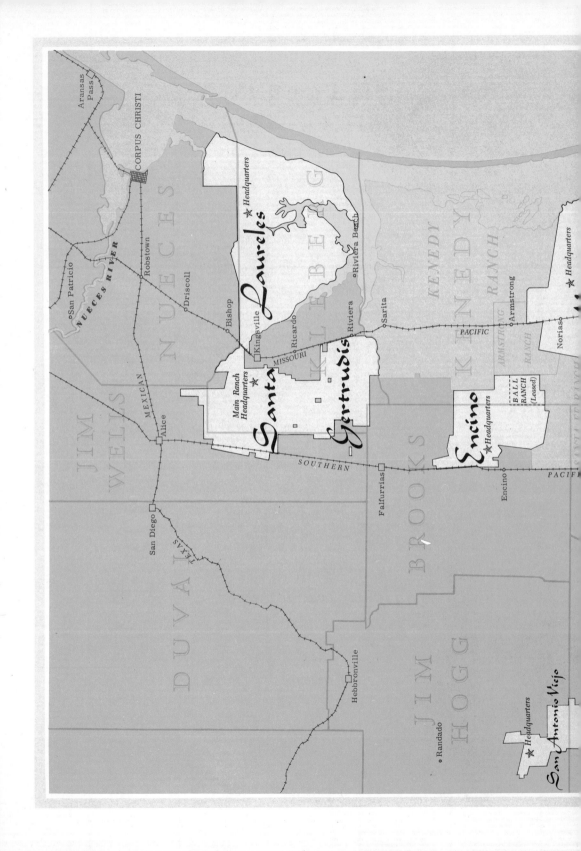

MAP OF THE COASTAL REGION
BETWEEN THE RIO GRANDE AND THE NUECES
SHOWING THE

KING RANCH

IN ITS CENTENNIAL YEAR 1953

SCALE, *approximately: One inch equals 15 miles*

ILLUSTRATIONS
DRAWINGS

FACSIMILES

1885-1953

XIII "The Same as I Might Do"

IT WAS THE FAITHFUL

friend Mifflin Kenedy who took charge of the King family's journey homeward from San Antonio and of affairs at the ranch during the first days after the sorrowing widow returned to the Santa Gertrudis. In her bereavement Henrietta King turned gratefully toward Kenedy: she saw him as the living link to treasured times shared so long with Richard King, times now past. Alice remained with her mother at the ranch house, attended often by Alice's fiancé Robert Kleberg, by a host of family friends, and by the *Kineños*. Richard King II returned to the nearby Agua Dulce; Ella King Welton went with her husband to St. Louis. Without the captain who had created it, the great ranch with its white house on the rise above the prairie seemed stripped of vitality. It faced new times. It sought a hand to guide it.

The captain had known whose hand was suited for the work. He had expressed his faith by the terms of his will, bequeathing everything to his wife "to be by her used and disposed of precisely the same as I myself might do were I living."

Henrietta King nourished the duty implied by these words. She understood it as a protraction of the effort she had shared with Richard King for thirty years: she would ranch as her husband had ranched. No other thought seems to have occurred to her. During the first months of her widowhood, seeking an antidote for her loneliness in her responsibility, she copied out a credo and pasted the written words upon a page of the scrapbook she kept:

> *What I Live For*
> I live for those who love me
> For all human ties that bind me
> For the good that I may do.[1]

There can be little doubt that during Richard King's final illness the captain and his wife privately discussed their regard for and confidence in the 31-year-old lawyer who was devoting his practice to the ranch's business. There is every reason to believe that they had agreed upon his promise not only as a son-in-law but as a most likely candidate for the wise administration of the manifold affairs and ranching works at the Santa Gertrudis. Shortly after her return from San Antonio, the widowed Henrietta King appointed Robert Justus Kleberg her Ranch Manager, to carry on as the captain had hoped, "as I myself might do were I living."

By the terms of the will, there were to be three executors of the estate: Henrietta M. King, Mifflin Kenedy, and the Corpus Christi banker and long-time friend, Perry Doddridge. Nine days after the captain's death, the Corpus Christi law firm of Stayton & Kleberg filed application to probate the will and it was recorded in Volume F, pages 13 and 14, of the Probate Minutes of Nueces County. On August 4, 1885, a court order admitting the will to probate was recorded in the same Minutes.[2] Sometime between April and August, Kenedy and Doddridge decided not to encumber the administration of the will by becoming joint executors with Mrs. King, a decision evidently occasioned by their opinion that in Manager Kleberg, Mrs. King had adequate aid for the settlement of the estate. Accordingly, Kenedy and Doddridge declined to qualify as executors, "thinking the interest of said estate to be best subserved thereby," and the court order of August 4 recorded the oath and issued letters testamentary to *Henrietta M. King, Sole Executrix.*[3]

Three appraisers of the estate were appointed by court order. A glance at their names makes it clear that all three were intimately acquainted with the ranch's affairs: Captain King's office manager, bookkeeper and amanuensis, Reuben Holbein, and John S. Greer and Thomas Beynon,[4] both ranch foremen and herd bosses on King cattle drives to Kansas. Their official appraisal estimated the value of the property being transferred to the sole beneficiary of the will: $564,784 worth of real estate, $496,700 worth of livestock and other property, making a total of $1,061,484.[5]

On the other side of the ledger, Richard King was in debt at the time of his death. It has been written repeatedly, so that it has become a kind of legend in round numbers, that King left his widow half a million acres along with half a million dollars debt. The legend is substantially correct, although the data to show the exact indebtedness cannot now be assembled. There are definite records of notes for $10,000 owed to Francisco Ytúrria and to William Kelly; there were other debts in varying amounts, some of them large, owed to Thomas Carson who represented the Stillman interests in Brownsville, Artemus Brown, José San Roman, the surveyor J. J. Cocke, the lawyer James B. Wells, and many accounts payable such as those owed William Headin, N. Gussett of Corpus Christi, and other houses with whom the ranch did business.[6]

Manager of Mrs. King's entire property and aide in the process of transferring this property to her hands, Robert Kleberg went to work at a massive task. As the business representative of the estate, writing to the lawyer for the estate, Kleberg outlined a plan of operation in a letter to "Friend James" B. Wells. He asked Wells for a copy of the "tax list of Capt. King for this year" and to "make out an inventory of his entire estate at the earliest possible time.... I apprehend but little trouble in setting up the estate as those who know Mrs. King will hardly object to her in place of Capt. King." Explaining his projected mode of procedure to Wells he wrote, "Let Mrs. King assume all the indebtedness of her husband—in other words let her step in his place....Everyone here that I have suggested this matter to is more than willing to do this—Mr. Gussett said certainly. I will just transfer my account which I held against Capt. King against her now and settle with her and everyone else here that I have approached is willing to do this. Mrs. King's obligations will be equally as good as her husband's—I wish you would see Mr. Brown and ask him if this will suit him. Also see Mr. J. J. Cocke—and Mr. Ytúrria—and ask them to accept Mrs. King in place of her husband in the settlement of their accounts... Let Mrs. King give her note instead of that given by the Captain." The debts incurred by the acquisition of *derechos* in the San Juan de Carricitos grant would be paid off: "Just take Mrs. King in the place of her husband—and be sure to make out an itemized account of your transactions just as soon as you can—Now do not fail to see to these matters at your earliest convenience and *do not fail* to answer this letter *promptly* direct to me at Collins—care of Mrs. H. M. King and believe me as ever your friend. R. J. Kleberg.'"[7]

An example of the actual mode of the transfer of Captain King's obligations to the continuing management of "King's Rancho, Santa Gertrudis," may be seen in a later letter from Kleberg to Wells, October 22, 1885:

Inclosed please find Mrs. H. M. Kings note for $10,000.00 payable to order of Wm. Kelly of Brownsville—this note is given in exchange of original note given by R. King to secure payment of purchase money due on Custom House Building—Note due April 1st 1885—Capt. King in settlement of this note gave his renewal note per same amt. payable to same party on or before April 1st 1887, both of these notes are in the hands of one Henry Charnock of N. O. La. who has agreed to surrender same upon receipt of the inclosed note, which is given in lieu of same—and which you will please deliver to Mr. Kelly or whoever delivers to you the original note or notes executed by the late Capt. R. King.[8]

Procedures for the settlement of the estate moved without obstruction or contestation. In due course, the sole executrix of the estate of Richard King became the sole proprietress of the ranch on the Santa Gertrudis and of all its dependent interests. The last of the debts of the estate appear to have been cleared from the books within ten years following the captain's death.

Settlement of the terms of a comparatively simple Last Will and Testament was a concern of Lawyer Kleberg working with Lawyer Wells. Beyond this was a far more complicated concern, for which Lawyer Kleberg by training and experience was far less prepared. It was necessary for him to fill the ranching boots of Richard King.

Only a few weeks after the death of the captain, the great western cattle boom of the early 1880's collapsed, leaving land and livestock prices depressed and uncertain for a decade. Added to the difficulties of a poor market in the first years of Kleberg's tenure as ranch manager, were the hardships of a drought that plagued the Santa Gertrudis area almost continuously from 1886 until 1893. Kleberg displayed faith in the ranch and confidence in himself as its director. With what appears to have been an unrelenting attention to every detail of a stockman's work, he set himself to learn what he did not know about practical ranching in South Texas, determined not merely to maintain the Santa Gertrudis as a great livestock operation but to extend and develop it further.

The confidence, the tenacity, the vigor that characterized him must be viewed in the light of the family and the background from which he sprang.

His father before him also bore the name Robert Justus Kleberg. Son of Lucas Kleberg, a merchant of Herstelle, Westphalia, this first Robert was born at Herstelle in 1803[9] and was educated at the University of Goettingen, graduating with a degree of *doctor juris*. When he had already embarked upon a promising career in the law, serving among other appointments as a young justice in the assizes of Nieheim, he abruptly made up his mind to emigrate to America. Explaining it later, he wrote, "I wished to live under a Republican form of government, with unbounded personal, religious and political liberty, free from the petty tyrannies, the many disadvantages and evils of old countries. Prussia, my former home, smarted at the time under a military despotism."[10]

There appears to have been additional reason for the young Judge Kleberg's decision to emigrate. He was engaged to be married to a young woman of the Prussian minor nobility, Rosalie von Roeder, whose brothers had been his schoolmates at Goettingen. The entire von Roeder family, consisting of the father and mother, six sons and four daughters, had planned a move to the New World and had decided upon Texas for their future home. The young judge decided to go with them. Four members of the family embarked in the spring of 1834 as an advance party to prepare for the arrival of the others. On September 4, 1834, Robert Justus Kleberg I married Rosalie von Roeder and on the last day of that month he and his bride, accompanied by the remaining members of the von Roeder family, sailed for Austin's colony.

After a passage of sixty rough days by sea to New Orleans and eight more days of sailing for Brazoria on the Texas coast, the emigrants were shipwrecked off Galveston Island three days before Christmas, 1834. Following months of hardship, by September of 1835 the von Roeder party managed to build two log houses and clear ten acres of land, to achieve a little wilderness settlement near Harrisburg in primitive Texas.

In the Texan struggle for independence from Mexico during the spring of 1836, the Klebergs and von Roeders were forced to abandon their hard-won settlement and to lose most of their possessions in the famed "Runaway Scrape" before the advancing army of Santa Anna. The elder von Roeder and some of his sons accompanied the family's womenfolk to give them protection in flight, while Robert Kleberg and two of his brothers-in-law joined the company of Captain Mosely Baker to fight as privates in the Texan army. At the battle of San Jacinto the young judge from Germany distinguished himself by his bravery; after the victory he was one of three trusted men Houston selected to guard the captured Santa Anna. Kleberg then took part in the marches of the Texan force which harried the defeated Mexican army south to a recrossing of the Rio Grande.

When the fighting was done, Kleberg and his wife Rosalie settled at Cat Spring in Austin County and later moved to another German settlement in DeWitt County, near Meyersville. The Republic of

Texas quickly recognized its able citizen Kleberg. In 1837 Sam Houston appointed him to the Land Commission; he became the Commission's president in 1838. Four years later, Mirabeau Lamar made Kleberg a Justice of Austin County; in 1846 he became County Judge of DeWitt County. One of the earliest and one of the most prominent of the Germans who contributed to the history of Texas, he held public office and public esteem for the remainder of his long life.

A reader of classic Greek and Latin and conversant in three modern languages, the scholarly Judge Kleberg was at the same time a robust pioneer who could and did work as energetically with his strong body as with his able mind. His aristocratic wife, gifted as a musician, was as remarkably able and vigorous as he. She not only adapted herself to the privation and the toil necessary to a pioneer woman's life, she found lifelong pride and joy in it. She bore her husband four daughters and four sons. One son, Otto, died in 1880; the other three, Rudolph, Marcellus and Robert, became Texan lawyers and citizens as eminent as their father. Rudolph practiced law in Cuero, served as United States District Attorney in San Antonio and as a member of Congress in Washington from 1896 to 1903. Marcellus, with law offices at Galveston, was one of the state's most prominent legislators; he also held a number of municipal positions in Galveston and was a regent of the University of Texas.

Their young brother, Robert Justus II, had been born on the family farm near Meyersville on December 5, 1853. He had grown up a country boy, disciplined son of a closely knit German family and hard worker at farm chores. He was barely eight when his eldest brother Otto rode away to fight for the South in the Civil War. Three years later when his brother Rudolph was old enough to join the Confederate forces, Robert and his fifteen-year-old brother Marcellus were left with most of the responsibility of providing for

and protecting their mother and sisters during wartime on the isolated farm: Judge Kleberg, sixty years of age and unable to serve in
the army, was occupied with civilian duties for the Confederacy and
was often away from his family.[11]

Robert had gone to neighborhood schools and then to a local
institution attended mostly by young Germans of the neighborhood, Concrete College, near the present town of Wharton. When
he had finished the courses there he had become a country school-
teacher himself, until he ran for and was elected to the county clerk-
ship of DeWitt County. While supporting himself by this means he
had read history and law in the office and under the tutelage of John
W. Stayton, later Chief Justice of the Supreme Court of Texas. In
pursuing his reading, the ambitious young Kleberg decided that he
must acquire like his father and his elder brothers a better education
if he would be prepared for a career in law. The funds enabling him
to attend a university came to him in a most unusual way.

His mother was the grandniece of a German nobleman deceased in
1791, Simon Heinrich Sack, of Glogau in Silesia, royal attorney
general and the possessor of a large fortune. He had bequeathed this
fortune in the form of a family trust fund in perpetuity, the proceeds
of which were to be distributed to the descendants of the Sack
family, wherever they might be, in the form of dowries to the
daughters, scholarships to the sons, and benefits to the widows and
orphans. The portion received by each of the many qualified Sack
descendants appears to have been the equivalent of about five hundred dollars.

The youngest brother of Simon Heinrich Sack was a distinguished
soldier, Philipp Wilhelm Sack, who is said to have saved the life of
Frederick the Great on a field of battle in the Seven Years War, and
to have been rewarded by Frederick with the tenancy of a royal
estate, *Der Rote Hof*,[12] with its old castle Hausberg, at Minden, where

Philipp Wilhelm resided as a landlord and a Royal Counsellor. His third daughter, Caroline Louise Sack, had married the nobleman Anton Sigismund von Roeder, orderly to the Duke of Braunschweig. Rosalie von Roeder was the ninth child of this union of Sacks and von Roeders; her sons were descendants clearly qualified for Sack scholarships. Upon application by correspondence to Germany, the young County Clerk of DeWitt County, Texas, received his grant, his legacy from a regime his family had left forever, which furnished him with the principal means to attend the University of Virginia and to receive a law degree there in 1880.[13]

The 27-year-old Robert Justus Kleberg had been admitted to the Texas Bar in 1881 and had entered the law firm of Stayton & Lackey at Cuero, county seat of DeWitt County. A few months later he had moved to Corpus Christi to hang out the shingle of Stayton & Kleberg, which was in effect a branch office of the Cuero firm.

It is certain that when Richard King put Robert Kleberg on retainer at Corpus Christi, the captain was well acquainted with the venerable Texan patriot, Judge Kleberg of Meyersville, with the lawyer and state legislator, Marcellus Kleberg of Galveston, and with the equally prominent lawyer and politician Rudolph Kleberg of Cuero and San Antonio — whose partner was Congressman William Henry Crain, intimate political and personal friend of James B. Wells. The young attorney who became manager of "King's Rancho" in 1885 had by no means entered upon the scene as a lone hand from a background of obscurity.

Son of a San Jacinto hero, member of an intellectually and physically vigorous family whose fortune resided not in cash but in character, Robert Justus Kleberg II displayed the strong traits of his heritage. His Prussian mettle, with its scientific bent, its passion for orderly method, appears not to have been too heavily encumbered with opinionated didacticism, that is, with squareheadedness. In the well-ordered space of Kleberg's mind he found room for honest self-appraisal as well as honest self-esteem. This quality, blended with a naturally sanguine temperament and a noticeable streak of sentimentality toward all things dear to him, gave warmth to his personality and made him effective—in spite of his actual inexperience—as administrator of the business affairs he encountered at the ranch on the Santa Gertrudis.

Within months, it was evident to all concerned that these affairs were being well directed. A finely weighted yet a most enduring balance had already been struck between the managerial entities of Sole Proprietress King and Manager Kleberg for the continuing operation of the ranch. Mrs. King, as all her family always observed, was "the *boss* wherever she was," and yet Robert Kleberg would say at the end of his life, "I like to think that in those nearly forty years the only instruction she ever gave was to do what I ought to do and tell her what she ought to do. And, when I told her, her reply would be, 'You know best'." It was a delicate yet stable adjustment between deference on the one hand and trust upon the other.

Business was only one concern in the growing and engrossing relationship of Robert Kleberg with the family of Richard King. In the spring of 1886, after the elapse of a proper interval following the captain's death, Alice Gertrudis King and the busy manager of her mother's ranch began to make definite plans for a wedding. Mrs. King approved; with glad preparation a date was set for the ceremony at the ranch house on the Santa Gertrudis.

It was a private affair celebrated with modest decorum early on a June morning, at an hour evidently dictated by the long coach ride to meet the train schedule for departure, at Collins Station, on a wedding journey. The *Corpus Christi Caller* recorded:

Alice G. K. Kleberg.

KLEBERG-KING—At the residence of the bride's mother, Rancho Santa Gertrudis, Nueces County, Thursday June 17, 1886 at 6 a.m. by Rev. J.R. Howerton, of Corpus Christi, Mr. Robert Justus Kleberg to Miss Alice Gertrudis King. No cards.

The marriage was very quiet, only Capt. M. Kenedy and Mr. U. Lott, outside of members of the immediate family, being present. The newly wedded couple left at once for the train at Collins, accompanied by Mrs. King, Capt. Kenedy and Mr. Lott. Mrs. King, Mr. and Mrs. Kleberg will go North for a summer trip. The Caller extends its congratulations and many good wishes to the happy couple.

In the letter written October 12, 1884, asking Captain and Mrs. King for their daughter's hand, Robert Kleberg had declared that in his relationship to Alice "No one knows better than I do — how well her parents love her and how the declining days of their life are brightened by her presence and devotion — and I can well understand how hard it must be for them to reconcile themselves to the thought that she should divide that devotion with another. Rest assured therefore that I shall never have the heart to ask her to leave you against your consent or wish."

Mrs. King accompanied the Klebergs on their honeymoon.

When they had returned to the Santa Gertrudis later in that summer of 1886 the bride settled to a quietly domestic contentment in the house where she had been born, in the house where she now lived not only with her mother but with a beloved husband. The daily care and maintenance of the household had already, for half a decade, been chiefly Alice's responsibility. It became her joy, while she watched her husband carry forward the enterprise her father had created.

The vitality the ranch had lacked in the first weeks following the death of Richard King flowed back again through the person of Robert Kleberg. In bringing more method to King's livestock operation, Kleberg would not lack imagination. One had been the pioneer; the other would become "the developer, the builder, the experimenter, the expander."[14]

It was not work to accomplish in a day or a year: it was work for a long lifetime. When he assumed management, Kleberg took over direction of a going concern: he knew he was on trial, not only before Mrs. King, but before the ranch employees—about three hundred of them. He kept the payrolls, the personnel and the operation about as he found it, initiating few changes until he was sure of his ground. No range rider or stockman to begin with, Kleberg's control of the key figures of the business, the horseback men who worked the pastures, the cow camps and corrals, was necessarily through experienced foremen and straw bosses already on the ranch.

James M. Doughty, an old Texas stockman who had been one of King's foremen and herd bosses on the roads to Kansas, had been put in charge of the ranch during the captain's last illness. Kleberg retained Doughty as a personal assistant and superintendent of range work. Doughty brought in his son, A. C. "Mack" Doughty, and made him one of the foremen of the works around headquarters. In addition to the Doughtys as foremen, there were the two cow bosses, Ramón Alvarado, "a man of great confidence of the family," and the competent "Jap" Clark. There were the two expert horse bosses, Luís Robles and Julián Cantú; there was Jim Sedwick who worked the headquarters' "Little Pasture"; there was José María Alegría who had charge of the sheep. For the southern division, on the San Juan de Carricitos lands, the head boss was the dependable E. B. Raymond,[15] veteran foreman, friend and business agent of Captain King. With Raymond was the redoubtable George "Josh" Durham, cow camp boss and former McNelly Texas Ranger.

Working under men of this strong stamp were *Kineños* who continued to serve the captain's family with the same spirit they had served the captain. In any such patriarchal establishment as the Rancho Santa Gertrudis, the very personal regard and responsibility of the *patrón* on the one hand and the very personal faith and loyalty of the *gente* on the other were required basic ingredients for all "labor relations." New Manager Kleberg grasped this. When he arrived at the ranch he spoke no Spanish and had little knowledge of the ways that went with that tongue. He studied the language as a basic requirement of his job.[16] While he learned to know the brand of loyalty, of wisdom and skill in his brown-faced centaurs, they came to understand "the son-in-law of *La Madama*." Growing in their estimation, he achieved a title. The old captain they had called with a kind of wry affection, *"El Cojo."* They called their new *patrón*, with the same affectionate acidity, *"El Abogao,"* The Lawyer.

New hands—like the Augustín Quintanilla who became one of the greatest of *Kineños*—went to work for *El Abogao;* while the ranch families of Alegría, Alvarado, Barrientes, Cantú, Castañeda, Cavazos, de Luna, Flores, García, Garza, Gutierrez, Longoria, López, Mendietta, Montalbo, Muñoz, Pérez, Quintanilla, Rodriguez, Silguero, Silva, Treviño, Villareal and many others, furnished the range work which was the foundation upon which Manager Kleberg built a continuing enterprise. Those families and that foundation remain the same seventy years later. Robert Kleberg used to say, "You can't get along in any kind of business without loyalty between employees and employer." *Kineños* say now, when they are asked, that they work with the Klebergs, not for them.

The ranch office has preserved no records to show stock sales or income figures during the first several years of Kleberg's management. At that time, however, county hide and cattle inspectors were required to keep official and presumably complete tallies on all livestock transactions. Though figures for sales from the southern division of the ranch, in Cameron County, are lacking, there are some figures from the Nueces County inspectors' records and these would indicate surprisingly few sales from the Santa Gertrudis property during the years 1885 to 1889. The only sale of the ranch's cattle recorded for the whole year of 1885 is 1707 head, sold to J. C. Stevens on June 4, less than two months after Captain King's death—and there were *no* King's Rancho cattle sales recorded in Nueces County from that date until May 11, 1887. That year, 3817 head were sold in three lots; the following year only 1681 head, in small bunches, are listed as sold. The figures show an increase in 1889: by April 21, 4450 head of grown stock and 606 calves had been sold. These Nueces County records also indicate small sales of horses and mules from the Santa Gertrudis: in 1885, 747; in 1886, only 49; in 1887, 392; and up to April 21, 1888, just 178 head. Though these tallies must surely be incomplete, and are probably misleading, it is safe to conclude that Kleberg was not selling anything like the numbers of livestock the ranch must have had available for market at the time. Yet by the year 1895 the ranch was branding something like 30,000 calves annually; with such an increased burden to the pastures each season, it is unreasonable to suppose that Kleberg was not selling far larger numbers of livestock than are now recorded.[17]

There is no record that the ranch ever engaged in cattle drives to Kansas after the death of Captain King; from 1885 on the ranch shipped its livestock to market on nearby rails.[18] Whatever the market figures may have been, drought and calamitous prices were dictating most of Kleberg's moves. Though the years 1886 and 1887 did not bring severest drought to the Santa Gertrudis itself, lack of rainfall brought crisis to many western ranching areas, forcing huge numbers of gaunted cattle into a market which had already collapsed. Prices remained disastrous through 1892—range cattle were worth no more than about $5 a head—and the cycle of low rainfall continued, culminating in the extreme drought years of 1891 and 1892, called "the great die-up" and remembered as the most severe South Texas ever experienced.[19]

In 1892 the pastures on the Santa Gertrudis were so parched Kleberg found it necessary to ship 12,000 head of cattle to grass in the Indian Territory. A ranch hand recounted that during these times *Kineños* carried skinning knives to save the hides of the dead cattle found starved on the range; the hand recalled that he himself skinned over 700 cattle that had died of thirst, and that he had pulled more than 2000 head out of Caesar Creek: "They would come to the almost dried up holes there and get stuck in the mud and often stay there until they died." He remembered the piles of whitened bones on the prairies.[20]

Detailed facts and figures to depict Kleberg's handling of the ranch's problems during this bitterly hard period are simply non-existent. Only by the end result, the progress and expansion of the ranch which is clearly discernible, can we judge that this period of Kleberg's management was somehow successful financially.

Desire for a more methodical, more scientific approach to the problems of livestock breeding and handling, and definite steps to improve the quality of the herds, marked Kleberg's ranch management from the very beginning.

One of his first acts was to order the cleaning out of the big headquarters Santa Gertrudis breeding pasture which was enclosed by the board fence Captain King had built, and which was holding a great herd the captain had allowed to breed unmolested, largely unworked and unbranded, for several seasons.

Ramón Alvarado's cow camp, bossed by the Doughtys, found the cattle wild and dangerous to handle and the pasture choked with jungles of thorny brush. It took five sweating weeks to make a round-up across the entire enclosure; when it was done and the herds had been worked over, sorted and moved out, there were still bunches of the snuffiest cattle left in the brush, uncaught. Jap Clark's outfit joined Alvarado's cowboys to finish the job. In the roping and castrating of the wild bulls, horses were killed or hurt almost every day and one of the men, Juan Pérez, was gored. The vaquero Victor Alvarado recalled with relish the sport he and the brush poppers found with the bulls: "Seeing what would happen and seeing the necessity of doing so, all the young boys that formed the camp agreed to take lessons in cape work. Every day that we brought bulls for the pens, after work was over, we would cut out one bull, cut off his horns and put him in the pen. There we disputed the championship. In place of *capote* (fighting cape) we used to use canvas sacks, and in a short while we had converted ourselves into true Gaonas."[21]

A determined effort was made to rid the ranch of the largely worthless herds of mustangs that ran wild in the fenced pastures. The scrub horses had no relation to production for ranch use and sale; they only ate valuable grass and made it difficult to keep other livestock under control. The clearing of the mustangs from the ranch's pastures was a rough, difficult and highly picturesque procedure.

At the time, most of the wild horses on the Santa Gertrudis were accustomed to watering at a big pond called Tulosa Lake. Kleberg had his men build an immense trap, with one funnel-shaped entrance, around the entire lake. The enclosure was made by chopping down big mesquite trees and dragging them into place with their tops turned in, so that they created a formidable wall of wood and thorn around the watering place. When the trap was completed, and after the wild horses had been allowed to become thoroughly accustomed to passage through the funnel-shaped entrance, the opening was closed.

The first time this was done, an estimated 4000 head of mustangs were caught in the enclosure, probably as large a band of wild horses as has ever been caught anywhere at any one time.

Between fifty and sixty of the best vaqueros on the ranch were called together; they were confident they could handle the captured animals. When an attempt was made to move them from the trap, they immediately broke into a violent stampede. Kleberg, in recounting it later, said he was mounted that day on a very powerful horse and when he saw what was happening, he managed to get to the front of the break away and tried to stop it, swinging and lashing a big quirt with a loaded iron handle. The plunging mustangs paid no attention whatsoever, to him or to the other riders. All 4000 wild horses got away; it was six months before they were coming again to water at Tulosa Lake.

When the entrance to the trap was blocked the second time, more or less the same number of horses were caught again — and did not escape. Vaqueros entered the enclosure and began to drive the captured horses around and around, without rest. After ten days of continual driving, the mustangs were so weakened by lack of feed and rest that they were manageable. One whole train load of them was eventually shipped to Mississippi and Tennessee, where Kleberg traded them for a few head of well-bred, gentle horses.[22]

It took decades finally to eliminate outlaw horses and cattle from the ranch. An old hand there, Wesley Stevens, who trapped mustangs in the 1890's, answered the query, "Was it civilized in those days?" with "Well, it didn't seem so wild and woolly to us then, but if anybody now had to go back to living like they did then, I reckon about half of us couldn't stand it."

When Kleberg had cleaned out the big board-fenced pasture and made it ready for a program of improved livestock breeding by building barbed wire cross fences, the new pasture areas were all dictated by the available supply of water. Each enclosure of course demanded its water hole or well. In planning smaller, handier, better controlled pastures, Kleberg came to grips with the single most trying problem connected with the ranch: there were not water sources enough, nor were there prospects of enough. A letter he wrote on February 11, 1889, was a characteristic report: "Cattle are dying daily. I lost 150 cows in the Mula [pasture] last month on account of bad water. I have been trying to sink a well deep enough to pass the salt water and reach the good water. But while I am down with the well 460 feet in the Mula I have found nothing but water too salty for any use."[23]

Kleberg allowed no difficulty to interfere with his effort to improve the beef qualities of cattle on the ranch. Shortly after assuming ranch management, he bought a purebred Shorthorn bull from his superintendent James M. Doughty's ranch at Rockport and ordered his foreman to put the bull with a hundred top cows cut from the herds on the Santa Gertrudis. In the second year of his management, Kleberg began a systematic purchase of Shorthorn bull stock to place with chosen herds of range cows, intensifying the attempts at up-breeding which Captain King had begun more than a decade before and which had, on the whole, yielded no discernible improvement in the stock. Yet Kleberg was convinced that an infusion of good blood from a British breed must produce a worthwhile result if that infusion were strong and constant enough. Writing years later, his wife Alice recorded: "R. J. made a division of the cattle in 1886. Bulls [were] brought in from breeding farms in Texas, Kansas, Mississippi, Kentucky, Illinois . . . and Canada. He said, 'The best blood in the market is none too good for the Ranch'."[24]

In 1892 the 68-year-old James M. Doughty died and Kleberg sought a new chief foreman. He looked for more than a capable range boss. He wanted a stockman with the technical knowledge and the practical experience to supervise a long-term program for better livestock breeding at the Santa Gertrudis. Searching for the man, Kleberg consulted with his friend Jim Wells. Out of a wide acquaintance with the cattlemen of Texas, Wells astutely suggested Samuel G.

Ragland, a Texan from Victoria and Rockport who happened to be Kleberg's age, and who had already proved himself an outstanding livestock handler and superintendent for ranching interests at Carrizo Springs and Eagle Pass. Wells brought Kleberg and Ragland together; Ragland's advent as the new Livestock Manager at the Santa Gertrudis happily implemented Kleberg's drive for improved ranching methods. Sam Ragland became the range mentor of Manager Kleberg and, later, the counselor of Kleberg's sons. One of them would say of Ragland, "All of our knowledge of ranching successfully was acquired from him."[25]

Ragland's first act as an employee of the Santa Gertrudis was the expert delivery to the ranch of a herd of 1200 purebred Shorthorns which Kleberg bought from Jot Gunter of Grayson County.[26] Ragland himself took charge of a road outfit and drove the valuable animals — which were not like tough, iron-legged Longhorns — across the six hundred miles from the north edge of Texas to the Santa Gertrudis. "The fact that Mr. Ragland brought this herd of fine-bred animals across the State of Texas in good condition and without the loss of one of their number was made possible by his thorough knowledge and understanding of cattle. This performance eclipses any drive made from these parts to the Kansas railheads by the old trail drivers of the early days."[27]

By 1895, Kleberg and Ragland had "highly departmentalized" the ranch's livestock production. Its most profitable single department was horse and mule breeding. Within the next decade the Santa Gertrudis ranch would become one of the world's largest commercial producers of horses and mules, breeding and selling thousands of head to the armies of the United States and of Mexico, to metropolitan police departments, to the carriage and saddle horse trade and to the market which supplied plow mules to the cotton farmers of the South.

In the horse and buggy days of the 1890's there was a steady demand, from city streets and country roads all over the nation, for grain-fed carriage horses. Kleberg keyed his breeding program to that volume demand. To produce a type suitable for the market, he carried on a breeding policy of consistently crossing his range mares with Standardbred and Thoroughbred stallions. The upbred get made a larger, more desirable horse for the carriage and commercial saddle horse trade, and in this Kleberg proved highly successful. The success, however, was at a sacrifice which became apparent later. By the time the market for carriage horses was a thing of the past, the ranch's range stock had been so altered by repeated infusions of hot blood that it was far less satisfactory as a working cow horse — for which there was still a demand — and had to be bred back toward its earlier qualities.

Manager Kleberg in the 1890's not only followed Captain King's practice of buying Kentucky stallions for his mare bands, he also began to buy Percherons and Clydesdales for the production of big strong mares to breed to Kentucky jacks. The outstanding mules that resulted were in demand all over the cotton states.

When opportunity arose, Kleberg rid the ranch of culls from the horse stock by swapping large numbers for a few fine-blooded animals. Upon one occasion he traded five hundred of the ranch's horses for five French Percherons; another time he swapped eighty mules for a Thoroughbred stallion named Octopus.[28]

Kleberg, educated in law, showed a natural bent for science. In 1889, his speculative mind and habit of careful observation led him toward a discovery of profound significance to the cattle industry of the United States.

Southern Cattle Fever, or Texas Fever as it had come to be called, stood as a menacing handicap to the prosperous development of the nation's cattle business. During the later years of the great drives to

Kansas, northern stockmen had frequently blocked entry of Texas cattle by locally organized "Winchester Quarantines"; by the early 1880's the problem had become so acute that the government had been forced to establish official quarantine lines and shipping regulations for the movement of southern cattle to northern markets. The quarantine lines were a bitter source of dissension. The shipping regulations, allowing the northern passage of southern cattle only during the three winter months of freezing weather when the disease seemed to be dormant, were odious to southern shippers whose cattle were in poorest market condition during those months.

The fever, which had been noted and described at Philadelphia as early as 1796,[29] attacked and destroyed red corpuscles in the bovine bloodstream, with usually fatal results. It was noticed that cattle native to the warmer climate of the southern states were nearly all immune and it was further noticed that the disease did not appear to be communicated by any direct contact between infected and uninfected herds. Contamination was indirect. Northern animals took the fever in warm weather merely by occupying pastures, pens, roads or stock cars used previously that season by the immune, apparently healthy southern cattle. No one knew what caused the ravages of the disease in northern cattle or how the fatal malady was transmitted.

The endemic existence of the fever was not only a serious handicap to southern stockmen shipping their cattle to northern markets, it was a prime reason for the difficulty in introducing highly bred imported stock to the ranges of South Texas. When cattle were shipped from northern states into the South or Southwest, they usually sickened and died. Survivors ordinarily remained immune for the rest of their lives and their calves were in most cases immune, but survivors from first arrival were few.

Without preliminary acclimatization in a southern climate elsewhere, the fine cattle Captain King had imported to his ranch had nearly all succumbed. When Robert Kleberg began to bring in grown purebred cattle from the North, he would watch them arrive at the ranch with fine, well-kept, glossy coats. Soon afterwards he would see them distressingly shingled with ticks. Observing them, he felt sure that "so many insects biting an animal was enough to make it sick."[30] It came to his increasing notice that cattle dead of the Texas Fever were infested with the blood-sucking tick. He had first a glimmer and then a growing conviction that there must exist some connection between the cattle ticks and the fatal disease.

When Kleberg and his family were vacationing at Deer Park, Maryland, in the summer of 1889, Kleberg became acquainted with Secretary of Agriculture J. M. Rusk. The two men found opportunity to discuss Texas Fever and the harassing regulatory problems it presented both to cattlemen and to the government. During the conversations Kleberg set forth his personal observations on the cattle tick as a suspected source of the disease. When Rusk indicated interest in such a theory, Kleberg offered the cattle, the locale, the laboratory and the necessary expenses for an investigation and study of the problem if Rusk would send a qualified authority to the Santa Gertrudis.[31]

Dr. Cooper Curtice of the Bureau of Animal Industry arrived at the ranch later in 1889 to begin studies which were to extend over a period of three years. Curtice's work on the life cycle of the cattle tick and its connection with observed facts in the incidence of Texas Fever was later incorporated into a full report by the Bureau's pathologist, Dr. Theobald Smith, who in 1893 proved conclusively that the miscroscopic parasite which attacked the red corpuscle in cattle and caused Texas Fever was transmitted by the cattle tick.[32]

When Curtice's first studies had indicated the truth, Kleberg set about searching for an effective method of destroying the tick. By 1891 he had invented, built and put into use at the ranch the world's first cattle dipping vat, a long chute-like tank fitted with an approachway ingeniously arranged so that the animal to be dipped was forced upon a swinging door and precipitated into the tank, emerging on the other side with every hair dripping.[33] The "wash" in the tank was made according to formulas Kleberg developed by trial and error — it eventually became an arsenical solution which would kill the ticks but not be injurious to the cattle.

As soon as its cause was understood, the fever began to be called "Tick Fever." Study of the tick explained much that had been observed about the conditions in which the disease appeared. The tick's eggs were deposited on the ground. By standing on ground where eggs had been laid, cattle were infested and reinfested by new ticks as they hatched and fastened themselves upon their bovine hosts. A season of freezing weather killed the tick eggs on the ground, which explained the absence of the cattle tick in northern climates and its prevalence in the mild South.

Because the life of the cattle tick was dependent upon a supply of animal blood, it was possible to eliminate ticks from a pasture by keeping the ground entirely clear of livestock for the full cycle of a year, in which period all deposited eggs would die. To keep ticks from the bodies of cattle on any infested pasture, it was found that the animals had to be put through the dipping vat every eighteen days.

It became a matter of proof that calves born and suckled on tick infested ground acquired immunity from the fever and ordinarily retained it as grown animals. This immunity, however, was often lost when the animals remained unexposed to ticks for a period of about two years. After that time, many formerly immune animals were as subject to the fever and its fatality as cattle which had never been exposed.

With so many complicated factors involved in the elimination of the tick, Kleberg quickly realized the prohibitive expense and the then unlikely cooperative effort which must attend any widespread and effective eradication campaign. He saw the impossibility of permanently clearing any limited area situated in a greater area infested by ticks. He saw the danger of such an attempt: tick-free cattle could lose their immunity and too easily become victims of fever contracted from surrounding tick infested areas. Consequently, Kleberg limited the use of his dipping vat to a control of ticks on Santa Gertrudis pastures, not an attempt at complete tick elimination. That would require in years to come a mass effort by all cattlemen concerned and could be achieved only by a rigorous and immense campaign for total eradication, working southward from the quarantine line and gradually shrinking the infested area until it was at last nonexistent.

Laboring toward this end, Kleberg sponsored the organization of the Texas Livestock Sanitary Commission and served as its first head. The Commission drew quarantine lines, studied and disseminated information on methods of tick control, worked with a national Quarantine Convention composed of the Livestock Sanitary Boards of eight states and territories, to improve and enforce quarantine regulations, to bring pressures upon cattlemen's associations and to influence legislation and seek governmental appropriations for the control and ultimate eradication of the tick and the large losses and vast hindrances caused annually by Texas Fever.[34]

The issue became bitterly controversial. It was difficult to convince great numbers of cattle ranchers that the gains of total tick eradication would be worth the stringent measures necessary: the expense of building and maintaining tight fences and dipping vats, of leaving pastures empty; the labor, the periodic, repeated botheration of dipping and re-dipping, moving and re-moving, patrolling and re-patrolling every cow brute in the South. One infested animal straying into a cleared pasture could bring on a quarantine there for another whole year.

In the end, the necessity for the elimination of Tick Fever became apparent to all but the most refractory stock owners. In 1906 the United States Department of Agriculture began a systematic campaign to clear the South of ticks. Starting its slow and thorough task at the northern tick line and working south, the official tick eradication program did not reach the far southern tip of Texas until 1922. The area of the Santa Gertrudis was not declared entirely free of the cattle tick until 1928 — thirty-nine laborious years after Kleberg had first mentioned the cause of Texas Fever to Secretary Rusk. Successful eradication of the tick was probably the most arduous and the most difficult range work ever accomplished on the King Ranch.[35]

In the early 1890's, Kleberg's range observations led him to anticipate another discovery concerning a previously undetected agent for the communication of disease among cattle. Kleberg suspected that buzzards in feeding upon cattle dead of anthrax spread that disease. Before scientists had proved that the carrion-eating birds were in fact carriers of the malady, Kleberg was following a policy of burning carcasses found on the range and waging his own shooting war against buzzards. At one of the earliest conventions of the Livestock Sanitary Board, Kleberg presented a resolution which recommended strong measures against the big bird as a bringer of anthrax. The resolution was adopted, the commission voting that "Mr. Kleberg's buzzard goes."[36]

Engaged in the outdoor work of a stockman who was beginning to make the Santa Gertrudis "an experimental range in many phases of Texas ranching," Kleberg was at the same time necessarily preoccupied with the indoor concerns of the ranch's business office, the fiscal affairs of Mrs. King's many properties. Chief among these affairs was the custodianship of the ranch's acreage.

Though charged with the departed Captain King's desire not to "let a foot of dear old Santa Gertrudis get away," and though the ranch's long-established policy was to "buy land and never sell," Manager Kleberg did find it necessary, shortly after the captain's death, to advise Mrs. King to sell certain tracts as the easiest means of settling some accounts owed by the estate.

In 1886, the ranch's banker and friend at Brownsville, Don Francisco Ytúrria, received title from Mrs. H. M. King to 4575 acres in the San Juan de Carricitos grant, for a consideration of one dollar per acre. At about the same time, the ranch's lawyer, James B. Wells, was sold 6420 acres from the Carricitos lands at the same price per acre. In October of the same year Wells was sold another 9142 acres, at a dollar an acre, in three separate tracts Captain King owned on the Rio Grande and which had not been a part of his ranch's operation. These sales to Wells and to Ytúrria in 1886 amounted to $20,137.

Land sales to pay debts did not mean that the ranch intended to discontinue its established policy of consolidating and clearing title to acreage surrounded by or contiguous to the ranch's pastures on the Santa Gertrudis headquarters grant. In 1885 and in 1886, Mrs. King paid a total of $8213 for titles to 7690 acres in several small parcels of such land. Yet the record shows that from late in the year 1886 until the spring of 1889, the ranch management was engaged in a retrenchment which allowed few land transactions. There were some exchanges of acreage, for convenience, with neighbors, and there was at least one sale of Nueces County land: in 1887 Mrs. King gave title to 3145½ acres to Charles Blucher, son of the pioneer surveyor Felix Blucher, for a stated consideration of only ten dollars, a transaction evidently satisfying a debt. In 1888 Mrs. King was borrowing money —there is record of a loan of $10,000 at eight per cent made by banker Ytúrria—and during that year not a single acre appears to have been added to the ranch. At this time partition by court action was being made of the various landholding interests in the Espíritu Santo grant; the deceased Captain King's interest was adjudged to be the title to 13,596 acres—which Mrs. King relinquished in 1889 to José San Roman for $8157.60 in settlement of a collection suit San Roman was bringing against her.

By 1890 the ranch had resumed a program of land buying, especially in the San Juan de Carricitos area, which would continue well beyond the turn of the century. In April of 1886, a year after the captain's death, Lawyer Wells had drawn up a list of the land titles owned by Mrs. King in Cameron County. The area within the San Juan de Carricitos totaled 312,279.70 acres.[37] Six years later, Mrs. King was shown on the tax rolls as the largest land owner in Cameron County, holding title to 334,469 acres.[38] All but a very small fraction of these were in the San Juan de Carricitos. In 1879, Lawyer Wells had brought friendly suit against the heirs and assigns of Narciso Cavazos, deceased, to define the boundaries of the lands the Kings had purchased in the San Juan de Carricitos grant. Ten years later the final decree was rendered and the boundaries had been established by court surveys. Meanwhile, Manager Kleberg, following the captain's old policy, had continued the standing order with Wells to consolidate and to extend the ranch's ownership in the area by purchase whenever worthwhile titles were offered for sale.[39]

The successive drought years of the late 1880's and early 1890's, the fallen cattle market, the widespread depression caused by a money panic in 1893, all brought a drop to the price of range land. With water holes drying up, pastures scorched, livestock starving, many small ranchers pulled out discouraged.

Land could be bought at the low price of fifty to seventy-five cents an acre. When such land could be made into advantageous extensions of the ranch's pastures, Manager Kleberg confidently added to Mrs. King's holdings: the big Rancho Santa Gertrudis grew bigger. In the period of the "great die-up," 1892-1894, when wagons moved along parched Texas prairies carrying signs like "In God we trusted; went west and got busted," Mrs. King—who had been west for a long time—bought more land. The very size of her ranch gave it an economic momentum, a credit when it needed cash, which was a built-in power to bridge a bad season or even a series of bad years. In adding to the ranch's lands during hard times, Manager Kleberg used the ranch's credit to borrow the cash required; the lenders found no fault with the soundness of the ranch's paper or the way it always paid off.

On January 21, 1895, nearly ten years after he became manager of the ranch, Kleberg received from Mrs. King a full and complete Power of Attorney for the handling of all legal and financial matters connected with all her property. It was in force for the remainder of Mrs. King's long life.[40]

In every legal aspect of Mrs. King's business and particularly in every land transaction entered into by her ranch, James B. Wells played a major rôle. Involved in many of the administrative decisions of the ranch's management, "Friend Jim" was also for a time Kleberg's law partner.[41] Sometime before 1889, Robert W. Stayton (brother of the John W. Stayton of Cuero) and Robert J. Kleberg who composed the Corpus Christi firm of Stayton & Kleberg entered into law partnership with Wells under the firm name of Wells, Stayton & Kleberg.[42] It is certain that the manager of the Rancho Santa Gertrudis found no time for any general practice of law, but at least nominal membership in the firm evidently presented advantages in the legal administration of Mrs. King's affairs which he and his partners considered too important to neglect. In the firm's actual operation it had two offices, Wells' in Brownsville and Stayton's in Corpus Christi, both of which Kleberg must have found helpful at the two county seats where most of Mrs. King's legal business had to be done. The firm stood as counsel for the ranch, managed its causes in court, acted as its agent in the handling of all land transactions, and examined, tabulated and paid the ranch's many taxes, using such political influence as it could muster to keep those taxes as low as possible in each of the counties where the ranch had property. Wells, Stayton & Kleberg withdrew from their partnership in 1895 and thereafter the great majority of legal work for the ranch was solely in the hands of Wells.

Too much emphasis cannot be placed upon the importance of Wells' continuing labor at buying, then proving, then piecing together in his office and in the courts, the titles which gave the ranch ownership of its lands. Its vast pastures were in more than a figurative sense the indefatigable legal handiwork of Wells, who created them by his unassailable knowledge of the law, by his probity and by his magnetic ability to persuade contestants to agreement.

Once when a visitor at the ranch asked Kleberg how much the ranch's land was worth, he explained "that the land wasn't worth anything until you did something with it." [43] Mere acreage was meaningless unless land was made useful, productive.

The land the ranch owned produced grass and grass could produce beef. It was a productive mechanism of elemental pastoral simplicity. Its actual operation — the efficient management of its productivity, the guardianship of the grass for the maximum nourishment of the beef — was anything but simple.

The land itself, wrested so recently from wilderness, was beginning to present a problem to men who had fenced it off for the use of its grass. When Richard King had first ranched by the water of the Santa Gertrudis, the Wild Horse Desert upon which his cattle grazed was nearly all an open prairie land covered with an almost unbroken mat of grass. Thickets of mesquite, of huisache, of brushy trees wickedly thorned, were uncommon and small, standing infrequently on low drainage pockets of the prairies or twisting like thin lonesome veins of taller green along a few dry creek beds.

In four decades the character of the prairies had noticeably changed. By 1890, the mat of grass was being invaded by tangles of brush which were spreading and growing into nearly impenetrable belts of thorn.

The most important single agency in the spread of the mesquite was the presence of great numbers of horses: they love to feed on the ripened bean pods of the mesquite. When the beans fall naturally from the tree to the ground, they rot, almost never germinating. On the other hand, when a horse eats the mesquite bean from the tree, it passes through the animal's digestive tract where the heat tends to crack the bean's hull, causing an almost unfailing subsequent germination. Surrounded by manure when dropped to the ground, the seed grows with a rich start in life.

There were also other causes for the encroachment of the brush. Grass fires no longer burned over the pastures, as in former days when Indians and chance travelers had set frequent fires on the wild prairies; flames then had consumed and kept down the growth of spreading thickets. Intensive cattle grazing was another contributing factor to brush growth: in areas where the primal matting of grass was broken or eaten away, especially in times of drought, the seeds of the brush found space to take hold and flourish and proliferate into thick-thorned jungles. Formerly fine pastures of open grass were becoming tangled *bosques* of useless mesquite over much of South Texas.

By early in the 1890's, the Rancho Santa Gertrudis found itself in a fight against the relentless advance of thorny brush over its pasture-lands, a fight which remains ceaseless to this day. The first attempts to kill off the spreading tentacles of the mesquite were made by foot camps of transient Mexican workers hired by the ranch to chop brush and grub roots with axes, picks, grubbing hoes, and strong backs. During the hard times of drought and depression in the 1890's, with unemployment everywhere, day laborers in gangs sought jobs at the Santa Gertrudis and were put to work clearing brush. They were paid five dollars for every acre they cleared, fifty cents for each cord of wood they cut, and varying prices for such pieces as could be used for fence, corral or gate posts. In addition, each worker was issued a weekly ration consisting of seven pounds of flour, one pound of coffee, two pounds of beans, one pound of rice, one quart of molasses, and one and a half pounds of bacon.[44] Sometimes workers would draw their issue of food at the ranch commissary and leave without doing any work. The ranch made no attempt to bring them back — the issue became a part of the standing order from Mrs. King that no hungry transient was ever to be turned away from her ranch without being offered employment and food.*

The problem of brush clearance was of relative unimportance compared to another concern, the most vital anxiety Manager Kleberg faced as a ranchman: water, lack of water. Soils of the region were fertile; abundant grass always sprang in the years when the rains came. Even in seasons of drought, the land generally maintained some nourishment — such as the tough *sacahuiste* grass, or the prickly pear which was edible when the thorns had been burned from its juicy, plate-like big leaves — sufficient to sustain herds through dry times. There seemed, in any event, little mankind could do about the rain that fell or did not fall from heaven, except to adapt the use of land to the observed average of rainfall and hope that the season might bring it. The real rub with ranching between the Nueces and the Rio Grande was not the undependability of annual precipitation, not a lack of grass — though more was always wished for. The real rub was the limited amount of, and lack of new sources for, potable

*See Appendix XI

surface water. Watering places for livestock were so few and far between that little use could be made of immense parts of ranges where grass did grow, wasted. It was the old complaint of Captain King: "Where I have grass, I have no water. And where I have water, I have no grass."

To a man of Kleberg's methodical and yet visionary mind the lack of water became a grating hindrance and intolerable flaw in the ranching operation he labored to develop. He dreamed of abundant water for the pastures in his care. He even allowed a zealous imagination — and a memory of farming — to transform pastures into richly bearing irrigated fields — if only there were water. He searched avidly for new sources, trying to add to the built tanks and dug shallow wells on the ranch, and he met largely with the kind of failure he encountered on the Mula pasture in 1889 when the drilling equipment available to him proved incapable of boring and casing deep enough to reach good water.

Late in the drought year of 1891, only a few months from the time when it would prove necessary to ship 12,000 of the ranch's cattle to Indian Territory grass to save their lives, when *Kineños* were pulling famished big steers from the mud of drying waterholes and skinning the dead cattle starved on the range,[45] Manager Kleberg was desperate for rain, and Mrs. King contributed a thousand dollars toward the expense of a novel experiment conducted by the Department of Agriculture in an effort to break the drought.[46] The rainmaking effort consisted of a noisy discharge of explosives directed skyward in the hope of bringing "rainfall by concussion." Location for one of these official experiments was set up about twenty-seven miles west and north of the Santa Gertrudis at San Diego. The concussion supplies, in charge of Lieutenant S. Allen Dyer of the 23rd Infantry and of an "aeronautic expert," George Castier, "consisted of 17 balloons filled with gas, 1600 charges of dynamite and rackorac, 250 charges for 12-pound cannon and 100 21-pound bombs for the mortar batteries." The first sky bombardment at San Diego on the night of October 16, 1891, brought no results; the next evening after another heavy barrage was fired into the air, clouds came up and at four o'clock on the morning of October 18 rain fell—"in torrents" in the vicinity of San Diego, yet perhaps not a thousand dollars worth at the Santa Gertrudis, where Robert Kleberg reported to the Department of Agriculture that "he was awakened by the rain falling on the roof of the house" but that "The rainfall at this place was very light—" Kleberg was inclined to believe that the result was encouraging enough to warrant "further experiments to produce rainfall," yet no more "bombardments" were set off in the vicinity. The government abandoned the experiments in 1892, not being able to decide "as to whether the rain was the result of the experiments or natural meteorological conditions," and the Santa Gertrudis had to await the breaking of its drought without further benefit of balloons and artillery.[47]

Kleberg steadfastly pursued his dream of providing pastures with a more adequate number of watering places. Reading, inquiring and studying on the subject of deep artesian waters, Kleberg grew determined to try for artesian wells at the ranch; his search for water became a search for the right equipment and the right man to do the job.

He found both. The result was of incalculable importance not only to the future operation of the ranch but to the future development of the whole region.

In October of 1898 Kleberg met Theodore L. Herring, who had dug water wells for years in the vicinity of New Braunfels, and who was convinced he could tap artesian water at the Santa Gertrudis if he could find suitable machinery. Kleberg had in his possession a clipping. It described a new make of heavy drilling rig and attached to it was a memorandum he had addressed to Mrs. King: "This will cost money but we need it to make land worth anything. Now you've got a year round use of about a 20th of the land — cause limit to how far cattle go to water. To make grass harvestable by cattle, must have it close enough to water." The heavy rig was made by the Dempster Mill Manufacturing Company at Beatrice, Nebraska.

T. L. Herring, staked by Kleberg, went to Nebraska. He came back with a "Dempster No. 6 Combined Hydraulic Rotating and Cable Drilling Machine," and with Tom Leary, drilling demonstrator and salesman for the Nebraska firm. In the spring of 1899, on a ranch pasture about five miles north and west of the present site of Kingsville, Herring set the new rig to work. Kleberg's instructions were to "keep right on boring until their drill came out on the other side of the earth unless they found water sooner." On the sixth of June, with the drill standing at a depth of 532 feet, a clear column of pure artesian drinking water burbled up and poured out upon the ground at the rate of seventy-five gallons a minute. Word was sent to headquarters.

It is not difficult to imagine how Robert Justus Kleberg whipped the horses, how the buggy wheels spun bumping along the ruts leading to where the spindly arm of the rig stood dancing in the heat of the summer sun over the miracle of flowing sweet water in a thirsty land. When Kleberg saw it, he was so overcome that tears filmed his eyes and rolled down his cheeks. He watched the water come splashing steadily from the well pipe.[48]

By October 6 there were four wells flowing; another rig had arrived from Nebraska and both Herring and Leary were busy bringing in successful wells on sites where the ranch needed watering places most.

Early in the first month of the first year of a new century which promised much, Kleberg wrote:

Santa Gertrudis or King's Rancho
Nueces Co Texas 1/8/1900
To The Dempster Mill Mfg Co
Beatrice Neb

Gentlemen

About ten months ago I first began the use of your No. 6 Hydraulic well boring Machine on this ranch—after having used four or five different kinds of well Machines—none of which filled the bill—All of my trouble for water is rapidly being dispelled by the use of your machine. I have now *ten flowing* wells made by your machine—the last just finished by Mr. Thos. Leary flows over 500,000 gallons per day—Your machine is easy and inexpensive to handle and does its work very rapidly—some days making 100 ft. in 10 hours—

Yours truly

Robt J Kleberg

Beneath the surface of the ranch, at depths ranging from 402 to 704 feet, he had found a giant subterranean flow which could be tapped at will. Within a year after his pioneering discovery, landowners over the entire region were drilling deep wells with equally successful results.[49] Irrigated farms became a possibility. Reporting the wells on December 21, 1900, the *Corpus Christi Caller* opined: "Flowing wells of good water in this part of Texas means a great deal, because of this section's rich soil and the early and late seasons, making it a popular garden spot of the Lone Star State."

As the number of deep wells on the Santa Gertrudis property increased—there were 22 by the end of 1900 and 67 by 1907—some of them were non-flowing. The water rose to within thirty feet of the wellhead and had to be pumped to the surface. Windmills soon became familiar features of the ranch's landscape, and a regular crew for windmill maintenance became a necessary part of the ranch's operation. The tanks by the wells, first scooped in the ground and later built of concrete, brought adequate and dependable watering places to the ranch's pastures.

The manager of the Rancho Santa Gertrudis was already thinking beyond pastures. Speaking of his first artesian well, he said, "The men wondered why I cried when we finally saw what we had all been praying for. But I knew that once a definite source of water was available I could induce railroad construction which in turn would lead to the development of South Texas."[50]

XIV · *The Family at the Santa Gertrudis*

ALICE AND ROBERT

Kleberg, and for the widowed Henrietta King, daily life at the big house was principally shaped by the domestic pleasures and duties revolving about an active family of young Klebergs. There were five.

All of them were born in town, at Corpus Christi where their mother went for each confinement to be attended by the family physician, Dr. Arthur E. Spohn; and all of them were inevitably christened, with small delay, in the Presbyterian Church.

The first child was a son. He was born in a rented two-story house called the "Greer House," on Carancahua Street, November 18, 1887. Christened Richard Mifflin Kleberg, he bore the first names of his grandfather and his grandfather's best friend. On July 17, 1889, a daughter arrived, to be named Henrietta Rosa Kleberg after two pioneers no less revered, her grandmothers Henrietta Chamberlain King and Rosalie von Roeder Kleberg. Three and a half years later, on January 9, 1893, another daughter was born and given her own mother's name, Alice Gertrudis; upon the advent of the second son, the twenty-ninth of March, 1896, he was christened Robert Justus Kleberg, Jr. The youngest of the children was Sarah Spohn Kleberg, born April 12, 1898, and named for Sarah Josephine Kenedy Spohn, the physician's wife, who was also Mifflin Kenedy's daughter.[1]

There was a difference of about ten and a half years between the eldest and the youngest of the Kleberg children, with the ages of the middle three spaced rather evenly in between. They grew up in a close circle of deep family affection which was demonstrative, and even indulgent, yet by no means lacking in disciplinary demands; obedience and industry were expected by the parents and by the grandmother, whose personalities evoked the pattern and wove the fabric of daily life for the children in the house.[2]

Their father was a stockily built man, a little below medium stature. His complexion was ruddy and he wore a bushy mustache the same sandy brown color as the thick shock of curly hair that crowned him. His blue eyes were usually mild and often merry—but they could level with a glint bearing sharp authority. As he grew older and stockier, he trimmed his mustache more brusquely, while the graying shock of his hair assumed a character almost like a mane, giving a leonine stamp to his solid presence. His spirit and manner were lively. Fond of company, he enjoyed good stories, told them well, and he loved to sing, especially the old German songs learned from his mother. Nor was he averse to a friendly glass, especially German beer, but in this he was by nature most temperate, as well as by circumstance most regardful of his mother-in-law's detestation of strong drink in her presence or on her premises. He had an abiding love for being out-of-doors and found few pleasures greater than loading a buckboard with companions and gear to go out hunting for deer, turkey, plover or quail on the ranch's great pastures, or to fish the water at the dam of the Tranquitas for the fifteen-pound German carp he found there.[3]

Strong ties bound him to his kindred from DeWitt County and these ties endured. The aged patriot, Judge Kleberg of Meyersville, died in 1888 and was buried according to his wish, under a great oak about twelve miles from Cuero on the ranch belonging to one of his daughters, Mrs. Caroline Eckhardt. His son Robert had a monument of granite erected over the grave. It was a massive stone carved to the shape of a soldier's tent bearing the inscription: "Robert J. Kleberg, A Hero of San Jacinto, Born Sept. 10, 1803; Died Oct. 30, 1888. He Did His Whole Duty to His Country and to His Family." At the monument's base were the words of the battle cry at San Jacinto: "Remember the Alamo." The judge's wife Rosalie survived him for nineteen years. She made a number of visits to her son Robert and his family at the Santa Gertrudis. Richard M. Kleberg remembered a notable evening in 1896, when his 83-year-old Grandmother Kleberg sat at the piano in the music room of the big ranch house, with her sons Marcellus, Rudolph and Robert about her. She played beautifully, joining her clear voice in harmony with the hearty voices of all her living sons, singing old songs in the tongue of her youth. Listeners in the room felt their hearts lift high in the rich lilt of the music. Suddenly Rosalie Kleberg stopped, bending her head, with her hands to her face. "The years—" she said in

German, "they are too many!" Eleven years later she was buried at the side of her husband. Upon the soldier's granite tent, for her there were carved the von Roeder shield and crest with its motto in German: *Hilf dir selbst, so hilft dir Gott.* To describe her ninety-five years on earth, there was this inscribed upon the stone: "She Lived the Simple Life; She Practiced the Religion of Duty."

Other Kleberg relatives were guests at the ranch where they were welcomed with affection and entertained with gusto. One of the nieces, Lula Kleberg, remembered the family banquets, the horseback lessons, the hunts, and how her Uncle Robert enjoyed sending the old King stagecoach, drawn by relays of white horses, to meet the train so that young visitors might have the jolting thrill of a dash across twenty-odd miles of prairie in high frontier style.

Mrs. King showed a marked regard for her son-in-law Robert's relations. In 1900 she gave Caesar Kleberg, a son of Robert's eldest brother Rudolph, a job at the ranch. The personable and engaging young Caesar had just served for two years as his father's Congressional secretary in Washington—and at that time, Caesar's ignorance of ranching was extensive. He was set to work repairing this ignorance in a Spartan school, as an assistant to Sam Ragland. One of Caesar's first lessons came upon one of the first mornings he rode out across the pastures with Ragland in a buggy. The boss reined abruptly, got out, and headed for high grass to tend to nature. "Young fellow," Ragland said as he hurried, "you watch the team." The recent secretary from the nation's Capitol dropped the reins to the dashboard and leisurely leaned back, preparing to read the newspaper he had folded into his pocket. The paper, as it opened, made a crackling rustle—and the horses bolted. While Caesar fought to pull them up, the clattering buggy came careening toward the engaged and enraged Sam. "Goddammit," shouted Ragland, "you got about a million acres out there! Don't you run over me!" Caesar's knowledge of the acres expanded rapidly; before long he became a key figure in the ranch's management. From the start he was an esteemed member of the household at headquarters. To the five children of that household, their father's nephew was much more like a beloved elder brother than a Cousin Caesar.

Every account of the children's mother Alice—whether from a relative, a friend or a chance visitor to the ranch in those days—speaks of the warmhearted gentility she displayed toward everyone around her. Brunette, rather plain save for the marked beauty of her large and expressive dark brown eyes, she carried in her very presence a generous and sweet-natured grace. The unaffected goodness of her heart made it difficult for her to consider hearts that might be otherwise: she believed the best, and expected it. There was an admirable selflessness in regard to her position within her own household. The duties of motherhood which she assumed with deep happiness and the responsibilities of the very large and busy ménage which she in fact supervised and maintained were never allowed to seem quite her own. All the home life she achieved was pervaded by the senior personality and presence of her mother. There is not a scintilla of evidence that Alice resented this. To the contrary, she displayed what appears to have been a native and never failing deference to her mother in all things. It was one of Alice's modes of happiness.

The tone of the headquarters household was set by the matriarchal presence of Henrietta King. Widowed at the age of fifty-three, her character was strong but her health was not. During the year following the captain's death, her infirmity was aggravated by a long-drawn emotional stress, suffered most acutely while the remains of her son Robert E. Lee King were being removed from the cemetery in St. Louis and reinterred at the side of Captain King's grave in San

Antonio. Ailing often, generally confined to a valetudinarian life, she was nevertheless entirely capable of summoning a vitality to match the remarkable strength of her spirit, and she would survive her husband for forty years.

Her widowhood was rigorously manifest. Until the very last years of her life, when she sometimes allowed herself gray or white, her dress and bonnet were severely black. The rooms she frequented most, she furnished with large portraits of her deceased husband; she wore his likeness prominently engraved in a brooch she pinned at her high collars; his portrait became an unchanging feature of the Santa Gertrudis business letterhead.

CAPT. RICHARD KING.

MRS. H. M. KING. PROPRIETOR. R. J. KLEBERG. MANAGER.

Santa Gertrud

KINGS RANCHE.

Alice, Nueces Co., Tex.

At the ranch her daily routine was marked by an early morning inspection trip through the garden to see what vegetables might be ready for the day's table, and an early evening walk to the front gate and back, on her daughter Alice's arm. In good weather she would have her rocking chair placed on one of the outside galleries where she sat with her sewing basket or her church paper and watched her grandchildren play around her. She told them stories, little homilies and reminiscences of earlier days. When the children were good, she gave them peppermints and hard candies she carried for them in her petticoat pocket. She was also capable of dealing with her invalid's cane a quick rap to the ankle of a disobedient child. A Kodak first appeared at the ranch in the 1890's and many of its earliest snapshots record the frail figure of Henrietta King presiding over gatherings of small grandchildren.

Oftentimes from her chair on the gallery, looking out into the sunlight, she discussed the ranch business of the day with her son-in-law Robert. He kept her informed and he made no decisions of consequence without her knowledge and approval. She was at all times the highest authority in the conduct of her properties' affairs and she was always consulted. Though her usual reply to a query was a smiling—and shrewd—"Just as you say, Robert," there were occasions when she said more. A story of one of these occasions demonstrates clearly how she used a quiet authority.

When Sam Ragland first came to the ranch, he asked Manager Kleberg for permission to abolish the big whips the vaqueros customarily used in handling the ranch's cattle. He believed that the whips were injurious to the beeves and Kleberg agreed. When ordered, the hands brought in their whips; Ragland proceeded to take out his pocketknife and cut through each one of them. One old vaquero who had been employed at the ranch since Captain King's time found it difficult to concede that he did not need a whip, and continued to use one. Ragland discharged him for failure to obey orders: the vaquero went to see *El Abogao* about it. Kleberg told him that Ragland was his superintendent, that orders must be obeyed, he must turn in his whip, or go. The old man chose to go. He found it unthinkable, however, to leave without reporting to *La Madama*. He approached her with a doffing of his hat and said that he had come sadly to pay his respects, to bid her farewell. She asked him why. He told her that the new *mayordomo*, Ragland, had discharged him. Henrietta King sent for her son-in-law to ask him about it.

When she learned the reason for Ragland's action, she expressed her regard for his decision — she delegated authority to no man without backing him to the hilt — and at the same time she could feel a very deep regret that an old employee was about to leave the ranch. When the several points of view had all been adjusted, the whips went — and the old vaquero stayed.[4]

Since the captain had built his first cow camp and brought the first *Kineños* to the Santa Gertrudis, the employer-employee relationship at the ranch was characterized by a bond of faithfulness on the one hand and of responsibility on the other. The tie that existed between the family of the ranching owners and the families of the ranching hands grew stronger with the passing years and decades. The faithfulness and responsibility became reciprocal, and became inherent in the continuing pattern of life and work on the ranch.

There was nothing soft or easy about that pattern. All men earned their pay, they worked for what they got.

They also knew that the wages they drew, the living quarters they and their families were furnished, the rations they were issued, were but one part of what their work brought to them. The other part was the daily challenge of the work itself. It had spirit in it. Meeting it, there was a response of spirit, and a reward: the work was a source of virile, energetic, open air pride. The ranch was home. Its character derived from all the people who lived there. Men made the ranch and the ranch made men.

If illness, misfortune or trouble struck a loyal hand, there was help waiting, according to the need. When old age came, a job was adjusted to a man's physical ability — with due regard for a man's self-respect in making a living, not taking a living as a gift.

The ranch rarely found it necessary to fire a man, though no insubordination was ever tolerated. *Kineños* themselves ordinarily found ways to rid the ranch of inept recruits, culling out by ridicule or by handing them the most disagreeable jobs, the newcomers who did not fit the work or contribute to the *esprit*.[5] Hands left the ranch by their own choice; they often chose to return. Most of them stayed, and their children after them carried on their work—not because they found it merely secure but rather because there was pride and interest in it.

The proud fidelity of the ranch's hands was never exemplified in more heroic form than by the *caporal* Ignacio Alvarado, one of the venerable bosses in the cow camps and on the roads to Kansas in Captain King's time, and one of Robert Kleberg's most trusted range aides later. One day Kleberg waited for Alvarado to arrive on the San Ignacio pasture on the southern sector of the ranch, to take charge of a herd of cattle gathered and ready to be moved north. Alvarado did not come at the expected time. The cow camp waited for the *caporal*. Several days later Kleberg saw Alvarado's son riding across the prairie and coming into camp. "Where is your father?" Kleberg asked him. The boy answered: "My father said to tell you he was sorry he could not come. He had to die."

Mrs. King's knowledge of the *Kineños* and their work was not limited to a view from a chair at headquarters. Twice each year, usually during the spring and autumn roundups, it was her custom to make an inspection tour of her property. Traveling as comfortably as she could over rough wagon roads in her heavy coach, accompanied by her family from the big house, she visited the cow camps where her herds were gathered and watched cow work in progress on the several divisions of her ranch. She saw for herself the condition of the cattle and of the grass, judging for herself the welfare of her stock, the efficiency of her horseback men, the efficacy of the range improvements being carried forward by her foot camps. What she saw she remembered in detail, and her approval or disapproval shaped the administration of all ranch business.

Her establishment on the Santa Gertrudis had achieved fame as the greatest ranch in the West. The fame attracted a stream of visitors, made the entertainment of guests a large concern of the headquarters household and its daily routine. Not long after the marriage of Robert and Alice Kleberg the big white frame house had been enlarged and refurbished for the third time. The one-story rear addition of the late 1860's, which extended from the two-story front unit of the house, was lengthened out and given a second story also, with pillared and lattice-railed outside galleries along the entire lengths of both floors to match the galleries on the house's existing square front. The remodeled living quarters of Robert and Alice Kleberg and their daughters were on the second floor of the original front unit; Mrs. King's bedroom was also there, across the hall, in the northeast corner. There were ten bedrooms in the new rear addition; Caesar Kleberg, Sam Ragland, and the two Kleberg boys Dick and Bob, had rooms there. Five to seven bedrooms were for the use of guests. Green shutters at windows and a certain amount of wooden scrollwork on cornices and gallery pillars gave an ornamental touch to the expanded house, which stood surrounded by a wide and increasingly tended lawn. Planted trees cast shade on the grass where Captain King's old cannons were still parked, and carriage driveways of crushed white shell led to the house's doors. The headquarters place on the rise above the prairie had mellowed since the bride of Richard King had lived there in a mud hut with her platters "fastened to the wall outside." Her dining hall, in a separate building between the new rear addition to the house and the stone kitchen building and servants' quarters farther on, was now graced with the amplitude of a table which could accommodate twenty-eight guests at a time, and often did.[6]

One of these guests was a writer. In *Harper's Weekly*, April 30, 1892, Richard Harding Davis told the nation of his visit to the ranch and became the first prominent journalist to report what he encountered there. Like a number of correspondents since, Davis was no man to let strict accuracy impede the reportorial dash. Making the ranch somewhat too big and certainly too slick, he created the journalistic grandpa of King Ranch descriptions:

It is rather difficult to imagine one solitary family occupying a territory larger than some of the Eastern States—an area of territory that would in the East support a State capitol, with a Governor and a Legislature, and numerous small towns, with competing railroad systems and rival baseball nines. And all that may be said of this side of the question of ranch life is that when one is within Mrs. King's house one would imagine it was one of twenty others touching shoulder to shoulder on Madison Avenue, and that the distant cry of the coyotes at night is all that tells one the hansoms are not rushing up and down before the door.

In the summer this ranch is covered with green, and little yellow and pink flowers carpet the range for miles. It is at its best then, and is as varied and beautiful in its changes as the ocean. . . .

The ladies who come to call on Mrs. King drive from her front gate, over as good a road as any in Central Park, for ten miles before they arrive at her front door, and the butcher and baker and iceman, if such existed, would have to drive thirty miles from the back gate before they reached her kitchen. This ranch is bounded by the Corpus Christi Bay for forty miles, and by barb-wire for three hundred miles more. It covers 700,000 acres in extent, and 100,000 head of cattle and 3000 broodmares wander over its different pastures.

This property is under the ruling of Robert J. Kleberg, Mrs. King's son-in-law, and he has under him a superintendent, or, as the Mexicans call one who holds that office, a major-domo, which is an unusual position for a major-domo, as this major-domo has the charge of 300 cowboys and 1200 ponies reserved for their use. The "Widow's" ranch, as the people about call it, is as carefully organized and moves on as conservative business principles as a bank. The cowboys do not ride over its range with both legs at right angles to the saddle and shooting joyfully into the air with both guns at once. Neither do they offer the casual visitor a bucking pony to ride, and then roll around on the prairie with glee when he is shot up into the air and comes down on his collar-bone; they are more likely to offer him as fine a Kentucky thoroughbred as ever wore a blue ribbon around the Madison Square Garden; and neither do they shoot at his feet to see if he can dance. In this way the Eastern man is constantly finding his dearest illusions abruptly dispelled. It is also trying when the cowboys stand up and take off their sombreros when one is leaving their camp. There are cowboys and cowboys, and I am speaking now of those I saw on the King ranch.

The thing that the wise man from the East cannot at first understand is how the 100,000 head of cattle wandering at large over the range are ever collected together. He sees a dozen or more steers here, a bunch of horses there, and a single steer or two a mile off, and even as he looks at them they disappear in the brush, and as far as his chance of finding them again would be, they might as well stand forty miles away at the other end of the ranch. But this is a very simple problem to the ranchman.

Mr. Kleberg, for instance, receives an order from a firm in Chicago calling for 1000 head of cattle. The breed of cattle the firm wants is grazing in a corner of the range fenced in by barb-wire, and marked pale blue for convenience on a beautiful map blocked out in colors, like a patch-work quilt, which hangs in Mr. Kleberg's office. When the order is received, he sends a Mexican on a pony to tell the men near that particular pale blue pasture to round up 1000 head of cattle, and at the same time directs his superintendent to send in a few days as many cowboys to that pasture as are needed to "hold" 1000 head of cattle on the way to the railroad station. The boys on the pasture, which we will suppose is ten miles square, will take ten of their number and five extra ponies apiece, which one man leads, and from one to another of which they shift their saddles as men do in polo, and go directly to the water-tanks in the ten square miles of land. A cow will not often wander more than two and a half miles from water, and so, with the water-tank, which on the King ranch may be either a well with a wind-mill or a dammed cañon full of rainwater, as a rendezvous, the finding of the cattle is comparatively easy, and ten men can round up 1000 head in a day or two. When they have them altogether, the cowboys who are to drive them to the station have arrived, and take them off.

At the station the agent of the Chicago firm and the agent of the King ranch ride through the herd together, and if they disagree as to the fitness of any one or more of the cattle, an outsider is called in, and his decision is final. The cattle are then driven on to the cars, and Mr. Kleberg's responsibility is at an end.[7]

Manager Kleberg and "major-domo" Ragland doubtless wished — especially in that drought year of 1892 — that ranching were as simple as this "wise man from the East" described it; and Mrs. King doubtless wished that her guest Mr. Davis had pointed out to his readers more clearly that similarity between life on Madison Avenue and life on the Santa Gertrudis was not exactly indicated by any similarity in parlor furnishings.

The ranch-style decorum prevailing about headquarters was especially evidenced at mealtime in the big house. Before each meal guests always heard three signal bells. The first was a preliminary notice to "clean up." Ladies were to appear in freshly changed dresses, and gentlemen — booted or not booted — were to wear coats at table. Propriety of dress was insisted upon by Mrs. King. A British noblewoman visiting the ranch once appeared at mealtime in a riding habit shockingly furnished with trousers; she was promptly requested to change. At the second signal bell guests gathered in the big parlor before moving to the dining room which stood detached from the dwelling house. When the third bell sounded Mrs. King led the procession of guests and family across the open passageway. Her grandson Richard Mifflin Kleberg remembered how his father would say to him, "Squire her in," and how he would offer his arm to his grandmother for the march to the table. In rainy weather Mrs. King would hold a newspaper over her head as she scurried across the open space to the dining room door.

She always presided at the head of the table. Her son-in-law Robert always sat at the other end of the plentiful board and carved the meat. Guests remembered his skill at slicing great roasts—and they remembered how Mrs. King always served the coffee and cereal from her end of the table at breakfast. Her question, "Will you have hot or cold cereal?" forestalled guests who would have preferred neither. It was her firm conviction that breakfast began with cereal; at her table it did. Alice, seated near her mother, graciously filled the rôle of the alert hostess, always knowing the names and the conversational gambits required by each of the new guests at table, sometimes more than a score of unfamiliar faces, and she made them feel at home.

After supper there were often songs at the piano in the music room. There were Robert Kleberg's old favorites, such as "Flee as a Bird," "The Lorelei," "*Heiden-röeslein*," and there were the songs the children learned in Spanish from the *Kineños,* and loved to sing. The last chorus before bedtime was usually a hearty rendering of Mrs. King's favorite, "Rock of Ages." On Wednesday evenings there was a gathering for family prayer; on Sundays Mrs. King approved no music but hymns.

The devout atmosphere of the household allowed neither dancing nor playing cards nor dominoes. The Kleberg children remember how they even had "to hide the Flinch cards" from their grandmother. Their mother, who was not so strict as Mrs. King, made certain allowances; Alice Kleberg would say to her husband's niece, Lula, visiting at the ranch: "Let's have a dance on the prairie!" Alcoholic beverages of course were forbidden to anyone in the precincts of headquarters, though it is patent that occasional guests came furnished with materials for an occasional swig on the sly.

Once a year Mrs. King allowed her disapproval of dancing to be overruled, to attend with all her family the festive Christmas *baile* the *Kineños* held at their quarters "beyond the stables." At this holiday celebration, *La Madama* made presents to everyone: for the grownups, gifts of "clothes, petticoats, jackets"; for the children, bright red tarlatan stockings bulging with candy and fruit. A prominent part of the preparations for Christmas at the big house each year was the cutting and sewing and filling of the many stockings, made from red tarlatan always ordered from Alkemeyer's in Houston.[8]

The Kleberg children found ranch headquarters the center of a happy life. Though there were town toys like velocipedes, Irish mails, coaster wagons and roller skates to rattle along the wood floors of the long outside galleries, and though the girls of the family might play at dolls and tea parties, there was also the whole wide outdoor life of the ranch to engage the hearty attention of small Klebergs, both boys and girls. From earliest memory they were aware of the outspreading range and the strength of the life it held. As soon as they were old enough to cling to a saddle they had begun to learn the land from horseback, to feel themselves a part of the ranch's life, to imitate the range work of the grownups around them. By the time Richard Mifflin was nine years old, his mother would be reporting, "Richard rode 26 miles yesterday."[9] At the age of four young Robert would be taking his first spill from a saddle, trying to gallop his pony. Healthy acquaintance with animals and their ways became a basic part of daily living: snapshots show very young Klebergs not only astride their own ponies, but standing with bird dogs, greyhounds, milk calves, big blooded bulls, pet lambs, a captive fawn, a coyote pup on a lariat leash. As small fry the Klebergs went horseback to the cow camps and began to acquire the vaquero arts of saddle and rope; they went hunting with their father in the buckboard, learning to shoot, to know field crafts and camp crafts under the open sky; they stood on the rails of the cattle pens, watching Sam Ragland and their father judge livestock. Robert Kleberg gave his sons daily ranch chores, while Alice Kleberg gave her daughters daily household tasks, to develop their sense of responsibility toward the work in which they lived. Their playmates on the ranch were young *Kineños*. Parents Robert and Alice Kleberg found it easy to fasten the strongest interests of their growing children to the vigorous range world that surrounded them.

Yet there was schooling to think of. In 1893 Mrs. King built a house in town next door to the Kenedys' on North Broadway in Corpus Christi, on the site of the old Mann house, property Captain King had acquired in 1862. From 1893, when Richard Mifflin entered first grade, until his sisters and his brothers had all graduated from the Corpus Christi public school, Mrs. King's house in town was home for that part of each year when school was in session. The week ends, the holidays and the summer months, all eagerly awaited, were spent at the ranch.

The Corpus Christi house was an ornately built and elaborately furnished mansion in the high Victorian manner. Henrietta King was proud to have her grandchildren come to town to stay there, to attend the public school built on land donated in earlier years by her husband, and she took pleasure in the ample headquarters — holding many conveniences her big ranch house did not possess — which she had established for her family in town. She was happy with its nearness to Doctor Spohn when she or any of her family were ailing; she especially enjoyed the closer communion with her church which town living gave to her: transferring her letter from Brownsville to the First Presbyterian Church of Corpus Christi, she became its spiritual pillar and strong financial support. In 1901 she contributed the funds for the erection of a new church building, in memory of her husband. Her imposing house in town and her position as one of Texas' wealthiest citizens she never used for the entertainment of "society," but for hospitality toward her friends and family and for church doings.

Her daughter Alice of course stayed in town caring for the children while they were in school—Robert Jr. and Sarah were both born in their grandmother's house on North Broadway—and during the school year Manager Kleberg at the Santa Gertrudis was often lonely for his family in town forty-five miles away, though he was with them nearly every week end. Some measure of his manner toward his loved ones is indicated in the letter he wrote his wife in Corpus Christi, from the ranch on April 10, 1897:

This is a bright but very windy day—Everything seems to be drying up rapidly—except the mesquite . . . its bright green leaves are glittering with sunlight as the wind tosses them about—making a mocking music which sounds like the rain was pouring down. . . . I am again reminded that *somebody* is not here—I wish she were—for this place doesn't seem right at all to me without her—but I will not write myself and you into a little case of the "blues." We have too many things to be thankful for—for that—so I will think of them.

Tell Richard Mifflin I found a big pair of steer horns in the woods & I am going to fix them up for him if he will be a good boy—Tell Henrietta there is a beautiful little fellow calling for her all day long in his sweetest notes, I never knew whom he was calling until Gov. Brockmeyer told me— "Henrietta La Favorito"! Tell Alice Tudis that—yesterday Marcello caught a coyote in a trap and brought him into the yard and all the little puppies except hers seemed afraid of the coyote for they ran off and howled terribly, but her little dog barked at him and finally grabbed hold of the coyote and tried to bite him—tell little Robt. J. that there are many "caas" here and I wish he were here to see them.

When Manager Kleberg did go to Corpus Christi to see his family, he and his wife enjoyed attending town parties amongst friends. Upon one such occasion, in February, 1898, at a festivity "given by Dr. and Mrs. Spohn in honor of Mrs. John G. Kenedy of La Parra," the *Corpus Christi Caller* reported that "Mr. Robert J. Kleberg, after much persuasion, sings 'In Days of Old, When Knights Were Bold' in a style that carries some of the company back to times when no entertainment was complete without him."[10]

Dr. Arthur E. Spohn, the family's doctor, neighbor and intimate friend, was one of the best physicians in Texas. Ten years previously he had spectacularly saved the life of Willie Chamberlain, the younger half brother of Henrietta King, when Chamberlain was bitten by a rabid coyote at the ranch. Dr. Spohn had rushed with his patient on a desperate voyage all the way to France and had arrived at Paris in time to have the great Pasteur administer his newly discovered inoculations against rabies. James Gordon Bennett in a copyrighted story from Paris, dated April 24, 1888, had quoted Pasteur as saying "Our Willie is saved" — and William Chamberlain, bitten by a mad coyote on the faraway Santa Gertrudis, had become one of the first of men to be delivered from the fatal horror of rabies by the Pasteur treatment.[11]

For his many skillful services to all her family, Alice Kleberg felt a deep indebtedness to Dr. Spohn. She set plans afoot for the building of a modern hospital in Corpus Christi, personally soliciting subscriptions from her many friends, and raising the greater portion of the money required. Among the contributions was the gift of a building site and $25,000 from Mrs. King. At one point in the campaign for funds a benefit amateur theatrical was presented, in which Clara Driscoll, daughter of a neighboring ranchman, played the rôle of Cleopatra to an enthusiastic and admiring audience. By dint of Alice Kleberg's continued interest and fund raising, the much needed Spohn Sanitarium was erected in 1900, set into operation, and presided over by the admirable physician for whom it was named.[12]

Though Mrs. King did not enter into the activities of Corpus Christi "society" she demonstrated a marked interest in the doings of the townsfolk, and she maintained a most extensive store of information on every current affair. When the *Caller* was delivered, Alice would often read the "locals" and the "town talk" items aloud to her mother for the subsequent discussion and elaboration which Mrs. King enjoyed. Mrs. King also grew fond of fastening upon the newspaper first, reading it all and then sitting upon it — so that no one else in the family could see it or ask to see it — until she had herself relished the pleasure of dispensing all the news of the day as she herself saw fit.

Her son Richard King II, his wife Pearl and their family from the Agua Dulce, were welcomed lovingly at the Santa Gertrudis and stayed often at the house in Corpus Christi. Young Richard Kleberg was usually called Richard Mifflin by the family, before he became known simply as Dick, in order not to be confused with his cousin and playmate Richard King III, a sturdy boy nearly three years older than the Klebergs' Richard. Mrs. King also exchanged warmly affectionate visits and communications with her daughter Ella Welton and her family, and with the Chamberlains. Her relationship with her daughter Nettie Atwood, however, had been clouded with reserve since before the death of Captain King; though there were exchanges of family news with Nettie, and occasional visits, the bond between Mrs. King and her eldest daughter and family was never as close as with her other children.

The kind of news the women of the family exchanged may be seen in the letter Alice Kleberg wrote on March 20, 1894, to Addie Gillette Chamberlain, the wife of Mrs. King's youngest half brother Edwin: "Alice Gertrudis is getting awfully cute . . . R. M. gets Henrietta into all sorts of mischief. Richard Mifflin wants to know what grade Fidelio is in and tell him to write so he can see his writing . . . Robert's away in Fort Worth . . . several cases of mumps on the ranch . . . Nettie wires the children are all better but Edwin . . .

Baby Alice has only seven teeth. I have weaned her . . . kiss little Edmund for me . . ."

Mrs. King, accustomed to much traveling before the captain's death, continued to take trips when the state of her health allowed. She went well outfitted for any contingency, traveling sometimes with as many as thirteen trunks. Most of her journeys were made in the summertime when Robert and Alice Kleberg and their children could accompany her, and almost every year a family entourage left the ranch for a few weeks, to see other members of Mrs. King's family at San Antonio and St. Louis, then to vacation in Maryland at Deer Park and to visit large cities of the East, or else to enjoy the cool of the Rocky Mountains from Colorado Springs. Robert Kleberg was anxious for his children to learn from these annual travels, and they remember how he would tell them as they sat on the trains, "Don't be a pig in a poke. Look out the window!" They also remember how they looked forward most of all to returning to the ranch life on the Santa Gertrudis, happiest vacation spot of all, before they returned to the house in Corpus Christi for another year at school.

Next door to that house lived the aging neighbor and friend, Mifflin Kenedy. Since the death of his wife Petra Vela, he had lived mostly in town and maintained an office in Corpus Christi. Only two of his six children survived into his old age: his daughter Sarah Josephine who lived nearby with her husband, Dr. Spohn; and his son John G. Kenedy who had married Miss Maria Stella Turcotte of New Orleans and who, with his wife and two children, John Jr. and Sarita, lived at La Parra as manager of the flourishing Kenedy ranch of 390,000 acres, south of Santa Gertrudis. The other members of Captain Kenedy's family were his adopted daughter, Carmen Morell Kenedy, who lived with him and presided over his household at

Corpus Christi; his four married stepdaughters—children of Petra Vela and her first husband Vidal—three of whom lived in Brownsville and the other in Laredo; his brother E. J. Kenedy who lived at Brownsville, and a sister in Pennsylvania.

In a deposition made in 1887, Mifflin Kenedy had stated that he was "69 years old, stockraiser and railroad contractor by occupation." During the last years of his life, the actual ranching and stockraising were mostly in the competent hands of his son John, while the captain himself was engaged in the business of acquiring more ranchland, proving his land titles, and sponsoring another railroad leading into the area. As a "railroad contractor" he had, since Captain King's death, backed another project of their good and faithful friend, the visionary Uriah Lott: Kenedy's financial aid and promotion had been chiefly responsible for Lott's completion of a line which at last linked San Antonio to Corpus Christi by direct rail. This line, built after several years of struggle with inadequate funding, was known as the San Antonio & Aransas Pass Railway, or less respectfully as the "SAP," and it was later purchased by and made a part of the spreading Southern Pacific system.

The impeccable and courtly Captain Mifflin Kenedy, mellowed with more years than three score and ten, was attached by bonds of lasting affection to all the family of his old partner. He felt an especial interest in the grandson named for both members of a well-remembered team: Richard Mifflin Kleberg. His grandmother found Richard Mifflin her favorite too: she saw in his dark-haired good looks and sturdy manner attributes to remind her strongly of Captain King. She admonished her lively grandson with pride "to know the names you bear."

A happy comradeship grew up between the two neighbors, the young boy and the old captain. On his way home from school,

Richard Mifflin would often stop by his elderly friend's office. Sometimes the two would ride in the captain's buggy on the roads outside of town. On one such day, looking out across the prairie, the old man said, "The country looks fine, sonny. No matter how rough this road is, it is never so rough as the Gulf of Mexico. Your grandfather used to say, 'Mifflin, one thing about the cattle business, you never have to crawl out on a cold stormy night and batten down —and you don't need a compass half as bad'." Once when the young boy opened the door to Captain Kenedy's office he found his friend sitting alone in silence, with head bowed. When greeted, the captain did not respond. Silence continued, the white-haired head remained bowed for an uncomfortably long time, until the greeting was finally acknowledged. The small visitor had unwittingly intruded upon Quaker Kenedy in silent communion with his Maker. In old age, the faith of Kenedy's youth dwelt strongly in him.

On his seventy-fifth birthday, his young namesake sent him a basket of fruit. Acknowledging the gift in a letter written June 18, 1893, Kenedy wrote Richard Mifflin: "My little grandchildren Georgie, Johnny and Sarita dined with me . . . and it would have pleased you indeed to see how their little eyes sparkled when the nice peaches, plums, apricots, oranges and cherries were set before them. I explained to them the basket of fruit was a Birth Day present from you. We then all drank the health of yourself, Henrietta Rosa and little Alice in a little sip of wine." The old captain ended his letter with "the kindest regards to your grand mother, and father and love to your mother, and love and kisses to your little sisters, and with a prayer that you will live to be a great big good man, and that grand ma, father and mother and your sisters will be proud of you, and that they will all say, what a good man Richard Mifflin has grown to be."

Three years later, when Richard Mifflin Kleberg received a birthday present himself from Captain Kenedy's son John, the nine-year-old namesake of the two captains wrote:

Dear Sir:

When I came to the ranch, I found a very beautiful little pony with a black stripe down his back and my saddle on him. I was told you had sent him to me as a present. I rode him and every one said he just suited me . . . we are both built alike—short and strong . . . I feel very grateful to you and thank you for making me as happy.

Yours truly and gratefully,

Richard Mifflin Kleberg

By that time both captains were gone. Mifflin Kenedy died suddenly of a heart attack on the morning of March 14, 1895, at his home on North Broadway. The next afternoon a sorrowing procession wound its way to the cemetery. There Corpus Christi's most eminent pioneer was buried "with full Masonic honors" while the Catholic Church bells, which he had presented in memory of Petra Vela, tolled his passing. The *Caller* reported, "A gloom was cast over our little city yesterday morning when the sad words 'Captain Kenedy is dead' were passed along our streets." His obituary[13] pointed out the abiding friendship which had existed between Kenedy and King, and with fitness summed up the accomplishment of both friends together: "—they were intimately associated and a biography of one cannot be written without reference to facts connected with the life of the other. They were equal to the important work of civilization assigned to them by Providence. Texas owes them no small debt of gratitude." Kenedy's death signalized in a very real sense the passing of the pioneer era. Almost exactly ten years after the death of Richard King, Mifflin Kenedy joined his old partner, beyond the remembered sound of steamboat whistles on the Rio Grande, beyond the remembered sound of Longhorn herds milling in the dust of the Wild Horse Desert.

XV A New Century Brings New Ventures

W HEN the twentieth century arrived, modernity had already begun to touch at the big ranch house. Telephone wires had put headquarters into a new kind of communication with town, with foremen on remote pastures. Lamplight had changed to the glare of acetylene which would soon be supplanted by the installation of Mr. Edison's incandescent electric bulbs. Water had been pumped to the house from one of the new deep wells Robert Kleberg had found, available at the turn of a tap, hot and cold. Those wells had brought a whole new augury for the future of the south tip of Texas — and new plans for the expansion of the ranch's enterprise. At the turn of the century Robert Kleberg was engaged in negotiating for a huge addition to the ranch's lands, the Laureles property which swept eastward from the edge of the Santa Gertrudis all the way to the shore of the Laguna Madre.

As early as 1862 Captain King had considered buying the Laureles from Charles Stillman; in some sort of arrangement with Stillman during the Civil War years King had in fact superintended the ranching there. Then in 1868 Mifflin Kenedy, not Richard King, had bought the Laureles, fenced it, and ranched it successfully until 1882 when the whole property had been sold to a syndicate incorporated in Dundee, Scotland, under the title of the Texas Land & Cattle Co., Ltd. The absentee investors had by no means found a bonanza ranching in Texas. By 1900 they had instructed their foreman at Laureles, crusty Scottish Captain John Tod, to seek a buyer, and had appointed as agents for the transaction the firm of Templeton, Brooks, Napier & Ogden of San Antonio. While negotiations dragged through the year 1900 and most of 1901, the Santa Gertrudis was already buying a part of the Laureles cattle.[1] On October 12, 1901, James B. Wells wrote Charles W. Ogden: "Mr. Kleberg and myself will meet Capt. Tod and yourself at your office in San Antonio on the afternoon of the 24th inst. to finally close the King-Laureles land deal."[2]

The purchase was negotiated in two sections. By an agreement which had been drawn and dated September 17, 1901, Mrs. Henrietta M. King bought about 60,000 acres contained in the grants of Las Comitas, El Infernillo and most of El Chiltipín, in return for six notes, each for $27,810.91. These were paid by September 15, 1904, and negotiations continued for the purchase of the remainder of the property. In 1906, Mrs. King finally gave Robert Duke, President of the Texas Land & Cattle Co., four notes at four per cent interest, each for approximately one fourth of a total sum of $531,930.60, for which she received title to the rest of Laureles, about 110,000 acres, comprising the entire Rincón de Los Laureles, a portion of the Rincón de Corpus Christi and 1266 acres of other lands. Livestock, improvements and equipment went with the title, and the Santa Gertrudis management assumed operation of the Laureles in 1906.[3] Among the properties acquired was the old Laurel Leaf brand Mifflin Kenedy had registered in 1868; Mrs. King returned the right to use it, with sentiment, to John G. Kenedy at La Parra.[4]

The Laureles purchase added a great new ranch to the livestock operation and brought the actual area of Mrs. King's property to the million acres which the popular mind had already attributed to her ranch. During the first decade of the century Mrs. King also bought some fifteen to twenty smaller tracts which put about 65,000 additional acres under her ownership.[5] Then for a period of about ten years her ranch made no further major purchases.

The turn of the century had brought a booming new interest in titles to Texas lands, an interest evoked by a wildly dramatic event presaging a new Texas economy: the Spindletop discovery of oil, near Beaumont in 1901. It brought from dusty files every old deed, warrant and faded record that might conceivably put the possessor in touch with a claim to possible riches in oil land. Exact boundary lines and absolutely clear titles assumed new importance; surveyors and land lawyers worked overtime. The government of the State of Texas became newly interested in titles to lands within its public domain and began instituting a wholesale series of lawsuits to challenge titles, especially of lands formerly composing Spanish and Mexican grants. In 1902 the Texas land commissioner reported:

It is believed that many of the claimants will be able to establish their titles, and some may be able to show they are entitled to hold the excess in area now claimed and held by them under a valid survey, but in such event the State will be in position to correctly abstract and enforce the collection of taxes on the whole amount claimed, which will be of great benefit to the State. On the other hand, it is believed that the State will recover at least 500,000 acres for the permanent school fund where the claimants have no title, or if title is shown, the excess will be recovered.[6]

Mrs. King, along with nearly every one of her neighbors south of the Nueces, found some of her titles under a new scrutiny. There is no question that the resulting series of suits performed a valuable service to the whole region in clearing up the validity of old titles, in causing careful new resurveys, and in most cases definitively settling claims against titleholders. The skill and acumen James B. Wells had so long wielded for his client Mrs. King became more than ever apparent during these litigations. In 1908 Alice Kleberg wrote Wells to thank him for not losing "a grain of old Santa Gertrudis soil yet."[7]

The oil excitement which brought about this re-examination of the area's land titles penetrated to the Santa Gertrudis following the opening of the great Lucas field at Beaumont. In 1901 Mrs. King leased the acreage of the ranch for oil exploration and drilling to A. J. Vick, who then transferred the lease to a Houston stockholders' corporation called the King Oil Co. Nothing came of it; the lease was canceled in 1902.[8] Though no actual oil development arrived in the vicinity until 1913 when wells were brought in at White Point twelve miles above Corpus Christi, and though it was not until 1919 that any further action was taken regarding oil leases on Mrs. King's property, the possibility of an oil discovery was not forgotten by the ranch management during the intervening years. Some estimate of the value of the Rancho Santa Gertrudis as it stood—with artesian well water but without oil wells—may be indicated by the fact that in 1907 a group of eastern capitalists and land promoters reportedly offered Mrs. King ten million dollars for her ranch, and was refused.[9]

During the first years of the new century Robert Kleberg lived in the productive prime of his busy life. The problems of managing a million acres of pasture land, on which grazed 75,000 head of cattle and nearly 10,000 head of horse stock, demanded only a portion of the astonishing energy Kleberg brought to his work. His mind was quick to fasten upon the far-reaching potentials of the artesian water supply he had discovered under the surface of coastal South Texas. Beyond the immediate benefits of water on thirsty ranching pastures, he studied the measurements of larger shapes, of future shapes: settlers arriving to create an area of irrigated farms, new crops, new towns, new values for lands—all served by a railroad inside the ranch's own front gate. Forging this vision into reality, he not only carried forward the huge livestock operation he managed, he experimented with new farm products for the land, he brought in a railroad, he built a city, he nourished a whole region into a new phase of enterprise.

Adequate rail transportation was the crux upon which shapes for the future depended. The Texas Mexican Railway which had gone into operation in 1881 pointed west instead of south from Corpus Christi, and went to Laredo on a roundabout way for connections with San Antonio and the rest of the nation. Its closest point convenient to the Santa Gertrudis was Collins Station, twenty miles northwest of ranch headquarters. In 1888, when the S. A. & A. P. had gone into operation from Corpus Christi north to San Antonio, the ranch had found itself with far better rail facilities than those offered by the Tex-Mex to Laredo: at the juncture of the S. A. & A. P. and the Tex-Mex tracks a village had grown up which had superseded Collins Station as the ranch's railway shipping point and postal address. This little town was named Alice—after Mrs. Robert J. Kleberg—and it was twenty miles from Santa Gertrudis headquarters. The lower tip of Texas from Corpus Christi straight south was still unserved by rails. The formerly important border town of Browns-ville had languished in the backwater of a merely local, diminishing trade, sunk in a sleepy isolation. It awaited in a rather desultory way a resurrection which only railway connection with the rest of the world could bring.[10]

Every attempt to achieve this connection had collapsed. As early as 1873 Richard King had sponsored an unsuccessful project for a line called the Corpus Christi & Rio Grande Railroad which would have linked Brownsville with Corpus Christi. Ten years later Count Joseph Telfener had planned a line through Brownsville into Mex-ico, but his plan had come to nothing.[11] The grandiose promoter Colonel E. H. Ropes had arrived in Corpus Christi in 1889, pro-posing to dredge a channel through Mustang Island to make Corpus Christi a real deep-water ocean port, and further proposing to build a railroad from there through Brownsville and on south as far as Panama. In 1890, twenty-five miles of actual grading had been done on his Corpus Christi & South American Railway; in 1891, the heavy dredge *Josephine* was actually chewing slowly across Mustang Island toward what was to be called "Port Ropes." But the Ropes ideas had far overreached their financial backing. During the money panic of 1893 the flamboyant Colonel Ropes left Corpus Christi for good, after a canewhipping administered by an irate local investor.[12] One of the bitterest scars left by "the Ropes boom" had been the failure of the bank and the loss of the personal fortune belonging to Perry Doddridge, Captain King's trusted friend, who died in 1902 with his fortune unrepaired.[13] Following the Ropes fiasco, yet an-other attempt to bring rail connections into Brownsville had failed in 1894, when the construction of the Pan-American Railway, a projected line from Victoria southward to the Rio Grande, ended in a sheriff's sale of the rails and equipment.[14] It was against this background of continued failure that some citizens of Brownsville even sponsored an aborted scheme for what was to be called the "Picket Line," a stub connection to be built from Laredo downriver.[15]

Meanwhile there had appeared a somewhat more solid possibility for the building of a line to serve the area south from Corpus Christi. The powerful Southern Pacific system had bought the S. A. & A. P.; in 1893 the famous Texas Ranger Major John B. Armstrong, who was ranching on his property in the La Barreta grant south of the Kenedy Ranch, approached Southern Pacific officials with a plea to extend their rails south from the S. A. & A. P. to Brownsville. Armstrong's petition was strongly supported by most of his ranching neighbors, notably Mifflin Kenedy and Mrs. King.[16] At the time, the Southern Pacific happened to be in straits with the Texas Railroad Commission over alleged monopolistic abuses, but when the dispute was settled there were no legal restraints against the right of the Southern Pacific to extend its S. A. & A. P. tracks to the Rio Grande if it so chose, and the big system forthwith considered the south tip of Texas "as its own preserve" into which it would extend rails at its leisure and design. Then after due consideration of the possibilities, the Southern Pacific chose to believe that the area south of Corpus Christi did not yet display sufficient promise to justify the expense of building and operating a line to serve it. In not deigning to make answer to Armstrong's repeated petition, the Southern Pacific succeeded in raising the ire of influential residents in Nueces, Hidalgo and Cameron counties. Pressures were building. Artesian wells came in, flowing strong, bringing visions, changing the economic prospect of the isolated area. Its citizens wanted a railroad, and they wanted action.[17]

In 1900 Robert Kleberg had plowed an experimental farm plot of fifteen acres near the Santa Gertrudis headquarters and had planted trial crops of cabbage and onions, irrigating them with the flow from one of the ranch's deep wells. The yields had been so spectacularly rich that Kleberg's imagination was fired.[18] Pursuing a bent for scientific inquiry, by 1902 he was engaged in a continuing series of pioneering experiments to determine commercial crop possibilities, and to disseminate the information thus gathered for the use of the farming communities he hoped to see grow in the region. Cultivating trial plots of irrigated vegetables and grain feeds for livestock, Kleberg also experimented with cotton. As a dry-farming crop it had been produced in Nueces County before 1890.[19] With the advent of artesian wells for irrigation, cotton planting began immediately to boom. To his experimental station at the Santa Gertrudis, Kleberg also brought experts to establish nurseries of semitropical fruit trees, dates, olives, citrus.[20] The citrus experiments, which in 1904 came under the skilled supervision of a horticulturist from California, Harvey C. Stiles, were the foundation for a highly successful citrus industry which now occupies a considerable part of the lower Rio Grande valley.[21] In the midst of these many new possibilities for the development of the land, Robert Kleberg was not unmindful of the basic dream of his pioneering predecessor Richard King: efficient transport for beef cattle directly from the ranch's pastures to the remote markets of the nation. It was time for a railroad.

Thoroughly tired of the Southern Pacific's dilatory tactics, Kleberg looked in another direction and found a new friend, Benjamin Franklin Yoakum, who had been employed by an old friend, Uriah Lott, during the construction and early operation of the S. A. & A. P. Since those strenuous days, Yoakum's business and promotional talents had carried him to a position of power in the railroading world, and had made him a magnate of the Frisco-Rock Island system.[22] The prime rôle Robert Kleberg played in turning Yoakum's aggressive attention toward a railroading project in South Texas is indicated by this letter written from St. Louis on June 8, 1902:

Mr. R. J. Kleberg,
            Alice, Nueces County, Texas

My Dear Mr. Kleberg—I am in receipt of yours of May 25th, which I find upon my return from Europe, where I have been killing time for the last few weeks. I thank you for your letter and information contained, which shall be treated confidentially, and should we decide to look further in the Southwest, shall be glad to take the matter up with you again. In fact, I shall be glad any time you are in St. Louis, or I am in Texas.

                     Yours very truly,
                       B. F. Yoakum[23]

The matter was taken up. Yoakum conferred with his old friend and former employer, the indefatigable Uriah Lott. It was he, that railroad visionary who with sweat and insufficient funds had created both the Tex-Mex and the S. A. & A. P. almost barehanded; it was Uriah Lott, that man destined to drive iron horses into so many wilderness miles with so little ability to garner any personal reward for his toil, who finally brought a railroad down to the tip of South Texas. On a preliminary scout for Yoakum and the interests he represented in St. Louis, Lott wrote from Quanah, Texas, on October 2, 1902:

Mr. Robert J. Kleberg, Esq.,
            Corpus Christi, Texas.

Friend Robert—I am on a confidential railroad mission through Texas from Red River to Rio Grande for one of the North and South lines that propose building to a Mexican connection. My business is to look over the entire line personally and make a full report, recommending what I think most advisable, and upon my report, I have no doubt, the road will be built at once. I have inspected the route from Concho County to this place and Vernon since Monday morning and the roads are too muddy for me to do much from here, and, after looking into Indian Territory and a piece from Vernon tomorrow, shall return to where I left my baggage and go from there South to Corpus, coming there next Tuesday night. I should like very much to see you, and if possible have you show me over the line where you prefer to have it go through Santa Gertrudis and Cameron County. Returning from Brownsville, I shall drive over the line North to San Antonio via Oakville and connect it up with Concho County from there and hasten North. If you cannot go with me, I should like to have you send some one perfectly familiar with the country whom you could instruct as to the route that would be satisfactory.

I do not want you to think I wish to impose any expense of such a trip upon you, for I am prepared to pay for the best and quickest that can be procured. There is just now great rivalry among the trunk lines and I think now is your time to secure the very best outlet to Kansas City, St. Louis and Chicago. I will give you more particulars when I see you.

With best wishes for Mrs. King, your wife, children and self, I am,

Truly your friend,

U. Lott.[24]

Three months later, as a result of Lott's trip, a charter was issued on January 12, 1903, to a corporation organized for the purpose of constructing, owning, maintaining and operating a railroad from Sinton in San Patricio County, south across Nueces, Hidalgo and Cameron counties 160 miles to the town of Brownsville. The line was to be known as the St. Louis, Brownsville & Mexico Railway and its incorporators were Robert J. Kleberg, A. E. Spohn, Robert Driscoll, Sr., Uriah Lott, Richard King II, John G. Kenedy, James B. Wells, Francisco Ytúrria, Thomas Carson, Robert Driscoll, Jr., E. H. Caldwell, George F. Evans, Caesar Kleberg, John B. Armstrong and John J. Welder. The first nine constituted the Board of Directors, with Uriah Lott, President; Robert J. Kleberg, Vice-President and Treasurer; and John G. Kenedy, Secretary.[25]

In April a five-day preliminary reconnaissance of the route was made by a survey group sent out by B. F. Yoakum.[26] During the course of sight-seeing in the Santa Gertrudis headquarters vicinity Robert Kleberg had stopped the wagon. "Here," he said, standing at a point about three miles due east of Mrs. King's house, "is where we want to build a town when Lott's railroad gets here."[27] The site became Kingsville.

Railroad builders in Texas, after the repeal of the land grant law in 1882, could not receive as rewards the great bonuses of public lands which had been handed out by the State for each mile of constructed roadbed.[28] In 1903 the acreage required by a new railroad, either for its right of way or for aid in its financing, had to come from private ownership; the problem of finding individual donors of sufficient acreage to make railroad building possible was a basic concern of Uriah Lott as president of the projected St. Louis, Brownsville & Mexico. Mrs. King, who owned the most land in the area, donated the most: a one-half interest in more than 75,000 acres, in addition to a right of way across her property.[29] Lott found a similar cooperation from other incorporators of the company, especially Robert Driscoll, John G. Kenedy and John B. Armstrong, who donated large tracts to meet the quota for lands required by railroad building contractors.[30] In the vicinity of Brownsville requisite donations accumulated more slowly. A score of interested citizens there made contributions of land and money to buy land, but it was not until Lott went to Brownsville and held a mass meeting on June 6, 1903, to promote the project and to put down the Southern Pacific attempts to block the project, that donations became adequate to meet contractors' stipulations. The total of these donations was in effect a down payment, in the form of land bonuses, made by local citizens to the railroad builders. The amount of the down payment required was set forth in the telegram sent from St. Elmo, Illinois, on May 28, 1903, by the railroad building contractors who had been chosen for the work:

To U. Lott,
　　　Alice, Texas

We will agree to construct your railroad from a connection with the Mex-National at some point between Alice and Corpus Christi to Brownsville, Texas, with a Branch to Hidalgo County on the Rio Grande River, providing owners of property will give us one-half interest in 240,000 acres of land to be selected by you free of debt and approved title with abstract of title with trustees within thirty days and furnish us free right of way for entire line and Branch, including depot grounds at all stations and terminal grounds at each end of the Line and Branch. We will commence work as soon as deeds have been deposited and title perfected. This proposition only good until June 25, 1903. Answer what we may expect.

　　　　　　　　　　　　　　　　　　　Johnston Brothers.[31]

The offer held good for another week: on July 1, 1903, the railway company entered into contract with the able and experienced Johnston Brothers. Beyond the donations of land, the hard cash required to construct the St. Louis, Brownsville & Mexico Railway came from the subscriptions of a "Brownsville Syndicate" of investors at St. Louis, brought together by B. F. Yoakum.[32] Before the end of July, construction offices were opened in Corpus Christi, and engineers were taking the field to establish the right of way.[33]

Meanwhile, at a directors' meeting held on the town site of Kingsville, officers for the actual operation of the railroad had been elected: Uriah Lott, President; Jeff N. Miller, Vice-President and General Manager. Shortly thereafter, the operational organization had been completed by the following appointments: Duval West, General Attorney; James B. Wells, General Counsel; R. J. McMillan, Assistant General Attorney; W. P. Homan, Chief Engineer; L. A. Guerenger, Resident Engineer; John D. Finnegan, Secretary and Treasurer; W. I. Church, Auditor; H. W. Adams, General Freight Agent; Finley W. Parker, Car Accountant; C. B. Chase, Superintendent

543

Motive Power; Herbert C. Dennett and C. J. Crane, Chief Clerks to General Manager; W. J. Carnahan, Stephen Daly and H. A. Jones, Construction Supervisors.[34]

Sixteen miles west of Corpus Christi a material yard was established at the point of juncture between the proposed north-south line and the east-west rails of the Tex-Mex; trackage rights having been secured for the use of the Tex-Mex line to that point, materials were soon piling up at the yard. This junction point stood in the middle of a pasture belonging to Robert Driscoll. The site was given the name of Robstown and it became the first of many towns born as the tracks moved south across unpopulated ranges to the Rio Grande.[35]

The construction organization worked without a hitch and track-laying progressed so rapidly that the railway was built and in operation within less than a year from the time construction began. A bunting-draped excursion train northbound from Brownsville to Corpus Christi made the first run over the completed line on July 4, 1904. Flags waved, cannons boomed, brass bands played in a salute to Independence and the "Brownie" Line.

Henrietta King rode down to the raw town site of Kingsville that day to await the arrival of the first train ever to move on a scheduled run over the prairie that had been her home for almost exactly half a century. When the train came in sight, "Mrs. King stood up in the wagon, and, with hands clasped, overjoyed almost to tears, said: 'Thank goodness, it is here!' "[36] That morning a telegram addressed to Mr. and Mrs. Robert J. Kleberg came from Brownsville:

THE FIRST PASSENGER TRAIN LEFT FOR CORPUS CHRISTI THIS MORNING. I HEARTILY CONGRATULATE YOU BOTH ON THIS EVENT WHICH COULD NOT HAVE HAPPENED BUT FOR YOUR EARNEST EFFORTS AND HEARTY AND LOYAL COOPERATION.

U. LOTT, PRESIDENT [37]

The first annual pass General Manager Miller issued was made out to Mrs. H. M. King.[38] The second was:

St. Louis, Brownsville & Mexico Railway Co.

Pass Mrs R. J. Kleberg & Children

Complimentary.

Until December 31 1904

SUBJECT TO CONDITIONS ON BACK

No. 2

Vice Pres't & Gen'l Manager

Time Table No. One was set up, effective Monday, July 4, 1904, at 12:01 A.M., for north- and southbound passenger trains running daily except Sunday.[39] It is said the line operated no Sunday train out of deference to Mrs. King's feelings regarding the Sabbath.[40] Scheduled time for the passenger run of 158.06 miles between Brownsville and Corpus Christi was nine hours (the stagecoach service from Brownsville to Alice took forty jolting hours), and scheduled freight trains ran each way three trips weekly.

Long before railroad surveyors had driven their stakes across the Santa Gertrudis, Robert Kleberg had chosen the site for the development of the town about three miles east of ranch headquarters. He had by no means awaited the arrival of the tracks to begin building the town. The railway company had received its charter in January, 1903; before that month was out another stockholders' corporation, the Kleberg Town & Improvement Co., had been organized. Its president was Robert J. Kleberg. It was not only a means to plan, promote and completely control the creation of a town and adjoining farm tracts, it was also the instrument through which the railway builders were given the land bonus donated to them by Mrs. King.

To go into business the Kleberg Town & Improvement Co. received from Mrs. King title to 41,820.6 acres lying along the railroad route including what is now Kingsville and 34,854.8 acres around what is now Raymondville, for subdivision into farm sites and town sites.[41] The company then issued stock, 5000 shares at $100 a share and made a gift of 2500 of these shares to the railroad builders, thus presenting them with their one-half interest not only in the land but in the profits to be made from an organized sale of the land. The remaining 2500 shares in the company were owned by Mrs. King, except for a qualifying share held by Robert J. Kleberg.[42]

By 1913 all but about 7000 of the 76,675.4 acres had been sold and the proceeds, "many hundred thousand dollars," divided between the railway builders on the one hand and Mrs. King on the other.[43] In 1914 a reorganization reduced the capital stock to 500 shares at $100 each;[44] subsequent subdivision and sale of farm sites in the vicinity of Alice and Bishop brought additional dividends in the continued operation of the company.

Kleberg kept that operation so firmly in hand, controlling sales, discouraging speculators, that Kingsville and its farming environs grew soundly. The Kleberg Town & Improvement Co. promoted; it did not exploit.[45] Kingsville developed unattended by the frontier phenomena of lawlessness and of economic boom and bust which ordinarily accompanied the arrival of a railroad and the hectic opening of new country.[46] If citizens accustomed to wider latitudes came to resent the tight monopolistic rein Kleberg maintained over the community he created, they must have been aware of that rein the day they arrived and chose to stay, and not even the fractious denied that Kingsville, compared to the doings closer to the Rio Grande when the railroad arrived, was born and grew up in an atmosphere of order unexampled in South Texas.

The survey of the town had been begun in May, 1903, embracing an area of 853 acres, divided into 226 city blocks defined by wide, straight streets. Alice Kleberg often conferred with the surveyor, Fred Warren, on the details of the town plan. Most of the streets were marked out on the prairie pasture and grubbed clean of brush by the time the railhead arrived from Robstown in February, 1904.[47]

When the tracks had moved past the town site on their way south, and a well driller had brought in a water supply for the Kingsville station, a caboose and a string of boxcars were shunted out on a siding to become headquarters of Vice-President and General Manager Jeff N. Miller, and field office for the railway under construction.[48] For the next few months the only other signs of habitation at Kingsville were a few temporary shacks and tents pitched along the tracks, where construction crews camped and could find a meal for a quarter at a tent café.[49]

In the early spring of 1904 a construction train brought in the first shipment of materials for the town's first permanent business establishment, the Kingsville Lumber Co. This key property was owned by Henrietta King and managed by the energetic Charles Flato, Jr., who immediately assumed a leading rôle in town development and was soon operating a banking venture in connection with the lumberyard, the Kleberg Bank, which financed the town's building, and which was owned jointly by Robert J. Kleberg and P. M. Johnston, of Johnston Brothers.[50] Sales promotion on town lots and farming tracts was soon under way; fifty dollars was the price for an ordinary lot and choice corners were listed at five hundred. The Kleberg Town & Improvement Co. was the source of title to every foot of property in the entire vicinity, and every deed contained a clause strictly prohibiting the sale of spirituous liquors under penalty of defaulting title. Mrs. King intended to see no saloons in her town, and there were none. Their continued absence was a pre-eminent factor in the peace and quiet which attended Kingsville's growth.[51]

As the spring of 1904 advanced, the railroad was busy building a depot, a general office and a roundhouse. John B. Ragland, brother of the foreman at the Santa Gertrudis, arrived to set up a general merchandise store in a shack "twelve by fourteen feet" financed largely by the Kleberg Bank. A little grocery shop with a dirt floor, a druggist's shack which also doubled as post office, a tent café, Ragland's minuscule General Merchandise, and an open air lumberyard comprised the "business district" of Kingsville which greeted the first excursion train on the Fourth of July, 1904.[52]

The advent of the trains brought the arrival of inquiring "home-seekers" and prospective customers to the Kleberg Town & Improvement Co., which opened an office in its own new Kingsville building before the end of 1904. In August of that year an able young newspaperman, Roy Miller — who would thenceforth be closely identified with the promotion of many of Robert Kleberg's enterprises — was employed as advertising agent of the St. Louis, Brownsville & Mexico Railway to publicize the attractions of the area.[53] Miller's promotional activities brought a widening publicity not only to the area but to the Santa Gertrudis ranch, and it brought increasing numbers of tourists and prospecting settlers to look over the land.

The Kleberg Town & Improvement Co. began to attract buyers of both town lots and farm sites. These last were usually in tracts of forty or eighty acres and, depending upon their location, were sold for prices ranging from fifteen to twenty-four dollars an acre, with no down payment required and on easy terms.[54] The sounds of carpenters' hammers and saws were heard increasingly along the streets of the new town; up at the ranch headquarters three miles away two kitchens and two cooks were almost constantly busy, feeding an influx of visitors and new customers of the Kleberg Town & Improvement Co. The company quickly saw the necessity of providing a decent hostelry for the new town, and early in 1905 it built a first class two-story hotel called the King's Inn, which was well furnished, with all the modern conveniences of the day and with a good dining room. The hotel immediately became the center of the town's social activity.[55] By the time Kingsville celebrated the first anniversary of its first passenger train the town built on the cow pasture had grown to a population of nearly 1000, "with two newspapers, a bank and sundry other buildings." It was there to stay, its real estate values were firm and Robert Kleberg was stating for publication in the *Texas Stockman & Farmer*, July 5, 1905:

We are not booming Kingsville and are not inviting boomers here.... To the man who is seeking a home where climate, soil, water and all other natural conditions are the best, and who knows how to work, we offer such opportunities as are not found in many places.

We believe this country is to be one of the richest agricultural sections of the world, and we are spending much thought and energy and money with the view of making the most of its possibilities.

I am satisfied after twenty years of experience and experimentation, that the soil is adapted to all semi-tropical fruits, vegetables and farm crops. With such soil and such climate, plenty of water and good railroad service, what is to prevent us from making a paradise where the prairie was . . .

The Kleberg Town & Improvement Co. lived up to all its name: it built a town and it provided improvements. In 1905 it financed and began the installation of a waterworks, which was completed in 1907 at a cost of about $75,000.[56] That same year the Kingsville Ice & Milling Co., built by Robert Kleberg and backed by Mrs. King, brought an ice factory to town.[57] The Kingsville Publishing Co., owned by Mrs. King, published a weekly newspaper.[58] The Kingsville Power Co., built mostly with Mrs. King's funds, lit Kingsville with electric light in 1908.[59] Outside of town, irrigated vegetable gardening and cotton growing burgeoned in a first surge of planting on the new farms. To create a system for supplying deep-well water to the local agriculture, Kleberg organized the Algodon Land & Irrigation Co. in 1905.[60]

This was the one large expectation which was doomed to a decisive disappointment. As early as 1907 it became clear that Robert Kleberg's dream of extensive irrigated farming would not be fulfilled. In the Kingsville vicinity it was found that most wells were inadequate to supply the large volumes of water required for irrigation purposes over any sustained period of time. Farther south, in parts of the Raymondville area, a small magnesium content in the deep-well water, flowing upon the irrigated fields, was found to be sufficient to clog the aeration of the cultivated soil to the increasing detriment of crops. Only a few seasons of general experience were required to prove that dry-farming of cotton, sorghum and other grain feeds was more feasible than irrigated farming which depended upon the local artesian water.

Kleberg then regretfully discontinued the project for which the Algodon Land & Irrigation Co. had been organized and turned his attention to dry farms of cotton and of grain feed — and to profits involved in processing and marketing the local cotton yield.[61] By 1907 Mrs. King had already financed the first cotton gin near Kingsville. This was the initial installation of what became the Gulf Coast Gin Co., owned solely by Mrs. King, which later built and operated nearly all the gins between Corpus Christi and Brownsville. Related to this interest in cotton growing and ginning was the Kingsville Cotton Oil Mill Co. in which Mrs. King invested $100,000 in 1911.[62]

The proliferating enterprise of the Kleberg Town & Improvement Co. — real estate promotion and development, soil and crop information and experimentation, cotton and stock feed planting, ginning and milling, public utilities, hotel operation, building material and construction, banking — was the burden of a man who was also engaged in actively managing the largest livestock ranch in the United States. To aid in the administration of the Kleberg Town & Improvement Co.'s daily business routine he set up the Kingsville Land & Investment Co. in 1910, and placed at its head a young man named John D. Finnegan, a native of St. Louis who had come to South Texas in 1904 as the Secretary and Treasurer of the St. Louis, Brownsville & Mexico.[63] Stationed as division superintendent at the railway offices in Kingsville, he divided his time between his railroad job and his duties with the land and investment company. Finnegan's knowledge of fiscal procedures and expert accounting practices made him a most welcome new element in Robert Kleberg's managerial affairs. In 1912 Finnegan resigned from the railroad to begin a long career as chief accountant and purchasing agent for the multiple King-Kleberg interests both in town and on the ranch.

While the major business enterprises of Kingsville were being created and controlled largely by money stemming from the Santa Gertrudis, Henrietta King did not neglect to direct a personal attention to other aspects of Kingsville's life. The first church service in the town was conducted by a Presbyterian minister in the unfinished building at Mrs. King's lumberyard. In 1905 she donated both a building site and the funds required for the construction of a Presbyterian Church, the first church building in town.[64] In 1907 Baptists built a church; during the following year Methodists, Episcopalians and Catholics each erected their own building; a Christian Church followed in 1910. To each of these congregations Mrs. King offered a gift of town property as a building site for a place of worship.[65] She provided Masons with a meeting place.[66] When the Kingsville Lodge was organized in June, 1905, it was designated "Chamberlain Lodge No. 913," in memory of a pioneer Mason of Brownsville, the

Reverend Hiram Chamberlain, and in gratitude to his daughter.[67]

The first public school opened at Kingsville in 1906 with thirteen pupils and one teacher;[68] by 1908 there were four teachers and 125 pupils crowded into inadequate classrooms. The next year Mrs. King donated the grounds and all the required funds, about $75,000, for the construction of an excellent two-story brick building of twenty-two rooms, which was open for the fall term of 1910. In her letter presenting this gift to the Board of Trustees of the Public Schools of Kingsville, Mrs. King wrote, "As I have carefully selected expert house builders for this work, so I would urge upon you the importance of employing expert character builders for the work within."[69] That same year the Presbyterian Synod of Texas began a movement for a school to be dedicated to vocational training for Mexican boys. Mrs. King donated a site for the school, 700 acres of land five miles south of Kingsville; and a most remarkable minister, Dr. J. W. Skinner, slowly and arduously created from this unadorned gift of land an admirable school, the Texas-Mexican Industrial Institute.[70]

On the rail line between Robstown and Brownsville there were twenty-one little stations, some destined to become thriving towns, others to remain little more than lonesome tanks and station houses, or sidings fitted with cattle pens, built in the brush by the side of the rails.[71] Those rails ran for fifty-eight miles on Henrietta King's pastures. The Kleberg Town & Improvement Co. by no means limited its interests to the development of Kingsville. When Surveyor Fred Warren had finished marking out the site for that town, Robert Kleberg had sent him immediately seventy-two miles south on the rail line to a station on Mrs. King's San Juan de Carricitos lands. There Warren had laid out the town sites of Raymondville and Lyford on property which had been conveyed to the Kleberg Town & Improvement Co. It proceeded to sponsor a development of that area, using much the same methods as those employed at Kingsville, though on a reduced scale and with slower success. By 1912 the Raymondville-Lyford community held about four hundred inhabitants, most of whom where engaged in dry cotton farming on small tracts in the vicinity.[72]

The company's interests were also involved at a station six miles northeast of Kingsville, on a tract of prairie blackland pasture bought from Robert Driscoll of Corpus Christi by a wandering promoter and colonizer, F. Z. Bishop. In developing a town site and in subdividing the adjacent farm land, Bishop appears to have been an agent working for Kleberg rather than an independent promoter.[73] The town Bishop founded took his name — the railroad had first named the station Julia — and the waxy soil of the prairie that surrounded the little town of Bishop was such extraordinarily rich cotton land that by 1912 hundreds of settlers had arrived to farm it.[74]

Another land development fifteen miles south of Kingsville, near a railway station designated as Spohn, grew in a different manner. Mrs. King sold a tract of her land there to Theodore F. Koch, a successful banker and land colonizer from St. Paul, Minnesota, who had been first attracted to pioneering business possibilities in the south tip of Texas by an illustrated article he read in the *Review of Reviews*,[75] a piece doubtless springing from the promotional endeavors of Roy Miller. Koch inspected land and land values from Brownsville to Corpus Christi, and in January of 1907 he bought from Mrs. King 18,881 acres in the Rincón de la Bóveda grant for $189,839. The purchase was later increased by 5000 acres, and Koch asked for and received additional rights as exclusive agent for the sale of certain nearby acreage owned by Mrs. King. The first step in Koch's program was the removal of Spohn station to a more favorable site a mile south, and rebuilding and rechristening it with a name more evocative for promotional purposes: Riviera.[76] By 1912 Koch had established a growing town, a community of small farms, two small dependent hamlets called Baffin Bay and Vatman, and a resort area nine miles east of the railway, Riviera Beach. Built on the shore of an inlet of the Laguna Madre called Baffin Bay, Riviera Beach achieved some currency as a resort served not only by a hotel and bathhouse, but by a little branch rail line built by Koch, the Baffins Bay & Western Railway.[77] A hurricane in 1916 brought havoc to the resort from which it never recovered, but the farm tracts sold by the Theo. F. Koch Land Co. survived as a permanent feature in the area's development.

Between Koch's Riviera subdivision and the Kingsville tracts of the Kleberg Town & Improvement Co. was the railroad flag stop called Ricardo, six miles south of Kingsville. In 1908 the Kleberg company appointed an agent to sell tracts at Ricardo; seven years later there was sufficient cotton acreage in the neighborhood to warrant the building of a local gin. Beginning in 1913, settlers there also brought in Jersey cattle, to establish what became a profitable dairying business in the Ricardo vicinity.[78]

Two other stations on the railroad became important as operational points on Mrs. King's ranch. Headquarters for the whole southern division was moved from the old site at El Sauz to the railway station Norias, named in Spanish for the ranch's (and the railroad's) lawyer and great friend: *norias* means *wells*. At Norias station the ranch made use of a two-story frame house built on railroad land only a few paces from the tracks; this gaunt, sunburned, hospitable edifice was to gain more than a local fame as the bachelor roost of Caesar Kleberg, the strenuous and genial superintendent who bossed the lower end of the King Ranch for thirty years. Norias was 50.7 miles south from Kingsville.[79] Three and a half miles north from Kingsville was a rail siding named Caesar. It was here that the ranch built its largest set of shipping pens to handle the cattle it sent to market, as Richard King had dreamed fifty years before. Fifty years later, with the railway a section of a great trunk system, a sign at Caesar still says:

THE LARGEST LIVESTOCK LOADING POINT
on the Missouri Pacific Lines
Santa Gertrudis Ranch

The economic growing-up of the area served by the St. Louis, Brownsville & Mexico Railway was not unaccompanied by growing pains. The railroad itself suffered in the growth process it created. It went into a receivership in 1913 after having been taken over by the Frisco system and renamed the Gulf Coast Line; three years later it became a part of the Missouri Pacific.

In 1904 the rails built across an almost completely unpopulated stretch of ranching country to a border town terminal of just seven thousand inhabitants opened up a territory so undeveloped that the profits of railroading through it were future potentials, not present actualities—as the Southern Pacific had accurately predicted, not choosing to gamble. There was admirable courage in the backers of the "Brownie," who did gamble. By their willingness to risk as pioneers must risk, they made the actual commerce of new land commensurate with its promise. In 1907 the three-year-old railway hauled about five hundred carloads of farm products from the lower Rio Grande valley. By 1925 the produce of that valley was moving in 35,362 cars to distant markets.[80]

Though the land development expressed by such figures was gradual, the arrival of the rails caused an immediate commercial quickening from Corpus Christi south to the Rio Grande. Brownsville awakened from its sleep. Soon a branch line of the rails, from Harlingen on the Arroyo Colorado to Fordyce above the old Mexican town of Reynosa, paralleled the river and opened a route to market for farm products from the rich alluvial soil of the valley. A widening network of canals, built by the private capital of a series of land development companies, brought a flow of river water to irrigate and make productive a constantly increasing acreage. Mesquite jungles along the margin of the Rio Grande became plowed fields. Land prices climbed. The kind of land that sold for \$4 an acre in 1905 sold for \$22 in 1910, unimproved.[81] The first bale of cotton produced in the United States during that season of 1910 came from Mercedes in the Rio Grande Valley;[82] the same year, oranges and grapefruit were first picked in commercial quantities from the newly planted citrus groves of the valley.[83] A modest resurgence of the old Brownsville-Matamoros trade, fed now by rails instead of boats, joined with the agricultural development of the area and added to a growth of prosperity. United States dollars instead of Mexican pesos became the currency in general circulation at Brownsville for the first time in that town's history.[84]

The increase in population which followed the advent of the railroad reshaped the politics as well as the economy of the south tip of Texas. Most of the newly arrived citizenry were Anglo-Americans who came carrying with them "the traditional ideas of local government and politics found in such states as Minnesota, Iowa and Kansas." The local government they encountered in southmost Texas, the sway of a kind of patriarchal border bossism practiced by a small minority of Anglo-American old settlers over the large majority of Latin-Americans who constituted decisive weight at the polls, was resented by many of the new arrivals who could not see how their own interests were furthered by such a body politic — and who were soon carrying, by their increasing numbers, a large voting weight themselves.[85] A shake-up was inevitable, and it was most notable in Cameron County, where politics were attended by great bitterness and by some bloodshed. When the heat and strain of the

1910 election came, James B. Wells, boss of the local Democrats, was too ill to participate, but his son, Joseph K. Wells, managed a Pyrrhic victory over combined Republican and Independent forces.[86]

The new citizenry on the farms and in the villages springing up on recent cow pastures were not only dissatisfied with their lack of voice in local county government as constituted, they found themselves and their interests physically isolated by inconvenient distances from the county seats. The Raymondville community, for instance, was forty-six miles from officialdom at Brownsville; Kingsville was forty miles from its county seat at Corpus Christi and farmers at Riviera were nearly sixty miles from their Nueces County courthouse. By 1910 there was a strong movement afoot for divisions within the old county lines to establish new counties and attendant new county governments to serve newly arrived clusters of population. The movement became insistent enough to bring action at Austin; the state legislature created several new counties of direct concern to the management of Mrs. King's ranch.

Willacy County was first established in 1911, named for state Senator John G. Willacy who represented the district. The first Willacy County's boundaries more or less enclosed what is now Kenedy County. It was not until a further division in 1921 that Willacy received its present location farther south, while most of its previously defined area became a newly created county named for pioneer Captain Mifflin Kenedy.[87] The original Willacy County's courthouse was at the town of Sarita; ten years later Sarita became the county seat of Kenedy[88] and Raymondville was designated the seat of the newly located Willacy County. Both these changes brought the southern divisions of the King Ranch — formerly in Cameron County — into new jurisdictions.

Two other new counties were formed by lopping sections from the western and southern sides of big Nueces. Jim Wells County, named for the most eminent lawyer in South Texas, was created in 1911 with the county seat at Alice.[89] Located northwest of the Santa Gertrudis headquarters, this new county contained a portion of the de la Garza Santa Gertrudis grant and some other pastures comprising the northwest sector of Mrs. King's ranch.

Two years later, by an act of the legislature dated February 27, 1913, Kingsville itself became the seat of a new county, named for the German-Texan soldier at the battle of San Jacinto, Robert Justus Kleberg. Carved from the southern part of Nueces, Kleberg County contained the heart of the Santa Gertrudis ranch.[90] The personal property of Henrietta King comprised approximately eighty per cent of Kleberg County's total acreage. Manager Kleberg administered a preponderant part of the land and of the business in the area, and he also assumed leadership in any movement he believed would contribute to that area's permanent development and prosperity. He heartily endorsed the creation of the new counties and worked for their establishment.

The resulting new county administrations were clearly not arrangements for the more convenient governing of a "private domain." On the contrary, the new county seats — particularly the one at Kingsville — made the King Ranch's political position much more complicated.[91] From Robert Kleberg's point of view, the situation related not merely to seeing friends holding local office, but to maintaining a strong voice in affairs which determined local tax rates. Public funds in increasing amounts were required for the expenses of local government. Bond issues were demanded for both municipal and county improvements, especially farm roads. All the funds of course derived from taxes; in owning the huge majority of taxable property, the Santa Gertrudis ranch bore the huge majority of county and municipal costs. The ranch accepted this as its proper obligation. At the same time, its predominance on the tax rolls went unmatched by any predominance at the voting polls: the interests represented by the ranch could be subject to a punishing tax rate created by the voting majority who would pay very little of the tax. "The development of South Texas," which Robert Kleberg had joyfully anticipated and then brought about, involved the Santa Gertrudis with a myriad ventures beyond its pasture fences, and planted a briar patch of politics within the front gate.

Until the creation of Kleberg County, the political influence the isolated ranch could muster was devoted mainly to delivering votes to help the rather remote campaigns led by its friend, James B. Wells. Both the King and the Kenedy ranches did all they could in answer to pleas like the telegram from Wells to Caesar Kleberg in 1908: "Partner, please get Robert to hoist Raymond to hold primary at Raymondville and other points and get out all the vote he possibly can. Answer."[92] In return, Party Boss Wells—never in his life a candidate for public office—did his level best to take care of his political friends. Wells' law associate, Harbert Davenport, noted that "the big cattle owners trusted him [Wells] in politics and usually suffered when they attempted politics on their own."[93]

The creation and existence of Kingsville and of Kleberg County necessarily focused the political attention and activity of the Santa Gertrudis ranch upon many local issues. In dealing with most of them, the aid and advice of James B. Wells were depended upon. His insight and effectiveness may be indicated by the record of peace and quiet, the absence of really bitter political rancor, which attended the growth of Kingsville and the development of Kleberg County.

In the midst of the changes brought to South Texas by a new century and a new railroad, the five Kleberg children began to grow up. The house on the rise of the prairie no longer stood isolated by miles of silent pastures crossed only by winding wagon roads.

When the school term opened at Corpus Christi in September,

1904, the new rails made a pleasant difference in the lives of the young Klebergs. On Friday afternoons General Manager Jeff Miller ordered a caboose hooked to an engine and sent it to Corpus Christi. When school let out the Kleberg kids found their own train waiting to take them home to the ranch for the week end. They usually raced to the tracks, then fought over who would climb up the ladder for the choice high seat, to look out the window in the cupola of their "private caboose" while it rattled and clacked over the forty-five cindery miles toward Kingsville — where horses were waiting.[94] That September of 1904 Richard Mifflin — who had long since come to be called plain Dick — was nearly seventeen and a junior at Corpus Christi High. His sister Henrietta, fifteen in July, was a year behind him at high school. Alice, eleven, was still in grammar school; the eight-year-old Bob was starting third grade and the baby sister Sarah, aged six, was just beginning school.

Altogether exceptional talents residing in Dick Kleberg displayed themselves long before he grew to manhood, manifesting a personality shaped by almost excessive competence and confidence, both physical and intellectual. He was as articulate as he was aggressive; excellent at his studies when he cared to be, lighthearted and handsome, gregarious, popular with his schoolmates, president of his high school senior class; he was also suspended from school for fist fighting. He played baseball as pitcher of the high school team or he sailed a boat on Corpus Christi Bay with the same skill he rode a wild horse or roped and tied an outlaw steer. He was a trick shot, a splendid hunter, able in the practice of prairie lore he learned from old men of the *campo* who lived close to the ways of the unsheltered earth and wild nature. The physically coordinated and competitive Dick was endowed with a mind of the same agile order as his body. He could use that mind with facile brilliance to store up information derived either from men or from books. He could permanently retain within the grip of a vise-like memory any oddment of fact that interested him. From his father's family he inherited talent for music: when he sang he could provide his own accompaniment on the guitar, accordion or piano. Brought up amongst *Kineños*, he spoke Spanish as naturally and as fluently as English; his gift of tongues was extended by a large smattering of German he absorbed from his father and the Kleberg kin, and by a command of French he acquired from a tutor.[95] A poetic feeling for and understanding of the range and its life, what it was and what it meant to a sentient being—very uncommon in a personality so capable of extroversion and action—distinguished the cast of his thought and marked his character as he matured. It was natural for his father who was a lawyer, the son and brother of lawyers, to want his eldest son to follow the family footsteps. Dick's vivid presence and gifted mind seemed exactly fitted for a career in leading and persuading men.

His sister Henrietta was a lively and engaging child with an impish mind fond enough of mischief and feminine frivolity to be called "the butterfly" by Mrs. King. "Grandmother," the butterfly would tease, with a charm that brought only the mildest imitation of reproof, "can't I *dance* instead of playing hymns?" As the young Henrietta grew, gaiety inclined her spirit toward parties and the pleasures of town doings. She did not take leave of the rigors of the saddle and dusty cow camps in the sun. She was a frequent visitor at Caesar's Norias, "though the accommodations were most primitive." Though she would live in faraway New York, her love for the Santa Gertrudis was abiding; she came back to visit whenever the opportunity presented itself.

Young Alice and Sarah as they grew up became tomboy hands at the cow works and roundups. Alice was especially unenthusiastic over school life and school studies at Corpus Christi. Her character —in her growing devotion to range life, to rides in solitude, to

knowledge of and communion with the land and the livestock —
bore a marked resemblance to that of her mother's beloved brother,
Robert E. Lee King.

Sarah, baby of the family, less Spartan than Alice, more at home
outdoors than Henrietta, became a skilled huntress and horsewoman
on the range, and the favorite of the *Kineños,* who admired her looks
and liked her sense of humor.

The young Robert of the Kleberg family, whose name naturally
became Bob, was eight and a half years younger than his brother,
a gap in age so wide that the two boys were able to share little
genuine companionship until they were well grown. Bob and his
sister Sarah, as the most junior members of the family, grew up with
a special bond of fellowship between them.

There were resemblances in the characters of the two Kleberg boys
and there were contrasts. Bob possessed self-assurance, but it was
unlike Dick's. Bob had to work for his. The gifts of mind and body
he possessed were neither so ready-made nor so diverse nor so amply
sufficient as his brother's. Bob had to strive. It gave his personality a
tension absent in Dick. Bob's wide grin was not his brother's confident smile. A self-sought discipline, a grapple for excellence, shaped
Bob's demeanor.

The two boys were alike in their love for the life of the cow camps
and their skills horseback. When Bob was six, he learned to do his
part in holding a herd at roundup; at that age he was riding out
before daylight with his father, brother, Caesar Kleberg and Sam
Ragland, working cattle. By the time he was twelve, Bob was more
expert with rifle and gun than most grown men, and was a regular
member of the adult hunting parties on the ranch.[96] He learned the
lore of the outdoors; he also learned every phase of the ranch's daily
work by doing manual labor as a plain cowhand. "I never wanted to

do anything else," Bob said, more than forty years later. "Nothing is more fun. I never liked town, and I don't like it now."

School was in town and at school he did not display his brother's easy aptitude with books, though his marks were good in subjects that interested him. Both brothers possessed highly perceptive and creative imaginations, yet the aptitudes springing from them were different. Dick's strongest abilities were contained within the humanities, the arts; while the proclivity of Bob's young engineering mind was more for the demonstrable fact and useful figure of practical science. The Spanish the two brothers spoke provided some index to their attitudes. Bob's less adept tongue spoke the utilitarian idiom of the cow camp, with more than a touch of gringo accent. Dick, though he employed no Castilian lisp, spoke Spanish rounded and undefiled, as if he were discoursing in his only tongue.

Bob entered school athletics as his brother did. He "played a little football" and earned a place on the baseball team, until he suffered a bad break in his pitching arm, cranking an automobile. In 1912, when he was fifteen and a sophomore at Corpus Christi High, motor cars were recent and strange and glamorous on the rough roads of South Texas. Bob's grandmother King in one of her rare extravagances presented him with a five thousand dollar Packard. The mechanically minded Bob proceeded to soup up its top speed from forty to sixty miles an hour, a feat which he still remembers as a "scientific accomplishment."

Beyond all else Bob's consuming and abiding passion was the ranch. He was fitted to its life; he was fascinated with its operation. From the time when he was a very small boy he had lived with a ranching mentor and exemplar; old bachelor Sam Ragland stayed in a cottage about a hundred yards from the big house, and Bob's father had sent Bob to live in a room next to the cattle manager's. The fledgling ranchman and the bluff cattleman had their meals at the big house with the other members of the family, but they had their quarters together at the cottage. In that companionship and in the long days on the pastures and in the corrals young Bob absorbed what the years had taught Sam Ragland about the complicated chemistry that produced beef from grass. Bob Kleberg as a man would remember the evenings when the rain came pounding on the cottage roof and old Sam in his nightshirt would come lighting up his pipe, strolling into Bob's room, to listen to the welcome rain, to talk, to think aloud about the coming grass and how best to use it. "When you can see the cow chips floating," Sam would say, "then we've had a rain."

Robert Kleberg, watching the characters of his two sons develop, in his affection and in his thoroughgoing Prussian way planned work for each of his boys when they were men ready to take their turns of responsibility at the Santa Gertrudis. Dick would become the lawyer-ranchman, capable of dealing not only with the work on the range but with other facets of the ranch's interests, its relations with government, business and men beyond the ranch's gates. Bob would become the scientifically trained stockman-agronomist, to help carry on the work Richard King had commenced and Robert Kleberg had continued, within the gates.

When he finished high school at Corpus Christi in 1906, Dick was entirely ready to be a ranchman but he was not so sure about being a lawyer. Whatever reluctance he felt was overcome by an affectionate regard for his father's plans and wishes, and by a habit of obedience. In the fall of 1906 Dick entered the University of Texas for a study of the law. He joined a fraternity, Sigma Chi, and entered with a characteristic gusto into college life, where he was active on the campus and outstanding in his studies. One of his professors, the jocular Judge W. E. Simkins,[97] ex-Rebel and great raconteur, provided a lively stimulus to the brilliant young ranchman's bouts with Torts and Equity. In 1911 Dick emerged from the university with a degree in law — and with another interest of a predominant fascination. He was engaged to be married to a student he had met at the university, the beautiful Miss Mamie Searcy of Brenham, Texas.

All the family from the Santa Gertrudis, including the matriarch Henrietta King, traveled in a railway private car to attend the wedding and festivities held at Brenham on June 12, 1911. Friends from far and near were present at the elaborate church ceremony. After a reception at the Searcy home the bride and groom left on a wedding trip to Colorado. The *Kingsville Record* reported:

> They will return to this city and make their future home at Santa Gertrudis, just west of town, one of the most beautiful ranch homes in Texas, where Mr. Kleberg was born and raised, where his family Mr. and Mrs. R. J. Kleberg and children and Mrs. H. M. King, his grandmother, owner of the immense King ranch, still make their home a good share of the time.
>
> The young couple are both graduates of the State University where they first met. Mr. Kleberg graduated with high honors from the law school of that institution but does not follow his profession further than it serves him in assisting his father in looking after the interests of their vast estates.
>
> The bride is a most accomplished young lady. She has the honor of carrying off all the highest honors of her class, in literature, domestic science and other studies.

Though Dick did become a member of the Texas Bar soon after leaving law school, he never entered a general practice of law.[98] Instead, he settled at the ranch with his bride and became the superintendent of the Laureles.

The ranch work, dealing with more than a million acres and about 80,000 head of cattle and 12,000 head of horses, had been divided for administrative purposes into three interrelated ranches, the Santa Gertrudis, the Norias-Sauz and the Laureles. Sam Ragland had charge of all ranching affairs on the lands comprising the Santa Gertrudis and related acreage. Caesar Kleberg at Norias bossed the "South Ranch," which was separated from the rest of the ranch by an intervening twenty-five miles of pasture belonging to the Kenedy and Armstrong ranches. Dick Kleberg took the job of supervising operations at the Laureles adjoining the Santa Gertrudis on the east. Each manager ran his sector at the orders of Robert Kleberg, whose ranching office at headquarters was now augmented by a town business office in Kingsville presided over by John D. Finnegan. Caesar's affable brother, Al Kleberg, a young electrical engineer, had also arrived to furnish a most able hand in the management of the lumber company and other town business enterprises owned by Mrs. King.

Twenty miles across a flat prairie from the Santa Gertrudis, Dick and Mamie Kleberg settled into the rambling big house at the old Laureles headquarters place. It was isolated, and it was oftentimes rigorous for the young university graduate who had taken Phi Beta Kappa honors in domestic science,[99] especially when there was illness and the nearest doctor was a score of miles away, but Mamie entered with zest into the life her husband loved and for which he was so colorfully suited. His skills beyond the daily range-riding management of a beef ranching operation were as diverse as the designing of a saddle tree which became commercially popular, the "Kleberg Special,"[100] and the development of one of the finest Jersey dairy herds in America. His sporting interests gave dash to life at the Laureles. He bought and bred fast horses which he himself rode at racing meets, and trotters which he drove in sulky races.[101] He raised champion bird dogs and taught them in the field. He coursed coyotes, sometimes with wolfhounds, sometimes with a fast horse and a quick loop of his rope. He bred strains of fighting chickens and pursued the laws of their genetics (which he applied to livestock breeding) with the same avidity he displayed in laying a few bets on his iron-spurred fowls at the pits. His mother, believing the best of her favorite son, once said, "Richard is the only one of my children interested in poultry."

Life at Laureles was further heightened by the range characters employed there: the Irishman Pat Cody, foreman during the regime of the Scottish syndicate, in the tea and scones days of Captain Tod and his tweedy wife; the *caporal* Augustín Quintanilla, who possessed in surpassing measure every *Kineño* skill; the incredibly strong and seemingly immortal Faustino Villa, who had been a deck hand on the *Colonel Cross* with Captain Richard King, and who at the age of one hundred years swam a half mile across the Santa Gertrudis Creek swollen in flood to deliver the mail to *El Abogao*.

"The year I was born," Faustino Villa said, "M E N were born."[102]

The size, the color, the wealth of Mrs. King's ranch commanded increasing attention from the press, increasing interest from the public. The aging widow in plain black who owned such a remarkable and picturesque property had long since become a personage, a *grande dame* of note far beyond the pastures of Texas. The President of the United States himself—though he had not been able to schedule a tour of the Santa Gertrudis—had called upon Mrs. King. On October 22, 1909, six days after he had held a meeting at El Paso with President Porfirio Díaz of Mexico, William Howard Taft on his way homeward by rail to the White House had paid a visit to Corpus Christi. After a short speech before the gathered crowds, in which he agreeably expressed interest in harbor improvements to make Corpus Christi the deep water port it had not yet become, President Taft had attended the formal opening of the Corpus Christi Country Club and then retired with his entourage to the Broadway mansion of Mrs. King, where he was entertained at luncheon and presented with a gift. The portly President carried to Washington a Running ⌄⌄ saddle made on the Santa Gertrudis, a *Kineño* bridle and a pair of spurs.[103]

That year of 1909 Henrietta King became a great-grandmother. Her grandson, Richard King III, after graduating as valedictorian of his class at the San Antonio Academy in 1903 and attending agricultural school at the University of Missouri, had married Miss Pierpont Heaney, daughter of a prominent physician of Corpus Christi, in 1907. The young couple had established their home at Corpus Christi where their first son, Richard Lee King, was born in 1909.

Only three of Mrs. King's own children, Richard II, Alice and Nettie, were still living. At the turn of the century, August 28, 1900, her daughter Ella King Welton had died at Concordville, Pennsylvania, after a long illness, and had been buried by the side of her father and brother in San Antonio. Ella's daughter, Henrietta Mary Welton, was an only child and much beloved by the grandmother for whom she was named. She married Nathaniel Burwell Page of Virginia; though the Pages lived in Virginia, they were regular visitors at the ranch.

With the improved railway service in the area and the increasing use of automobiles, Mrs. King's big houses both in town and on the ranch were used more often for gatherings and visits with her children and grandchildren, and to entertain the large circle of her family's friends.

The attic spaces on the original front unit of her big ranch house had been converted to third-story rooms, fitted with dormer windows and finished with a front gallery railed and ornamented with scrollwork to match the larger porches below. Standing high and well groomed in new white, mellow and inviting in the midst of a smooth wide lawn and the shade of big trees, the old house on the rise above the prairie—and above the growing town of Kingsville—was a literal embodiment of the gradual growth and increasing grace of the Santa Gertrudis, different indeed from the plain shape of the one-story frame ranch house built on bare wilderness ground half a century before.

In the early morning hours of January 4, 1912, Henrietta King, nearly eighty years of age, saw this home which represented so much of her life burn to the ground.

A group of visitors from the East had been hunting at the ranch and had departed for the train at Kingsville early in the evening, leaving only Mr. and Mrs. Jeff N. Miller as guests in the house with the Klebergs and Mrs. King. While everyone was asleep, sometime before 4:00 A.M., fire broke out within the highly inflammable wooden walls. It was later established that a cranky gardener named Mahoney, employed at headquarters, had a long record as an arsonist and probably set the blaze.

Dick Kleberg's bulldog awakened Caesar and Al Kleberg in their downstairs room by barking and pulling at their bedcovers. At about the same time, the Millers discovered smoke and flame. They were in one of the upstairs bedrooms in the long addition built on the rear of the original house, and without waiting to dress they dashed along the bitterly cold outside second-story porch to warn the Klebergs at the front of the house. The Klebergs and Mrs. King were able to hurry down the stairway in their part of the house, but the interior stairs in the rear addition were already blocked by flame, so that the Millers were forced to climb and slide down from the outside porch to escape. In a fall to the ground Mrs. Miller broke two ribs.

Meanwhile Mrs. King had very calmly emerged from the burning house, wearing a black dress and carrying two small bags, one with medicines and another with a few valuables.

Someone in the family, counting heads, suddenly called out, "Where's Alice?" Al Kleberg dashed into the house and came back out carrying young Alice Kleberg, who had not awakened in the excitement and was still half-asleep.

Robert Kleberg, with his nightshirt tucked into his trousers, went with Al into the smoky office and vault at the southwest corner room of the downstairs. Together they were able to toss some of the ranch records and papers to safety outside. Sam Ragland, who was trying to move the piano, was ordered by Mrs. King to come out of the house. "Let nobody get hurt," she said. "We can build a new home. We can't replace a life."

The eighteen-year-old Alice, now entirely awake, ran to the bell tower by the kitchen building and rang the big bell there, long and hard. Its clang awoke every hand around headquarters; the sound carried to Kingsville. Flames burst suddenly from the house roof, lighting the sky, making the fire visible for miles across the prairie.

No fire fighting equipment was available. The family, the Millers, the *Kineños* stood dazed at the leap of the flame, the red tumble of falling timbers, the furious clouds of yellow sparks knocked whirling into the far dark. As the helpless and half-dressed crowd moved back from the bite of the heat and great sheets of licking fire ate the walls away, someone suggested to Mrs. King that she go with the rest of her family for shelter at the commissary.

More than forty years later, Al Kleberg remembered how she came out of the house, moved away from the baleful glare and taint of smoke. "I can see her now," Al Kleberg said. "All dressed in black with a little black bag in her hand. She turned and threw a kiss at the burning house."

In the gray light of the winter morning after daybreak there were two forty-foot brick chimneys standing black and alone over a mound of smouldering rubble at a queerly empty place by burned stumps of trees and scorched grass. The wires along the railroad tracks away from Kingsville carried stories; distant newsrooms wrote headlines, "Famous King Ranch House Is Burned," "Occupants Escape Death."[104]

Aside from the records and papers rescued from the office, and a few small keepsakes haphazardly carried away from the flames, the house and all its contents were utterly destroyed. Ashes and rubble, which were carefully sifted in an attempt to find valuable jewelry lost by Mrs. Miller, yielded nothing. The fire cut the Santa Gertrudis home place totally and irretrievably away from the physical setting and the accumulated mementos of its past.

Three days after the fire Robert Kleberg sent a message to his friend B. F. Yoakum in New York, to answer a telegram in which Yoakum had expressed his sorrow over the destruction of the hospitable house. In a style heavily reminiscent of another well-known visitor at the ranch, Edgar A. Guest, Kleberg wired:

THEY MAY DESTROY, THEY MAY BURN THE BUILDINGS OF SANTA GER-
TRUDIS IF THEY WILL, BUT THE SPIRIT OF HOSPITALITY AND FRIENDSHIP
WILL HANG AROUND HER STILL. HER GATES ARE OPEN WIDE AND ALL HER
FRIENDS MAY ENTER AND NONE WILL BE DENIED.

A one-story structure of five rooms, devised as temporary housing, was hastily erected about fifty yards from the ruin,[105] while the manager of the Rancho Santa Gertrudis turned his thought toward a replacement of what had been lost. Mrs. King set forth one condition for it: "Build a house," she said, "that anybody could walk in in boots." The rest she left to her son-in-law and the architects he engaged.[106]

It was Robert Kleberg's aim to build what he termed "a monument to Mrs. King's hospitality." In that monumentality he based his conception fittingly enough upon the memory of an impressive casa grande he had once seen at the casco of a hacienda in Mexico.

Participating in the design and planning, he supervised creation of a grandiose house which required two years and $350,000 to build.

Its walls of hollow tile and stuccoed concrete rose up fireproof and massive upon the site of the old frame ranch house. The dazzling whiteness of its great size, its complexity of juts, turns and trims, of crenelations and corbels, archways and tiles, its pierced tower, all combined to produce the effect of a mammoth villa built to stand in the florid light of a hot southern sun. If its scrambled elements of Mexican, Moorish and California Mission, of Long Island and Wild Horse Desert, left something to be desired by captious critics of architecture, the building also had a strong presence, a curious grandeur that somehow mellowed to fit the pastures of South Texas and to grow attractive with the passage of time.

The great house had twenty-five rooms, each with its fireplace; there were nearly as many baths; it had wide and cool verandas, a grand salon with murals of the Alamo, of ranch landscape and of its wild life and livestock. There was a dining hall for fifty guests, and a patio planted with tropical trees, shrubs, blossoming vines and vivid flowers. Tower windows overlooking the patio were fitted with stained glass by Tiffany. Italian bronze balustrades lined the main marble stairway. The floor of the salon was made of mesquite boards, cut from the ranch, polished and pegged with ebony. There were especially loomed rugs on the tiled floors of other rooms; mounted heads of Longhorn steers and antlered bucks hung on the walls. Only in the matter of furniture is Robert Kleberg said to have displayed a hand not lavish: the house took a great deal of furniture and he bought it in sets which were utilitarian, plain and mostly uncomfortable. In the baronial-ranch atmosphere of the vasty rooms and halls "nothing showed a trace of the feminine touch"; it took years to provide them with a measure of the graceful comfort the family had enjoyed at the old house.

Though the new home was not entirely completed until 1915, it was finished enough for the family to move into by late 1913. In the course of its construction numerous additions and improvements were made on outlying buildings around headquarters. A new carriage house, a ten-car garage and a modern dairy barn were built. A kitchen and dining room were installed in the second floor of the commissary, for the use of chance visitors, job hunters and wayfarers who came constantly to the ranch. The old commissary building, the nearby servants' quarters, and the fireproof stables which had been built in 1911 were all refurbished and newly painted. A major landscaping program was initiated to develop a setting appropriate to the big house. The lawn was enlarged, planted with a smooth and thick mat of carpet grass. Tall date palms, big-leafed banana trees and feathery lines of pink-blossoming tamarisk, shrubs and beds of flowers, grew to contrast handsomely with the native willow, ebony, huisache and big gnarled mesquite. The roadway leading into this Texan *casco* became an avenue lined with alternating palms and ebony. When the building and planting were completed in 1915, ranch headquarters had assumed the aspect which in every essential regard forms its appearance today, forty years later.

Two daughters of the family were married in the big house when it was very newly finished. In a ceremony held at 8:30 on the morning of January 30, 1915, Alice Gertrudis Kleberg married a young cattleman, Tom T. East. Henrietta was her sister's wedding attendant and Caesar Kleberg was East's best man. Minerva King, daughter of Richard King II, played the piano and Dick Kleberg sang "Til the Sands of the Desert Grow Cold." Following a big family wedding breakfast, the newlyweds left directly for San Antonio Viejo, the groom's ranch south of Hebbronville in Jim Hogg County about seventy-five miles from the Santa Gertrudis, where the young couple established their home and shared the arduous ranch life they both knew and loved.

Six months later, on June 26, 1915, the big house was the scene of far more elaborate festivity when Henrietta Rosa Kleberg married John Adrian Larkin of New York. Larkin, who later became Vice President of the Celanese Corporation, was a companion and Princeton classmate of Tom Armstrong, son of the ranger and ranchman, John B. Armstrong. Tom had introduced Henrietta to his college friend; at the wedding Armstrong was Larkin's best man. The ceremony—with bridesmaids, groomsmen and a flower girl in attendance—was performed at an altar of flowers beneath the Tiffany windows in the patio. Henrietta's brother Dick sang "Because," accompanied by Cousin Emilie Kleberg of Galveston; at the altar Robert Kleberg gave his daughter in marriage. The bridal couple took their leave while Princetonians of the wedding party sang "Old Nassau" then gave the Princeton cheer, speeding the happy Larkins on their way to a honeymoon in the Adirondacks, a summer home at Croton-on-Hudson and a town life far removed from South Texas. Among the wedding gifts were a loving cup from the cowboys at Norias and a painting of Texas bluebonnets from the Santa Gertrudis hands.

With Mamie and Dick Kleberg at Laureles, Alice and Tom East at San Antonio Viejo, Henrietta and John Larkin in New York, only the two youngest Kleberg children lived at the Santa Gertrudis— and Bob was away for most of the year at college.

After graduation from Corpus Christi High School in 1914 Bob, at the strong request of his father, had enrolled in the school of agriculture at the University of Wisconsin. Recounting it later, Bob said, "The discussion with father was what I should study, not that I did not want to go. It was understood that I would go. It was my idea at the time to study electrical engineering. My father told me he had always felt handicapped that he did not have the training or education he needed for the agricultural and ranching side of his responsibility in managing the ranch. He wanted me to study agriculture for a year; if I was not interested in it by that time, I could shift to any other course of study. Needless to say, I did become interested, and continued in that course."

He joined Sigma Chi and applied himself as much to the fun of campus life as he did to books. He went out for track, sailed ice boats on Lake Mendota and learned to ski in the Wisconsin winter weather. During the two years he attended university his grades were average.

Events at home summoned him early in 1916. The ranch management was shorthanded. A bitter drought had begun to wither the grass at the Santa Gertrudis. And its big house had been built to greet a time of trouble. A new cycle of violence had come again to the old contentious place south of the Nueces. Lashed by a great revolutionary upheaval in Mexico, fired by old hatreds on the north bank of the Rio Grande, bandits were riding again where Richard King had fought them forty years before.

XVI *Troublous Times and a Long Life's End*

PRESIDENT PORFIRIO DIAZ

had ruled the Republic of Mexico since 1884. In the twenty-seven years of his iron-handed regime Mexico had enjoyed peace. Natural resources had been developed, internal improvements had been made, national solvency and firm foreign credits had been achieved, prosperity hitherto unknown in Mexico had appeared. Yet there had been a monstrous governmental fault within this outward betterment. The Díaz prosperity was slanted. It reached only the rich and the powerful. The working population grew poorer while a small class of property holders grew richer. A chasm between the few rich and the many poor grew too wide for any despotism to bridge.

The collapse of the Díaz government was somewhat strangely brought about by the mild and unmilitary son of a rich family of *hacendados* in Coahuila, Francisco Madero. This studious and idealistic little man with a dark goatee had written a book, a temperate and reasonable tract on Mexico's need for political freedom, entitled *The Presidential Succession of 1910*.[1] The ideas expressed in it were by no means those of an incendiary, yet in the fevered series of events attendant to Díaz' re-election that year the modest Madero by force of circumstance and in spite of himself became the voice and then the militant rallying agent of all Mexico's long repressed malcontents. After being thrown in jail at San Luis Potosí (and released through the influence of his family), and after a flight to refuge in Texas (where he declared the Díaz re-election null and void and proclaimed himself ready to assume the provisional presidency pending new elections), Madero recrossed the international boundary in the desert west of El Paso on February 14, 1911, to join with and take command of armed revolutionists who had already gathered to lay siege to the border town of Ciudad Juárez, Chihuahua. Amongst the rebels were two leaders Madero could not control: Pascual Orozco, a storekeeper from southern Chihuahua, and Pancho Villa, a cow thief and bandit from Durango. While emissaries of Madero were negotiating with officialdom in Mexico City, Orozco and Villa took the siege of Ciudad Juárez into their own hands; on May 10, 1911, they assaulted and took the town. The battle was in defiance of Madero's orders, yet the victory made Madero the sudden master of northern Mexico, and sent revolt pounding through the land. The rotten structure of the old regime fell with a crash. In less than three weeks after the battle for Ciudad Juárez the eighty-year-old dictator Díaz was in flight for a haven in Europe, and the 37-year-old doctrinaire Madero was on his triumphant passage to the capital, where he was hailed as "the semi-divine deliverer of the masses from bondage."[2]

By character and by experience Madero was incapable of coping with the situation he had shaped, the anarchy he had unchained. The unchecked defiance of the first two real toughs he confronted, Villa and Orozco at Ciudad Juárez, was an early and clear indication of the tragedy in store. Francisco Madero was in essence a prophet, not a leader. He was soon a victim, caught up and enmeshed in violent events and with ambitious men beyond his capacity to measure or to control. After a sorrowful series of uprisings and betrayals, plots and counterplots, on the night of February 21, 1913, while being transferred from the National Palace to the federal prison, the deposed President Madero was brutally shot at the orders of the reactionary military man who had manipulated himself into the usurpation of the power of the presidency, General Victoriano Huerta. The assassination of Madero cast the revolutionary struggles of Mexico into a deeper dimension and into a labyrinthine violence which lasted for seven more ravaging years, until the nation was worn out with bloodshed.

Huerta managed to stay in power for a year and a half before he was driven from the country. His most formidable opposition was that which bore the large label of the Constitutionalist Party—which was itself split into factions waging war with each other—nominally headed by Venustiano Carranza, a singularly self-righteous, be-whiskered ex-governor and landowner of Coahuila. By the time Carranza succeeded to the provisional presidency, his tenure at the National Palace and the troops who sustained him in office were bitterly opposed by many forces: the actual leadership of the revolution was military rather than political, and had frayed out into a wide assortment of more or less autonomous chieftains living by their own warring devices. Soldiery and banditry became largely indeterminable.

From the multitude of leaders three great field chieftains emerged: Pancho Villa in the North, Emiliano Zapata in the South, Alvaro Obregón in the West and at the middle. It was the battle alignment of these three major figures in relation to Carranza that created the large pattern of events for the five last years of the revolution. Villa fought Carranza. Obregón fought for Carranza against Villa. Zapata opposed both Carranza and Obregón, but only by defensive action within Zapata's own territory.

The dynamics of the duel for power favored Obregón. In battle he eventually reduced Villa to military impotence, while other forces were working to Obregón's advantage. After a *Carranzista* general had murdered Zapata, after Carranza himself had been murdered in flight from a revolt led by Obregón's friends, after an interim government had bribed Villa to peace by the gift of a great hacienda, after surviving *Zapatistas* were quieted with a grant of lands and a promise of agrarian reforms, the strongest survivor of the revolution stepped up. In November of 1920 Obregón became the president of a Mexico peaceful by exhaustion: the revolution was over. Though it is true that the decade of travail gave birth to political, economic and social reforms which shape present-day Mexico, the revolution itself was tragically marked more by bloody grapples for personal power than by struggles to correct the abuses which had caused the national upheaval in 1911.

During the Díaz regime foreign capital had been cordially invited to Mexico and it had often received special privilege. The country's rich resources in metals and oil, the railroads, the industries and utilities, had been so dominated by foreign investment that the mass of the Mexican population had begun to feel cheated of its own economic birthright, of its own economic destiny. The national uprising was a surge of passionate nationalism. *Mexico for Mexicans* became a battle cry. A hatred of Americans, for whatever influence the "dollar diplomacy" of "the Colossus of the North" might or might not have on the Mexican economy, became part and parcel of the Mexican revolutionary spirit. Its virulence—manifested in bloodshed, pillage, confiscation of property—racked at American residents in Mexico. Its threat became an immediate concern of Americans living along fifteen hundred miles of border facing Mexico, and a vital concern of the United States government.[3]

The Díaz *Rurales* who had patrolled the Mexican frontier, maintaining order with a deadly efficiency, were suddenly dispersed in the spring of 1911. During March, President Taft ordered the mobilization of 25,000 United States troops for stations at points close to the Mexican border.[4] A watchful tension gripped citizens along the Rio Grande. Yet no revolutionary turbulences appeared along the lower reaches of the river opposite the south tip of Texas until early in 1913 when a revolt against Madero, shortly before his death, brought stirrings to the garrison at Matamoros.[5] Late in February the Governor of Texas sent four companies of Texas militia and eight Texas Rangers to Brownsville; a troop of Army Regulars from the 14th United States Cavalry arrived at the same time.[6]

Scattered bands of Constitutionalist forces opposing the federal garrisons of Huerta began to operate that spring in Nuevo León and Tamaulipas. In May they took Reynosa; in June they stormed Matamoros and captured it. Refugees poured across the border into Texas; there were wholesale executions of prisoners by the Constitutionalist commander; harsh tributes in cash were extorted from Matamoros business houses. The rabidly anti-American Constitutionalists made threats, and in the growing atmosphere of rapine and brutality the citizens of South Texas saw the ghosts of old times and old hates rise up and begin to ride.[7]

President Woodrow Wilson was engaged in a policy of backing the Constitutionalists and their "First Chief" Carranza against the Federals of Huerta, and in a policy of turning the other cheek, whilst writing a high-minded note of protest, as his official answer to violence against United States citizens and their property in Mexico. When revolutionary leaders observed no other punishment or retaliation, they mistook Wilson's forbearance for weakness and proceeded to abuse Americans at will. In 1914, bands of Mexican raiders began to cross the river for plunder on the Texas side. A United States Navy and Army landing against *Huertistas* at Vera Cruz in April of that year, and an American military occupation of that port for six months, did not help to convince Mexicans that they had no business on the north bank of the Rio Grande.[8]

In August a great war broke out in Europe. The German foreign office quickly measured the American sympathy for the Allies, and just as quickly calculated the uses of the Mexican antipathy for the United States. Foreseeing eventualities, the Germans lost no time in setting up an undercover apparatus in Mexico, not only as a headquarters for spying on the United States but as an agency to fan hate and foment war between the Mexicans and Americans. Soon "German agents were scattered all over Mexico, German army officers were teaching military science and tactics to Mexican soldiers and revolutionists, and a powerful wireless station in Mexico City was sending information from the United States to the Central Powers."[9]

Late in the spring of 1915 there were increasing raids on outlying ranches and farms and roads north of the Rio Grande. Anglo residents near the border in the south tip of Texas were not only wrathful over such criminality itself, they began to be aware of a mystifying conspiratorial strangeness in the Mexican people they knew and amongst whom they lived. The manners of friendly Texan-Mexicans changed. They withdrew in reserve; some became furtive, some became sullen. Unknown horsemen were seen riding in the brush. Disturbed Americans felt an alien wrongness in the very air. One of them spoke out, "What in the name of goodness is the matter with you Mexicans; are you all going crazy here?"[10]

The matter with the Mexicans was the work of German agents.[11]

It was revealed later when the United States entered the war in 1917 that Germany was actually toying with the propaganda possibilities of a crackpot scheme "to unite Mexico and Japan with Germany in a general war on the United States for the purpose of restoring the Southwest to Mexico and giving the Far West to Japan."[12] Some measure of the absurd fantasy to which Mexican dupes were led by a promise of German help came to United States officials early in 1915, when a deputy sheriff of Cameron County happened to arrest the Mexican by the name of Basilio Ramos, *alias* B. R. García, who had in his possession a paper which explained the curious behavior of many border Mexicans. This paper, written in Mexico, achieved notoriety as "The Plan of San Diego." It had a pipe dream weirdness that bulged old border men's eyes:

The Plan of San Diego provided that on February 20, 1915, at two o'clock in the morning, the Mexicans were to arise in arms against the United States and proclaim their liberty and their independence of Yankee tyranny. At the same time they would declare the independence of Texas, New Mexico, Arizona, Colorado, and California. The army would be the 'Liberating Army for Races and People'; and the red flag with its white diagonal fringe would bear the inscription 'Equality and Independence.' Funds would be provided by levies on captured towns, and state governments would be set up in the state capitals.

Every North American man over sixteen would be put to death as soon as his captors could extract from him all his funds or 'loans'; every stranger found armed should be executed regardless of race or nationality; no leader should enroll a stranger in the ranks unless he were Latin, negro, or Japanese. The Apaches of Arizona and other Indians were to receive every guarantee and have their lands returned to them.

The five states were to be organized as an independent Mexican republic, which at an appropriate time would seek annexation to Mexico. When success had crowned the initial effort, six more states north of those named— evidently Oklahoma, Kansas, Nebraska, South Dakota, Wyoming, and Utah—were to be taken from the United States and given to the negroes who were to select a suitable banner for their republic. This buffer negro state would lie between the Mexicans and what one of the signers of the Plan called 'the damned big-footed creatures' of the north.[13]

All that ever came of this outreaching fever of the imagination was a long series of ragged raids and large threats upon the lives and property of border Texans. Even so, events were sinister enough from mid-1915 through 1917 to disrupt ordinary daily existence and commerce. Life between the Rio Grande and the Nueces became almost constantly complicated with alarm. Hatreds flared at each new report of outrage committed by the revolutionists and bandits who came raiding across the border. New companies of Texas Rangers were enlisted. An aroused citizenry armed itself in fear of an actual invasion from the south. There were heated requests for more United States troops to guard the river.

During the first days of August, 1915, a formidable band of Mexican horsemen rode the brush more than fifty miles north of Brownsville. When their presence on the Sauz division of the King Ranch was reported to Caesar Kleberg, who was at Kingsville for the week end, he telephoned to the rangers at Brownsville and to the Army command at Fort Brown, requesting immediate help for the handful of cowboys, headed by foreman Tom Tate, who were charged with the protection of the southern end of the ranch. Early in the afternoon of August 8 a special train left Brownsville, bound for Norias. It carried an Army captain, a squad of eight troopers from the 12th Cavalry, two Texas Ranger captains, several rangers and a group of local peace officers. Upon their arrival at Norias, they found King Ranch horses ready and waiting. The whole armed party, except for the squad of troopers, mounted and rode southeastward with Tom Tate and several King Ranch cowhands, looking for a fight in the direction of the Sauz pastures where the Mexicans had been reported.

An hour and a half after the special train's departure, the regular afternoon northbound had left Brownsville. Aboard it for the ride, stirred by curiosity over the purposes of the special train ahead, were three adventuresome customs inspectors—Portus Gay, Joe Taylor, Marcus Hinds, and their friend Gordon Hill, a deputy sheriff of Cameron County—all of them armed, all of them ready for any excitement they might encounter up the line. They had it.[14]

Alighting from the train at Norias in the hot sun of late afternoon, the four men walked to the porch of Caesar Kleberg's two-story frame headquarters house, which stood isolated and exposed on the flat and bare ground a few feet from the railroad tracks.[15] The new-comers found the recently arrived corporal, his seven troopers, and eight ranch people at the house: Frank Martin and Lauro Cavazos, King Ranch cowboys; George Forbes, a ranch carpenter, and his wife; the colored cook Albert, and his wife Edna; and two Mexican servant women. Supper was ready. The four newest arrivals were invited in to eat with the others—and told of the armed party which had earlier ridden off toward Sauz looking for bandits.

A few moments after supper when the men had walked out of the house into the still brightly lighted summer evening, they saw riders approaching from the east and Marcus Hinds said, "There come the rangers back."

They were not rangers. As they came loping in the dust—there were fifty-eight horsemen—the sixteen men at the Norias ranch house saw the big Mexican hats on the riders, saw their red flag waving, heard the sudden cutting whine and pop of Mauser rifles opening fire at a range of 250 yards.

The besieged men grabbed up their own guns, ran for quick cover behind the railroad embankment, and returned the fire. They at once realized that they were being enfiladed from the south and the west as well as attacked frontally from the east: Frank Martin and two of the troopers were hit in the cross fire during the first few moments of the fight. The corporal and the rest of his squad maintained a steady fire with their Springfields and Lauro Cavazos killed the bandit leader's horse, stopping the advance, while the Norias defenders managed to move their three wounded into the house and to regroup and resume firing from behind two big rolls of barbed wire and a heavy steel form used to make round water troughs, which were inside the yard fence around the house.

The attackers then maneuvered to the south, gathering and taking cover in the section house by the railroad tracks and behind a nearby outhouse and a pile of cross ties. The exchange of fire grew hot and heavy, though the ranch defenders were reluctant to shoot into the section house, knowing that the section foreman, his wife and some of the section hands with their families were huddled inside. The bandits' bullets raked the ranch house, drilling through its thin plank walls. George Forbes was shot through the right lung; one of the wounded soldiers was hit again in the leg as he lay on a bed. The four women in the house hugged the floor and were not hit.

The Negro cook Albert, dumping a mattress over his scared wife Edna, yelled, "Woman, you don't know what a *fightin'* man you married!" and ran to the telephone which was fastened to the exposed outside wall on the ranch house porch. With bullets whistling at his back, Albert rang Kingsville and actually got his boss on the phone. "Mister Caesar! We need help NOW!" Albert bellowed. Caesar helplessly stuttered that there was a train ready in Kingsville, loaded with men and guns, but that he could find nobody to run the engine. "You just turn that engine loose and start that train this-away!" Albert shouted. "G'bye Mister Caesar—I got to go fight some more—"

The fight lasted from six o'clock all through the fading evening light. In the last glow of dusk about eight-thirty the bandits charged, shooting and yelling. Cool marksmanship on the part of the men in the ranch house yard again stopped the advance; Joe Taylor killed the wildly cursing leader of the charge as he came within forty yards of the fence. Firing eased off into silence. The beleaguered men, with little ammunition left, stayed at their posts in the dark.

A little over an hour later they heard hoofbeats and voices noisily approaching from the southwest. It was the party of rangers and peace officers riding in from their unsuccessful scout, totally un-aware of what had happened at Norias. They would have been fired upon had not one of the edgy men in the ranch yard, Lauro Cavazos, recognized the familiar voice of Tom Tate. No one yet knew that the raiders had slipped away in the darkness carrying a number of their wounded, leaving ten dead. Of the party at Norias, a Mexican woman had been killed by the bandits at the section house, and there were four wounded in the bullet-torn headquarters. Shortly after the return of the scouting party, trains both from Kingsville and Brownsville arrived with doctors, nurses and reinforcements with ammunition to spare.[16]

The weary defenders of Norias were then assaulted through most of the night with the freely given advice of the lately arrived non-combatants. Portus Gay said, "We were told over and over again what we should have done, and had to listen to several of them that were not in the fight tell what they would have done if they had been there. This kept up until Ranger Captain Henry Ransom started to tell what he would have done under the circumstances, when he was stopped by Joe Taylor with: 'Listen, WE were here—we did not get a man killed—we were here when they came, we were here when they left, and we are still here, and I don't know what you all would have done if you had been here, but I do know that there *was not a goddam son of a bitch of you here!*''

A wounded bandit was found near the section house and he talked, before he "died." He said the raiders had not expected "to find anyone at the ranch house except three or four cowboys, that they were going to rob the ranch and the ranch store, and also the south-bound night train. He said they thought they would find supplies, saddles, guns and ammunition at the ranch, and that they thought they would get money from the mail, express and passengers on the train, then they were going to burn the ranch house and the train."[17]

The next morning the raiders were followed as they headed south toward the river, but they were not caught. Some of them had been identified, however; and more than a dozen were later tracked down and killed.

Within the next six months there were in the immediate area twenty-six recorded clashes with Mexican incursionists. They made vicious raids on isolated ranches, they derailed two trains and shot and robbed the victims in the wrecks. There were bloody ambushes, running battles in the brush, brutal shootings of helpless captives. Alarms grew so great that thousands of National Guardsmen were mobilized and sent into military camps along the Rio Grande. Major General Frederick Funston, commanding border troops from headquarters at Fort Sam Houston, got so frazzled at trying to catch the elusive raiders north of the river that he made official request of the War Department for a pack of bloodhounds and a band of Apache scouts.[18]

The troubles nearly brought on a fullfledged war. Late in the night of March 9, 1916, on the desert 850 miles north and west from the south tip of Texas, a large force operating under orders from Pancho Villa swooped down upon the little border garrison town of Columbus, New Mexico. Ten American civilians and eight American soldiers were killed in fighting off this surprise assault and violation of the international boundary. President Wilson was forced to put down his pen and pick up a sword: six days after the Columbus raid, Major General John J. Pershing led a punitive expedition into Mexico with orders to capture Villa alive or dead, an objective Pershing and his men would pursue without success but with bloodshed during the next ten months in the sandy deserts and rough sierras of Chihuahua.

In that same month of March, 1916, the border banditry touched directly at a member of the family from the Santa Gertrudis. Just before nightfall on March 17, Alice and Tom East drove in from a cow camp to their headquarters place on the San Antonio Viejo. East got out of the car and went into the barn to see about some stock feed, while his wife drove their car toward the corral around the other side of the barn. When East started to open the barn door opposite the one he had entered, he looked out and was astonished to see about forty armed Mexicans "just standing around" in the barnyard. He quietly shut the door without being seen. Unwarned, Alice East drove into the barnyard; the bandits surrounded the car.

"They didn't harm me at all," she said later.

She was allowed to walk, accompanied by the bandits, to the house of the Franklin family who lived on the place and worked for the Easts. There the bandit leader demanded food.

In the cover of darkness, East thrashed his way afoot several miles to the cow camp where he dispatched a messenger to the rangers stationed at Hebbronville, thirty-five miles away.

Meanwhile the bandits' conduct was singularly mild. During the night they robbed the ranch commissary, taking ninety dollars and all the shoes, clothes and groceries they could find. At daybreak they caught some of the East horses and rode away.[19]

By mid-morning the ranger party from Hebbronville, a dozen men, arrived in a truck loaded with their saddles and guns. East mounted them on ranch horses and they all started in pursuit of the raiders. After twenty-five miles of trailing, the party surprised the Mexicans in their camp. During the ensuing fight in thick chaparral one bandit was killed and an unknown number wounded; they ran, and seven of their stolen horses, two mules, saddles, bridles, pistols and rifles were captured.[20]

A short time later threats were made against the Santa Gertrudis headquarters. One morning a telephone call from a peace officer in Kingsville warned the ranch that a band of raiders was reportedly gathering to attempt an assault, probably that night, upon the big house itself. The Klebergs, smarting yet from the Norias raid and the inept preparation for it, took the warning seriously.

Bob Kleberg had recently arrived home from the University of Wisconsin; he took a leading part in organizing the measures for meeting an attack. High-powered rifles, ammunition and field glasses were gathered and carried to the roof of the big house; a searchlight was hastily rigged atop the tower. Trustworthy *Kineños* were issued guns; vantage points all around headquarters were manned with armed men.

Toward evening the Klebergs repaired to the roof, to the rifles set handily behind the crenelations crowning the high white walls. The matriarch Henrietta King insisted upon a personal tour of the defense. When she had been shown where her people were posted and exactly how they were alerted and armed, she expressed a very sensible satisfaction. "I'm going to bed," she said. "Everything seems in order."

No attack took shape — but the night did not quite pass without a shot. One of the house servants, Severo Lucio, posted in the lonely blackness at the south entrance to the great downstairs hallway of the house, tripped himself and his shotgun went off, shattering a chunk of plaster from the edge of a doorway in the hall. When the sudden bang had finished echoing through the startled dark, there was a military reaction from the elder Kleberg's Irish chauffeur, posted with a gun at the head of the bronze-railed staircase.

"*Frrrriend or foe?*" he bellowed. Receiving no answer he added, tentatively, "If frrrriend, whistle—"

No raiders ever approached the Santa Gertrudis, yet the ranch exercised due caution. The possibility of real violence was not disregarded. In the excitement of the times, guards and fence riders patrolled. The searchlight on the tower stood ready to stab its chalky beam into the darkness each night, to probe the pastures and the thickets around the rise on the prairie. Ranch bosses never went out unarmed. Bob Kleberg said later, "We were careful, riding or even standing around in camp, about who came up behind us."[21]

On May 13, 1916, Robert Kleberg was in San Antonio, wiring his wife in New York:

WE ARE HERE TO KEEP YOU FROM WORRYING. MEXICAN CONDITIONS LOCALLY SAME AS WHEN YOU LEFT. ALL WELL. GRANDMA FINE. ENJOYING CHANGE. DON'T HURRY HOME. ENJOY YOUR STAY. TRUST ME I DON'T LIE.

ROBT.

By June of that turbulent year, heavy Army forces commanded by Brigadier General James Parker had taken station along the lower Rio Grande. Up to that time, it had been clearly evident that the Mexican marauders had been operating in Texas with the sanction of the Constitutionalist "First Chief," Venustiano Carranza. General Parker at Brownsville suddenly got rough. On June 17 he ordered half a company of infantry equipped with a wireless, and five troops of cavalry, including a machine gun unit, to cross the Rio Grande in pursuit of a Mexican raiding party, about ten miles upriver from Matamoros. Orders from Washington recalled the United States troops next day, yet their few hours of presence on Mexican soil brought a panic to Matamoros. The *Carranzista* commander there evacuated his garrison and ordered the citizenry to leave the town, in flight from an assault he believed impending.[22]

The menace of Parker's machine guns was heightened at the time by reports of Pershing's operations against Villa in Chihuahua. Threat of action by United States soldiery, and the formal recognition the United States State Department granted the Carranza government at Mexico City that summer, had a marked effect along the lower border. Armed incursion by formidable bands of Mexican raiders thenceforth ceased in South Texas, though the threats and alarms continued.

"Mexican troubles" were only a part of the worries of South Texas ranchmen. Drought gripped the land. Rainfall at the Santa Gertrudis in normal years averages about twenty-six inches annually. During the period from early 1916 through 1918 that average fell below eight inches on parts of the ranch.

While the King Ranch watched for raiders, it had to gather and to ship thousands of its cattle to leased pastures in the North; it was necessary to buy and distribute daily feed, mostly cottonseed cake, for some 20,000 head left on the suffering headquarters pastures, and to shift another 25,000 head from the Santa Gertrudis and Laureles to the Norias-Sauz area where stock could subsist on the drought-resistant sacahuiste grass and on prickly pear from which the thorns had been burned.

One man armed with a kerosene torch made for such work could burn off enough pear each day to sustain life in about a hundred head of cattle. Crews of these pear burners had to be maintained and supplied across the vastness of the ranch pastures. Early in 1918 cold northers killed much of the pear. Some idea of range conditions may be had from the fact that the ranch offered for sale three hundred head of good riding horses at one dollar a head—and found no takers.[23]

Early in this crisis of providing for the herds, the 63-year-old Robert Kleberg was stricken with illness. In 1916 palsy broke the robust health he had enjoyed and seriously impeded most of his outdoor activity.

While in Colorado that year Dick Kleberg had appendicitis, and the appendix ruptured. He nearly died; his recovery took many months. Preoccupied with her husband's illness and the care of their three-year-old daughter Mary Etta, Mamie Kleberg was also expecting another child. A son, Richard Mifflin Kleberg, Jr.—"Little Dick"—was born November 20, 1916.

When war came in the spring of 1917 and Dick Kleberg's health had started to mend, he devoted only a minor portion of his time to ranch work. Holding a Texas Ranger's commission, he found duty connected with Army Intelligence on the border, and in Mexico became one of the operatives against the sundry German subversive agents who flourished during the days of Franz von Papen's activities.[24]

The United States entered World War I eight days after Bob Kleberg's twenty-first birthday. With his brother engaged in other service, with his father physically unequal to the task of overseeing the ranch's operation, the recent student from the University of Wisconsin found a large weight of ranching responsibility riding his young shoulders. They were ready shoulders, and they were to prove tireless. Moreover they were not alone. "Sam Ragland and Caesar Kleberg had the experience and the knowledge to give. I asked for it all the time," Bob said. He became the acting — and tensely active — manager of the nation's biggest beef ranch in a monster drought at a crucial time of war.

When his draft number came up on January 14, 1918, there was a decision to make. His father made it. Robert J. Kleberg, Sr., demanded that Robert J. Kleberg, Jr., file an appeal for draft deferment, as an essential manager in an essential operation. The appeal was filed; the deferment was granted.

During the hard months of 1918 while the war wore to its end, there was time for nothing but the grinding daily work, time for no preoccupation but that of keeping scores of thousands of cattle alive, keeping hundreds of thousands of acres in operation, producing beef. The drought continued unabated. The range work was performed shorthanded. Bob Kleberg was away from the ranch for only two days during the war. The difficulties inherent in his job may be read in the profit and loss totals of the time. In the year 1916, when the drought had just begun, Mrs. King's whole ranching operation made a net profit of $277,496.55; in 1917 net profit had melted away to a net loss of $77,266.63. During 1918, in the midst of a war boom with most industries riding high, Mrs. King's ranch suffered a net loss of $144,475.37.[25]

In only one regard were the operational worries of the Santa Gertrudis lessened during 1918. Tension concerning raids from Mexico eased off. There were still scattered acts of violence, yet the border teemed with such numbers of Army troops, Texas Rangers and special officers that the threat represented by Mexicans suspected of conspiring with German spy rings, and just plain horse thieves and grudge holders was not a very grave threat. It had faded by the time the war was over.[26]

During the border disturbances there were Texas Rangers and peace officers who dealt summary injustice and reprisal to many innocent Mexicans. Some of these acts were as reprehensible as some of the raids they were intended to punish. Early in 1919, the Honorable J. T. Canales of Brownsville, representative in the Texas Legislature, brought about an investigation concerning outrages suffered by Mexicans in Texas during the period of the border trouble. Two thousand pages of evidence were adduced by the Canales hearings.[27] To more than match these, another record of bloodshed and wrong and racial hate was compiled by a senatorial investigating committee from Washington later in 1919: it brought together 3500 pages of testimony setting forth the American losses of life and property in Mexico and on the border during the revolution.[28]

The drought broke and the rains began to restore the pastures in 1919,[29] yet the Santa Gertrudis management was sharply aware of the losses its livestock operation had sustained during the two preceding years—and of the approach of a general postwar slump. The elder Kleberg considered that a sale of land might be an advisable way to provide a cash balance for use in the uncertain times. He found a buyer for a choice sector of the ranch's Laureles property. On June 13, 1919, Mrs. King sold to P. A. Chapman, a wealthy oil man from Waxahachie, 34,833 acres of the land which later became the model farming development known as Chapman Ranch, sixteen miles south of Corpus Christi. The price Chapman paid for this rich blackland was $22.50 an acre.[30] Shortly thereafter he bought 6000 adjoining acres at the same rate.[31] These two transactions together brought nearly a million dollars cash to Mrs. King's account.

Bob Kleberg could not share his father's enthusiasm for farm land developments. He had two reasons. Bob was convinced that all but a minute fraction of the land would ultimately prove better suited to grazing than to farming. Moreover, agricultural development, no matter how marginal, is accompanied by a climbing tax rate— which some day a ranch with immense acreage might not be able to pay.

Bob foresaw the necessity, despite "the development of South Texas" so dear to his father, for a firm decision which in its largest aspect deals not with any desirable rise of land values or with any undesirable rise of tax rates, but with something of infinitely greater consequence: how men may most beneficially use a given piece of land with a given average annual rainfall. Decades before, Captain King had considered the land a pasture and had put it to a pasture's natural uses. Bob Kleberg would return to his grandfather's original idea. From early in the century until 1924 the ranch was operating more than 15,000 acres of farm land— some 10,000 west of Bishop and 5000 at Santa Gertrudis — growing cotton and grain feeds. Commercial farming ceased on King Ranch land at Bob Kleberg's insistence.

His bias for the branding iron and prejudice against the plow was forcibly expressed to his father when the elder Kleberg was enthusiastically considering a new land promotion project along a rail line to be built by the Southern Pacific south from Alice to Harlingen. The railroad asked and hoped for a land bonus from the King Ranch, a tract in the western part of the Norias-Sauz division. It was the railway's promotional plan to transform the sandy dry pastures there to irrigated citrus farms. Kleberg asked his son for an opinion. "Biggest fool thing you could think about," Bob told him. When consulted, James B. Wells agreed with the younger Robert. The elder Kleberg quietly dropped his proposal for the promotion of more agriculture in the area.

The transaction with P. A. Chapman was the King Ranch's last sale of any considerable piece of its pastures. Thenceforth the ranch retained the acreage it owned—and acquired more. In 1921 Mrs. King added to her holdings in the San Salvador del Tule grant when she took title to 21,122.4 acres, in payment of notes owed to her since 1913 by Fred W. Sprague.[32] This acreage became the extreme southwest corner of the Norias-Sauz properties—close by *La Sal del Rey*, an important regional source of salt since early Spanish times. (Mrs. King owned a quarter interest in the 4605-acre tract which held the lake and saline-crusted shores of *La Sal del Rey*. It furnished salt for her cattle.)

The ranch properties were further enlarged in 1922 when Tom East transferred title to his San Antonio Viejo ranch of 76,870.4 acres to Henrietta M. King in full cancellation of the indebtedness he had contracted during the ruinous years of drought and falling market. She leased the whole property back to East and his wife Alice, who continued to operate it as before.[33]

During the last decade of her long life the widow of Richard King became the august survivor of an era immensely remote from the tumultuous times that arrived in the wake of world war. Confronted with the changes those times were bringing, conscious of a mortal hour that must find her soon, Henrietta King did what she could to safeguard that which she cherished most in a mutable world: her family and her ranch. On the fifth of July in the war year of 1918, she signed a lengthy new last will and testament, drawn up at her request by her trusted friend James B. Wells.[34] Its provisions were designed to assure a just partition of her many properties among the many members of her family, and also to assure by a ten-year period of trusteeship the unbroken continuance of her ranch's operation while it was being prepared for ultimate division amongst heirs. The will was an instrument which projected her ranch, her family, her own spirit, into the future.

Henrietta M. King

The future was much in the mind of the matriarch who had lived through so long a past. Three months after she signed her will she decided to make one of its articles an immediate gift rather than a delayed bequest. She gave to the daughter who had "faithfully devoted practically her whole life to my care, comfort, consolation and aid," the land which had been that daughter's home since her birth in the midst of another war, fifty-six eventful years before.

By a "General Warranty Deed of Gift and Bill of Sale" from her mother, on October 28, 1918,[35] Alice Gertrudis King Kleberg became the owner of Santa Gertrudis headquarters, embracing 30,439.23 acres and all the improvements thereon, including the great house. The gift also included an additional 8111.89 acres of a rich blackland farming tract known as the Palo Alto Farms, in the Bishop vicinity. Alice leased back to the ranch management the property to which she now held full title, and its operation continued unchanged.

Six years later Alice Kleberg executed a deed of gift by which she gave the Palo Alto farm tract to her son Robert J. Kleberg, Jr., as Trustee for all her children, including himself, and for Caesar Kleberg, who participated in the gift.[36]

Meanwhile Bob, as Trustee for his brother, sisters, himself and Caesar, made two major land purchases. The first of these, dated June 13, 1924, was the 34,924 acres comprising the old Cornelius Stillman property in the San Salvador del Tule; the price paid was $157,158.00.[37] Two weeks later, June 30, he bought the Ed C. Lasater ranch of "approximately 107,030 acres" south of Falfurrias for a sum of $547,619.19. Both purchases, financed through the San Antonio Loan & Trust Company, were made possible through the sale of the land in the choice Palo Alto tract.[38]

Bob Kleberg, as Trustee, in effect thus converted eight thousand acres of rich farm land to some one hundred forty thousand sandy acres of ranch land, a transaction of immense significance to the Kleberg family's ranching future. Bob said of it later: "It is evident that I believe more in ranching than I do in farming. The purchase was made not only because it was a good purchase but also because it was known that large parts of the sandy country of the ranch would be partitioned to the King and Atwood families. It would be dangerous to operate the King Ranch without sandy land in conjunction with the other heavy black lands of the ranch. There was also a vast difference in the mineral interest under 8000 and 143,000 acres. It was part of a long-range view to keep the King Ranch intact. Mother and father concurred in this."

Bob leased both the Lasater and the Stillman acreage to Mrs. King immediately after purchase. In the reorganization of the ranch after the death of Mrs. King, the Stillman pasture, Robert J. Kleberg, Jr., Trustee, would be leased and operated as part of the King Ranch's Norias Division. Under the same trusteeship arrangement, the Lasater property would create a new division of the ranch, called the Encino.

Four months after Mrs. King had deeded the Santa Gertrudis to her daughter Alice, the aging matriarch made another kind of a gift to the son-in-law who for thirty-four years had been devoting all his mind and all his heart to the Santa Gertrudis and its interests. A part of these interests was the possibility of oil in the earth under the ranch's pastures. Petroleum had become a titan, a prime mover in the conduct of the world's business; the search for new petroleum sources had sharpened. Probing at the promise of the long coast all the way from the black pools at Beaumont to the crude-soaked rigs at Tampico, searchers were looking again at Mrs. King's ranch. To deal with them she gave Robert J. Kleberg, Sr., a new and full power of attorney, and, along with it, a small gift "for the Trust and Confidence reposed in him by me." On March 1, 1919, by an instrument titled "Power of Attorney Coupled with an Interest," she gave him for his own a $3/32$ interest in any oil, gas or other mineral which might be found "upon, in, or under" any of the land she owned "in each or any of the Counties of Cameron, Hidalgo, Starr, Willacy, Brooks, Jim Hogg, Jim Wells, Kleberg, Nueces and San Patricio."[39]

Beginning later in 1919, Robert Kleberg made various leases and watched several oil exploration and drilling projects operating upon the ranch's land. With the exception of a single gasser six miles southeast of Kingsville, brought in on February 3, 1920, and then capped, there was no successful petroleum development upon the ranch's land during his lifetime. Yet the 3/32 interest which Mrs. King had presented to him became a part of his estate. It proved to be a rich gift to Robert Kleberg's children.

Mrs. King survived all her own children except Alice. In April of 1918 a message brought news of Nettie King Atwood's death. Her brother Richard traveled to Chicago to represent the King family at the obsequies; through the years Nettie and her mother had never entirely repaired the breach in their relationship.[40]

Four years after Nettie's death the son and namesake of Captain King died suddenly of a stroke while on a visit in St. Louis, September 27, 1922. He was buried there in the family cemetery plot of his wife, Pearl Ashbrook King, who died three years later, on November 17, 1925. The *Corpus Christi Caller-Times* wrote of the generous and openhearted Richard King II on the day after his death, "There is probably no other man in South Texas who held the regard of his fellow man more than did Mr. King." *The Cattleman*, in its issue of October, 1922, pointed out that "Mr. King was one of the first to introduce agriculture to South Texas. The first farm was on his La Puerta ranch nearly half a century ago." He had lived to see the cotton lands in the vicinity of Corpus Christi become one of the richest farming areas in the nation.

In that year of 1922 Corpus Christi reached a milestone in its development as an important coastal city. For decades its citizens had been trying to find a means to make it a deep water port open to the ocean shipping of the world. In 1919 there had been a new and stronger agitation for an adequate harbor, following the destruction brought to the jerry-built port facilities by a fierce hurricane that year. A body of leading citizens, headed by Robert J. Kleberg, Sr., had formed an aggressively promotional organization known as the Deep Water Harbor Association for South and West Texas. After prodigious labors in compiling data and preparing harbor surveys, in promotion and publicity, in rallying civic and commercial support throughout all Texas south of San Antonio, in lobbying (by Roy Miller, mostly with funds furnished by Robert Kleberg)[41] for the necessary political assent in Washington, the association had its reward. On May 25, 1922, Congress passed an appropriation to begin work on a real harbor for ocean-borne commerce at Corpus Christi. The port's total cost came to about five million dollars, derived from federal and state funds and a local bond issue, and it required four years to build.

Robert Kleberg's health did not allow his presence at the dedication ceremonies opening the new port on September 14, 1926, yet this occasion represented one of the largest satisfactions of the career he had spent in "the development of South Texas." His predecessor Captain King had hoped and worked for such a port since he and his partner Legs Lewis had first dreamed of transport for the cattle they raised on the wilderness pastures by the Santa Gertrudis. Seventy years later the captain's son-in-law saw that vision become reality.[42] The Nueces County Navigation Commission said in 1953:

No citizen of Texas contributed more to the founding of the Port of Corpus Christi than the Honorable Robert J. Kleberg. Thirty-three years ago as chairman of the General Executive Committee of the Deep Water Association for South and West Texas, he led the nation-wide campaign which brought about the Port's establishment, donating munificently of his talents and his funds to bring into reality a facility which made Corpus Christi the great city it has become.[43]

In the years of change that followed the first World War the ranch on the Santa Gertrudis suffered the loss of the lawyer who had served it for forty faithful years. After long and wasting illness, James B. Wells died at Brownsville on December 21, 1923. This brilliant attorney and remarkable man — "loved by his friends and respected by his enemies"[44] — left a name written large in the annals of the Texas Bar and in the political history of southmost Texas. In his relationship to Mrs. King, to her family and to her ranch people, Jim Wells was an affectionate friend as well as a professional counselor. His death was a grief. Twenty-nine years later Bob Kleberg wrote: "Certainly Judge Wells, more than anyone else, helped in putting together the original ranch and I know every member of our family will be eternally grateful to his memory."[45]

The long life of the famed matriarch of the Santa Gertrudis had a quality of legend. As her age advanced beyond ninety, the frail figure in widow's black seemed invested with the stateliness of a lone survivor from a former chapter of history. Henrietta King lived out the last of her years in an unassailable calmness "with a hope full of immortality as my change draws near."[46] The world about her, the house she lived in, the pastures she owned, the people she loved, grew misty with great time.

Death came to her at the age of ninety-two, about ten o'clock on a spring night at the Santa Gertrudis, March 31, 1925.

Her body lay in state in a bronze casket in the flower-banked big front room of her great house, while her family, her friends, her employees, came to the rise on the prairie where she had lived for seventy brave and useful years. Messages to her family sped along the wires leading to Kingsville. Relatives and friends arrived on the iron rails from the four quarters, from far cities. News of the death traveled over country roads, carried by the lips of sunburned drivers behind the steering wheels of dusty, brush-scratched automobiles, men with harness reins in their hard hands, men spurring sweated horses through tall grass and thickets of thorn to rough settlements and lonely camps.

From the farthest corners of far South Texas pastures there began a great convergence upon the Santa Gertrudis. Men came with their wide-brimmed hats in their hands. They brought their wives who dabbed damp handkerchiefs at weather-rough faces. They brought their solemn-eyed children. They parked their wagons and their cars to camp on the grass and under the trees.

All the *Kineños* came. Some of them rode horses two days and a night to arrive in time. The foremen of the cow camps gathered as a body at headquarters and went to present themselves to Alice Kleberg, to express their sorrow formally and in the ancient style to *La Madama's* daughter, to pledge again their faithfulness to her family.

A great throng crowded to the simple funeral rite at the big house on April 4, at three-thirty in the sunny afternoon. When the service conducted by the Reverend S. E. Chandler was concluded, a cortege more than a mile long moved behind the black hearse down the gentle slope from the Santa Gertrudis on the road to town, to the cemetery of Kingsville which Henrietta King had planted and named Chamberlain Park in honor of her father.

An honor guard unlike any other on the face of the earth led the slow procession. The ranch's cowboys, nearly two hundred of them, wearing their range clothes, riding their range horses, accompanied *La Patrona*, who had always been their partisan, upon her final journey.

At her crowded graveside, during the hymns, eulogies and last prayers, gray-haired bankers from Manhattan rubbed shoulders with leather-faced brush choppers from the lonely *callos* of El Sauz.

When the casket was lowered into the earth there was a stir at the edge of the crowd where the bare-headed horsemen stood. They mounted to their saddles. They came reining forward in single file, unbidden and uncommanded save by their hearts, to canter with a centaur dash once around the open grave, their hats down at side salute to Henrietta King. Then her vaqueros rode away in the silence, toward the herds they had watched for her and would go on watching.

Among the funeral wreaths and florists' arrangements in the banked mound of color left upon the grave's raw earth, was a home-made bouquet of huisache blooms; there was a Running W woven of wild flowers.

That fall, the remains of her captain, her son Lee and her daughter Ella were brought to Kingsville from San Antonio and reinterred at the indomitable Henrietta King's side. They sleep there under a tall shaft of granite marked simply: KING.

XVII *Trusteeship and Transition*

THE RANCH

management set about adjusting itself, without delay, to the stipulations set forth in the will of Henrietta King. That complex instrument, twenty-two typewritten pages long, called for a ten-year trusteeship preliminary to partition of the estate among the heirs. To direct ranch operations during the ten years and then to administer the division of the property, her will appointed eight trustees. These were her son-in-law Robert J. Kleberg, Sr.; Caesar Kleberg, assistant general manager of her ranch; Samuel G. Ragland, her ranch's livestock manager; John D. Finnegan, office manager; James B. Wells, her lawyer (whose death preceded Mrs. King's); and her three grandsons, Richard King III, Richard M. Kleberg and Robert J. Kleberg, Jr. Of these trustees, the will named as executors Robert J. Kleberg, Sr., James B. Wells, Caesar Kleberg and Richard King III. Wells was not replaced in either appointment; actually, seven trustees and three executors would administer the settlement of the estate.

It was imperative, however, to seek from the court the immediate appointment of temporary administrators empowered to disburse and receive estate funds while the will was in legal process of being recorded and admitted to probate. On April 4, 1925, three days before the will was filed, the probate court of Kleberg County was petitioned for the appointment of two such temporary administrators.[1] One of these was Robert Driscoll, a close personal and business friend of the family and president of the Corpus Christi National Bank. The other was Richard King III, vice-president of the same bank. They were duly appointed by the court, and served the estate until probate enabled the three executors appointed by the will to assume their duties.[2]

The court also named three appraisers for the estate, qualified by knowledge and experience to evaluate land and livestock in the vicinity: J. C. McGill, operator of the Santa Rosa Ranch in Kenedy County; Joe H. Keepers, Jr., stockman and inspector for the Texas Livestock Sanitary Commission; and W. M. Doughty, former county judge of Hidalgo County, ranching neighbor and lessee of Mrs. King's La Coma tract in the San Salvador del Tule grant.

The detailed inventory of Mrs. King's properties — listing everything down to such items as "50# lard can," "8 hame straps," "3 1¼ lock nuts," "2 sugar bowls" — recorded the scope of her enterprise. Totals on the appraisers' work sheets[3] indicated that the estate was the owner of 997,444.56 acres of ranching and miscellaneous lands — not including the related King Ranch acreage of the Santa

Gertrudis headquarters or the Stillman and Lasater tracts which were properties of the Klebergs, not of the estate. Upon the estate's pastures there were tallied 94,347 head of cattle, 3782 head of horse stock, 802 mules, 47 jennies, 355 goats, 595 sheep and lambs. The *Statement of Gross Estate, Mrs. H. M. King,*[4] as prepared by the appraisers, read thus:

ASSETS

REAL ESTATE

Ranch Lands	$4,784,324.27	
City Property.	73,555.00	$4,857,879.27

PERSONAL PROPERTY

Cattle and Horse Stock	1,086,119.00
Cash Account	52,079.82
Land Notes	559,475.50
Secured & Unsecured Notes	315,756.41
Rincon Improvement Co.	1,287.50
Stocks and Bonds	132,625.00
Accounts Receivable	68,959.20
Merchandise at Stores	7,741.97
Office Furniture	1,079.45
Automobiles and Trucks	8,470.00
Machinery and Supplies	10,000.00
	$7,101,473.12

LIABILITIES

Bills Payable	$1,151,545.89
Bills Payable State Lands	47,639.44
Vouchers Payable	16,823.32
Accounts Payable	323,489.97
Commission due Agents	9,784.49
Funeral Expenses	10,860.50
Probating Will	387.52
Legal Expenses	135,000.00
	$1,695,531.13

Total Assets	$7,101,473.12	
Total Liabilities	1,695,531.13	
NET TOTAL . .	$5,405,941.99	

The board of trustees took over management after the probate of the will late in the summer of 1925. The estate gave each trustee a monthly salary of $416.66; the three executors received added compensation in the form of commissions.[5]

The year 1925 was marked not only with drought but with the lowest ebb of the postwar deflation in the cattle industry. From 1920 to 1925 there had been a steady decline in the livestock market; in the latter year, ninety-five per cent of western cattle loan companies went into liquidation.[6] Thousands of stockmen lost their ranches. At such a time Mrs. King's estate faced liabilities totaling more than a million and a half dollars, together with the certainty of having to raise cash to pay huge estate taxes. Prospects for finding the cash were poor. Money had to be borrowed—and the ranch operation itself had been losing money steadily, every year but 1922 when a small profit was shown, since the war's end.

General economic conditions created part of the unsatisfactory balance. It was also becoming increasingly clear to the ranch's management that a part of its trouble stemmed from its own cattle herds. They were not doing well.

Since 1886 Robert Kleberg had been engaged in upgrading the ranch's tough Longhorn range stock by continued infusions of blood from two fine British beef breeds, the Shorthorn (earlier called "Durham" or "Teeswater")[7] and the Hereford. For years the ranch had been maintaining carefully separated herds of about 4000 purebred Shorthorns and 2500 purebred Herefords to supply the stud for the upbreeding of the range stock. This continuous upbreeding had changed the character of the ranch's commercial herds. Though they made more desirable beef, they had perceptibly "lost in hardihood, reproductiveness and rustling ability." It was found that Shorthorns and Herefords ran two to four degrees of fever when they stood exposed to the blazing South Texas summer sun. The swarming insect pests of the coastal flats plagued them; they suffered from screw worm, cancer-eye and other diseases. In unfavorable seasons the ranch's range cows produced meager crops of small-boned calves.[8] During the roundups following the 1925 drought, for example, the ranch branded only 15,773 calves, the smallest number in years, and only fifty per cent of a normal calf crop. For more than a decade the ranch had been watching what was unmistakably a gradual weakening of its "improved" commercial beef herds.[9]

Though the Klebergs were at that time in the midst of an intensive and extensive experimental program to create cattle better suited to thrive upon their ranges — by crossing the Shorthorn with the Brahman blood from India — the results were promises rather than fulfillments in the year 1925. During that first season of the trusteeship, neither the herds nor the financial statements of Mrs. King's estate were in comfortable condition.

The senior Kleberg attended to every matter of ranch or estate business brought to his attention, but his growing infirmity had by now confined him largely to a wheel chair. By common consent of the board of trustees, the 29-year-old Bob Kleberg continued as General Manager of the ranch. With a vehemence which had grown to be a part of his character and his conduct, he addressed himself to the difficulties at hand, both on the pastures and in the ledgers.

A predominant worry was the amount of tax the estate would be required to pay the Federal and State governments. This amount of course depended upon an officially acceptable appraisal, for tax purposes, of the estate's lands and livestock. Valuations on nearly a million acres of many varying grades of grazing lands and on nearly a hundred thousand head of different kinds and qualities of livestock were necessarily arbitrary opinions, however informed. The properties were not for sale; and even if placed on sale the prices they might or might not reasonably fetch in an actual market — their actual worth — were very widely open to question.

Tax officials were naturally anxious to establish the highest valuations possible. Trustees of the estate were understandably just as anxious to keep appraisals low. They were painfully aware that too high a tax could very well bring the ruin and the breaking up of the ranch — as various newspaper stories and rumors were pointing out at the time.[10]

The valuations on the lands and livestock submitted by the estate's appointed appraisers were not accepted by the taxing authorities. They sent their own appraisers, who proceeded radically to hoist the valuations.[11] The trustees protested. The issue over fair and just appraisal of the estate's property went before the Federal tax commissioners and remained in contest. The estate's trustees and its attorneys spent painstaking months accumulating evidence to support the estate's tax return, obtaining volumes of affidavits, and proofs of land and livestock sales, to demonstrate values. Bob Kleberg spent six months in Washington helping to compile the presentation of the estate's case to the Treasury; when he had to return to the ranch's operation Caesar Kleberg worked in Washington for another six months.

Exploring a possible source for part of the tax money which would be required, the King estate took the occasion in 1926 formally to remind the Government again of claims filed and ignored for half a century, styled *Richard King v. United Mexican States*, for total losses of $396,950 suffered in the old border depredations and still unpaid. These claims, set forth in a lengthily documented *Memorial*, were submitted before the General Claims Commission.[12] Sixteen years later, by the Settlement of Mexican Claims Act of 1942, the estate was actually awarded damages which, when the installment payments are all made, will amount to a total of $81,000.

Meanwhile, in 1926, the estate's tax contest went right on. "The values we made were correct and fair values for the times," Bob Kleberg says. "A valuation of four to five dollars an acre on a million acres of raw ranchland was about right, but it took a long time for the Government to admit it."

There was another aspect to the determination of the amount of Federal tax due. The Revenue Act of 1924, which became effective June 2 of that year, very substantially increased tax rates applicable to net estates in excess of $100,000 as compared to the rates previously in force under the Revenue Act of 1921. A retroactive provision became law in the Revenue Act of 1926 and wiped out the increase of rates for the period which included the date of Mrs. King's death in 1925. The lower rates contained in the Revenue Act of 1921 therefore became the applicable rates in the payment of the tax owed by Mrs. King's estate.

When the contest concerning the taxable evaluation of her property was finally terminated by mutual agreement late in 1928, the Government had very materially reduced the amount of tax it had at first sought to collect. Mrs. King's estate paid death taxes in a total of $859,416.07. The Federal tax amounted to $530,017.52, plus interest of $74,016.44; the total of $604,033.76 was paid in three installments, in 1927, 1928, 1929. The Texas inheritance tax of $225,382.31 was all paid in 1929.[13]

The trustees had to borrow the money to pay, bringing the ranch the nearest it has ever been to financial peril. When the national economy crashed late in 1929 Mrs. King's estate owed creditors more than three million dollars.[14]

Four years later, Bob Kleberg astutely found the means to carry the ranch's burden of debt.

The Humble Oil and Refining Co. of Houston had leased certain of Mrs. King's lands and explored for oil there early in the 1920's.* Oil indications had been found, but no producing wells had been brought in and the leases had been allowed to lapse. A decade later Bob Kleberg suggested to Humble executives, among whom were some good friends, a careful reconsideration of the oil potentials at the ranch. To support an argument in favor of the possibilities, Kleberg mentioned that he doubted if oil men could show him any million acres along the Gulf Coast between the Louisiana line and Tampico where oil was not present. If the Humble company would obligate itself to explore and develop the minerals and to make annual bonus payments large enough to cover the interest on the debts owed by Mrs. King's estate, it could have exclusive drilling rights on about a million acres. Negotiations were opened.

An agreement of momentous import was signed on September 26, 1933, when Humble leased the lands to be partitioned among Mrs. King's heirs, 971,711.43 acres, as well as the Lasater and Stillman acreages of which Bob Kleberg was Trustee, and the Santa Gertrudis headquarters tract owned by Alice Kleberg. In all, the oil company received exclusive exploration and drilling rights on 1,133,156.31 acres. Further terms of the agreement gave the ranch an annual bonus of thirteen cents an acre for drilling rights; the lease also granted the usual royalty of one barrel out of every eight of all oil extracted from the property. The estate received a cash loan of $3,223,645, secured by a first mortgage on the King Ranch land. Interest was at five per cent; $500,000 of the principal was due in five years and the remainder in twenty.[15]

The three million-odd dollars of the loan were used to clear away the debts of the estate. Oil and gas were found on the estate's land beginning in May, 1939, almost six years after the signing of the lease.

* See Appendix XII for the story of oil development on the King Ranch.

It is necessary to point out that oil at no time and by no means "saved" the King Ranch. Strictly as a livestock ranching operation it had become irrefutably sound. During 1926 the cattle market took an upward trend; rains brought good grass. When that year's ranching returns were tabulated Manager Bob Kleberg could show his fellow trustees not a loss but a net profit of $227,382.08[16]—despite the expenses involved in the administration of Mrs. King's estate. From then on, the beef the ranch produced made money. There were 25,000 calves branded with the ᭐ in 1927; 18,000 ᭐ steers and spayed heifers went to the nation's markets. By 1931 the ranch was shipping 25,000 beeves a year and, even in the hardest Depression years that followed, was selling an annual gross of nearly a million dollars worth of meat on the hoof.

For three years before Mrs. King's death and for three years following, the ranch was engaged—along with its other problems—in the final elimination of the southern cattle tick from all its livestock and from all its pastures, in the concluding phase of the Department of Agriculture's long campaign to eradicate the tick from the United States. The ranch found its operating costs heavily increased with the extra expense entailed by the campaign: the building of a total of twenty-four dipping vats at strategic points on ranch property; the replacement of hundreds of miles of fence by higher, heavier, stronger, tighter wire to insure the control of stock within the ranch's enclosures and to stop any possible passage of tick-infested strays from the outside; and the straining labor, requiring many extra hands, of rounding up, herding, moving, dipping, re-dipping, examining and patrolling every head of stock on the ranch. The difficulty and expense paid off finally in 1928 when southmost Texas was declared entirely free of the tick which had hampered cattle breeding and beef marketing there for sixty years.

Farming operations at the ranch changed radically during the early years of the trusteeship. Cotton and other commercial row crop growing was abandoned in favor of range grass planting and a very limited cultivation of grain feeds. In 1914 Robert J. Kleberg, Sr., had first plowed a pasture to sow it experimentally with Rhodes grass. This import from Africa seemed exactly suited to South Texas soil and weather. By 1931 the ranch had a stand of 17,000 handsome acres in Rhodes grass. It grew so well that it was harvested for hay; at the same time, the planted pastures served as choice grazing enclosures for selected herds. Special barns for the storage of the Rhodes grass hay were designed and built on these pastures. Each barn had a capacity of 175 tons and cattle could self-feed from them. "Agriculture" at the ranch became pasture improvement. By 1940 about 75,000 acres of the property would be plowed and successfully sown with Rhodes grass.[17]

Topography, soil and natural pasturage varied greatly within the ninety-three miles between the south line of the lower Sauz and the northern fence of the Santa Gertrudis. The wide coastal flats and open prairielands were found most suitable for breeding ranges, while the brushier and more broken country, far more difficult to work, was generally used to support the steers which would go to market as beef. The ranch management, explaining its operation in 1926, wrote that it used its lands "under a system which contemplated the breeding part of the range producing enough calves to stock that part of the Ranch which is not suitable for breeding purposes. It is only by operating these pastures as one ranch that it is possible to get the cattle produced on the different ranges in condition to realize the most money."[18] The management was acutely aware of the advantage it enjoyed by possessing diversity in its ranges. The sands of the Norias-Sauz provided a vital complement to the loam and blackland pastures of the Santa Gertrudis-Laureles. Though these last contained richer soils and provided more nourishing grasses for livestock *when it rained,* the poorer sand country to the south was in effect a kind of ranching insurance; it grew a hardier herbage better capable of sustaining life in cattle when drought gripped the land, and drought often did.

In good years, most of the W beef steers—from which the ranch derived most of its income—were placed on a blackland pasture at the Laureles, to gain weight before shipment. A large portion of these beeves was then sent to stouter grass on pastures located in the best part of the old Osage Nation—between Pawhuska, Oklahoma, and Cedarvale, Kansas—belonging to James L. Barroum and to the firm of Chapman & Barnard, to fatten on these ranges for three or four months before shipment to the markets of St. Louis, Kansas City or Chicago. Through the years Barroum and Chapman & Barnard handled well over a hundred thousand head of King Ranch beeves.

Moving the right cattle to the right pasture at the right time, and then to market, could be compared to a curious game of chess. It was played with thousands of perishable pieces. Wrong moves were ruinous. A combination of right moves made money. The pieces themselves and even the grass on the board were alive, and must not wait. It was a game that absorbed the hearts and minds of the ranching family of Klebergs. The elder Robert with his sons Bob and Dick and their Cousin Caesar were engaged at the time in experiments which were leading to the creation of a new breed of cattle: they were literally carving new pieces and, by range grass planting, attempting to build a better board for their creative game of cattle chess. As in any game of chess, they played by planning ahead.

The ranch's vast and various pastures were integrated so that their different values and uses had become dependent parts of a whole mechanism operating for a single purpose: the large-scale conversion of grass to marketable beef. To lop any important pasture away from the working mechanism would maim the procedure—and this was the prospect in store for Mrs. King's property when it would be partitioned to the various heirs at the end of the ten-year trusteeship.

The Klebergs wanted to see the operation of the ranch remain intact after partition, through some future management agreement with the other heirs as shareholders in a continuing great enterprise. When it became clear that no large family arrangement would be agreed upon, the Klebergs surveyed the possibility of purchases from other heirs, for the future maintenance of the enterprise under one ownership. To explore this possibility and to act upon it, Bob Kleberg was appointed his family's business agent and manager by a full power of attorney from his father on May 27, 1926,[19] and another from his mother, dated July 6, 1928.[20] Thus, while he managed the ranch's current operations for the trustees of his grandmother's estate, he also became the custodian of the Kleberg's future plans.

His own future plans were indissolubly bonded to the Santa Gertrudis and to a new household he had established there.

About the middle of February, 1926, less than a year after the trustees had made him manager of the ranch, and while he was engulfed in the first great wave of the estate's problems, he had gone to San Antonio for a day of business. That evening he was introduced to a young visitor in the city. Her name was Helen Campbell. Slender, bronze-haired and brown-eyed, she was as pretty as she was poised. Her father, the Honorable Philip Pitt Campbell, was a Congressman from Kansas for more than twenty years. His daughter had grown up at the capital and across the Potomac in Virginia; she had gone to school at National Cathedral; she had toured Europe; she had attained a cool, easy grace. She rocked Bob Kleberg.

Ranch business had to wait. The impetuous man from the Santa Gertrudis courted Miss Helen Campbell at about the same speed he used a rope at a roundup. Seventeen days later, March 2, 1926, they were married at Corpus Christi. After a ten-day wedding trip to New York, they hurried to the Santa Gertrudis, to unending rounds of responsibility in a ranching world new to Helen Kleberg.

She entered it with perceptive eyes, estimating the meanings as well as the vibrant colors of her husband's world of wide grasslands and great herds, of hatted centaurs in the blazing sun. With level intelligence she sought and found adjustment to the strong savor of the life into which she was plunged. In it she came to provide the calm, articulate counterpoise to her husband's tensely driving force.

They lived at first in the big house with other members of the family, then they moved to a more modest menage they arranged for themselves. A white frame cottage stood at the edge of the garden behind the big house, beyond the garage. Half-hidden in thick greenery, under the shade of big hackberry trees at the end of a walk bordered with date palms, flowering shrubs and the big tropical leaves of banana trees, the cottage had charm and it had privacy. The Klebergs took it over and built additions which converted the small house into a three-bedroom country lodge. It was as comfortable as it was rambling. Its ranch-style porch, extending along the entire face of the house's L-shape, was glassed in and furnished to make a handsome and inviting front room, in a visible setting of leafy, sunny green. The simple and sequestered house beyond the garage became the permanent home of the Bob Klebergs, and the real headquarters of the ranch. A daughter, destined to be their only child, was born to Bob and Helen Kleberg on October 20, 1927. Christened with her mother's name, Helen King Kleberg, the little girl was promptly dubbed "Helenita."

With Bob married and settled at the ranch, the elder Klebergs saw all their children save Sarah busy with family lives of their own. When Sarah had finished school at Miss Spence's in New York, she had returned to the big house to live with her parents, and to become a part of the ranching life she loved at the Santa Gertrudis. She worked there, keeping accounts at the headquarters commissary; she rode skillfully as a cow hand at the roundups; she often joined her brother Bob and his friend Tom Armstrong on strenuous hunting trips as an expert huntress and good company in camp.

When she was thirty years old she fell in love with Henry Belton Johnson, Jr., a ranch employee whose father had managed farming operations at the Palo Alto Farms. She was married to the handsome young Johnson in a ceremony held at the Santa Gertrudis on July 23, 1928. Tragedy came to them. The husband was stricken with brain tumor a few months after marriage. A son, Belton Dandy Kleberg Johnson, was born in 1929. His father died in 1931. The next year Sarah married Dr. Joseph H. Shelton of Kingsville, a physician fifteen years her senior. Another son, Robert Richard Shelton, and a daughter Sarita, who died in early childhood, were born of this marriage, which ended with the death of Dr. Shelton by heart attack in 1939. Sarah's own ill-starred life ended in a motor accident three years later. Her two strong sons, "B" and Bobby, went to live with their uncle Bob and Aunt Helen, who raised them to manhood.

By the time Bobby Shelton was born in 1935, the family springing from the union of R. J. Kleberg, Sr., and Alice Gertrudis King counted fourteen grandchildren. Sarah had two sons, Bob had one daughter. Up in New York, the Larkins were parents of John Jr., Peter, Henrietta and Ida. Over at the San Antonio Viejo the Easts had Tom Jr., Robert and Alice Hattie; and since the birth of the Dick Kleberg's first two children, Mary Etta and Dick Jr., there had been two additions to the family, Katherine and Alice.

Under the terms of Mrs. King's will her favorite grandson, Richard Mifflin Kleberg, inherited the house on Broadway in Corpus Christi. In 1925 the lawyer-ranchman and his wife moved their family, to take up residence at the big house in town where their children could have the advantages of city schooling.

Since R. J. Kleberg, Sr.'s, invalidism, his son Dick had been charged not only with bearing a hand in the ranch's management and livestock breeding programs, but also with carrying on much of the elder R. J.'s outside interests in public service. Among these was the work of the Texas and Southwestern Cattle Raisers Association. The senior Kleberg had served as its president twice, in 1899 and again in 1901; his son Dick had served on the Executive Committee for eleven years, from 1913 to 1924. In 1926 he was elected president, "the only instance in the history of the Association where both father and son have been honored with its highest office." Dick's effectiveness as head of the association and as an aggressive leader in campaigns for association aims (such as lower freight rates for cattlemen, modern beef grading, fair weighing, stricter brand registration, tariff protection, tick eradication, predatory animal control) caused the overthrow of a long established precedent: fellow members elected him president for two consecutive terms.[21]

His public activities for the association, his successful work for the establishment of the South Texas Normal School at Kingsville (which in 1929 became the flourishing Texas College of Arts and Industries), his energetic rôles in such organizations as the Kleberg County Standard Dairy & Livestock Association, American Jersey Cattle Club, American Brahman Breeders Association, Better Beef Association and many others, all pointed toward his capacity for politics. Though he sought no political office, his timber as a possible public figure did not go unnoticed in South Texas. An editorial in the *Hebbronville News*, October 12, 1927, said: "He is a man of strong ideas, and while he has played politics only to the extent of assisting in electing good men to office, yet, if at some future time he should aspire to political honors, and he is still a young man, there is good reason to believe that he may become Governor of his native State."

Early in November, 1931, Harry M. Wurzbach, Republican incumbent of the 14th Congressional District of Texas for eleven years, died suddenly. His district comprised eleven counties in south central Texas and contained two sizeable cities, San Antonio and Corpus Christi. A special election was set for November 24, 1931, to elect Wurzbach's successor. His party chose C. W. Anderson of San Antonio as the Republican candidate. The Democratic party machine of urban San Antonio put up Carl Johnson, and three or four less prominent contenders were entering the race. Friends of Dick Kleberg called on him and urged him to run.

Before he consented, he went to see his father. The aged R. J. momentarily forgot that his son's legal residence was now in Nueces County instead of the district containing the King Ranch—which had been the bailiwick of good friend John Nance Garner since 1902.

"You're not going to run against John Garner!" R. J. said.

"No, Dad, we're now in different districts."

"Then run like hell," was the answer.

On a whirlwind campaign Dick managed to speak in every county of the 14th District during the ten days left before the election. He ran on a platform of seven enumerated planks. These stated his adherence to the fundamental principles of his party, his desire to see government "the servant not the master of the people," his strong advocacy for "a modification of the Prohibition laws," his promise to diligently represent his whole district and each of its varied interests, his special devotion to the welfare of the farmer and livestock raiser, his desire to support legislation to aid and benefit the laboring man and to fulfill all governmental obligations to ex-servicemen,

and his pledge to protect the interests of the American people in all questions of foreign policy. His campaign fliers were headed:

A VOTE FOR RICHARD M. KLEBERG *is a Vote for a DEMOCRAT*
Who Believes in State Rights, Local Self Government
and All the Old-Time Principles of His Party.

His party was crucially interested in seeing a Democrat replace the deceased Republican Wurzbach: Democrats were building to a majority in the House of Representatives after thirteen years of Republican dominance. When the ballots of the 14th District were in, Democrat R. M. Kleberg had a clear plurality of more than 5000 votes. Next morning, November 25, 1931, the *New York Times* ran a picture of the new cowman-Congressman with a headline TEXAS CLINCHES HOUSE CONTROL and a tally of the new line-up— Democrats 218, Republicans 214. Democrat John Nance Garner became Speaker of the House. His ranching friend from the adjoining district moved to Washington with Mamie and the children, and took up new duties a long way from Laureles pastures.

After serving out Wurzbach's unexpired term, Dick Kleberg was elected to six successive terms, 1932-1944. During his entire tenure he served with noticeable energy and effectiveness as a member of the House Committee on Agriculture. His work as a legislator was principally directed toward the field he knew best and cared for most, the nation's farms and ranches. He was the author of a number of agricultural bills, the most important of which was the act establishing the Farm Credit Administration as an independent agency of the government; he had a prominent part in writing much of the farm legislation enacted during the years he spent in Washington. His interests as an outdoorsman were strongly voiced in his support of such bills as the Migratory Bird Conservation Act; he was active in the writing of the Duck Stamp Law.

His command of the Spanish language and his rapport with those who spoke it made him extremely useful to Congressional groups working toward better cooperation between the United States and Latin America. On an official mission to South America in 1942 his understanding of the Latin mind and his public addresses in Spanish made new friends for his country; his friends mentioned him more than once as eminently suited for an ambassadorship south of the Rio Grande.

At home his popularity was not exactly diminished by his conduct at grass roots affairs like the Robstown rodeo. There the Solon from the Capitol got on a horse, entered a breakaway calf roping event and proceeded to rope and tie a calf in sixteen seconds flat — no purse winner, but clearly a Congressional record.

Re-districting had changed the boundaries of his constituency in 1934. Three of the northern counties, including Bexar which contained San Antonio, were dropped from the 14th District. Eleven counties were added — including Kleberg, Kenedy and Jim Wells — and most of the ranch became a part of the district he served.

The record shows that Kleberg was generally a staunch supporter of his party's legislative program, of Franklin Delano Roosevelt and of the New Deal, until about 1938 when Kleberg became convinced that the Democratic Party was violating "the Old-Time Principles." He spoke his convictions, and he voted often with the opposition. In the 1940's all other considerations were submerged in the exigencies created by a world war, yet Kleberg's inner cleavage with his party's conduct of domestic affairs grew continually wider. When he ran for re-election in 1944, he was defeated in the Democratic primaries by John E. Lyle of Corpus Christi.

Dick Kleberg came home from Congress maintaining that he was as staunch a Democrat as ever. He said that he didn't leave the party, but that the party left him. After spending thirteen of his fifty-seven years in public service at Washington, he returned to the Santa Gertrudis and the felicities of ranching again.

In 1925 when the elder Robert Kleberg assumed his duties as the senior executor and trustee of Mrs. King's estate he was seventy-two years old. The following year he suffered a mild stroke; a partial paralysis poignantly extended his infirmity. It did not destroy the vitality of his spirit or his constant concern with the operation of the ranch. Each day he was lifted from his wheel chair into his automobile; on its seat he made an inspection tour daily.[22] The physical handicap by no means injured his mental power. His invalid's chair was the seat of senior authority in the administration of the estate's business until the day of his death. Unable to hold a pen to sign documents brought to him, he provided himself with a rubber stamp of his signature, which he himself applied when required.

His invalidism was mitigated by the warmth of his family's affection. He lived in the big house as the beloved paterfamilias, taking cheer from his wife, who adored him, from all his sons and daughters, from his growing number of grandchildren, from his friends who came to see him.

Of these friends none brought him more cheer than a gifted traveler who for years was in the habit of stopping at the Santa Gertrudis whenever he could—Will Rogers, with his rope, his grin, his forelock. The family remembers how he ate quickly at the dinner table; how, before the meal was done, he would hurry upstairs to the invalid's room, and how the laughter would ring from that room and sound along the halls. Rogers venerated Robert Kleberg both for his humanity and for his mastery as a ranchman; as he became more enfeebled, Rogers' visits became more frequent. From visit to visit, his host would collect stories to trade: Rogers' appearances became shining occasions to the aged gentleman in the wheel chair. How Will saw the ranch, how he enjoyed himself when he came, he wrote in his newspaper column on December 6, 1931:

Well, all I know is just what I read in the papers or what I see from hither to yon. A few weeks ago I was coming out of Mexico and stopped over at San Antonio to broadcast on the Rockne memorial programme, and the next day I went out to the King ranch at Kingsville, Texas.

Of course, you could write whole magazine stories, in fact books, on the King ranch. But I am going to leave that for a while till I am able to get over more of it. It's just about the biggest ranch we have in our land. Been in this same family for years, and they are real ranch folks.

Their hospitality is as big as the ranch, and it's a million and a half acres. But what I am going to tell you about now, the "roping." That's the thing I wanted to see.

Old Paddy Mayes, the old Cherokee boy from Pryor Creek, Okla., had been sent up to the big league. He had been up there a few weeks when I run onto him in Chicago. He was with the Philly Nationals. I met him and asked him how it was going with him. He said:

"Well, all my life I have always heard of the big leagues, and heard so much about how they played ball and how good they were. Well, I have been up here just two weeks. Well, they wasn't overestimated any."

Well, that's the way with the ropers on the King ranch. They hadn't been overestimated any.

Now, I had just seen some mighty good roping. I had just come out of Mexico, where they had given me a special exhibition. They have a great thing there. It's called the Charro club. Charro means cowpunchers. Well they have a regular place, like a big corral, and smaller ones, and all, and some good wild cattle, and all the fellows in the City of Mexico that used to be cowboys, and lots of them that are yet, why they all belong, and on Sundays they go there, and have these Mexican cowboy sports, like "Tailing the Bull." That's one we don't do up here.

You run up on a fast pony, grab the steer by the tail, get a good hold, then throw your leg (which is still in the stirrup) over the tail. Then that gives you a good brace. Then turn your horse to the left, and if you do it right you turn the old critter tail in front of head.

You don't tip him an exact somersault. It's a kind of a side-twister, but he slides along looking back where he come from. Well, they had some fine roping there, mostly fancy, as the Mexicans are the real originators, and the best in the world as ropers.

Well, Sarah, that's the daughter, and Alice, that's another one, and Bob's wife, that's the one that's got charge of the cattle, they took us to the "wagon," where one of their round-ups were working. They was dragging out calves for the branding, and when I say calves I mean little fellows, kinder scrawney, weigh about seven fifty to eight hundred, just about the size of a horse.

It's brushy down there, and they can't miss. They have practiced all their lives. (They are all Mexican boys that not only them, but their fathers and grandfathers were raised on this same ranch). They are a real bunch of cow-hands. They use grass ropes, not rawhide.

They can follow a steer through that thick brush so fast and so close to him that they haven't got a chance to throw at his head for the brush, but they put their horse right on his heels, then throw and get his hind feet without swinging, and do it, too.

They brand right out on the range. Bob Cleyberg [sic] wanted me to try it, and I did; but, Lord, I was in there swinging around and messing things all up. I would hit where the calf had been just previously. They had boys that would rope 'em out all day, and NOT swing, just pitch away out to the end and get veal on the end.

Head, hind feet, "mongano" (front feet), and they got good horses. They had two or three hundred saddle horses on this "remuther," and good beans. That's what makes a good cow outfit, is good beans. Just give me some good beans and I will follow you off. I sure wish I was on a ranch.

I would like to stay a year on that outfit. But I got to get back and see what Mr. Hoover is doing and kinder keep my eye on Calvin and encourage the Democrats. But I like roping the best.[23]

The senior Kleberg's last days were warm not only with affection from his family and friends but with great pride in the work of his two sons. He saw them fulfilling his hopes and plans. He lived for ten months after Dick's election to Congress, taking immense satisfaction in the knowledge that his forthright elder son was ably serving South Texas and the nation—while he saw his younger son, with altogether exceptional gifts both as a stock breeder and as a business head, stand up worthy of the ranching responsibilities and the ranching dreams at which his father and his grandfather had labored.

Well content, forty-seven years after he had joined his own hardworking destiny to that of the ranch on the Santa Gertrudis, Robert Justus Kleberg, nearly seventy-nine, put down the burden. He died in his upstairs room, with his family present, early in the afternoon of October 10, 1932.

Scenes resembling those of seven years before were repeated. Like Mrs. King's, his body lay in state at the big house. There were the gatherings of the quiet crowds from the ranch, from the region, from afar, and the paying of homage to the memory of a strong and straight friend, of a distinguished citizen.

All the *Kineños* came to the bier, to see *El Abogao* for a last time. Candido Garza, a small gray-haired man who had worked for the ranch all his life, stood a long time before the *patrón*. He cried silently but he said aloud, with the voice of all his people, "*Adiós, amigo mío.*"[24]

Three Presbyterian ministers conducted services at the ranch on the afternoon of October 12; five thousand people reportedly stood at the graveside in Chamberlain Park at Kingsville later that afternoon. When the Masonic ceremony came to a close, the cowboys from the farthest reaches of the ranch again rode by an open grave in a final salute.

For half a century at the Santa Gertrudis Robert Justus Kleberg had been faithful to a trust. Fidelity was the fundamental substance of his life. To it he had added another element springing from the

deeps of his own nature, from his own quality of mind and spirit. This was the obligation to excel. All his life he aimed not to labor passably, but rather to labor surpassingly well. He was not content with the merely adequate. His cast of mind made progress a tangible entity: it was to be continuously sought and eventually found. To his sons he spoke of progress as "a road paved with past mistakes corrected." Yet it was more. Before there could be a road to pave, there was a course to lay and a faith to tread it. He built Richard King's ranch from half a million to more than a million acres. He ranched them with skill, through good times and bad. He stocked them with scores of thousands of the best livestock he knew how to breed. He found a way to provide them with unfailing water; he improved their pastures with new grasses. He made experimental science a part of his husbandry.

His services as a citizen extended far beyond the ranch. He was a prime mover in bringing a railroad to the land, and ocean shipping to that land's edge. He brought permanent populations and a prospering commerce to formerly empty prairies, found new products for yet untilled prairie soil. He created towns and he built a city. Across the span of a fruitful life spent in "the development of South Texas," he lived to see young men in roaring aircraft speed high over pastures where once he had watched young "Kansas Men" on horseback.

He died with the shape of his accomplishment assured, with his desire for excellence visibly projected into the future, through his sons—that was the true achievement. The continuity, more than that, the increasing genius of the ranch's management through the three generations of its existence, and the continuing promise of genius in the fourth generation, is the most conspicuous and the most impressive fact in the story of the ranch. Ranchers, not scions, spring from the Santa Gertrudis.

The senior Kleberg died three years before the termination of the trusteeship. Seeking some means to keep the ranch — or as much of it as possible — intact for future operation after the division stipulated in Mrs. King's will, Robert Kleberg's family had already on March 12 and on November 30 of 1929 negotiated for the purchase of interests held by two other heirs, Henrietta Welton Page and Elizabeth Atwood Baldwin.

On December 14, 1934, with the end of the trusteeship less than four months away, the widowed Alice Kleberg and her two sons organized a family corporation for the purpose of operating that part of the ranch which the Klebergs would own after partition. The company was incorporated under the name KING RANCH. It is to be noted that although the Santa Gertrudis property had been popularly referred to as the King Ranch for decades, it did not officially name itself the King Ranch until 1934.

When the company was formed the 72-year-old Alice Kleberg conveyed to it her real estate and livestock properties and the holdings devised to her by Mrs. King's will. Dick and Bob Kleberg, as trustees for themselves and their three sisters in equal shares, then purchased from their mother all the stock in the corporation. They elected their corporation officers: Dick, chairman of the board; Bob, president and general manager; their mother, secretary and treasurer. The trust under which Dick and Bob held the stock was to endure for a term of twenty years. Thus organized, the Klebergs prepared for the division of Mrs. King's estate.[25]

On March 30 and 31, 1935, transfers for final partition according to the terms of the will were delivered by the trustees and executors who had set aside the respective shares of each heir, executing all deeds and conveyances. Next morning, April 1, 1935, ten years after the death of Henrietta M. King, her heirs received their inheritances.

By far the most salient item in each bequest was its piece of the big ranch. The will apportioned to each of Mrs. King's four children, or their heirs, a specified area of the ranch's land, together with all the equipment, improvements and livestock thereon.

Alice Kleberg was devised the northern sector, the entire Santa Gertrudis and Laureles divisions. The southern sector of the ranch, comprising all the Norias and Sauz divisions, was divided into two portions designated as the "Norias West Ranch" and the "Norias East Ranch." The heirs of Richard King II received all the Norias West Ranch (called the Santa Fe). Under the will, the other portion, the Norias East, was to be divided into two equal parts. One half was to go to Henrietta Welton Page, sole heir of Ella King Welton. The other one half was devised to the heirs of Nettie King Atwood. In 1929 Henrietta Welton Page had sold her inheritance including her 161,895.12-acre interest in the eastern sector of the Norias Division to Alice G. K. Kleberg for about four dollars an acre and other consideration — Mrs. Kleberg assumed Mrs. Page's share of the King Estate debt — so that at the time of the partition in 1935 this land was conveyed by the trustees directly to the Klebergs' corporation, King Ranch.

By a transaction similar in every respect to Mrs. Page's, one of the Atwood heirs, Elizabeth Atwood Baldwin, had sold her inheritance including her 40,473.78-acre interest in the eastern sector of the Norias Division to Mrs. Kleberg, so that in 1935 this land too was conveyed to King Ranch. The result was that in the partition the trustees conveyed the north five-eighths of the Norias East Ranch to King Ranch and the south three-eighths, called the Sauz Ranch, to Edwin, Alice and Richard Atwood.

When this ranch partition had been made, there remained for division a residuary estate consisting of cash, miscellaneous real estate and personal property. In her will Mrs. King disposed of three-fourths of this residuary — one-fourth to Alice Kleberg, one-fourth to the heirs of Richard King II, one-eighth to Henrietta Welton Page, and one-eighth to the Atwoods—but did not dispose of the remaining one-fourth. The trustees decided that this remaining one-fourth should be divided equally among Alice Kleberg, the heirs of Richard King II, Mrs. Page and the Atwoods, and so partitioned the residuary estate. Their decision was later upheld in court litigation with the Atwoods.

The San Antonio Viejo Ranch in Jim Hogg County was a part of this residuary estate and its acreage was apportioned accordingly. Mrs. Kleberg by her purchase from Mrs. Page and Mrs. Baldwin had added their shares to her interest in the residuary so that King Ranch received title to a total of 42,038.5 acres of that property—to which it added 24,022 acres by purchase from the heirs of Richard King II; Alice and Tom East continued to ranch it.

Richard King II's three heirs, Richard King III and his two sisters, Minerva King Patch and Mary King Estill, chose to set up their own ranching operation, as their own family enterprise, at the Santa Fe Ranch which they received in the partition. This property, comprising 147,258.5 acres and an approximate 20,000 head of cattle, was thenceforth completely severed from the King Ranch. To align the separate holdings more conveniently after the partition, the heirs of Richard King II acquired from King Ranch some of the stock partitioned to it in the Corpus Christi National Bank and its interest in lands in Bee and Goliad counties amounting to 3834.41 acres. The Kings also sold to King Ranch their interest in some of the cattle on the San Antonio Viejo and the Lasater and Stillman pastures.

The King family, maintaining the historic firm name of R. King & Co., has operated the Santa Fe Ranch and the 10,000 acres of the Agua Dulce Ranch which remain in the family's ownership, as a flourishing enterprise to the present day, branding its livestock with the first officially recorded brand of Captain King's original ranch, the venerable HK, which Richard King II received when his parents presented him the Agua Dulce in 1883. Among other properties devised to his heirs by Mrs. King was title to 112 sections of land (71,680 acres) in the arid western Texas counties of Crane, Upton, Edwards, Val Verde and Crockett. This land was not subject to the ten-year trust under the will, and therefore passed to the Kings immediately upon their grandmother's death in 1925 and was later disposed of by them.

In her will Mrs. King made special provisions for her grandson Richard W. Atwood who was a mental patient in a sanitarium near Chicago. She directed the trustees to set up a trust fund which would yield three hundred dollars monthly for his care and maintenance for the rest of his life, and provided that unless he recovered his mental competence his share as a legatee in the Norias East property was forfeited to his brother and sisters. Accordingly the trustees set up the trust for him, consisting primarily of his one-third interest in the Atwood three-eighths of the Norias East Ranch.

Edwin and Alice Atwood were both residents of Chicago, not interested in South Texas ranching, bitterly hostile and resentful concerning their ranching relatives there, and dissatisfied with the terms of the legacy from their grandmother — from whom they had been estranged for thirty years.[26]

Two years before the end of the trusteeship and division of the estate, the Atwoods instituted a rancorous and prolonged litigation designed to impugn the trustees in their administration of the estate, to challenge the correctness of the estate's partition, and to contest the validity of the Humble oil lease on the King Estate's land.

The first suit, brought in 1933, asked that an "accounting be had of all the acts and doings and of all the failures to act of said trustees"; that the trust estate be reimbursed "for money, property, and other assets found to be due by reason of improper actions or failure to act pursuant to the will"; and that "Robert J. Kleberg, Jr., Richard Mifflin Kleberg, Caesar Kleberg and John D. Finnegan be removed as trustees under the will of the late Mrs. Henrietta M. King and suitable and qualified persons be appointed in their places."[27]

The court rejected the Atwood allegations and demands. Judge T. M. Kennerly, United States District Court for the Southern District of Texas at Houston, ruled: "I think and find that the plan of partition was fair and that the partition itself was fairly, properly, equitably and lawfully made, except as to the creation of the special trust for Richard W. Atwood." In that matter, which was vaguely phrased in the will, the court held that the trust fund should have been set up separately in cash and the cost apportioned to all the heirs, including the Atwoods, instead of to Richard Atwood's share only. The trust fund was altered to conform to the court ruling. This was the extent of fault found after a rigorously complete probe into the administration of the estate and every minute item of its accounts.

Edwin and Alice Atwood refused to accept partition of Mrs. King's estate as set forth by the terms of her will. The acrimonious litigation persisted in by their Chicago lawyer went on and on. Their suit was defeated, the decision against them was upheld on appeal to the United States Circuit Court of Appeals, and the United States Supreme Court refused to review it — yet the Chicago lawyer went on suing.[28]

Discovery of a rich oil field on their own Sauz Ranch in 1944 was not unwelcome to the Atwoods, however.

At the time of the estate's partition on April 1, 1935,[29] the first Atwood suit was in court and, pending settlement, Edwin and Alice Atwood disavowed partition under the existing terms. Trustees of the estate were compelled to maintain the operation of the Sauz Ranch, in mitigation of damages and as responsible managers for the absentee Chicagoans, for fifteen years: it was not until April 20, 1950, in Judge Kennerly's court in Houston, that Edwin Atwood finally accepted the legal delivery of the Sauz property. In court that day Edwin Atwood also testified that he and his sister Alice had conveyed forty-five percent of their interest in Mrs. King's estate to their lawyer, Thomas Hart Fisher, as compensation for his services.

With the disposition of the lands partitioned to the Atwoods, the Kings and Mrs. Page thus outlined, it is easier to describe the lands to which the Kleberg family corporation retained title and which now comprise the King Ranch.

Neither the acreage nor the ranching operation was radically changed by the partition. The heart of the ranch, containing head-quarters and the ranch's finest herds, was the Santa Gertrudis Division. All of it and all of the Laureles Division, together totaling 428,055.43 acres, in addition to the Santa Gertrudis headquarters tract of 30,439.29 acres which she already owned by gift from her mother, were devised to Alice Kleberg. The King Ranch retained the entire northern sector of the old ranch intact. According to the terms of the will, on the morning of April 1, 1935, 471,383.86 acres were to be separated from the old ranch's southern sector, yet the new King Ranch corporation retained 202,368.90 acres of the Norias-Sauz through the purchase of the Page and the Baldwin interests. To these the King Ranch added, by leasing from Robert J. Kleberg, Jr., Trustee, the lands which he had purchased in 1924, the Stillman and Lasater properties totaling 141,734.98 acres.[30] Altogether, these southern pastures comprised 344,103.88 acres. When these were added to the Santa Gertrudis and Laureles, the Klebergs owned a formidable expanse of 802,542.54 acres, not including the San Antonio Viejo and some noncontiguous parcels of real estate which were also a part of Alice Kleberg's legacy. With all the lands, she received as her portion approximately 60,000 head of cattle.

The Kleberg-owned King Ranch was organized into four administrative divisions, an arrangement it retains to this day. The Santa Gertrudis of 203,468.19 acres and the Laureles of 255,026.53 acres remained exactly as they were before partition.

At the Norias the Klebergs added their Stillman pasture to their Page and Baldwin purchases, making a newly bounded Norias Division composed of 237,348.96 acres—with headquarters still at the ramshackle old two-story house by the railroad tracks at Norias Station.

An entirely new division named the Encino was formed from the Lasater land located west and north of the Norias and separated from it by the King family's Santa Fe Ranch. To enlarge the Encino Division the Klebergs made a ten-year lease, later renewed, on an adjoining tract known as the Ball Ranch. The leased acreage when combined with the Lasater land made the Encino a working unit of 131,017.07 acres.

The San Antonio Viejo was not a part of the King Ranch proper; though the 66,060.5 acres over in Jim Hogg County did belong to the family corporation, it was in fact the ranching realm of the Tom East family.

When the San Antonio Viejo and the leased Ball land were included in the total, the entire ranching acreage *operated* by the King Ranch corporation and by the East family came to 889,463.1 acres. Though the corporation would acquire land in other states and in three foreign countries during the next two decades, the size of the home ranch itself would not be further expanded. Contrary to press reports and the popular belief that the King Ranch embraces a million acres, the actual area of the land the corporation now *owns* in South Texas is exactly 726,924.12 acres.[31]

The many ramifications of the business attending the trusteeship and partition of Mrs. King's estate, the Atwood trouble, the shaping of the King Ranch family corporation, the continuing operation of a great land and cattle enterprise, of course made legal counsel enormously important. The scholarly Joseph K. Wells represented the ranch in the years immediately following his father's death in 1923; so did attorney Edward Kleberg of Corpus Christi.

In 1924, negotiations for the purchase of the Lasater land brought Bob Kleberg into a first business contact with Leroy G. Denman of San Antonio. Denman's father, Judge Leroy G. Denman, had upon occasion represented Mrs. King's ranch. He had been eminent at the Texas Bar as a member of the firm of Denman, Franklin & McGowan, and in banking circles both as a director of the San Antonio National Bank and as the president of the San Antonio Loan & Trust Co. He had died in 1917; his 25-year-old son had capably stepped into his place as a leading lawyer and as a banker at San Antonio.

When the two young men, Leroy Denman and Bob Kleberg, met for business in 1924, they became fast friends. Denman arranged for the financing of both the Lasater and Stillman purchases through his San Antonio Loan & Trust Co., while the Kleberg's Palo Alto farm tracts were being sold; thenceforth Bob Kleberg called for Leroy Denman's aid and advice with increasing frequency.

By 1930 the able Denman had become the principal legal counsel for the ranch and one of the Kleberg family's most respected friends. In the twenty years that followed, until his death in 1950, Denman's services were prodigious. He brought the ranch through the maze of legalities incident to the trusteeship and partition, grappled with its debts and taxes, built the legal structure for the King Ranch corporation, guided it through the muddied waters stirred by the Atwoods' litigations and left a brilliant lawyer-banker son, Leroy G. Denman, Jr., who would follow in his father's footsteps as the devoted attorney for the ranch.

In the course of the years through the trusteeship, new men had found places in the ranch's management. The ancient and sapient Sam Ragland, boss of headquarters division and a trustee of Mrs. King's estate, had retired from active range work; he died in 1935. In 1926 Lauro F. Cavazos had replaced Ragland as working foreman of the Santa Gertrudis Division. Cavazos, a descendant of the José Narciso Cavazos who in 1781 had received the San Juan de Carricitos grant from the Spanish Crown, had come to work as a young cowboy on Mrs. King's ranch in 1912. He had been one of the steadiest of men under fire in the Norias raid in 1916; he had seen action as an artilleryman in France during World War I, and he had returned to work on the ranch in 1921. His ability had made him foreman five years later.

Over at the Laureles, Charlie Burwell had become Dick Kleberg's successor as boss of the work on that division. The big, powerfully built, highly competent Burwell had been a Texas Ranger, then an employee of the Cattle Raisers' Association. He had first come to the ranch in 1921 with a tick eradication crew. When he was offered the foremanship of the Laureles in 1930, he was planning a pursuit of his ambition to study law and to become a member of the Texas Bar; it took him several months to decide upon the course of his future. Then he had chosen: not the law but the Laureles.

Jim McBride had been the hard-working foreman on the Lasater land which Bob Kleberg bought in 1924. When the property changed hands, McBride stayed on as the able headman there. His son, Billy McBride, after graduation from Texas A & M and a return in 1946 from service in the North African and Italian campaigns of World War II, would one day join his father at the Encino Division.

The years had brought a profound knowledge of men, land, livestock and practical ranching to Caesar Kleberg. His knowledge was blended with such acumen, with such diplomatic and dependable managerial ability, that on the ranch he was referred to sometimes as "the old master." His contribution to the working administration of the ranch was immense. Though he was still superintendent at Norias, that was only part of his labor: he and Richard King III carried the burden as the surviving executors of Mrs. King's estate, and Caesar was in fact the senior assistant administrator for the entire ranching operation.

To manage the actual range work at the south end of the ranch Caesar had three top men; the gifted chief foreman Eppse Goodwyn at the Norias who had worked for the ranch since 1911;[32] Tom R. Tate, an ex-ranger who looked like the prototype of all Texas range men carved out of the old rock, and who presided over operations at the Tordilla Ranch on the "Stillman pasture"; and George Durham, headman at the Sauz.

Durham was the son and namesake of one of the belegended McNelly rangers who had delivered Captain King's stolen cattle from Las Cuevas in 1875. The elder George Durham saw three of his sons assume his own potent stamp.

George Jr. followed his father as boss at the Sauz. He died young, of a heart attack while building a fire to brand calves. He was succeeded by his brother Bland. Ed Durham, another brother, would later become the formidable foreman of the whole Norias Division and would be, like Bland, a pillar of strength in the King Ranch management. A measure of all the Durham family's impressiveness is suggested by the remark of Carl Hertzog, printer of this volume, who visited the Sauz in 1952. "If Bland had asked me to leave, I would have hurried," Hertzog said.

Another ex-ranger, Sam Chesshire, went to work at the Norias in 1921. There he maintained a position not only as a top horseback man, hunter, and trainer of Caesar's bird dogs, but also as an unmatchable raconteur whose burning narratives fried the ears of visitors at Caesar's strictly bachelor diggings by the railroad tracks.

One of these guests, after an hour or so of post-poker sleep in the Olympian Norias atmosphere, complained at 4:30 A. M.: "Well, Caesar, it don't take very long to spend the night with you."

The range bosses of the King Ranch, presiding over cow camps of skilled and faithful *Kineños*, made a closely knit and exceedingly adept organization for performance of the never-ending toil over the long reaches of the ranch's quiet grass. There were other less picturesque phases of the ranch's work which required fully as much devotion, and skill of another kind: the business office kept the whole operation going.

Since 1912 John D. Finnegan's able management of fiscal affairs had been a prime factor in the ranch's evolution. He knew nothing about livestock but he knew a very great deal about sound business practice. That knowledge was woven into the fabric of the King Ranch's business routine and business success. Finnegan created and maintained a detailed system of accounting for the whole enterprise, grappled with its tax schedules, took the burden of daily office detail, and trained young men, like Cy Yeary and J. B. Fisher, for key office jobs of the future. Bob Kleberg said, "Mr. Finnegan gave the bone and sinew to the big development of the ranch."

In 1932 when illness forced Finnegan's semi-retirement, the ranch was fortunate to have at hand another man of like caliber. Al Kleberg, after an absence in the Army during the war and after six years as an engineer with the Humble Oil Company, had returned to the ranch's employ. He assumed Finnegan's position as general manager of the business office in Kingsville, and for the next twenty years filled that position with the same degree of competence as his predecessor.

Another figure of prime importance was J. K. Northway—no cow camp boss or business executive, but a Doctor of Veterinary Medicine. He had first come to the ranch in 1916, a young man fresh from college. He had remained—and he remains to this day—demonstrating not only a veterinarian's skill but a remarkable eye for the conformation of livestock and a thorough-going gift for genetics. His work at the ranch was soon extended beyond a guardianship of the health of the herds. In the Klebergs' experimental program of crossbreeding, which led to the creation of Santa Gertrudis cattle and to a great family of Quarter Horses, the records "Doc" Northway kept became a vital department of the ranch's enterprise.[33]

Over all departments, divisions, cow corrals or office desks, the driving force was Bob Kleberg. A torrential vitality poured from him and reached to the remotest fence corners. With his steamboating grandfather's gift of command, Bob Kleberg ran a taut ranch. He held it together, he sparked it, he made it go, he kept it going. He had seen his father's life quota of vital energy spread thin in the business complications attending "the development of South Texas." Expending his own welling flood of vigor, Bob Kleberg channeled it to the development of the King Ranch.

From crack of dawn till after dark he rode strong horses, drove stripped-down ranching cars, paced at office desks. He pushed others hard. With his own energy he was pitiless. He had opinions and he held to them, hotly and volubly. He had supreme confidence in what he was doing and in how he did it. There was a creative power, like that of an authentic artist at work with living animals and grass, in the way he handled the pastures, shaped the herds, bred the beef, dominated the works and made the ranch the most accomplished, most prosperous, most famed livestock ranching operation of his time.

His driving force, his push, his engrossment with his task shaped all his behavior and his talk, and tinged each moment of his consciousness. Yet his preoccupations by no means warped him away

from sociability. A natural conviviality was part of his unquench-
able energy: his friendships were strong and so were the pleasures he
drew from companionship. He was tempered by a robust animal
health he absorbed from the outdoors; moreover, he possessed the
interior happiness of a man living for his work.

There were responsibilities connected with his work which he
found far from happy. The King Ranch had its enemies as well as its
friends. Animosity toward the ranch, toward its manager, and especially toward its fence, reached a high tide in the 1930's. Richness
was suspect: during the Depression bigness was badness. There was
no question about the size of the King Ranch. Whether or not it was
bad, it got a bad time—from some of its neighbors, a few of its
kinsfolk, and from the press.

In 1931 the King Ranch became involved in a bitter controversy
over the building of a state highway through Kenedy County. The
proposed route passed for fifteen of its fifty miles across the Norias
Division. At the beginning Bob Kleberg stated that he would accede
to public demand, and he prepared to donate to the state a hundred-
foot-wide right of way through the Norias.

State engineers then questioned feasibility of construction through
the heavy drifting sands along the route. Local and state political
pressures embroiled procurement of funds for the proposed highway. Examining their own interest and convenience, a majority of
the big ranchers in Kenedy County (five of them, including the
King Ranch, owned ninety per cent of the county's land and controlled its tax rate) came to the conclusion that a paved route across
the county was to them neither necessary nor desirable. Bob Kleberg,
the Kenedys, Armstrongs, Ytúrrias and McGills opposed the project.

As a substitute for the Kenedy County road, Kleberg led in the
proposal of a seashore highway up the entire length of Padre Island,
which would offer the shortest, straightest route to connect Browns-

ville with Corpus Christi, and be a scenic drive for the attraction of tourists to the area.

A majority of residents in the lower Rio Grande valley rejected the Padre Island proposal, and demanded as a rightful public convenience the elimination of the then current detour around Kenedy County and the building of a paved overland traffic outlet from Raymondville straight north, through the closed fifty miles of Kenedy County, to Riviera in southern Kleberg County where the highway already led on to the coastal cities of Texas.

After two hard years of damnations and recriminations, key ranchmen of Kenedy County consented to the highway through their pastures. Though the right of way was agreed to and deeded without cost to the state in 1933, the highway department did not bring the road to actual completion until 1940.[34]

At the height of the storm the *Houston Press*, January 10, 1933, had coined a phrase with a headline: TEXAS' WALLED KINGDOM OF KENEDY— *Cattle Princes Bar Way With Barbed Wire While Valley Begs For Highway*. The "walled kingdom" stuck. The opprobrium of the phrase outlasted the contention that had created it, and became attached not to Kenedy County but to the King Ranch.

The epithet and its implications derived from the fact that the ranch in spite of its size stoutly maintained its rights against trespass. Its fence, built to protect its livestock, also enclosed a state game preserve. It was patrolled by wardens appointed by and responsible only to the state, but paid in part by the ranch. Implementing a long-sighted program for game preservation within its own area, the ranch's self-imposed hunting regulations were far more stringent than state game laws.[35] The results were apparent in the flourishing wildlife populations on the ranch's pastures. Easy targets for hunters' guns made trespass a temptation to many, and greatly helped to make the words "walled kingdom" a pat allusion.

The physical presence of frequently patrolled King Ranch fences along scores of miles of public highways had evoked a collection of local tales which were as hardy as folklore, about dire punishments said to be awaiting hapless intruders upon the ranch's vast spread. The stories, insofar as their origins can be traced, stemmed from the undocumented but real shootings and hangings of cow thieves and bandits in the brush during the cattle wars before 1885, and from hazy but probably true incidents of hard treatment dealt to suspicious Mexican vagrants during the border violence of 1915 and 1916. More recently poachers—some of them engaged in a ruthless slaughtering of game for regular markets—had been arrested or else roughly ejected from behind the King Ranch fence; embellished and baseless local gossip springing from such incidents furnished nourishment for a continuing body of warped information concerning the ranch's purported measures against trespass. Late in 1936 much-publicized circumstances surrounding the unsolved disappearance of two men in the King Ranch vicinity lent a specious measure of substance to the old legends and rumors. "The Blanton Case" and the press stories that accompanied it imbued a large public with a lasting impression that the "walled kingdom" was a "proven" fact.

A 57-year-old farm worker named Luther Blanton and his son John, twenty-four, lived at the hamlet of San Perlita, eight miles east of Raymondville and two miles from the west fence of the game preserve on the Sauz Ranch. On the afternoon of November 18, 1936, the two Blantons went out with their guns, presumably to hunt. Mrs. Blanton later stated she heard three distant shots sometime after her husband and son left. She said she heard no other shots. When her men failed to return that night, she notified neighbors and a search began.

The identity of the Blantons' tracks, or their direction, was not established. Some of the neighbors nevertheless decided that if the Blantons had disappeared, it must be because they had entered the Sauz preserve.

Though the Sauz Ranch had been partitioned to the Atwoods the previous year, they had not accepted it, and the property was still being maintained by the King Estate. Employed for all the ranch work on the more than hundred thousand acres of the Sauz were exactly fifteen vaqueros and two state game wardens.

A local faction quickly made the disappearance of the Blantons an opportunity to vent a personal animosity against the King Ranch, its fence and the men who patrolled it. A handful of troublemakers set afoot the accusation that the Blantons had met with violence at the hands of Sauz Ranch game wardens or fence riders.

The ranch's stiff-necked and angry denial of the accusation was scorned as nothing less than proof of guilt — while hours, then days passed without the reappearance of the missing men. Accusations, bearing only incidentally any solicitude for the fate of the Blantons, became hotter. When the ranch grimly refused to be intimidated by demands for a mob entry upon the Sauz premises to search for the Blantons, the people at the Sauz received inflamed threats that an outraged local citizenry would "tear up the fences and burn down the ranch."

The steady Sheriff of Willacy County, Howard Cragg, after a deadend investigation of the Blantons' departure from their house with their guns in their hands, found himself with no clue to the Blantons' whereabouts, but with every prospect of having to put down a bloody battle if troublemakers persisted and tried to force the Sauz Ranch gate. The sheriff watched newspaper reporters arrive and knew he was in trouble. Three days after the Blantons disappeared, the situation became so tense that Governor James Allred ordered a company of Texas Rangers to San Perlita.

The threats of violence—not the malice against the ranch—subsided when the rangers arrived. Ranger Captain Bill McMurray's extended investigation of the Blantons' disappearance yielded no more results than Sheriff Cragg's. A game warden and a fence rider employed on the Sauz were among those questioned and released. The rangers went over the ground, took testimony, conducted a series of searches through the tangled brush in the vicinity, on and off the Sauz property. A deputized citizens' posse led by Constable Ernest Oakes of San Sebastian also made a search on the Sauz Ranch.

The Blantons, living or dead, in South Texas or elsewhere, have not been traced. The incidents of that baleful November afternoon when the Blantons vanished from sight have not been ascertained. Continued investigation never uncovered a useful clue; the King Ranch never made a statement except to repeat that it had no knowledge of what happened to the Blantons. Local discussion of the case, complete with endless varieties of the "inside story," continues to this day and continues to leave the mystery unsolved.[36]

Two things are clear. The virulent personal bitterness of a very few inhabitants of Willacy County, not the unknown fate of the Blantons, stirred the furor against the ranch—and the inordinate publicity it received was a natural consequence of what the press had already created and called a "walled kingdom."

The Blanton incident was the harsh climax to a phase of King Ranch history marred by controversies in the public eye, and marked by a skeptical, often hostile press. Contentions and antagonisms began to ease in 1937. From the trying period of trusteeship and transition through which Mrs. King's estate had passed, a King Ranch emerged in the modern guise of a business corporation with vast interests, multifold ramifications, public obligations—and unique achievements in livestock breeding and range improvement.

The King Ranch Achievement

AS ITS OWN

solution to its own ranching problem, the King Ranch created its own breed of domestic kine. It brought into flourishing existence the only recognized new breed of beef cattle ever developed upon the shores of the New World.

By 1915 Manager Robert Kleberg had established at Mrs. King's ranch the largest purebred Shorthorn and Hereford herds in the United States. He was understandably proud of them, and he became reluctantly aware of the fact that these two British breeds, superbly adapted to more temperate climates, were not the ideal stock for subtropical rangelands. In the course of the years since 1886 he had infused the ranch's original Longhorn herds with large proportions of Shorthorn or Hereford blood, and while he watched them make better quality beef, he also watched them fare poorly and lose their former hardihood under the hot sun of coastal Texas.

A few of the tough and prolific Brahman cattle from India were creating notice in East Texas at the turn of the century. These big beasts were often vicious, hard to handle, and they lacked quality as fine beef, but they were adapted to tropical heat, they had high tolerance to insect pests, and they demonstrated an ability to fend for themselves on coarse or scarce pasturage. Stockmen along the Gulf Coast eyed the Brahmans with interest, but government import regulations at the time severely restricted the number of these cattle, and ranchmen found it next to impossible to procure pure Brahman stock for introduction to their ranges.

The first Brahman blood arrived on Mrs. King's ranch in 1910, in the form of a huge black half-bred Brahman-Shorthorn bull, the gift of Tom O'Connor of Victoria.[1] As a tentative experiment, Robert J. Kleberg, Sr., added this bull to the Shorthorn bulls in a pasture with some four thousand purebred Shorthorn cows. All the resulting male offspring of the O'Connor bull were castrated except for one promising red bull calf called Chemera, and all the heifers were turned back with Shorthorn bulls. It became apparent within the next several seasons that this experimental cross of Brahman blood with the ranch's Shorthorn stock had produced the best range cattle for hardihood, size, and ability to fatten yet seen on the ranch.

Meanwhile cattle of Brahman blood had become more easily available to stockmen in the warm Gulf Coast states. In 1918 the senior Kleberg, at the strong behest of his son Bob, was able to procure from the leading Brahman importer, A. P. Borden of Houston, fifty-two selected three-year-old bulls of three-fourths to seven-eighths Brahman blood.

To initiate a breeding program conceived by young Bob Kleberg, endorsed by his brother Dick and cousin Caesar, and somewhat hesitantly approved by Bob's father, the Borden bulls were divided and placed among eight different breeding herds composed of twenty-five hundred excellent purebred Shorthorn cows and bulls. Bob's program was a highly iconoclastic procedure — all textbooks deplored the crossbreeding of purebreds — and Bob's father had been working for more than thirty years to develop his purebred Shorthorn and Hereford herds.[2]

The placing of the Brahman bulls in the ranch's best Shorthorn breeding herds indicates two things clearly: by 1918 Mrs. King's ranch faced a vital dollars-and-cents necessity for a more productive range animal, and the ranch management felt persuaded that it must take radical measures in an attempt to develop such an animal.

The mere crossbreeding of common South Texas range stock with Brahman blood was by no means unorthodox by that time; many stockmen were using Brahman bulls and were enthusiastic about the results. Ed C. Lasater was saying, "Brahman cattle raise the value of South Texas rangeland two dollars an acre." Tom East, replying to a visitor's query about the wildness of Brahmans, was saying dryly, "I'd a lot rather say 'Yonder they go!' than 'There they lay'." The stout Brahman crossbreds were becoming a widespread and visible boon to most ranchmen in the area.

Yet a crossbreed was by no means what the King Ranch looked for. The Klebergs were breeders, not mere multipliers, of cattle. Studying their first crosses and second crosses, they looked for a type and they evolved a breeding plan aimed at *fixing* a type — a big and strong, solid red, heavily fleshed beef producer of about five-eighths Shorthorn and three-eighths Brahman ancestry. Dick Kleberg said, "Cattle are machines to gather and sell grass. We want a big rack to hang the grass on."

The instrument enabling the Klebergs to fix the type they looked for appeared in the auspicious shape of an extraordinary red bull named Monkey, sired by one of the Borden Brahman bulls, Vinotero, out of a Shorthorn milk cow at the Laureles[3] which carried about one-sixteenth of Brahman blood through the original O'Connor bull and his King Ranch son Chemera.

The prepotent great bull Monkey, born in 1920, turned into a selected breeding herd in 1923, active as a sire until his death in 1932, fixed desirable characteristics so firmly into his offspring—he had more than a hundred and fifty useful sons—that through him the Klebergs were able to create a new breed of cattle. Monkey was the foundation sire from whose progeny the Santa Gertrudis breed took shape.[4]

The first distinctive American breed of cattle was created not by trained geneticists equipped with a research laboratory and a scientific experimental station, but by a family of practicing ranchers using their own judgment, their own livestock, their own pastures and their own money to shape what they themselves needed for the profitable pursuit of their own business.

Three current misconceptions about their work ought to be dispelled. The creation of the breed was no "haphazard" affair; it was the result of an astutely executed breeding program. The bull Monkey was not "an accident" of breeding; his appearance was no more and no less an accident than the appearance of any outstanding individual in planned matings. Finally, the development of the Santa Gertrudis breed was not the result of having "millions of dollars poured into it." On the contrary, the breed was a child of necessity, created to check the financial losses suffered by the ranch, and an actual lack of funds, during the years 1918-1925. The presence of Monkey and his robust offspring upon the ranch pastures after 1925 is the principal explanation for the change, after several unsatisfactory years, from annual losses to annual profits in the ranch's livestock operation.[5]

The new breed "originated through the necessity of finding a beef type animal which was better suited to the climatic and range conditions of South Texas."[6] The Santa Gertrudis inherits from its Brahman blood the loose skin which enables it to withstand great heat, and the tough skin which renders it nearly immune to noxious pests.[7] From the Brahman the breed derives its marked ability to rustle for a living under a blazing sun either in humid tropics or upon ranges parched with drought.[8] The breed also carries the Brahman characteristic of being able to gain weight with exceptional rapidity on grass. From the Shorthorn ancestry the Santa Gertrudis receives its rich red color, made solid red and of a deeper hue by its blend with the Brahman pigmentation. The beef qualities of the Santa Gertrudis derive from the Shorthorn, displaying a heavier, deeper meat-making conformation for the larger production of the most desirable cuts. The Santa Gertrudis carcass has an unusually high dressing percentage and its beef, capable of remarkable marbling, meets every grading test for highest quality.

The United States Department of Agriculture, Bureau of Animal Industry, in 1940 officially recognized the Santa Gertrudis as a new and separate breed of cattle, with its own characteristics as defined and firmly fixed as those of any other recognized breed.[9]

The admirable adaptability of the Santa Gertrudis to environments in which the British beef breeds did not flourish had been carefully noted by many stockmen long before 1940. Though the King Ranch from the first phases of the breed's development maintained a policy of retaining all Santa Gertrudis cows and heifers for disposition within its own herds, it sold each year, or else presented, a limited number of its Santa Gertrudis bulls to interested ranchmen and to friends.[10] The Santa Gertrudis blood was thus dispersed through these bulls to many other herds and a growing number of breeders began to develop their own Santa Gertrudis stock by a crossbreeding and "grading-up" program pioneered on the King Ranch.* The improvement of their own range animals, in hardihood and in beef qualities, was so clearly perceptible that a growing number of Santa Gertrudis enthusiasts appeared. Herds of red cattle with increasing proportions of Santa Gertrudis blood came into beefy existence from South Texas to Florida, spreading through the warm southern states, to Cuba, and thence to Central and South America.

On November 10, 1950, the King Ranch held its first annual auction sale of Santa Gertrudis bulls. Two thousand people watched the bidding in a circus tent pitched on a ranch pasture, and the top bull brought $10,000. Two years later the highest price for a Santa Gertrudis bull would reach $40,000.[11]

Upon the day following the first auction in 1950 a number of Santa Gertrudis breeders who had attended the sale met in the schoolhouse at King Ranch headquarters to discuss the formation of a breeders' association. Five months later the Santa Gertrudis Breeders International, with 169 charter members, was formally established.[12]

In 1954 the association issued its first herd book, *Santa Gertrudis Breeders International Recorded Herds*, Volume I, containing a splendidly written technical and historical presentation of the origin of the breed, its Standard of Excellence, a listing of the composition of the recorded herds of its members, and other papers relating to the founding of the breed and of the association.

Both the breed and the breeders' organization listing more than six hundred members[13] are now well launched upon a program bearing unmeasured potentials for the future of livestock raising upon

* Appendix XIII, "Breeding Techniques," discusses the ranch's breeding and grading-up program.

all those areas of the earth's surface where stockmen look for cattle capable of producing heavy beef while subjected to the punishments of harsh rangelands, whether they be arid sandy prairies or steaming tropical jungles. The Santa Gertrudis breed is built for them.[14]

The King Ranch at the present time finds itself engaged in two distinct but related operations with its cattle. It develops its fountainhead breeding stock of top purebred Santa Gertrudis in choice pastures close by headquarters, maintaining in these selected herds approximately five thousand head. And the ranch pursues its basic business, that of producing commercial beef from its tens of thousands of range cattle upon its hundreds of thousands of acres. These commercial herds are being continually upgraded, every new generation of calves, through the use of Santa Gertrudis sires from the ranch's own purebred stud. By a consistently maintained program of improvement and selection, all the range stock on the King Ranch within a few more years will qualify as purebred Santa Gertrudis cattle.

Amid many satisfactions over the breed of cattle he brought to being, Bob Kleberg remembers a sentimental story. His mother particularly cared for the Shorthorns she saw so often in the Santa Gertrudis pastures during the early years of the century. When the Brahman crossbreeding program began, she told her son, "I hate to see the red cattle go." She lived to a day when Bob could say to her, looking out upon the same Santa Gertrudis pasture, "Well, mother, you got your red cattle back."

The ranch's achievement in the breeding of horses has been little less spectacular than its work with cattle.

It may be remembered that from the very first year of its operation it has displayed a propensity for fine horseflesh: in 1854 Captain Richard King paid six hundred dollars for a sorrel stud horse named Whirlpool—twice as much as he had just paid for the whole Rincón

SANTA GERTRUDIS BULL — BUEN AMIGO

de Santa Gertrudis land grant. Throughout his life the captain bought good horses, and bred good horses which were in demand because of their superiority over the range ponies common to the area. At one point Captain King wrote of his ranching: "Horses made this a success." His son-in-law Robert Kleberg paid no less attention to the horse stock when he came to run the ranch. For many years the market for good horses and mules provided Mrs. King's ranch with a considerable portion of its annual income.

Over the course of decades both King and Kleberg added Thoroughbred and Standard blood to the horses they raised for sale and the horses their vaqueros used in ranch remudas. Up to a certain point the infusion of better blood into the original tough Spanish and mustang stock was a good thing — as Doc Northway says, "The *right* kind of Thoroughbred blood never hurt *any* horse."

In 1910, about the time the race tracks in Texas were closed by state law, Kleberg bought a band of thirty Thoroughbred mares and two stallions from Sam Lazarus of Fort Worth, and hot blood became predominant in many of the ranch's remudas.[15] These halfbreds were often too large, too leggy and too nervous to make good working horses on the range; the three-fourths and seven-eighths Thoroughbreds were even less satisfactory. The necessity for breeding back to a more compact type of range mount with more "cow sense" became increasingly apparent on Mrs. King's ranch.

George Clegg, one of the shrewdest breeders of Quarter Horses the country has ever seen, had a place near the town of Alice. On a trip to Clegg's one day in 1915, Bob Kleberg was shown a group of twenty beautiful mares. Clegg was so proud of them he called them his "wax dolls." Bob returned home with the "wax dolls" so fixed in his mind that he could not forget them. He was only nineteen at the time, without authority to buy stock for the ranch, so he told his cousin Caesar about the mares. He asked Caesar, who did have authority, to see if he could buy a good stud colt out of one of Clegg's "wax dolls." In 1916 Caesar visited Clegg's and was shown the mares. Caesar pointed at one of them with a superb sorrel colt at her side.

"How much would a colt like that sell for?" he asked, casually.

Clegg said, "A hundred and twenty-five dollars."

Caesar said, "I'll take him!"

Clegg said, "Not that one—"

Caesar held Clegg to his "bargain." The suckling colt was driven at his mother's side the twenty-five miles to the King Ranch. When he was weaned a few months later his mother was returned to Alice. When he grew up, the sorrel stallion—who never received any name but "the Sorrel Horse," and later, "the Old Sorrel"—changed the character and the quality of the King Ranch's horse stock and influenced the type of the quality stock horse over much of the United States.

As a young horse he was trained for the saddle and used hard at working cattle. He displayed such intelligence, such inborn ability and agility as a roping and cutting horse, and he was so properly built and muscled that Robert J. Kleberg, Sr., seeing the horse work at a roundup, suggested that the sorrel might be tried at stud. This permission was all Bob waited for; he placed the stallion with some of the ranch's best dams, including his own pet saddle mare, Brisa.

Old Sorrel, a contemporary and a superb red equine parallel to the ranch's red bull Monkey, became the foundation sire of a distinctive strain of range saddle horses. Through Old Sorrel and through a perceptive, long-term breeding program using his get, the King Ranch has made a notable contribution to the breeding and improvement of the American Quarter Horse.*

Such an animal is bred for certain qualifications. He must have

*See Appendix XIV, "The Development of a Quarter Horse Family."

the intelligence to learn and to remember well what is expected of him; his temperament must be alert, yet without nervousness. He must be strong-muscled enough to carry good weights, yet be agile under the saddle. He must be speedy enough to outrun the fastest steer, yet compact enough to have an easy and ready maneuverability.

Possessing such attributes, a King Ranch Quarter Horse is obviously a utility mount fitted for more than cow work. He becomes a polo pony par excellence, or a winner at the quarter-mile stakes, from which his breed derives its name.[16] As a pleasing saddle horse he has few equals; he is a consistent prize winner at horse shows. He even becomes a circus horse: the present "Liberty Act" in Ringling Brothers Circus buys and uses King Ranch Quarter Horses only. Their intelligence and temperament fit them for elaborate training.

The King Ranch now has approximately two thousand Quarter Horses in its breeding bands and working remudas, all bearing blood stemming from their extraordinary forebear, the Old Sorrel. They carry his stamp and with few exceptions they bear his color.

In earlier days there were brutality and waste in the usual methods employed by western ranchmen for the breaking of their plentiful range horse stock. Full-grown horses, totally unaccustomed to any handling whatever, were abruptly driven in wild from the pastures, roughly roped in a corral, then blindfolded and, with one leg tied up, saddled by main force. A hard-riding horse breaker climbed in the saddle. The horse was turned loose with the terrifying burden on its back and ridden until the pitching and running stopped, until the horse was literally worn into subjugation. Good horses were ruined often: their high spirits as well as their strong bodies were damaged, spoiled, broken.

The wasteful harshness of "bronc busting" has long been forbidden at the King Ranch.

Horses there begin their training for work when they are foals by

KR QUARTER HORSE
W I M P Y

their dams' sides. As such, they are brought in and made entirely unafraid of the presence of man and of being continually handled by him. When they are grown and ready to ride, they have been so gentled — so quietly and gradually accustomed to what is demanded of them, to a bit in the mouth, to the weight of a saddle and the feel of a cinch — that when man steps in the stirrup at last, the horse is ready — not with violence but with confidence. The animal has been *trained*, not broken, to use. The ranch is proud of the effectiveness of its horse-training procedure.[17]

Kineños in all their daily range work ride the splendid progeny of the Old Sorrel. There is a singular esthetic character in a King Ranch scene of men mounted upon rich red horses matched to the rich red of Santa Gertrudis cattle against a background of tall green grass.

Each year, concurrent with the bull sale, the ranch sells at auction from thirty to fifty of its Quarter Horse colts and fillies. They handsomely make their sorrel ways not only upon their home pastures but in the wide world.[18]

The development of this family of superior horses for range use led Bob Kleberg and the King Ranch toward the development of superior horses for quite another purpose — toward that ultimate summit of horse breeding, the establishment of a Thoroughbred racing stable.

No phase of animal breeding is surrounded by so much interest or glamour; no breeding enterprise requires more consummate judgment and skill. The ranch's entry into the field came not from any sudden decision or explicit choice in the matter, but by a set of circumstances which became so compelling that King Ranch race horses seem to have been inevitable.

The prime circumstance, of course, was the Klebergs' experience and consuming interest in successful animal breeding. Then there was an obscure Thoroughbred stallion at Goliad, Texas; there was the fact that a certain Thoroughbred mare in Kentucky could not be bought except in a lot of mares at a Saratoga sale; and there was a most knowledgeable trainer named Max Hirsch. Such elements were conjoined with that inadvertence fate often displays—and the King Ranch found itself in an exciting new business.

The Klebergs were always watching for horses they thought might be brought into the ranch's breeding program for the improvement of its Quarter Horse line. "We wanted to get for Old Sorrel the best Quarter mares in the world," Bob Kleberg says. In 1934 he found one such animal, the roan mare named Ada Jones. She was owned by John W. Dial of Goliad, Texas, a Quarter Horse man of the same high caliber as George Clegg, who bred the Old Sorrel. The mare Ada Jones was fourteen years old; Kleberg bought her nevertheless, and hoped for a foal.[19]

While he was at Dial's, Bob was shown as a random matter of interest a Thoroughbred stallion. His name was Chicaro and he had seen unhappy times. When Dial found him, he had been raced unsuccessfully at New Orleans; he had been left unsheltered and misused by his owner, and had nearly died of pneumonia. Dial, who knew a real horse when he saw one and who also happened to know Chicaro's breeding, had bought the stallion cheap, brought him to Goliad and nursed him back to fine condition—with a shrewd eye to his possible use at stud.

Chicaro was a splendid blood bay with black points. Although he was much bigger than a Quarter Horse—he stood sixteen hands three and weighed over fourteen hundred pounds—he had the type, the compactness of build, the muscled strength of line the Klebergs looked for in the finest conformation of their Quarter Horses. Estimating Chicaro's possibilities as a desirable sire, Bob persuaded John Dial to sell the horse, and the stallion went to the King Ranch to be bred to some of the mares.

The ranch had owned many Thoroughbreds before, but the truth was that none of them had ever been of top class; some of them had been good, but most of them had been what turfmen would call "weeds." Chicaro was something else. His dam was Wendy; Wendy's sister was Elf, the dam of Boojum, one of the fastest race horses of the time.[20] Chicaro received his stamp, his powerfully muscled conformation, not only from his sire Chicle but even more through his dam Wendy who was out of Remembrance who was out of Forget, a great English jumper. Remembrance was also dam of Bonus whose son was Twenty Grand, winner of the fastest Kentucky Derby.[21] The big stallion Chicaro had very great blood. It was his presence on the King Ranch which set Bob Kleberg to an inquiry, and then to an intense and more and more engrossing study of the blood lines of the top Thoroughbred families and their characteristics. His interest at that time sprang solely from the use to which those characteristics might be put in improving the Old Sorrel line of Quarter Horses on the ranch.

Pursuing that interest, he went to Kentucky. The specific object of his trip was to look for Thoroughbreds with conformation to match Chicaro's, to study them if he found them — and maybe to buy a mare. Major Louie Beard introduced Bob and his wife Helen to horse people in Kentucky and showed the Klebergs around the bluegrass country.

One day, driving near Lexington with Thomas Cromwell and John Dial, Bob Kleberg looked out at a paddock by the side of the road.

"Stop the car," he said, looking, "I see the mare I want!"

He learned later that the mare's name was Cornsilk, and he still says, "She had the best conformation of any mare I ever saw, Quarter or Thoroughbred." He learned something else, which offers a measure for estimating the kind of eye Bob Kleberg has for a horse. It turned out that the mare Cornsilk, spotted from a distance on a chance drive along a country road, was by Chicle—Chicaro's sire!

Cornsilk could not be bought at the time: she was one of a stud of mares their owner Morton Schwartz would offer for sale at the next Saratoga. Determined to get her, Bob went to the Saratoga sale of August, 1936.

Asking, learning, looking, studying, he reached an opinion at Saratoga that the whole string offered by Schwartz was "the best small stud of mares in America." The bug bit Bob Kleberg. He bought not only Cornsilk, he bought seven more: Sunset Gun, Dawn Play, Science, Easter, Footprint, Chocalula *and* Split Second. Together they cost him nearly forty thousand dollars.

Not long afterward, Bob found occasion to ask the renowned owner of the Idle Hour Stud, the redoubtable Colonel E.R.Bradley, what he thought of Split Second.

"Never heard of the horse," the colonel snorted at the tyro from Texas.

Someone present reminded Bradley that the coal black two-year-old filly Split Second was the one that had just beaten Bennie M., the colonel's filly. Bradley turned on Bob Kleberg.

"Well," the colonel said, "I don't know what you think of your filly, but I wouldn't take a hundred thousand dollars for the one she beat!"

It happily appeared that out of an initial desire to improve King Ranch Quarter Horses with a certain infusion of suitable Thoroughbred blood, the ranch now found itself in the Thoroughbred race horse business.

It was not entirely inadvertent: the sport of kings was a natural outgrowth of the Klebergs' interest in fine horseflesh, and it was also a challenge. Could the same skills and experience used in creating the Santa Gertrudis cattle and the Old Sorrel family of Quarter

Horses be applied with equal success to the breeding of Thorough-breds? Could big-time winning race horses be bred on the hot dry prairie pastures of Texas as well as on the bluegrass of Kentucky? And could the breeding of racing Thoroughbreds be made a profit-able business venture in spite of the risks and expenses involved?

As far as racing itself was concerned, the ranching Klebergs first of all stood in great need of a racing expert's professional guidance. They began with luck, for they found their guide in the able person of Trainer Max Hirsch. He and Caesar Kleberg had been friends for years; Bob Kleberg says, "I don't know if I would have gone into racing the way I did if it hadn't been for Max and my confidence in him."

It was Hirsch, in the employ of Morton Schwartz, who had a large hand in putting together the stud of mares Kleberg bought at Saratoga, a stud splendid for two reasons: not only for their breeding but for the physical condition Trainer Hirsch had given them. It was he from whom Kleberg bought Split Second—Hirsch had pre-viously acquired that choice filly from Schwartz. It was Hirsch who gave Kleberg some of the earliest and best advice he got from the racing world. It was Hirsch who in that year of 1936 guided Schwartz's Bold Venture to victory in both the Kentucky Derby and the Preakness. And it was Hirsch whom the Klebergs asked to direct the racing destiny of their nascent stable. He and his son, W.J. "Buddy" Hirsch, have brilliantly handled the racing of King Ranch horses ever since.

"One of the things that particularly interests me in racing," Bob Kleberg says, "is the fact that it has such a marvelous literature." As he began to delve into it, and into the labyrinthine records of the stud book, he was soon aware of a curious fact: the horses with qualities he liked best in Thoroughbreds—beginning from his in-terest in Chicaro and then Cornsilk—*all* proved to have blood stemming from the illustrious race horse Domino, through Commando. Max Hirsch shared Kleberg's interest in the characteristics of that strain. Out of his vast practical knowledge of racing, he corroborated Kleberg's discernment of the breeding merit residing in the Domino-Commando blood.

In the meeting of minds between Kleberg and Hirsch, it was no extraneous fact that Bold Venture was a horse of the Domino-Commando blood through his dam Possible, one of Schwartz's fine mares. The King Ranch had an eye on Bold Venture. Dick Kleberg had seen him run and win the Derby and Bob "had been watching him since he was a two-year-old." In 1938 they bought him from Schwartz in Lexington, and Bold Venture became the first important stud of the new stable.

In addition to Domino and his descendants, another great performer and certain of his progeny engaged the Klebergs' professional attention as breeders—those of Fair Play through Man o' War. In general the breeding program of the King Ranch stable became the studied effort to develop winning horses by a concentration and a blending of the Domino-Commando and the Fair Play-Man o' War strains.*

When in 1946 some of the most desirable blood of these lines was to be dispersed from the Idle Hour stable following the death of Colonel Bradley, Bob Kleberg wanted certain Bradley horses very much. Under the administration of the Bradley estate, no horses could be bought out: the entire bulk of the estate was to be sold as one property—and the price was $2,900,000. Kleberg went to his racing friends Jock Whitney and Ogden Phipps with a proposition. The three of them formed a syndicate, bought the Bradley estate and then worked out a three-way dispersal of the horses and other property. By this transaction the King Ranch's top racing and breeding stock was increased materially.

*See Appendix XIII, "Breeding Techniques."

In a phenomenally short time from its beginnings in 1936, the King Ranch bred not one but several great and remembered horses, including one of the eight horses in American turf history that have won the Triple Crown.[22] Most of the stable's horses were bred on the ranch's own pastures within three miles of the Santa Gertrudis headquarters. And for a period of nearly twenty years the King Ranch racing stable, with its accounts kept separate from other ranch business, has bred enough winning race horses to show an actual operating profit, instead of a loss, at this most expensive and finical of all breeding enterprises.

The first outstanding horses raced by the King Ranch were fillies: Split Second, Dawn Play and Ciencia. Split Second was the ranch's first stake winner, in the Selima at Laurel in 1936. The three-year-old Dawn Play, after winning the Coaching Club American Oaks[23] and the Acorn Stakes at Belmont and the American Derby at Washington Park in 1937, was struck by a bolt of lightning which ended her racing career; unfortunately she died some months later without producing a foal. The next year Ciencia came along, and in 1939 she became the first and only filly to win the big Santa Anita Derby.

By 1943 the King Ranch had bred one of the great purse winners of all time—and had failed to recognize it. That year the stable sold for $1500, in a claiming race at Belmont, a rather "unpromising" two-year-old. He was Stymie, who won for his owner Hirsch Jacobs a record $918,485.

The same year Stymie was sold, Assault was born on the King Ranch. This chestnut son of Bold Venture out of Igual won the Triple Crown in 1946.[24] His speed and gameness made him one of the noble champions of the turf; his winnings amounted to $675,470 before he retired to Santa Gertrudis pastures at the end of 1950.

That year another son of Bold Venture nearly brought the Triple Crown to the King Ranch again. In 1950 Middleground won the

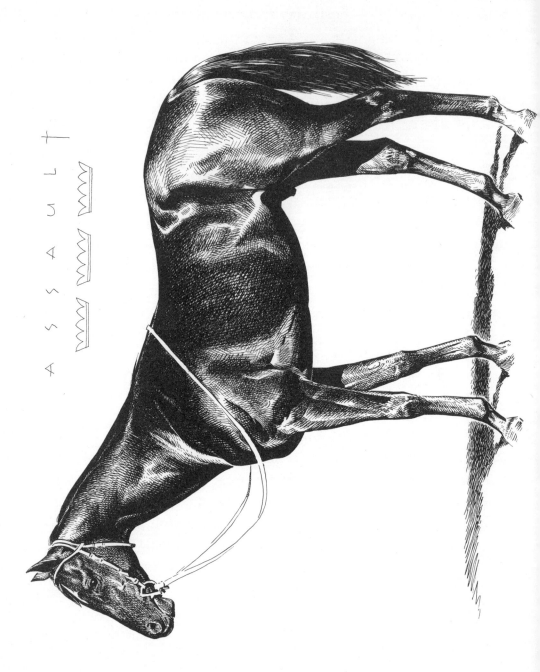

Kentucky Derby, lost the Preakness and came back to win the Belmont. A sesamoid fracture in his right foreleg forced his retirement later that season, and he was put to stud at the ranch where — unlike Assault who was found to be sterile — he became a promising sire.

In the years since 1936 more than a score of notable horses bearing names like Curandero, Flying Missel, Scattered, Better Self, Too Timely, Bridal Flower, But Why Not, Encantadora, Bea Ann Mac, On Your Own, Dispose, Riverina, To Market, Rejected and High Gun have pounded down the stretch wearing the King Ranch silks of brown and white, to win classic racing events and to contribute to the ranch's reputation as one of the most colorful and most consistently successful racing stables in operation.*

The King Ranch has bred the large majority of the horses it has sent to the starting gates, but it has by no means neglected to buy promising young horses from other stables. Equestrian, To Market, High Scud and High Gun are examples. High Gun caught Max Hirsch's eye at a Kentucky yearling sale in 1953 while Bob Kleberg was in Australia; the colt was bought for $10,200. This brown son of Heliopolis out of Rocket Gun may well be one of the best horses that ever carried the ranch's silks. It is important to note that in any such purchase Bob Kleberg acquires the Domino and Man o' War strains which engage his attention as a breeder.

A part of the Bradley estate which became property of the King Ranch in 1946 was the Patrick Farm of 680 acres in Fayette County near Lexington, Kentucky. With horseman Howard Rouse installed as its manager, the farm is now an important adjunct to the facilities of the King Ranch stable. Brood mares are kept there, convenient to service by outside stallions of the region when such breeding is desirable; similarly the ranch's top studs can stand at the Kentucky farm convenient to many other horse breeding establishments. Approximately half of the King Ranch brood mares and breeding

*See Appendix XV, "Ranch Thoroughbreds and Their Winnings."

stallions are usually found at the Kentucky farm. The colts born there remain until weaned, when they are all sent to the Santa Gertrudis, to grow up and to receive their initial training for the track with the Texas-born colts on wider, tougher prairie pastures, an environment Bob Kleberg believes brings a stronger growth to his young horses.

Their preparation for a racing career begins shortly after weaning, by watchful care and feeding and by an unvarying routine at a training barn where the growing horses are gentled and made accustomed to a constant handling. The gentling leads gradually to bridle and saddle at about the age of fourteen months, and then to cautious "breezing" on a training track where natural form and possible performance are first estimated. By the time candidates for the track are eighteen months old, one-eighth mile speed trials against a stop watch make further estimates of future performance possible, though some horses develop much faster than others, and most race horses at one time or another, or all the time, are plagued—their trainers and owners are anguished—by trouble with those most maddeningly delicate mechanisms in a powerful horse, the forelegs, which bear the weight and brunt of the racing action. When young horses show speed, show a spirited desire to move out ahead of their running mates, display a general health, and possess legs in reasonable working order, as young two-years-olds (all racing Thoroughbreds' birthdays are arbitrarily designated as the first of January of the year during which they are born) they are ready to send to Max or Buddy Hirsch to get their final training and eventually a try at racing.

For eighteen years, until his death in 1953, an old-time race horse man, William F. "Bill" Egan, was in charge of the training of the young horses before they went to Hirsch. Egan's work was supervised by Doc Northway, who manages all the work now; the whole program and every horse in it bears the constant scrutiny and operates under the direct orders of Bob Kleberg.

The ranch's present excellent facilities for handling its Thoroughbreds were built in 1948 and 1949 about two miles west of the big house at the Santa Gertrudis. Doc Northway's air-conditioned one-story office building houses private offices, breeding books and records, a clerical staff, a veterinarian's laboratory, and a lounge and dormitory and commissary for "horse people" who visit the ranch on business. Close by the office building with its lawn and landscaping stand completely equipped training barns combining forty-five stalls, and a building containing trainers' quarters and a school for apprentice jockeys and horse handlers. Past these buildings is a beautifully maintained oval training track with a measured one-mile course. Stallion barns and a number of paddocks are in the area. Out beyond are fenced pastures for Thoroughbred mare bands and their leggy foals.

About ninety brood mares and ten stallions are currently used in the breeding; annually about thirty two-year-olds start to the tracks under Hirsch's tutelage. By the very nature of horse racing, most horses fail to make their mark. Few seasons have passed, however, in which the King Ranch has failed to produce notable horses and a long string of wins. From 1935 through 1953 the stable spent $1,773,000 in buying horses to breed or race. During those eighteen years enough King Ranch horses crossed the finish line fast enough to bring their stable $4,009,991.12 in purse winnings.

The excitements and satisfactions can be contained in no purse. They reach to the breeder's heart. At a dinner given by the Thoroughbred Club of America in Lexington, Kentucky, on October 25, 1946, a Testimonial presented to the King Ranch's Bob Kleberg ended with the words, "the breeding paddocks of tomorrow will benefit by his accomplishments of today."

Max Hirsch, with something similar in mind, spoke of Sportsman Kleberg with somewhat less formality: "Why the hell should I be arguing with him? He has already won more races than anybody I know of who has been in the business the same length of time. He has won practically every race in the country. Some people in a lifetime don't win any of them. Hell, he's won the Belmont twice, for instance, and some people who have been racing all their lives have never been in the money in the Belmont."

Bob Kleberg said, "At the start I didn't know if I was going into racing or not. But if I was—it was going to be a part of building the reputation of King Ranch breeding, something to show what the ranch could do as a breeding thing."

Its racing stable, its Quarter Horse family, its Santa Gertrudis cattle furnish living evidence of what the ranch can do "as a breeding thing." But to keep apace with its livestock, the King Ranch must also improve its lands—the very reason for the animals' being.

The natural pastures of southmost Texas, growing their native grasses in normal seasons of something like twenty-five inches of average annual rainfall, have carrying capacities which range from about ten acres to as many as twenty acres for the support of one cow with a calf. The variation from ten in the best to twenty or more in the weakest is caused by the kind of soil, and consequently the kind of herbage, present in that pasture: richer soils generally grow stronger and more nourishing grasses. There is, however, a far more basic factor to dominate the yield of any pastureland. When moisture fails, so does grass. During some seasons fifty acres are not enough to keep a cow alive. Any ranching operation in South Texas is shaped by the paucity and the uncertainty of rain. Recurrent drought is an attribute of the land.

Failing the means to bring down water from the skies when needed, any effort toward the production of more or better range

grass for livestock is attended by large expense and, to date, only partial success. The best chance for full fruition of any such effort is indicated in the sentiment voiced by the King Ranch's manager riding on a pasture recently cleared, root-plowed and seeded with new grass, "Now if the Lord wants to make it good, I've done all I can."

The King Ranch takes a manifold approach to doing all it can. By an extensive program of brush clearance, it extensively increases the quantity of the grass available to livestock. It prepares earth to hold more moisture and grow more grass by the building of retaining and spreader dams and by pasture terracing. It fertilizes large areas with phosphates to enrich the soil and its grass. It plows and sows immense tracts with new range grasses; it plants prickly pear along miles of fences and in wide fields for use as stock feed during drought.

Brush control began on the ranch in the early 1890's. By 1915 about 17,000 acres had been tediously cleared, mostly in the head-quarters pastures, by transient workers the ranch from time to time hired and armed with axes and grubbing hoes. Real progress against the steady invasion of the mesquite had to wait for the advent of heavy power-driven machines. The ranch built and tried many types of equipment over a period of many years before it developed effective machinery for the work.*

An astonishingly efficient solution to the problem was finally custom built for the ranch in 1951: a giant funnel dozer and root plow powered by dual tractors and weighing 110,000 pounds.[25] The behemoth in a single passage over the ground knocks down trees, funnels them beneath the center of the tractor, leaves the shattered debris in windrows, and at the same time pulls a sixteen-foot-wide subterranean plow blade which not only cuts the tree roots below the bud line, at about sixteen inches beneath the ground surface, but

*See Appendix XI, "Defense Against Brush Encroachment."

also efficiently subsoils that ground. The monster destroys about four acres of brush jungle an hour, at an approximate operating cost of four dollars an acre. Two of these machines are in continuous use, working day and night shifts at the ranch.

During the eighteen years from 1936 through 1953, the King Ranch in its fight to control brush and to increase the acreage of available grass has cabled 10,700 acres,[26] dozed 103,998 acres and root-plowed 141,264 acres of its rangeland, and has spent $751,259.75 to do it. In addition, it has experimented with the use of herbicide to kill brush. At a cost of $2.32 an acre, planes have sprayed 100,162 acres with generally unsatisfactory results. Except when preceded by cabling, the "2,4,5-T" spray was ineffective and regrowth occurred.

Heavy earth-moving machinery owned and operated by the ranch is in continual use, sculpturing and scratching ranges to aid grass growth. A series of retaining and spreader dams are built across twelve of the drainage courses. In the area surrounding the rise upon which the Santa Gertrudis headquarters stands, an extensive system of plowed terraces holds the moisture from rains; grass grows in these terraced pockets when the rest of the earth is brown.

In a novel approach to the problem of conserving surplus surface waters after rain, the ranch built an unusual installation in 1951. It drilled what might be called a well in reverse, below a retaining dam on the Tranquitas, and installed pumps to force surplus surface water *down* to subterranean sands in an attempt to recharge the water sand so as to restore pressure and also replenish water.[27] Conclusive judgment on the value of the project was suspended until more rain falls on the Tranquitas drainage and until revisions are made in the well's equipment; yet the experiment itself indicates the energy with which the ranch pursues any promising measure for water conservation in a region where the pressure and amount of underground water are being depleted.

The ranch has studied and labored with tangible results at the improvement of grasses upon its pastures. Intensive planting of the imported African Rhodes grass began in the early 1920's; a decade later, with 75,000 acres successfully sown, Rhodes grass seemingly offered the definitive solution to the problem of growing more and better grass. It not only provided splendid grazing grounds, it made rich hay. About 100,000 bales were harvested annually from the planted pastures.

A dire misfortune was in the making. In 1943 the ranch made its last crop of Rhodes grass. Five years later, for all practical purposes, the wonderfully promising Rhodes grass was gone from the King Ranch.

A noxious scale, *Antonina gramines*, killed it. This scale, never seen before in South Texas, was suddenly discovered in the autumn of 1942. Rhodes grass attacked by it turned yellow and died. No practical means to effectively combat the parasite could be found. The ranch helplessly watched the green pasture-fields it had developed with much hope and great expense go dead.

Shortly after the scale was discovered, Nico Díaz, a trained agronomist and grass specialist, was employed to come to the ranch and devote himself to furthering the development of range grasses on King Ranch pastures. Many joined in the attack but were unable to find any effective countermeasure to the inroads of the scale, so Díaz began intensive studies and experiments to find replacements for the perishing Rhodes grass. In the years since his arrival at the ranch, in February, 1943, Díaz has made himself the greatest practical authority on southwestern range grasses, and the greatest practical planter of such grasses in the United States today.

Out of the hundreds of alien grasses Díaz has tested and studied for adaptability to the South Texas environment, he has developed two, KR bluestem and Kleberg grass, which have proven themselves on the range; and one other, named Caesar grass, as yet unproven but of similar promise. An unrelinquishing search continues.

Díaz demands three requisites for an "introduced" grass: it must be "aggressive," that is, show a marked tendency to spread and take over ground from weaker grasses; it must be palatable to livestock; and it must be hardy, so that it needs neither protection nor stimulus under actual range conditions where livestock are grazing and trampling, and where plentiful rain may or may not arrive.*

Commenting upon Díaz's approach to his work, Bob Kleberg says: "I think that the whole problem of grass for South Texas or other similar areas has been to find the grass that could hold its own under the climatic changes in periods of drought and pasture stress. So many of our pasture men have gone on the theory of protecting grasses to maintain them whether they are hardy or not. Nick's approach is not the standstill approach. He is attempting to find hardier and better grasses, just as the Santa Gertrudis cattle are hardier and better. We could have built shades and kept the old cattle breeds. We didn't do that. We found cattle more suitable to our set of conditions here. In like manner, we have found hardier grasses and we expect to develop still others."

In addition to his duties as a scientific sleuth after new grasses, Díaz is charged with growing grass seed sufficient for the planting of all newly cleared and plowed King Ranch pastures. The great funnel dozers and the lighter range plowing equipment all carry seed planters. When the soil is turned, Díaz's grass seeds automatically go into the ground, to await rain and germination. Few men, including Johnny Appleseed, have devoted themselves to work of a more benign aspect, closer to the mystery of Mother Earth, than Nick Díaz trying to make the good grass grow.

The improvement of pasture soils, concurrent with the improve-

*See Appendix XVI, "The Grass Program."

ment of pasture grasses, has engaged the active attention of the King Ranch. On a tract of land at the Encino Division, the United States Department of Agriculture and scientists from Texas A. & M. College working together and with the ranch, for a number of years have conducted pioneering experiments in procedures to correct deficiencies in rangeland soils. The ranch has put to effectual use the knowledge thus gained. Among other results, the experiments have indicated the cause and the cure for a nutritional disease of cattle known as "creeps."*

Soil analysis of certain sections of the ranch, particularly the pastures in the San Juan de Carricitos and San Salvador del Tule grants where creeps was frequently observed during bad seasons, showed a phosphorus deficiency. After intensive experimentation with livestock upon limited grazing plots of the Encino pasture, the King Ranch set about correcting phosphorus deficiencies, where they were indicated, on large areas of the ranch. Using one method, in the nine years from 1943 to 1952, the ranch fertilized 138,175 of its acres with phosphate pellets distributed by "crop dusting" aircraft.

Another more immediately effectual method was also evolved to supply phosphorus to livestock upon pastures where that mineral is deficient. Working with a commercial company,[28] the King Ranch developed an ingenious range device, a machine that meters into water at drinking troughs the proper amount of monosodium phosphate, which is thus fed directly to cattle through the water they drink at pasture wells. About 350 of these machines have been installed and are now in use over many sections of the King Ranch. The application of phosphorus to these areas has caused a complete disappearance of creeps, increased the weight of breeding cows from 100 to 200 pounds, and increased the calf crop approximately twenty per cent.

*See Appendix XVII, "Experiments in Supplying Phosphorus Deficiency."

Studies of the values of eighteen other trace minerals in soils, of copper, iron, iodine, magnesium, molybdenum, and the like, are now receiving attention. These experiments show some promise of providing further benefits to range grass and hence to livestock production on the ranch's pastures.

In recent years, with rainfall far below its annual average in South Texas, common prickly pear has assumed a position of real importance as a crop to sustain cattle when grass fails. This cactus, frequently berated as a nuisance, is a growth so designed by nature that a field of it is in effect a rich warehouse of livestock feed handily protected and stored up for dry times. Vicious thorns protect its big, thick, plate-like leaves; at the same time a thin skin covering much like cellophane efficiently packages the juiciness and the green nutriment stored within each leaf. When needed, that store may be unlocked simply by burning off the thorns. Cattle eat the freshly de-thorned leaves with appetite and sustain themselves well by it; they may even fatten if two pounds of cottonseed cake are added daily to their pear feed.

The King Ranch pursues a firm policy of cultivating prickly pear. It is planted along fences, and the plentiful spread of big pear fields is encouraged in many pastures. Equipment to burn off the thorns is being constantly improved. The latest pear burner rigged at the ranch is a jeep, fitted with a trailer carrying a 250-gallon tank of butane and equipped with a pair of burners fed by two well-mounted fifty-foot hoses, each sending butane at thirty-two pounds of pressure into the nozzle to cast a flame jet more than six feet long. The four-man crew operating this twin unit burns pear enough each day for eight hundred head of hungry cattle. Further improvements in the technique and equipment are inevitable. They are in reality livestock insurance for years when rains do not come.

Game conservation is another important feature, and one of the most interesting achievements, of pasture management at the King Ranch.

During all the nineteenth century, South Texas teemed with game. Yet the increase of hunters and the lack of enforced hunting laws by 1910 had very nearly destroyed the formerly abundant deer and wild turkey of the region. In the fall of 1920 a party of six experienced hunters camping for a week on the Norias were able to kill just one deer. At about that time, it was estimated that few more than a dozen flocks of wild turkeys were left on the entire ranch.

Sportsman Caesar Kleberg, with strong opinions on wildlife conservation, took action. At his Norias Division he clapped a stringent limitation upon the hunting allowed; at Austin he mustered all the influence he could find to bring legislation for strong game laws. Alice Kleberg's aid was enlisted. On one of Governor Pat Neff's visits to the ranch, Mrs. Kleberg so interested him in the plight of the disappearing wild turkey that he was persuaded to sign a bill declaring a closed season of ten years on these great birds. The number of wild turkey now in Texas is largely due to the saving effects of that closed season.

Meanwhile, the elder Robert Kleberg had imposed rigid regulations upon the family and upon all ranch employees and ranch guests for the preservation of the game still existing at the ranch. These self-imposed game regulations, far stricter than the game laws, produced results. With the ranch posted and patrolled against hunters from the outside, and with hunting by ranch residents and guests severely curtailed, the game gradually came back. The increase of deer and wild turkey behind the ranch's fence was concurrent with their continued decrease elsewhere in the region. The contrast became pointed; in choosing to maintain its hunting regulations the King Ranch made enemies. It persisted nevertheless, believing that a program to preserve the area's game was a worthwhile obligation to assume. The State of Texas made certain portions of the ranch state game preserves closed to all shooting, and the ranch management paid state wardens to patrol the property. The dense populations of deer, turkey and quail on the ranch today demonstrate one of the most effective game restoration programs ever conducted by private enterprise in this country.

This restoration, beautiful to see, is not without its problems. At the Norias recently Bob Kleberg said, "Twenty per cent of the edible meat on the eastern part of this division is game and should be used. How to harvest it, now that it's here, is a hard proposition." The Texas Game and Fish Commission each year uses the reservoir of game at the King Ranch to provide hundreds of deer and wild turkey for the stocking of other areas. Each season a certain amount of game is also taken by sportsmen invited to the ranch. Yet only a portion of the available game can be taken by these means under present state restrictions. If the present program continues with success the problem of a growing surplus must eventually be met by legislative action.

In 1945 the ranch employed as a full-time member of its staff V.W. Lehmann, a trained conservationist and one of the nation's leading wildlife authorities, to administer a program for the scientific study and protection of game on the ranch. His expert discussion of game conservation and management as practiced on the King Ranch forms Appendix XVIII of this volume.

The ranch's pastures produce livestock and game — and they produce oil.

After the signing of its lease in 1933, the Humble Oil and Refining Company spent six years in careful exploratory work before it drilled a well on the King Ranch. Oil fields developed by other operators stood promisingly near the northern margin of the Laureles Division and not far outside both the northern and the western boundaries of the Santa Gertrudis Division; the first drilling by the Humble Company was not to wildcat for new fields at the interior of the property but to explore already known oil structures for such extension as they might show within the north and west edges of the King Ranch.

The ranch's first producing oil well was found on the San Antonio Viejo, where the Colorado Field of Jim Hogg County touched the boundary of the King Ranch property. The Humble Company completed this first well in May of 1939; in September it brought in another producer barely within the northern line of the Laureles Division on what proved to be a very limited southern extension of the Luby Field in Nueces County. Neither of these first wells was of consequence in establishing sites for further oil development.

Continuing with its drilling on the King Ranch periphery near proven fields, the Humble Company in 1941 found what it looked for when it encountered a rich extension of the Stratton Field on a northern sector of the Santa Gertrudis not far from headquarters. More than a hundred producing wells were later drilled in the King Ranch's Stratton and West Stratton fields. In 1942 an even larger extension of an already proven field, the Seeligson, was richly tapped on the western edge of the Santa Gertrudis Division.

Twelve years after the signing of the lease, the Humble Company in 1945 drilled its first wildcat on the ranch, and brought in the Borregos Field, a major discovery, lying entirely within the boundaries of the King Ranch in the south central sector of the de la Garza Santa Gertrudis grant.

Subsequent operations on widely scattered locations over the ranch have resulted in no discoveries comparable to the Borregos, Stratton and Seeligson, except the Willamar Field found on the Atwoods' Sauz Ranch.

Since 1945 four minor oil locations have been discovered on the

King Ranch, and the Humble Company's long-range program of exploration and drilling strongly continues.* By the end of 1953 there were 650 producing oil and gas wells on the Kleberg family's property.

Oil activity brought astonishingly little change to the physical appearance of the ranch pastures. Following terms agreed upon in the lease and, more than that, displaying a friendly partnership co-operation with the ranch, the Humble Company has conducted its operation year after year with such neatness and planned good order that the land is unscarred by any of the rusty trash or stained desolation that generally arrives with oil. Grass grows to the bases of the "Christmas trees"[29] standing unexpectedly in quiet pastures; pumps and valves and tanks stand trim and tidy upon cleaned ground against backgrounds of green mesquite and country silence. Livestock and wildlife go undisturbed by the field crews and the paraphernalia of oil production.

The King Ranch operated without oil for eighty-five years, and did well; with oil, it does better. Oil income provides the management not with an excuse to quit working so hard but rather with the means to carry on that work harder. The oil royalties furnish money to use upon improvements and facilities the ranch could not have previously afforded. Moreover, the extra income has created for the King Ranch an enviable cushion against adversity, a margin of financial safety against the seasonal vicissitudes connected with the conversion of grass to beef to dollars.

In a somewhat indirect and unforeseen and interesting way, the arrival of the oil wells marked an end of an era: they radically changed the operation of the range work at the King Ranch. Oil activity created a necessity for roads to carry heavy equipment across every far reach of the ranch. When good all-weather roads appeared

*See Appendix XII, "Oil Development."

in a widening network connecting division with division, pasture to pasture, and joining the whole to headquarters, the old horseback isolation of the work camps, the slow cattle drives from remote corners of the ranch, were relegated to the past. Time and distance shrank. Following the oil roads, combustion engines and motor vehicles became ranching implements as basic as cow horses.

Heavy stock trailers now move the King Ranch cattle from pasture to pasture, or to a shipping point. King Ranch cow camps are mobile units, speedily transported by truck, with saddles and supplies, to any remote set of working pens—and as quickly brought home. Vaqueros no longer need to live for weeks at isolated camps; the work of the *corridas* is faster and easier. Carried by motor transport, maintenance crews and foot workers now operate from a central base at division headquarters. Holding a steering wheel, not a pair of bridle reins, a foreman in a single day can look over a very large sector of his division. The farthest pasture of the King Ranch is now no more than a two-hour drive from the big house at the Santa Gertrudis or from the movies in Kingsville. Good roads have quickened the daily ranching operation, made it more efficient, centralized its administration and its supply.

Initially a large proportion of these roads were adequately surfaced by a novel method which used simple and comparatively inexpensive means. Bob Kleberg says, "I don't believe any other roads were ever built exactly like those on the ranch." Without preliminary surveying or grading as in conventional roads, the ranch employed a standard Wood's road-mixing machine to move along digging up the packed soil in the ranch's already existing unimproved, winding dirt roads. The machine as it moved scooped up the dirt, mixed it with asphalt and deposited the resultant mixture, making a road eight to ten feet wide and about eight inches deep after rolling. This soil-asphalt stabilizer dried hard and firm, fairly smooth, and surprisingly durable. Most of it was later reinforced by a further topping of gravel-asphalt mix. These tough ribbons of hardtop embedded along the natural winding contours of the land were found to require minimum maintenance and to serve with complete effectiveness all ordinary vehicular ranching traffic. Other roads, under hard use and heavy trucking, were graded, graveled and blacktopped in the conventional way by the Humble Company to serve its oil fields in production. By 1954 there were 287.64 miles of improved roads within the ranch. The cost of this work, $1,209,922.96, by previous agreement was shared equally between the ranch and the oil company. For the extension and maintenance of its road network the King Ranch has its own equipment and crew bossed by the energetic and salty Foreman Jack Seth, who came to work for the ranch in 1946.

A growing use of automotive and mechanized equipment has made a large motor pool and shop a ranching necessity. The handling and the maintenance of its many machines, from giant dozers to jeeps, is presided over by an extremely able superintendent, L. F. "Red" Wilkinson. His department is a vital element in the daily operation of an increasingly motorized King Ranch.[30]

The ranch buys top-quality material for its range installations. Some of these are manufactured to order and are models for fine ranching equipment. In so far as possible, basic items like fences, gates, wells, windmills, watering troughs and pens are standarized for facility in installation and replacement, so that range work is performed with the least waste in man hours and money.

Good ranch fences are usually an indication of good management behind them. After decades of experience, in which planking, 4-gauge smooth galvanized wire, and some barbed wire were used, the King Ranch has devised its own type of fencing, fabricated to order in 38-inch and 49-inch widths.[31] Designed and first ordered by

Bob Kleberg in 1933, it is gradually replacing all older fencing on the ranch, and now encloses approximately seventy per cent of the pastures.

This fencing is a heavy-gauge galvanized net wire with its mesh just small enough to keep livestock from getting heads or feet hung in it, and its wire is woven with a crimp so that the net retains resilience even when very tightly strung. It is usually strung on eight-foot steel fence posts along the outside boundaries of the ranch; on most inside pasture fences posts of mountain cedar are used. The net is secured not by staples but by heavy wire passed through holes bored through each fence post.

A freight car holds ten miles of the King Ranch's special net wire, and the ranch buys about four carloads a year. Before World War II such fencing cost about $425 a mile, installed; it now costs from $1100 to $1200 a mile—yet its proven effectiveness and its great durability make it economical. In the twenty years from 1934 to 1954 the King Ranch has put up eight hundred miles of net wire, most of it in the 49-inch width. On coastal flats where corrosive salt air used to destroy galvanized wire in three or four years, the ranch installed fourteen miles of its net fencing especially fabricated of stainless steel. Its cost was three times that of the galvanized variety—and twenty years after installation it is as good as new.

Gates in all the ranch's fences are being modernized. More than five hundred aluminum gates, to replace wooden ones, have been installed since 1947. Wherever a pasture fence crosses an oil road, the Humble Company has built a heavy "bump gate," which opens by the push of an auto bumper and swings shut when the car has passed through. There are about seventy-five of these Humble-built conveniences now on the ranch.

The magnitude of the ranch operation may be suggested by the number of water wells it requires. There are 381 of them. A hundred and one are flowing wells, fourteen are worked by power pumps, and 266 use windmills. Each division has a full-time windmill crew; the ranch continuously employs twenty-five men on this work.

The watering troughs at all the wells are of concrete, poured to a standard pattern, circular in form, usually thirty feet in diameter and three feet deep. Most of them are now fitted with the feeder which adds monosodium phosphate in solution to the water. To increase the facility with which both livestock and game may drink, two-thirds of the trough's depth is built below ground level, so that the concrete rim stands only about a foot above the surface of the surrounding ground. A part of road builder Jack Seth's job is to keep the ground around the hundreds of water troughs level and firm. A caliche-, clay- and asphalt-sand mix is used for this purpose.

Captain King built his first corrals of roughly chopped mesquite posts which were set side by side upright in the ground and then laced together with wet rawhide which dried like iron. At the ranch today the peeled and creosoted posts the diameter of telephone poles, the heavy sawed timbers and planking morticed and bolted for strength and permanence, the massive gates, the complicated cutting and squeeze chutes — one of them hand-fashioned of *quebracho* and *lapacho* woods and imported complete from the Argentine in 1929[32] — the care with which sharp edges have been smoothed and injurious protrusions eliminated, the convenient viewing walks and platforms around the tops of high pens, the efficient loading chutes, are all a far cry from the founder's primitive ranch corrals.

Though the King Ranch prefers and clings to the old way of working its big roundup herds on open pastures, pens and corrals are fundamental to the whole ranching operation. For the various purposes of holding, sorting, doctoring and shipping livestock, the ranch now maintains twenty-seven pens at widely scattered locations over the property. If placed together, these labyrinths of strong timber would cover about 160 acres. The largest are the shipping pens at Caesar; they take up seven and a half acres and handle three thousand head of cattle at one time. The most interesting are the Calandria pens, looked upon by visiting cattlemen as a model arrangement for the efficient handling of livestock.

Camp houses have been built at salient points, often near a set of pens, to provide ranch hands with convenient eating and sleeping quarters during cow work in that vicinity. There are twenty-three such camp houses, six on the Santa Gertrudis, eight on the Laureles, five on the Norias, and four on the Encino. Built according to varying plans over a period of years from 1935 to 1954, they are all stoutly made and pleasantly designed to fit their various settings. Each is equipped with a kitchen, shower, good water, firewood, a screened porch the length of the house for shade and a dormitory with room for the bedrolls of about twenty men. Replacing tents formerly in use, the camp houses are an advantage both to the health and to the efficiency of the cowboys.

In 1938 the King Ranch corporation began the construction of an entirely new headquarters for its Norias Division. The old site, astride the railroad tracks and a motor highway under construction, was no longer practicable; a new location was chosen on a pleasing rise of ground five miles east of the old headquarters. The rise was solidly matted with a jungle of thorny brush, and extensive clearing had to be done before construction began. When completed three years later, the new Norias headquarters consisted of a long rectangular white ranch-style main house—designed with great taste and for handsome ranch living by Helen and Bob Kleberg—a foreman's house, a ranch school, a commissary, garage, barns and twenty-one modern and well-made employees' cottages.

Caesar Kleberg's historic and ramshackle frame museum piece at Norias Station was regretfully but definitively demolished. The new headquarters with its simple white buildings, gravel drives, green lawns, newly planted trees, on the rise where the southeast breeze from the sea seldom fails, became the most attractive place on the King Ranch. About the same time a similar building program on a smaller scale created an excellent new headquarters under great live-oak trees at the Encino Division.

There are today approximately 1200 people living on the King Ranch; the payroll lists 504 employees. A clear indication of the many kinds of work required for such a ranch's development and daily operation may be seen in the relatively small number of horse-back men: a scant hundred *Kineños* now earn their wages in the saddle.

Most of the ranch people live at the Santa Gertrudis. In 1950 and 1951 the King Ranch created a model housing project on uncrowded, pleasant grounds west of the big house. "The Colony" now consists of 103 modern units, one-, two- and three-bedroom cottages, which provide convenient and comfortable housing for a majority of the employees and their families on the headquarters division. In the vicinity the ranch has also built several larger and more elaborate houses for foremen and managers of departments. Modern houses for employees, the equal of those at the Santa Gertrudis, have also been built for the fewer workers on the other divisions: there are thirty-nine cottages at Laureles headquarters, twenty-nine at Norias and eight at Encino. Except at the small Encino, schoolhouses are maintained for the ranch families' children at each division head-quarters.[33] The schoolhouses have been built by the ranch; the teaching staffs and the elementary school courses are under the ad-ministration of either independent or county school systems.

The venerable ties of faithfulness and of responsibility in the employee-employer relationship on the ranch have strengthened through the years. Bob Kleberg says the management's aim is to have employees "as interested in the ranch as the owners of the ranch. To that end they are provided with better homes than they would ordinarily find in the same situation in life anywhere else; they are supplied with milk needed for their families and children, and with other food necessities in better amount and at times of better quality. Employees ordinarily do not retire at any certain age or by choice: most of them are prone to want to work and do something as long as they possibly can. For that reason, as time goes on their employment situation is changed to fit their physical abilities and dependence insofar as possible. Many employees of the ranch require no help when they become infirm or want to retire; many of them have never asked for anything. Though there is no fixed sum guaranteed to them as pensions at any time, it is the aim of the ranch to help those that need help when help is needed. They feel that King Ranch is their lifetime home if they devote their best energy and efforts to it." The King Ranch continues to be distinguished for the loyalty of its people, and for the challenge its people feel in the work they are given to do there. Their spirit is evident in the ranch's daily operation.

The administrative center of the King Ranch corporation is the business office it maintains on the second floor of the Kleberg First National Bank Building, on Kleberg Street, in Kingsville. Ten staff members there handle the daily business detail and the correspondence connected with the corporation's activities.

The business office director is James H. Clement, who came to work as an assistant to Al Kleberg in 1947, and who assumed charge of the office after Kleberg's death on October 20, 1952. Clement supervises the corporation's accounts through J. C. "Cy" Yeary, the purchasing agent, whose desk functions as a daily point of contact between the business management and the needs of the range men at work on the King Ranch pastures, and through the chief accountant J. B. "Bud" Fisher.

The business administration of the ranch is not Clement's only concern, for the King Ranch corporation also owns and operates half a dozen firms in Kingsville, most of them legacies from the varied enterprises in which the elder Robert Kleberg engaged to promote Kingsville's early growth and welfare.

Clement receives and evaluates reports from each of these corporation properties: the thriving Kingsville Lumber Co. and its Saddle Shop; Ragland's, transformed from a fusty purveyor of general merchandise to a fine department store complete with modern *décor* — under the supervision of Clement's energetic and pretty wife, Ida Larkin Clement; the Kingsville Publishing Co., which publishes the *Kingsville Record*, a weekly newspaper, and operates a busy commercial print shop; Jersey Products Co., a commercial dairy; and the Kingsville Milling Co. which, amidst its other general business, grinds and mixes all livestock feeds for the King Ranch, six to eight million pounds of grain, and from a half to three-quarters of a million pounds of ground mixed feeds annually. The King Ranch is one of the shareholders in the Kleberg First National Bank, the oldest bank in Kingsville. In the half century since its founding, Kingsville has become a city of nearly 25,000 people, and its volume of trade flourishes accordingly.

In 1950 Robert C. Wells, son of James B. Wells and a namesake of the elder Robert Kleberg, returned to Texas after twenty-five years' residence in South America to take a position with the King Ranch as its land and tax consultant and as its public relations head. His affability, his acumen and his wide experience make him a skillful diplomatist and an invaluable aide in the conduct of the corporation's affairs, in its dealings with the public, with officialdom both in the United States and Latin America, and with the press. He is ably assisted at the office in Kingsville by John Cypher, Jr., who is charged with meeting many of the inquiries addressed to the ranch and with conducting most of the visitors' tours about the ranch.

In 1951 Bob Kleberg asked an eminent geneticist and authority on animal husbandry, Albert O. Rhoad, to become a full-time member of the King Ranch staff in order to devote himself to the study and analysis of the ranch's livestock breeding programs. Rhoad's work with ⩗ animals, his papers concerning that work, his continuing scientific studies, have already made an incalculable contribution to the King Ranch achievement. In speaking of the genial Geneticist Rhoad, a ranch denizen opined, "He's the best thing that's come to the King Ranch since Monkey was born."[34]

The fundamental enterprise of the King Ranch remains the commercial production of livestock. All its other activities are adjuncts or appendages to this basic operation. Livestock has provided two-thirds of the total gross income earned by the ranch during the twenty years from 1934 to 1954. Petroleum products have provided the other third. Though oil and gas royalties were hardly appreciable before 1942, they have increased steadily since that time. By 1952 the ranch's annual gross from oil and gas royalties became equal, for the first time, to the year's gross from livestock sales. Whether or not this trend continues, petroleum production is the province of the Humble Company. The occupation and preoccupation of the ranch is raising beef.

In the crucial year of 1926 when the trustees of Mrs. King's estate pondered the payment of its debts and taxes, the sale of some more of the ranch's land was discussed as a panacea. Bob Kleberg was hotly against it. "I can make more money selling cattle than selling land," he told Leroy Denman. His confidence stemmed from his faith in the development of the Santa Gertrudis breed, and that confidence was not misplaced. By 1932 Bob Kleberg, using the same acres, had doubled the ranch's beef production of 1925.[35] During the twenty

years from 1935 to 1954—through the end of a depression, the
course of a world war, a postwar inflation and a severe drought—
the King Ranch has marketed an average of 19,814 head of cattle
annually, which is "a turn-off," as the rancher puts it, of approximately one-third.

At the time of Mrs. King's death in 1925 the appraisers of her
estate tallied nearly 95,000 head of cattle, which included approximately 20,000 calves, on about 1,150,000 acres. Using the round
number of 75,000 head of grown cattle, and making no special
category of cows with calves, it may be seen that all the varying
pastures, grouped together for an average, supported one head of
cattle on about fifteen acres. Ten years later when the Kleberg family
organized the King Ranch corporation, the approximately 60,000
head of cattle bequeathed to Alice Kleberg were pastured on the
890,000 acres which then and now comprise the King Ranch: in
1935 it was still using almost fifteen acres for each head of stock.
In the management's experience since, such a figure represents a
carrying capacity possible only in years of plentiful rain. With rainfall far below normal since mid-1950, the carrying capacity of many
pastures has been reduced as much as a third, and the sizes of the
King Ranch commercial herds have been reduced accordingly.[36]

As an integral part of its beef production enterprise, the King
Ranch in 1946 bought 4300 acres of splendid pastureland near
Coatsville, Chester County, Pennsylvania, and later enlarged the
property to 9200 acres. Every year now the ranch ships from 4000
to 5000 of its best beef steers from Texas to the lush grass on the
"Pennsylvania Division," where they are fattened to top market
condition and delivered by truck in three hours—without loss of
weight—to a packer in Baltimore or Philadelphia or New York. The
operation replaces with incomparable efficiency the ranch's former
practice of sending a portion of its stocker cattle each spring to

leased pastures in Oklahoma or elsewhere.[37] Now the ranch owns its own rich and fattening grass, handily close to the big consumer markets of the East.*

There is one other chief outlet for the ranch's beef crop. Every year about 6000 calves, after a hundred days in the feed lots at Rancho Plomo on the Santa Gertrudis Division, are shipped from the Caesar pens to Swift & Co. at Lake Charles, Louisiana. These steers and those sent to Pennsylvania comprise approximately two-thirds of the annual beef production on the King Ranch.

At the age of eight months a Santa Gertrudis calf will usually out-weigh a Hereford of the same age by from one hundred to two hundred pounds.[38] The "big rack" Dick Kleberg wanted to hang the grass on is certainly there; the Santa Gertrudis steer is not only bigger to begin with, but repeated tests show that the Santa Gertru-dis will outgain other breeds on the same feed.[39]

As a result of retail merchandising systems which have taught the American housewife to ask for small cuts, the demand current in the United States today is for an animal weighing from 1000 to 1150 pounds which will give a carcass yield of from 600 to 700 pounds.[40] Santa Gertrudis calves at the normal time of weaning, at eight months, will usually weigh from 500 to 600 pounds; to produce the currently most desired grade of beef this same weaned calf should be grain fed, either on pasture or in dry feed lot, from six to eight months, depending on the finish desired. This means that the carcass now most suited to customer demand in this country can be produced from a Santa Gertrudis at fourteen to eighteen months of age, provided grain or other concentrated supplement is used either with grass or in the dry lot.

This also means a radical change in the King Ranch's beef pro-duction and management practices — for originally the Santa Ger-trudis breed was designed to produce three-year-old steers for grass

*See Appendix XIX, "Expansion Outside of Texas."

finish in South Texas brush pastures, and to produce fat calves for direct shipment to market. Fortunately the Santa Gertrudis animal lends itself to the change which will meet the new demand and which will spell out to Santa Gertrudis owners larger production of a higher grade product at an earlier age.

King Ranch acreage in South Texas has not been enlarged since the time of the ranch's incorporation by the Kleberg family. The expansion of the enterprise is taking place in another way and by other directions, of immense potential importance to the future of the corporation. In recent years its pastures have outspread not only to Kentucky and Pennsylvania, but to foreign countries.

A King Ranch livestock operation flourishes in Cuba, another on the far side of the globe in Australia, and yet another in Brazil. Each is a joint venture: in Cuba with a sugar company, in Australia with a land and cattle syndicate organized for the purpose, and in Brazil with a Brazilian meat packing firm. Each venture is designed to introduce Santa Gertrudis cattle, and to demonstrate and exploit their great utility in other lands where climate, range conditions or other factors have hampered beef production.

Before the King Ranch acquired its interest in the Cuban property near Camagüey, some of the best stockmen on the island had already begun development of Santa Gertrudis herds, and the ranch's enterprise has confirmed rather than introduced the advantages of the big red cattle in Cuba.

Their first introduction "down under" came in 1952 when the ranch shipped 202 fine young cows and 73 top young bulls to the syndicate's Queensland properties. The Santa Gertrudis beef qualities plus their quickly proven adaptability to the Australian continent and climate awakened strong interest among stockmen there, and brought spirited bidding to the first bull sale held on the syndicate's Risdon Stud near Brisbane in November of 1952. At Twin

Hills, farther north in Queensland, the King Ranch and its Australian partners have begun to breed Santa Gertrudis bulls to commercial range herds. These promise not only to prosper but to affect by example the Australian livestock industry.

The most recent of the foreign ventures was organized in 1953, when the King Ranch entered a partnership agreement with Companhia Swift do Brasil, S. A., to establish commercial beef herds on some 147,000 acres of largely undeveloped land in the interior of Brazil. Half of this acreage is owned by the ranch, half by the Brazilian company. Ranching installations have been built, the land is being cleared and improved, the first Santa Gertrudis imports are firmly acclimated, and some idea of the rich promise of the property may be gained from the fact that the 147,000 acres of Brazilian land, once in grass, can have a carrying capacity equal to the entire King Ranch in South Texas.

Notwithstanding mineral revenue, racing purses and numerous subsidiary ventures which may or may not show profit when it comes time for the annual accounting, the King Ranch is basically a cattle ranch: its business is breeding and raising and selling cattle; its lifeblood is the cattle on its ranges. Every year since 1936 the ranch has sold more than a million dollars worth of beef on the hoof. In the exceptional year of 1951, when prices were at an all-time high, the King Ranch's stock cattle sales grossed five million dollars.

The Klebergs draw the sustaining force which distinguishes them, as a family and as individuals, from a direct participation in the ranch's work. Their vitality comes from the roots which still attach them to the land and to the rigorous life of that land. For as long as that strong attachment is manifest, the entity of the King Ranch will endure — and not longer.

Alice Kleberg survived her husband for nearly twelve years. Until the day of her death she mourned his absence from the house he had

built. With a gentler force of Christian character than her mother had displayed, with a deeper kindness and humanity, Alice Kleberg continued to devote herself actively to duties within her household, to the welfare of her ranch, her children, her growing grandchildren who called her "Mana." She died at the age of eighty-two on the thirtieth of July, 1944, at the ranch where she was born. Its continuance was Alice Kleberg's handiwork, a task which had quietly, selflessly and happily composed her life.

Two years later the family lost the last senior member of the household. Caesar Kleberg died at the Santa Gertrudis, April 14, 1946. In him wisdom and warmheartedness were joined; no man who ever rode King Ranch pastures numbered as many friends of as many kinds as "Mister Caesar." He lived as a bachelor at the ranch for forty-six years, devoting to it his astute judgment, his keen wit and his genial heart. In his sympathetic regard for others, his character carried a parallel to that of his uncle's wife, Alice Kleberg.

Alice Kleberg's eldest daughter Henrietta lost her eldest son, John Larkin, Jr., in combat on the European front in 1944; the senior John Larkin died four years later in New York. The following year, in 1949, Henrietta married Major Thomas R. Armstrong, who had introduced her to Larkin and had been the best man at their wedding in 1915. The late marriage of Henrietta and Tom Armstrong is a most happy one; it brought them both back to residence in South Texas and to active ranching on the Armstrong property north of the Norias. Their presence there as beloved kinfolk and neighbors enhances life at the King Ranch.

The eldest son of Robert and Alice Kleberg, home from Washington in 1945, became the senior resident at the big house, sharing the direction of the range work and the corporation's business with his brother Bob, and watching his son Richard Jr. assume responsibilities in the ranch's management.

Young Dick Kleberg had lived his early boyhood on the Laureles. His schoolmates there were the sons of *Kineños* and he spoke their tongue as his own. He learned to rope and ride with them. He played their games; he knew their jokes. He heard what the old vaqueros of the brush had to say. They called him *Ricardito*, Little Dick, and he spent most of his early years close to their lives and their daily confidence.

He had also been away, at Corpus Christi, Washington, Virginia Military Institute, and to the University of Texas, where he received a bachelor of arts degree in 1937, and where he studied law, like his father, for three more years.

At the university in the spring of 1940 he met and courted a sophomore coed of striking beauty and vivacity. Her father was a prominent Austin physician; her name was Mary Lewis Scott. In November of that year she became Mary Lewis Kleberg, and went with her 24-year-old husband to live at the ranch where his uncle had started him at a man-sized job.

Young Dick became managerial assistant to Bob Kleberg, to learn the incessantly demanding range and office business of running the King Ranch from a saddle, a car seat, a cutting chute or a desk. It is a work for which Dick was born, for which he is being trained by a mentor of authentic ranching genius, and for which he has already proven his mettle. His drive and ability both as a stockman and as a corporation executive of the King Ranch is the clearly evident promise of his generation. It is shared by other young members of the family, like Jim Clement and Belton Johnson. It foretells the strong continuing character of the King Ranch achievement.

XIX *Centenary*

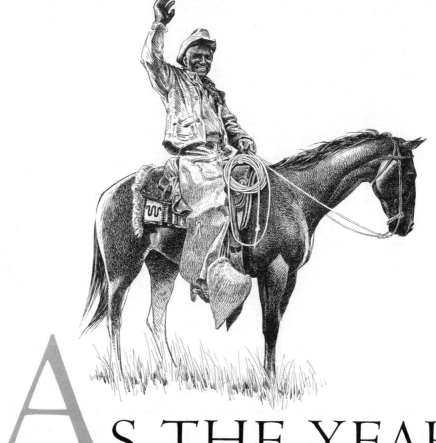

AS THE YEAR

1953 drew near, a vivid century spent at ranching called for observance. The King Ranch considered how it might appropriately celebrate the centenary of Captain Richard King's first purchase of land on the Santa Gertrudis. The long chain of events created by the captain's advent upon wilderness pastures formed a stout chapter in the history of South Texas and of the livestock industry as it developed in the American West, but no comprehensive account of those events had ever been assembled. They were worthy of accurate record. The issuance of a volume of history was conceived as an essential part of the ranch's centennial observance.

Yet a survey of the past did not suffice. In the minds of the Kleberg family, the orientation of their ranching enterprise toward a productive future held a greater meaning than any summing up of a productive past. For the real celebration of its centenary, the King Ranch planned an unprecedented birthday party.

To attend it, and by their presence to make the occasion significant and useful, specialists from the animal industries and from learned institutions on five continents were issued invitations to be guests of the ranch at a Centennial Conference. Distinguished geneticists, nutritionists, botanists, veterinary scientists, climatologists, were asked to participate in a symposium to be held at the King Ranch for the purpose of providing a serious meeting and a fruitful exchange of ideas between a group of practicing ranchmen and a group of authorities whose fields of scientific knowledge were related to ranchmen's daily work, and to their future.

The Centennial Conference opened on October 17, 1953, at the big house on the Santa Gertrudis. Formal sessions, lively discussions, field trips upon the ranch's various divisions, social gatherings, crowded the next three days and evenings. Present for these unexampled proceedings were about 150 guests "including members of faculties of sixteen North American colleges or universities, Cambridge University (England), the University of São Paulo (Brazil), and the University of Adelaide (Australia)." Agricultural technicians and cattle breeders were present from Argentina, Australia, Brazil, Colombia, Cuba, Great Britain, Venezuela, and the Union of South Africa, as well as from cattle-raising areas of the United States. Ranchers, newsmen and friends of the King Ranch were the other participants.[1]

In his Address of Welcome, Dick Kleberg, Sr., said, "Here on this continent, undoubtedly, there exists an entirely new technological frontier wide enough to stagger the imaginations of modern men.... We cattlemen are glad to share with you men of science the challenge and the opportunities of this new frontier. We feel confident that out of this conference will come a means of greater service to mankind."[2]

Eighteen technical papers were read and discussed in open forum during the course of the conference, and in order that they might have widespread future usefulness the complete texts of all the papers were later prepared for publication, edited by Albert O. Rhoad, and issued under title of the symposium itself, *Breeding Beef Cattle for Unfavorable Environments*, by the University of Texas Press. The excellent format of the volume with its full report of the entire proceedings of the conference make it the worthy record of a worthy occasion.

The character of the ranch management is patent in the fact that it chose to organize such an occasion. In his speech at the dinner during the closing session, Bob Kleberg told the gathering, "We wanted to mark the centenary of the ranch as a livestock operation, not by a big parade or pageant, or a 'blowout,' but by something that would be representative and significant of your efforts and our efforts. We wanted to give recognition to the industry and to the animal sciences which have contributed so much to the progress of this ranch.

"We felt that the emphasis should be on the breeding of beef cattle adapted to unfavorable environments, for we believe that the future expansion of large-scale beef production will be in the wet and dry tropics and the semidesert areas of the world. That is where the largest undeveloped regions lie. Many of you are contributing to such a future. We, too, want to contribute to that future. And I believe we can."[3]

Earlier in his talk, he reviewed the labors of his grandfather and his father at the Santa Gertrudis, saying that they had left "a considerable example and a considerable responsibility." Guests left the centenary celebration of the King Ranch certain that neither the example nor the responsibility had been neglected.

Ranching today is a highly competitive business enterprise. Most of the economic factors sustaining such business are shaped now far beyond a pasture's horizon, by men and money in remote market places, by uncertainties of distant demands and unseen supplies, by governments and great events, by the world's huge commerce. And yet the success of a modern ranch, in terms of commercial profit which enables it to survive as a business venture in an aggressive business economy, still wholly depends upon basic elements which have been the fundamental concerns of pastoral husbandmen since ancient times: weather, herd welfare, land use, range skills.

Grappling with these changeable yet changeless elements for a hundred years in a changing world, carrying on a ranching business strenuously and with success, the King Ranch has vitalized its business venture with creative imagination. But business has not been and could not be the final essence of that venture.

No set of figures in a ledger, no account of physical size or cash valuation, can contain the ranch's rightful significance. Its only true measure is alive, in the reality of the pastures themselves and the life they engender.

Rains have come, ending drought, spilling water from the sky, bringing great seas of grass which now testify to the care this land has had. The strong new grasses sown widespread upon these pastures supplement the native growth, cover the land with a sturdier turf than existed when men first found it.

Its users here have been concerned with the beauty as well as the

utility of living grassland. The small evidences of humankind on the immense pastures, whether they be fence lines or petroleum installations, are made unobtrusive; they blend with unmarred landscape behind margins of brush and planted pear. Roads follow easy winding contours of natural terrain rather than the brusque rectitude of surveyors' geometry. Windmills, weather-mellowed in the breeze from the sea, stand in islands of high green chaparral, like small and

solitary beacons on enormous prairie horizons. The air of an un-
touched and untrammeled original world envelopes these efficient
and highly productive pastures.

   Wildlife in greatest abundance animates this land. Slender deer
move with bounding swift grace toward coverts within tangled
mottes on the prairie. Coveys of quail break whirring to sail up suddenly from tall-tasseled grass. Wild turkeys in flocks preen and strut

and gobble, their metallic plumage shining in the mottled sunlight of liveoak glades. Above lonely *callos* undulating patterns of interlacing *V's* of flying waterfowl in multitudes—ducks, geese, sandhill cranes—make music in twilit winter skies.

Upon this grassland which no hand has abused or broken, or squeezed dry of its original nutriment, or left squalid or forlorn, a superb breed of cattle has its origin, a true new breed springing from this continent. The strong, mellow red Santa Gertrudis cattle "fit this land and this land fits them. They were made for each other."[4] Upon these same pastures are bred superior horses to work Santa Gertrudis herds—horses to match the quality, and even the color, of the cattle this ranch created.

The essential source of this creation is too apt to be obscured by the massive material substance, the exemplary excellence, of the installations which confront and impress a visitor who enters the ranch at its Santa Gertrudis main headquarters.

The living spirit that made the ranch what it is, that built the headquarters, the big house, the barns, the stables, the show pens, the paddocks, and created all else, must be discerned beyond headquarters gates. It is alive in the land itself, in the far quietness of growing grass and grazing herds.

It is a spirit which pervades the ranch's cow camps at roundup, a spirit palpable and pronounced in the vitality, skill, work, fun, gusto shared together by Klebergs and *Kineños,* old and young, all of them horseback people *at work* in the bonds of their trade, the strenuous old trade of the range.

It is a high spirit. It creates a pattern, a unity, sets a rhythm and a pace, for the grinning, sweating, thorn-scratching, bruising, rope-burning, hard-riding work day of a King Ranch *corrida* gathering, driving, holding, cutting, roping, throwing, branding, castrating, earmarking, inoculating, doctoring, sorting, loading, shipping herds of big red cattle.

There can be few things like it anywhere.

There can be few remudas of so many splendid horses waiting at dawn by a camp while cowhands take their last coffees before saddling to ride.

There can be few sights — few experiences — like watching an autumn sun come up to make a prairie of high grass into an outreaching, shining golden cloud — through which there move, flowing in a potent and rich red stream, a thousand head of King Ranch cattle, their invisible hooves sounding *sish sish sish* across the golden cloud to the roundup ground.

There can be few outdoor exhibitions like the handling and cutting of the gathered herd in the open space, the sudden breakaway dart of a snuffy steer, the lashing hellbent run of a hatted centaur through a rattling thorn thicket to turn the fugitive back to the herd; there can be few more exhilarating skills than a horseman's unerring toss of his rope's loop; the bouncing, bawling dragging of the calves toward the fire where the iron is hot; the order within the seeming confusion of the hustlers afoot, heeling, mugging, wrestling, holding the kicking calves, to apply the W — in a ten-ring circus-rodeo with the sky for a tent and continuous music from the bellowing of the herd.

There can be few warmer fellowships than those at the cow camp fire after a voracious supper of savory meat, with the *patrón* Mister Bob grinning in the light of a Coleman lamp, with the foreman Ed Durham talkin' quiet stories with points as sharp as tasajillo thorns, with vaqueros playing cards, with eddy and flow of Spanish and tang of mesquite smoke in the night air with the stars, and a bedroll waiting, and another day coming in which to have it all again.

No summary of mere fact, set forth upon the page of a book, can contain the living force of the spirit that quickens inheritors of a tradition born from the riders of a Wild Horse Desert.

706

And there are no statistics to convey the ranch's final meaning, the profound sense of surety and strength men find springing from earth's fruitfulness, from the inerrant cycle of the journeying sun and changing season, from the everlasting chemistry conjoining soil and sky. The final meaning lives in the worthy use of those two primal elements envisioned by Richard King in a new land long ago:

HERDS AND GRASS

APPENDICES

XI

Defense Against Brush Encroachment

XII

Oil Development

XIII

Breeding Techniques

XIV

The Development of a Quarter Horse Family

XV

Ranch Thoroughbreds and Their Winnings

XVI

The Grass Program

XVII

Experiments in Supplying Phosphorus Deficiency

XVIII

Game Conservation and Management

XIX

Expansion Outside of Texas

DEFENSE AGAINST BRUSH ENCROACHMENT

by L. F. WILKINSON

WHEN CAPTAIN KING began his stock-raising enterprise a large part of the lands which now form the King Ranch were still open prairie country. The heaviest brush was on the southern tip of the area that was to become his ranch, with the exception of the live oak country and lands immediately adjacent to creeks. There was heavy brush on each side of Santa Gertrudis Creek, but the rest of the area was either prairie or very nearly so. However, during the years leading up to the turn of the century there was a gradual encroachment of brush.

It was recognized early that control or eradication of brush, particularly mesquite, would be one of the great problems of maintaining range lands in productive form. During the 1890's distressed economic conditions brought thousands of starving Mexican families to this country in search of food and work. Approximately a thousand families were employed by the ranch to dig out mesquite and other obnoxious growth with hand axes and grubbing hoes. One man could clear less than an acre a week. These workers were supplied with food and sufficient money to care for their immediate needs. This type of hand clearing required close supervision to see that the roots were grubbed to the proper depth. Even then it was impossible to see if all the roots were taken out.

From about 1900 to a comparatively few years ago, the management of the ranch followed the practice of burning off during the winter months when the ground was wet and grass roots would not be injured by fire. To some extent this held down the encroachment of brush; however, broadly speaking, brush has been spreading and increasing in density for many years at a cumulative rate.

Caesar Kleberg and Robert J. Kleberg, Sr., tried many different eradication methods during the early days. One of the first was piling dead wood around the trunks of mesquite trees and firing it; this was to some extent successful, but it was much too slow and too expensive for extensive use.

In the year 1910 the ranch secured a stump puller manufactured by the Hercules Company of Centerville, Iowa. Operation of this equipment involved attaching a cable to the largest tree in the immediate vicinity as a dead man to anchor a large drum. Then a second cable was attached to the tree to be pulled. Mechanical advantage was obtained by means of the drum, powered by two mules. As the mules were driven to turn the drum, the winding cable slowly pulled the tree. This was a tedious, time-consuming operation, but it was considered necessary in view of the heavy encroachment of mesquite.

Ranch records indicate the first mechanized pasture improvement started on the ranch in the year 1915. Two Buffalo Pitts Traction Engines—great iron-wheeled steam tractors—were secured. A Mr. Rarig of Robstown built plows for this equipment in his machine shop. The plows had to be extremely heavy to provide the necessary strength. They were of the three-blade mole-board type. It is believed that this was the first time a plow was pulled by tractor equipment for pasture maintenance in a cattle ranching operation.

Richard M. Kleberg, Sr., was delegated to maintain and operate this equipment. The plan was to have a number of men follow the plows, pulling up and stacking the mesquite roots for future use as fuel for the steam tractor. These tractors weighed approximately ten tons each. Old-timers report this equipment was of little value due to the expense of operation, the tremendous weight and lack of traction on the steel wheels, and numerous mechanical breakdowns.

The old steam-powered tractors were superseded about 1918 by the more efficient Twin City gasoline tractors. These were used to pull plows. Within a couple of years the Ford Motor Company built an iron-wheeled four-cylinder gasoline tractor, the Fordson. Ten of these units were purchased, along with suitable plow equipment. These tractors were placed in operation over the area which had been cleared by hand grubbing. Approximately 17,000 acres were reclaimed by this method. Worth Wright was the agricultural foreman in charge of this operation, assisted by Johnny Cavazos.

Plowing operations were greatly improved by the advent of the Caterpillar tractor, and some very effective land clearing was accomplished by using a very heavy disk plow especially designed to be pulled by these powerful tractors. However, this method of land clearing continued to be very expen-sive. Trees had to be cut down by hand before plowing. The cost was as much as $15 per acre for plowing alone. Only the land adjacent to the headquarters was cleared in this fashion, some 17,000 acres, since the cost of the operation made it prohibitive for preparing land for grazing purposes. However, at a later date some farming land was cleared in this manner.

The first markedly rapid progress in the land clearing program began in 1923. Samuel G. Ragland, cattle manager for the ranch, was also county commissioner. The county was operating several tractors. Robert J. Kleberg, Jr., asked why such a tractor couldn't be used to pull a mesquite tree directly from the ground, just like pulling a tooth. The idea was tested with one of the county tractors, and the first test was so successful that the ranch purchased several tractors of this type and put them into operation pulling trees. By 1925 a considerable number of Model 60 tractors had been put into operation on the ranch.

Each tractor was operated with a crew of eight men. Short cables were looped about the trees to be pulled; a long cable from the tractor was attached to these short cables, with the tractor working from tree to tree back and forth across the land to be cleared. Though not economical by any means, the cost was far below any previous land clearing operation. During the next five years some 15,000 acres were cleared by this method in the Santa Cruz area.

Seeking to do away with the excessive manpower involved in the operation, Mr. Kleberg secured a "crawler" shovel made by the Insley Machinery people. He had the equipment modified so that instead of a shovel the tractor was equipped with a holding device that could be compared to a claw hammer on a large scale. It pulled trees from the ground as one might pull a nail from a plank. This was another step forward, but still too slow and costly for large scale use. Only one person was required to operate it, and it cleared from an acre to an acre and a half per day. For the most part it was used to clear some of the small pastures around the ranch headquarters.

This method of pasture improvement was used until 1935. That year proved to be the transition point in this department of the ranch's development. At that time the writer was a salesman for the William K. Holt Machinery Company, Caterpillar dealers. Permission was secured to try a new model, the RD-8 Diesel Caterpillar tractor, on the ranch. Mr. Kleberg conceived the idea of attaching a knockdown bar, or ram, and a V-blade to pull stumps after the trees were knocked down. The LeTourneau Manufacturing Company of Peoria, Illinois, built this equipment to specifications. Both the V-blade and the knockdown bar were controlled by the operator from the tractor seat. Thus was born the tree-dozer, a mechanical land clearing device which was to spread throughout the world.

Naturally, Mr. Kleberg was proud of the unit and its achievement, but he was not at all satisfied with the performance; only a percentage of the roots were being removed. We went back to LeTourneau and requested that they build a large steel half-round plow blade to be pulled by the tractor. When completed this "loop" was pulled beneath the surface of the ground, slicing a four-foot swathe. From this developed the idea of a wedge-shaped blade, which was eventually produced in a nine-foot model.

This was the first practical root plow. The blade traveled underground at an approximate depth of twelve inches. It cut all lateral and horizontal roots, but it did not disturb existing turf on the surface.

Also in 1935, concurrently with the development of the root plow, the first cabling operation, or "chaining" as it came to be called, was carried out. This involved the use of two tractors attached to each end of a heavy chain some three hundred feet in length. The chain was dragged through the brush, pulling down mesquite trees and other obnoxious growth. However, this left many stumps and roots imbedded in the ground to sprout and cause heavy regrowth.

In 1949 Mr. Kleberg conceived the idea of building a tractor of sufficient weight and horsepower to perform the entire brush clearing job in one operation: To knock down the trees in front while pulling the root plow behind. The first machine was a heavy iron-wheeled tractor weighing more than a hundred tons, known as "The Mesquiter." After months of trial and disappointment, it was determined that this tractor did not possess sufficient strength to perform the job at a sufficiently economical cost. However, from this first experiment knowledge was gained to determine that the idea was feasible.

The William K. Holt Company was contacted. They were furnished specifications and a guarantee that the ranch would accept the resulting machine upon delivery if it operated successfully for a thousand hours. It did. This unit, known as the Twin D-8, was delivered to the ranch in March, 1951 —a 110,000-pound leviathan. It consisted of two 130-horsepower diesel tractor motors side by side, together developing 270 horsepower at 1110 rpm, with each motor transmitting power to a single Caterpillar track.

The front was equipped with a knockdown bar capable of pushing over trees from 12 to 40 feet high and up to 20 inches in diameter. Beneath the motors, between the two tracks, there was 36-inch vertical clearance. This was the Funnel Dozer—another invention of Robert J. Kleberg, Jr.—which consisted of two blades angling in beneath the knockdown bar. The bar pushed brush over; the blades, forming an 18-foot-wide mouth, funneled it between the tracks under the machine, piling the uprooted brush into windrows. The piled brush protected the young grass from grazing cattle and added humus to the soil as it rotted. Behind the Twin D-8 a 16-foot-wide blade was pulled underground, cutting roots below the bud line, loosening the soil and providing a subterranean reservoir to hold rainfall. In addition, a seeding attachment was installed which automatically seeds the land as it is cleared. Thus, in one operation and with one operator, heavy brush growth is grubbed, and the land is plowed and seeded.

At the present writing the first Twin D-8 has operated a total of 10,250 hours. A second machine was delivered in March of 1952; it has piled up 8,500 hours, making a gross of 18,750 tractor hours. One of these machines will clear four acres per hour. The cost of operation—including all expenses: salaries, depreciation, et cetera—is $16 an hour, or $4 per acre. During their operation the blades of these two machines have traveled underground more than 25,000 miles, a distance greater than the circumference of the earth at the equator.

Since the development of the root plow the ranch has also operated four standard D-8's with angle dozers on the front and 9-foot cable-controlled root plows on the rear, clearing mesquite, *granjeno** and other undesirable growth. Approximately 72,000 acres have been cleared with this equipment at a cost of about $2.75 per acre. These tractors have also been used on other work about the ranch, such as the construction of terraces, dams and roads.

In addition the ranch owns and operates some seventeen John Deere and International tractors on rubber tires for pulling rolling cutters, disk harrows, and other pasture maintenance tools. The ranch also uses a small loop or blade, operated by hydraulic control, on a wheeled tractor as a spot grubbing unit. This machine will run under the root system to grub out pasture regrowth. It can remove as many as a hundred regrowth spots per acre at a cost of approximately fifty cents an acre.

The King Ranch's operation in Cuba is using four D-8's, complete with root plows, angle dozers, stacking racks, blade graders, and Towner-type heavy duty cutaway disk harrowing plows. This was the first heavy mechanical land clearing equipment ever to be used on the island of Cuba in a ranching enterprise. The units have been operating there less than three years and have converted about 20,000 acres from jungle growth to high production pasture. The Cuban ranch is also using a Caterpillar D-4 equipped with a dozer on the fence building operation, another first in Cuba.

On the King Ranch's Brazilian properties two D-8's are in use, equipped with root plows and angle dozers; there are also four D-6's equipped with Towner-type disk harrowing plows. All of this equipment is involved in land clearing and tank building. Here again the use of heavy land clearing equipment was a pioneer venture.

---

* Western hackberry (*Celtis pallida*).

OIL DEVELOPMENT

by Frank T. Fields

Oil did not come quickly or easily to the King Ranch. It was not until 1939 that production worthy of the name was established and oil began to take its place among the natural resources of the ranch. And 1939 was exactly twenty years after Humble Oil and Refining Company leased King Ranch acreage for the first time!

Humble took its first lease on the King Ranch in 1919. The first exploratory work began in 1922, when surface geology surveys were made. Results were most disappointing, leading to the almost doleful opinion that "There appears to be nothing on the King Ranch to indicate any favorable area for drilling wells for oil or gas . . ."

The report did leave the way open for some small hope. "These lands," it continued, "can be considered as wildcat territory and if a sharp structure could be determined there is a possibility of developing oil or gas on the uplift. However, there is small likelihood of one being able to determine the presence of a structure from surface geology . . ."

That prediction was borne out by surface geology activity which continued in 1923. Again, results left little room for optimism. The report stated, in part, that "The greater portion of the Ranch is so thickly coated with loose sand that many of the accepted indications of salt domes in all probability did not show up at the surface and there are no pronounced elevations which are not obviously the results of erosion rather than an uplift . . ."

The report went on, tolling off one pessimistic view after another: ". . . there are no seepages of oil, gas or sulphur water . . . the shallow and artesian water wells offer no evidence of favorable structural conditions . . . mounds and depressions of small relief are so frequent that this type of topography is of no value as an indication of salt domes." The report closed, like the final curtain on a tragic drama, with the cold recommendation that ". . . failing to find any favorable indications of salt domes being present on this part of the King Ranch there is not sufficient justification for a test well to be drilled."

With surface geology bowing off the stage as a means of exploring for oil, it was time for a new method—geophysics—to make its entry. In 1924, Humble entered into an agreement with a German seismograph crew to explore an area of not less than 50,000 acres.

Results of the seismograph work indicated that two nine-section units showed favorable promise. To check the findings of the seismologic survey, Humble geologists recommended that four shallow wells be drilled. The last of the four was completed on May 24, 1925.

It was determined from the results of these wells that additional information would be needed, and core tests were made on other portions of the King Ranch. Altogether, twenty-six core tests were made, the last being completed on July 22, 1925. In all this work, nothing was found to change the oil outlook for the ranch from one of pessimism to one of optimism. The first venture had failed. Only a small amount of oil had been obtained from one well drilled as an extension of the previously discovered Kingsville Field. Humble, with so little promise of success, began about 1926 to surrender its King Ranch leases.

Humble Leases Again

THERE WERE THOSE who never gave up hope of finding oil on the ranch, even after early exploration and drilling had proved fruitless. Prominent among these was Wallace E. Pratt, then in charge of Humble's exploration. In 1933, Humble leased the King Ranch for the second time, taking more than a million acres. Two years later, the ranch was partitioned in accordance with the will of Mrs. Henrietta M. King, wife of the founder. Mrs. King had died in 1925 and had stipulated in her will that the ranch remain intact for ten years after her death. All leases held by Humble remained unaffected by the partitioning; it merely meant that a separate accounting for royalties would be made on any oil and gas which might be produced from the now-separate ranches.

Later Exploration

AFTER TAKING LEASES in 1933, Humble spent the next six years carrying on a comprehensive program of exploration before a well was drilled. This time, the land was explored intensively with all types of equipment—the torsion balance, the gravity meter, the core drill, and the seismograph, which had been greatly improved since it was first used on the ranch in 1924.

The torsion balance is an exploration tool that measures differences in the pull of gravity which sometimes indicate favorable underground structures. It was the forerunner of the gravity meter, a new and greatly improved device for doing the same kind of work as the torsion balance.

Core drilling consisted of taking samples, or cores, from underground formations at relatively shallow depths. This work began on the ranch about 1936 and continued for the next ten or twelve years.

In 1938, Humble sent a seismograph crew of some twenty men to the King Ranch, and exploratory work of this nature is still not completed there. In seismograph exploration, a small charge of dynamite is exploded in a shallow hole drilled every 1200 to 1500 feet for that purpose. The explosion creates an artificial earthquake from which vibrations are recorded on photographic film. Geophysicists study and interpret these vibration patterns to determine what structures may lie below.

During the past seventeen years or so, virtually all acreage under lease on the King Ranch has been "shot" with the seismograph. Geophysical crews, using improved equipment and new techniques, periodically go back over portions of the ranch to take a new look at areas where satisfactory results were not obtained with earlier work.

Development of Proved Fields

BEFORE HUMBLE BEGAN any wildcat drilling following its second entry into the King Ranch, several fields discovered by other operators extended onto the ranch. The work of drilling in these extensions on ranch property occupied Humble rigs for the next several years.

In May of 1939, the company completed its first well as an oil producer in the Colorado Field of Jim Hogg County. Excluding the small oil producer drilled in the old Kingsville Field in 1923, the Colorado well was Humble's first on the King Ranch.

The second well came closely after the first, but on a different part of the ranch. In September of 1939, a producer was drilled in the Luby Field of Nueces County, a small portion of which extended onto the northeastern part of the ranch.

Two years later, in 1941, Humble completed its King Ranch-Paso Ancho No. 1, the company's first well in the Stratton Field, near Kingsville. The following year a number of wells were completed in the Seeligson Field, southwest of the Stratton Field. Also in 1942, Humble completed its first producer in the West Stratton Field.

In 1944, moving southward, Humble began to develop the extreme southern end of the ranch in the Willamar Field of Willacy County (in what had become El Sauz Ranch). Here, another oil field discovered by others extended onto the ranch. Also in 1944, development of the ranch's part of the Tijerina-Canales-Blucher Field began, with the first well completed in January, 1945.

By that time Humble was ready to begin its wildcat drilling program on the King Ranch.

Exploratory Drilling

HUMBLE DRILLED its first wildcat well on the King Ranch in 1945, just twelve years after the land had been leased for the second time in 1933.

That first wildcat discovered the Borregas Field, rated at that time as the most important discovery in South Texas in eight years. The Borregas Field, which lies between the Stratton and Seeligson fields, was unlike other King Ranch fields in one important respect: it lay entirely within ranch boundaries. It has since proved to be a major field.

But, just to prove the unpredictability of the oil business, the second wildcat well (also drilled in 1945) brought in what has proved so far to be a one-well field! This was the Monte Negra (or Motas Negras) area southwest of production in the Stratton Field. The well has flowed only a very small amount of oil, and two other wells drilled there—one in 1946 and one in 1947—were dry holes. Here was a striking example of contrast in the oil business. Two wells were drilled, on a wildcat basis, not too many miles apart. One discovered a major field; the other proved no more than a brief "flash in the pan." Actually, oilmen would be delighted with odds as favorable as that. As a national average in rank wildcat drilling, only one well in nine finds any oil at all.

Two wildcat wells were drilled on El Sauz Ranch during 1946. Both were dry holes. As if to offset that disappointment, however, drilling elsewhere in proved fields on the ranch found new oil sands. These discoveries continued during 1947, although no new fields were discovered on the ranch during that year. Three more wildcats on El Sauz Ranch were dry holes.

Activity during 1948 followed the generally disappointing pattern set by the two preceding years. Increased wildcat drilling during 1948 discovered shallow gas sands in the Boedecker area of eastern Brooks County. Oil and gas were also discovered that year at West Borregas and on the Santa Fe Ranch. But these discoveries proved of only minor significance. In all during the year, eight dry wildcat wells were drilled. One of them, the Sauz Ranch-Tenerias No. 3, went down to 13,509 feet, a record for Humble operations in the Southwest Texas Division. Almost exactly two and a half miles of expensive hole had yielded nothing but geologic information.

During 1949 six wildcat wells resulted in three gas discoveries. One was the Viboras Field in Brooks County on lands held by Robert J. Kleberg, Jr., Trustee. The other two were the South Santa Fe and the Laguna Larga.

Exploratory drilling discovered two more fields on the King Ranch in 1950. These were the Julian Field in southwestern Kenedy County and the Canelo Field, seven miles west and slightly south of Riviera in Kleberg County. No oil has been found in the Julian Field, but the discovery well produced condensate at a high rate. Three other wells drilled there resulted in two dry holes and one gas well. The Canelo Field proved to be of minor significance. Three wildcat wells drilled there during 1951 were dry holes.

No oil or gas fields were discovered on the King Ranch in 1951. One, the Calandria gas field, was discovered in 1952, but a second well drilled there was a dry hole.

In 1953, Humble wildcatting brought in two new gas fields on El Sauz Ranch in Willacy County. One was in the North Willamar (Tenerias) area and the other was in the Southeast Willamar area. The most recent gas discovery was made in 1954 on the Laureles Division of the ranch, brought in by successful completion of the King Ranch Alazan No. 2 well. Indications are, however, that this gas field will prove of limited importance, and the discovery well has been shut in.

Burden of Wildcatting Carried by One Operator

WILDCAT DRILLING on the King Ranch is complicated by the large area involved. Successful wildcatting in Southwest Texas usually makes use of subsurface information gained from the dry holes—the mistakes, as well as the producers, drilled by all operators. On the King Ranch there are no other operators. All exploratory drilling information must come from Humble's wells alone. This slows down the rate and increases the difficulty of finding oil and gas. On the other hand, it enables better planning and less interference with ranch operations.

By the end of 1954, a total of sixty-seven wildcat wells had been drilled on King Ranch leases. Of these, fifty were dry holes, seven produced oil, and ten were completed as gas wells.

Of the five oil fields discovered by Humble on the ranch, only one—the Borregas—is of major importance at present. Two oil fields—the Monte Negra and the Santa Fe—have been abandoned. The other two—the South Santa Fe and the Canelo—have been of limited importance.

Two of the discovered gas fields, Viboras and Laguna Larga, are promising; two others, West Borregas and Julian, are of uncertain importance. The Boedecker gas field has been abandoned. All other gas fields, including the Calandria, North Willamar (Tenerias), Southeast Willamar, and Alazan, are probably small productive areas.

Drilling and Production

DRILLING ON THE King Ranch ranges from about 3,000 feet below the surface in the Colorado Field to below 13,000 feet in the Sauz Ranch-Tenerias area. High pressures in some areas make it necessary to use heavy muds for drilling; mud weights range from nine to eighteen and one-half pounds per gallon.

Producing wells range from shallow pumping, low-capacity wells in the Colorado

Field to wells that could, if they were allowed to, flow almost 300 barrels per day through a one-eighth inch choke. Reservoir types vary from a single reservoir in the Colorado Field to a total of forty-nine separate reservoirs underlying various portions of the Seeligson Field.

Since oil was first produced from the Colorado Field on the ranch in 1939, there have been at all times no fewer than two and sometimes as many as sixteen drilling rigs in operation on the ranch.

Workovers and Formation
Stimulation

THE OIL INDUSTRY'S problems with a particular well are by no means at an end when the well is brought in as a producer. In many cases, when it stops flowing or does not produce regularly, a well may have to be "worked over." In some cases, the trouble may be the impermeability of the producing formation itself, and the formation may have to be acidized or "fractured" in some way to stimulate the flow or production of oil. In other cases wells must be plugged back and reperforated in oil saturated sands lying above zones where encroaching water has drowned out production. In each case, intensive studies of reservoirs and reservoir behavior are the basis for deciding what shall be done with individual wells.

Oil operations on the King Ranch call for a rather extensive program of workovers and formation stimulation, particularly in the Stratton District, where problems are intensified by the large number of separate reservoirs in the Seeligson Field.

In 1954 alone, for example, the program of workovers and formation stimulation in-cluded four formation fracturing jobs, sixteen acidizing jobs, three mechanical repairs to wells, ten recompletions in the same zone, nine recompletions in new zones, and thirty-one dual completions.

In a dual completion, one hole is drilled to serve as two wells. Production flows from one reservoir up through the tubing. Simultaneously, a different completion is made in a separate reservoir above the first producing horizon, and oil from this zone flows up between the tubing and the casing (the annulus). In this two-well arrangement from one drilled hole, two separate flow lines emerge at the surface and each well has its own allowable. It is an economical arrangement that is most practicable in fields that contain several reservoirs, or separate layers of oil-producing sands, such as the Seeligson Field.

Problems Peculiar to
the King Ranch

IT IS UNLIKELY that development of any single oil lease has ever met with the variety of problems that Humble has had in its operation on the King Ranch.

Topography of the ranch ranges from marshes adjoining bodies of salt water to rich, black farmland. Between these two extremes are densely wooded mesquite areas, smooth rolling grasslands, desert-like sand dunes, fresh water lakes, live oak and shin oak country, and soils and vegetation of other natures. Visualize the magnitude of this empire by realizing that three drilling rigs can operate on the King Ranch at the same time and still be separated from each other by seventy-five to more than a hundred miles!

Marsh buggies or amphibious jeeps called

"weasels" may be required in preparing some drilling locations. Other locations may fall in sand dunes fifty feet high and many acres wide. Or they may fall in a perfectly dry flat that might overnight become a lake two or three feet deep.

If the location is in a live oak motte, clearing is held to a minimum and no very large oak trees are disturbed, so that refuge for wild game can remain as natural as possible.

If the location falls in heavy mesquite, as it frequently does, it must be cleared with a bulldozer and the roots plowed up to prevent regrowth of this hardy shrub-like tree. A specially-made giant machine* is used for this clearing-and-rooting job on the ranch.

A wildcat location may require construction of a road fifteen or more miles long, probably built of caliche or clay. Many of the frequently used roads are hard-topped, and hundreds of miles of them have been built by Humble and the ranch jointly. Road-building, in fact, was a major project in the early years of oil development on the King Ranch. And every foot of road was built carefully, with the idea constantly in mind that the ranch's natural assets are grass and shade. Roads did not go through oak mottes or other groves of trees; they went around them. Care was also taken while building roads not to set up conditions that would encourage or lead to soil erosion.

Each fence crossing inside the ranch has been equipped with a "bump gate," or "push gate," which a driver can go through without getting out of his car and which closes itself afterward. These are used instead of cattle guards to minimize the danger of injuring thoroughbred horses or purebred cattle.

Some roads, of course, have to be elevated to prevent inundation during heavy rains which have, on occasion, turned low places into flooded areas. Travel on all roads, in all kinds of weather, is done carefully to avoid injuring or killing the ranch's livestock and wild game.

Gas Conservation

BOTH THE KING RANCH and Humble have been leaders in conservation; the former primarily concerned with conservation of soil, water, wildlife, cattle and horses, and with the best uses of the land; the latter dedicated to the conservation of oil and gas. As a result, it is natural that the two should work harmoniously together. Humble has kept the idea of conservation constantly in mind in all of its drilling and producing operations, thus assuring efficient development and production and the greatest ultimate recovery of oil and gas.

Early in the development of the King Ranch leases the importance of casinghead gas conservation was recognized and steps were taken to conserve this gas. This recognition has resulted in a comprehensive gas conservation program on the ranch, which includes gas injection projects to effect increased oil recovery through pressure maintenance, for gas storage, to carry on net-ratio operations, and for cycling purposes.

During 1945 a gas-gathering system was built to utilize Seeligson and Tijerina-Canales separator gas for rig and lease fuel. This system was later extended to the Borregas and Stratton fields. When the Texas Railroad Commission issued a no-flare order for April, 1947, prohibiting production of oil in the Seeligson Field unless the gas produced with that oil was utilized for legal purposes, Humble was in a position to comply with the order.

A year later, in 1948, a similar order was

* See Appendix XI.

issued for the Tijerina - Canales Field. Humble complied by installing a portable compressor which returned casinghead gas to the producing formation.

Gas compressor plants have been built in the Seeligson and Stratton fields for compressing and returning gas to formations in those fields. Casinghead gas from the Willamar and Luby fields is processed through gasoline plants operated by other companies, then returned to the reservoirs.

In the Stratton area, some wells are operated under a net gas-oil ratio ruling which permits the production of high gas-oil ratio wells at the full allowable rate so long as the produced gas is returned to the reservoir from which it is produced. This allows production of considerably more oil than otherwise could be produced.

In the Seeligson and Stratton fields, gas cycling operations are being carried on where the high pressure gas wells are produced, the condensate removed, and the dry gas is returned to the reservoir.

Current King Ranch Operations

HUMBLE'S CURRENT operations on the King Ranch are supervised by four headquarters districts: Stratton, Colorado, Scott & Hopper, and Willamar. At this time,* some 338 employees work in the four districts.

The Colorado District in Jim Hogg County was the first district headquarters to be established by Humble on the King Ranch. It was established there in 1940, following the initial drilling in 1939 under supervision of the Kelsey District. At present, some twenty-seven Humble employees work in the Colorado District.

The district supervises the small San Pablo

and Armstrong fields located off the King Ranch, in addition to that portion of the Colorado Field lying on the ranch. Drilling operations have not been particularly heavy in this area during recent years. Several years ago in the Colorado Field, salt water was returned to the producing reservoir on an experimental basis in an effort to increase ultimate recovery of oil. This experiment proved the feasibility of "water-flooding" the field, and the five-spot pilot flood has been extended to encompass the entire southern half of the field.

The Stratton District has its headquarters in the Stratton Field, near Kingsville. It supervises operations in the Stratton, Borregas, Seeligson, Tijerina-Canales-Blucher, Luby, Kingsville, West Borregas, Laguna Larga, and West Bishop fields on the King Ranch. Fields off the ranch also under Stratton supervision are the Brownlee, North Magnolia City, Rita, Sarita, El Paistle, and Mifflin fields.

In addition to production, Stratton supervises two gas compressor plants to eliminate flaring of gas.

Operations in the Stratton District at present require 255 employees engaged principally in drilling and production operations. A great deal of remedial work has to be done on wells in this district. Multiple reservoir conditions prevail, and the presence of numerous sands which frequently "lens out," plus the complexity of faulted structures throughout the field, make analyses of recompletions difficult.

The Scott & Hopper District was established in 1944, primarily to supervise operations on the Scott & Hopper, Rachal, and Sullivan ranches. When wildcat operations began on the Encino Division of the King Ranch in 1948, the district began to super-

* November, 1955.

vise those operations. In that year, also, the district took on the job of supervision of operations on the Santa Fe Ranch, but in recent years those operations have been abandoned. With abandonment of the Santa Fe and Boedecker fields in this district, Scott & Hopper now supervises the Julian gas field, the South Santa Fe Field (a 1949 oil discovery), and the Viboras Field, a 1949 gas discovery. At present there are thirty-six employees in the Scott & Hopper District.

The Willamar District, also established in 1944, is near Raymondville in Willacy County. This district supervises only Humble's operations in the Sauz Ranch part of the Willamar Field.

Beginning with twenty-six persons in 1944, the number of employees in the Willamar District rose to 111 by the end of 1946. As drilling was reduced, personnel was transferred accordingly, and at present there are only twenty employees in the district. Development of producing properties is essentially complete, and Humble is now evaluating secondary recovery projects.

Cooperation

HUMBLE IS CAREFUL on the King Ranch to carry on operations in such way as to protect ranch property. For example, guards built around "Christmas trees" (arrangements of valves and pipes protruding above the ground for flowing wells) were altered to suit the best interests of the ranch. Normally, such guards are built of angle iron, but it was feared that edges and sharp corners might, on some locations, injure prize livestock. The ranch designed and Humble built a special guard of smooth, round pipe to prevent injury.

In the earliest years of operation, a valuable mare broke her leg going over a cattle guard and had to be destroyed. Humble forthwith removed cattle guards through fences and replaced them with the bump gates described earlier.

Whenever Humble people spot a fence break, or a section that appears in need of repair, they either mend it themselves, if it is a simple job, or report it immediately to ranch officials.

Preservation and protection of wild game on the ranch is a matter of as much interest to Humble people employed there as it is to ranch personnel. The King Ranch is understandably proud of its game, and goes to much effort and expense to protect and preserve it. There are several game preserves on the ranch, with deer and turkeys being shipped from the ranch to other areas throughout the state. Humble takes care that neither the game, its food nor its cover is mistreated or destroyed.

For its part, the King Ranch has from the very first demonstrated a warm and sympathetic understanding of Humble's problems connected with oil and gas operations. A most cordial relationship exists; faith and confidence between the two parties have grown with years of experience. This was demonstrated in one of the earliest meetings between Humble and the King Ranch owners. One of the latter is said to have remarked at that time: "We are ranchers, not oil men. You run the oil business here, and we'll run the ranch."

It is that attitude which prompts Humble men concerned with King Ranch operations to describe the producer-landowner relationship as "one of the most pleasant we have ever known."

BREEDING TECHNIQUES

by ALBERT O. RHOAD

ABREEDING ESTABLISHMENT the size and scope of the King Ranch—with its extensive herds of commercial beef cattle, large herds of its own breed of purebred Santa Gertrudis cattle, its stable of Thoroughbred race horses, its bands of registered Quarter Horses, its barn of fine Jersey cattle—requires of its manager and members of his staff knowledge and skill in the selection and mating of livestock sufficient to embrace a large segment of the entire field of theoretical and practical animal breeding. The attainment of a forward position in breeding efficient cattle and fine horses indicates that sound breeding principles have been applied with consummate skill.

Because the skill required in designing adequate breeding plans and selecting and mating the proper individuals is largely a matter of personal qualifications, constructive breeding is still very much an art. When this art is fortified by an understanding of the scientific principles involved, many pitfalls in animal breeding may be avoided; progress toward desired goals is made with more confidence and disappointments are passed off with less concern.

The art of animal breeding has been accumulating down through the centuries from those remote times when man first domesticated animals. With knowledge gained through experience, man has created and perfected most of the present-day breeds. The science of breeding came into the picture with the rediscovery and verification of Mendel's laws of heredity, in 1900. Scientific knowledge related to animal breeding has been gathering appreciable momentum only during the last twenty-five years, reaching at the present time a level of completeness that permits man to manipulate, with considerable insight, the hereditary patrimony of our present-day breeds.

Scientific research has given man an explanation of the biological phenomenon underlying time honored breeding practices without, in many cases, changing the practices. Research has pointed out many of the fallacies of some breeding practices and beliefs that have come down through the ages, but only in very recent years has animal genetics as a science reached a point where entirely new breeding procedures and techniques are emerging into the practice of livestock improvement.

In King Ranch breeding operations the art and the science of breeding are so interwoven into the structure of improving livestock that it is not always discernible where one begins and the other ends. It can be stated, however, that experience takes precedence over theory in shaping breeding plans and that new techniques must be proven before they are incorporated into ranch breeding practices.

Breeding techniques employed on the King Ranch cover a wide range, based upon the desired ends and the class of livestock involved. Techniques in crossbreeding, grading-up, purebreeding, line breeding, inbreeding and outbreeding are constantly in use, involving in some cases thousands of head of livestock. The very numbers add in some respects to the complexity of the operations; yet, on the other hand, large numbers offer a broad genetic base to build upon, permitting greater latitude in selection and more flexibility in designing mating systems. All of these factors add to the rate at which progress can be made in attaining desired ends.

There are no trade secrets or magic formulae that guarantee success in breeding livestock. Yet breeders, through experience, are clearly aware that certain systems of mating lead more consistently to desired ends than other systems. It is in this field of experience and practice that differences in opinion between breeders, and between breeders and researchers, arise as to the most desirable mating systems to use in specific breeding problems. The King Ranch has consistently followed certain mating systems that have produced desired results under its conditions and with its class of livestock. It is reasonable to believe that under similar conditions the same techniques would produce similar results.

Cattle

IN BREEDING range cattle the development of adapted types is basic to all breeding operations on the King Ranch, because without an adapted type any breeding system aimed at improving type or efficiency could not be fully successful. This was learned through experiences in purebreeding and grading-up with high quality but unadapted breeds. Crossbreeding to the hardy Zebu was necessary and was used by the King Ranch and other breeders along the Gulf

Coast of Texas for more than thirty years before research at government experiment stations verified the necessity for this type of crossbreeding and gave sound biological explanations for the system's success.

In crossbreeding, the King Ranch has frequently followed a modified technique derived from long experience with many crossbreeding experiments: Under conditions where it is desired that the characteristics of one of the parent breeds should predominate in the crossbred offspring, the heredity complex (i.e., gene combinations) of the other parent breed should be broken up by outcrossing (i.e., made as heterozygous as possible). By then mating linebred individuals of the preferred breed with outcross individuals of the other parent breed, the crossbred individuals would more closely resemble the desired parent breed. This technique, in effect, was followed in developing the crossbred foundation of the Santa Gertrudis breed when predominantly Lavender Viscount linebred Shorthorns were crossed with Brahman bulls showing various strains of *Bos indicus* breeding.

The King Ranch commercial herds are based on a crossbred foundation of Hereford-Brahman and Shorthorn-Brahman. With these the relatively simple grading-up technique is employed through continuous top crossing to purebred Santa Gertrudis bulls. On the King Ranch the system has been perfected in at least one respect. Because of the large numbers involved it is possible to grade the breeding herds on type and to some extent on percentage of Santa Gertrudis breeding. As a result, some of the commercial herds closely resemble the purebred Santa Gertrudis while others still have large numbers of original foundation-type cows. In time these latter herds

[722]

will also closely resemble the purebred Santa Gertrudis.

Creating a new breed from the Brahman-Shorthorn crossbred foundation has been the most significant of the King Ranch's contributions to livestock breeding. Since the formative period of our modern specialized breeds of cattle (in England and Continental Europe almost two hundred years ago) no entirely new breed of bovines has appeared on the scene until 1940 when the Santa Gertrudis was officially recognized as a breed.

What is meant by creating "an entirely new breed"?

Basically it is putting together combinations of genes that heretofore had not existed and concentrating the desirable new combinations into a uniform breeding population.

The Santa Gertrudis breed was the result of just such a procedure. In crossbreeding the Brahman with the Shorthorn, genes from the Brahman paired with genes from the Shorthorn to form new combinations in the offspring. This gave to these cattle characteristics and qualities which distinguished them from either parent breed. Many of their distinguishing characteristics and qualities represented desirable new gene combinations; other characteristics and qualities represented undesirable combinations. In mating the crossbreds, the desirable new gene combinations had to be retained and even increased in concentration while the undesirable combinations were concurrently being reduced and even eliminated.

The undesirable gene combinations were reduced or eliminated through culling; the desirable combinations were retained through selection, and their concentration was increased through inbreeding.

The art and science of breeding have their greatest play in application of the difficult and often complex detail procedural techniques necessary to effect each step in the above: The breeder has a choice of various bases for culling. Volumes have been written on the numerous techniques of selection and on the many systems of inbreeding. Each technique has a place in breeding procedures where it is the most effective technique in attaining desired ends.

In all breeding operations, however, there is the element of chance. Breeding techniques—no matter how refined they may be or how intricate the formulae they may follow—are subject to the hereditary phenomenon governing random assortment and recombination of genes.

Recognizing this fact, skilled breeders in mating their animals follow a plan in which the chance recombinations of genes they desire will happen with greater probability than if a different plan were followed. The results cannot be classified as luck in breeding; luck is the production of outstanding individuals without forethought of the probabilities or contrary to probabilities.

Monkey, the foundation sire of the Santa Gertrudis breed, is a case in point. His sire, the Vinotero bull, and a group of Brahman-Shorthorn crossbred cows were moved from the Santa Gertrudis Division of the ranch during the protracted drought of 1917-1918 to better grazing conditions on the Laureles Division. To this group Richard M. Kleberg, Sr., then manager of the Laureles Division, added some select part Brahman-Shorthorn cows out of a small herd retained at Laureles headquarters as milk cows. The probability was high that this particular group of cows when mated to this particular bull would produce good offspring. It was a matter of chance, however, when and which would produce an outstanding individual good enough to serve as the foundation sire of the projected new breed. It turned out to be one of the cows from the milk herd. Although chance was a factor in the breeding of Monkey, as it is in all animals, his breeding was not an accident of luck.*

On the other hand, it was fortuitous that Monkey appeared early in the accelerated crossbreeding program, because this enabled the King Ranch to start the second phase of breed building, i.e., increasing in the herd the concentration of the desirable gene combinations that Monkey possessed. This was done by inbreeding and later linebreeding to Monkey. But before this could be effected a long-range master plan had to be designed that would facilitate manipulation of the thousands of head of cattle that were eventually involved in converting the crossbreds into a uniform breeding population. For this purpose Robert J. Kleberg, Jr., designed in 1925 the single-sire, multiple-sire herd combination breeding plan. This plan, still in use, is unique in large scale cattle breeding. It concentrates superior individuals in a series of single-sire herds in which matings are controlled and the offspring scored, marked and pedigree recorded. By bulling large select cow herds with pedigreed offspring the multiple-sire herd part of the plan permits the rapid dissemination of their superior gene combinations into all herds.

---

* As a long yearling, however, a bit of luck entered the life of Monkey. He, with several other Brahman X Shorthorn bulls, was sent to the 1922 Fort Worth Stock Show for exhibit purposes. The exhibit cattle were to be sold after the show closed. Robert J. Kleberg, Jr., obtained his father's consent to have the impressive red yearling bull, Monkey, returned to the ranch; the others were sold. Monkey started his career as a sire the following season.

Another essential part of the master plan is placing superior type heifers born in the multiple-sire herds in the single-sire herds on an equal preference basis with superior type pedigreed heifers. This means that type takes precedence over pedigree in the selection of heifers. This is better understood when one realizes that there are less than four hundred cows in the various single-sire herds and from five to six thousand cows in the multiple-sire herds. Mass selection based on type is the basic method of selection.

Pedigree selection, although only an accessory method, has a very important part in the plan because the sires featured in the single-sire herds are pedigreed sons of the current best pedigreed male descendant of Monkey. Because only Monkey and his best male descendants were in the single-sire herds, with one exception,† from the very start and because their best male descendants went as sires into all other herds, all purebred Santa Gertrudis cattle on the King Ranch today are descendants of the foundation sire, Monkey.

Through the effective execution of this unique plan, the desirable gene combina-

---

† The one exception was the Bob Tail bull, a Brahman-Shorthorn bull used in making an outcross on inbred granddaughters of Monkey. A few sons of the Bob Tail bull were retained, and placed in large multiple-sire herds. His best daughters were placed in single-sire herds and bred to sons or grandsons of Monkey. Only after the third generation of linebreeding to Monkey were any bulls carrying Bob Tail breeding used in the single-sire herds.

The Bob Tail outcross was made early in the program because only Monkey and his sons and their daughters were in the single-sire herds. This would have led to continuous, close inbreeding with its insidious effects if the herd had been closed entirely to outside blood at that early date. The Bob Tail outcross was made to offset any tendencies toward insidious effects.

tions of the original Brahman-Shorthorn crossbreds reached, in a period of twenty years, a concentration level in the Santa Gertrudis of a uniform breeding population which was officially recognized as a new breed in 1940.

The plan, designed and executed by Robert J. Kleberg, Jr., is unique in two important respects: First, no previous bovine breed had been formed in like manner from a planned species cross through controlled steps to a recognized new breed.

Second, genetic investigations on estimates of hereditability in livestock, made since 1940, have shown that mass selection is the most effective breeding method to follow where production is expressed in both sexes and where hereditability is high. These studies not only verified that Mr. Kleberg's plan was the most effective one that could be designed for this purpose under ranch conditions but they also explained, in part, the rapid genetic progress that was made in converting the original crossbred into a purebred population.

As mass selection is the mating of "like with like" on the basis of type, a type objective or goal was determined, in its general form, before the breeding plan was set up as a procedure through which the type objective was attained. It was in designing the type and setting up performance goals that practical considerations of the functional and artistic considerations of the aesthetic came into play in creating a useful and pleasing whole. Robert J. Kleberg, Jr., was both the architect and the engineer in building the Santa Gertrudis breed.

Functionally the Santa Gertrudis had various specifications to meet, specifications not common to other beef breeds in this country at that time, some twenty-five years ago. It had to be hardy, i.e., adapted to local climate and range conditions. It had to be an efficient producer of quality beef from grass. Aesthetically the Santa Gertrudis was designed to have a solid red coat, a pleasing color for cattle, and good heads, distinctive of the breed.

To the extent these characteristics are expressed in the conformation and hair coat they were included in the type-standard designed and used by Mr. Kleberg as a basis for selection. The adaptability to heat, as expressed by loose hide and short hair coat contributed by the Brahman parent, was combined with the easy fleshing qualities and early maturity of the Shorthorn parent as expressed in deep fleshing in the areas of primal cuts and good weight for age. The red coat color came from the Shorthorn while the solid color pattern came from the Brahman parent breed. The characteristic Santa Gertrudis head, on the other hand, represents a harmonious blend of the cranial types of both parent breeds. In temperament the breed also manifests blending qualities, although in this respect it more closely resembles its Shorthorn parentage. By culling poor doers on the range during prolonged droughts a degree of adaptability to drought has been attained.

In one very important respect the type-standard of the Santa Gertrudis departed markedly from the type-standard of other beef breeds. The popular trend of the day toward small compact types was studiously avoided in developing the Santa Gertrudis. Experiences on the King Ranch with the small, short-coupled, close - to - the - ground type clearly indicated this was not the most efficient or economical type of beef cattle to produce or fatten on the range. Current investigations at many experiment stations on type as related to production have shown that the popular trend toward the small compressed type has brought about an unsatisfactory situation in a large segment of the purebred beef cattle industry today.

Beef type in the Santa Gertrudis is expressed in good weight at all ages with both cows and bulls showing considerable length, depth and size. The Santa Gertrudis is a large breed, but size in the extreme is not the objective, for this may lead to coarse, bony types. Instead, good size combined with mellowness and quality is the objective. That the Santa Gertrudis type is closely associated with high rate and efficiency of gain was demonstrated in 1954 in a rate-of-gain test on the King Ranch. Mr. Kleberg, following a practice of many years, set aside a group of good yearling bulls as replacement bulls for the ranch. Of these an extreme top group was selected and individually marked for use in the top breeding herds and another group marked for use in the commercial herds. Subsequently they were placed in feed lot on full feed for ninety days preparatory to placing them in service. The average daily rate-of-gain for the entire group was 3.20 pounds, for the extreme tops 3.29 pounds per day, and for the others 3.02 pounds per day. Experiment station reports give 2.25 pounds per day as the average gain for bulls of other breeds of similar age.

An important point from these figures is that the Santa Gertrudis type as selected on the King Ranch for many years has been a fast-gaining type, although only since 1953 have these gains been systematically measured. As efficiency-of-gain is closely related to rate-of-gain, Santa Gertrudis cattle are efficient converters of feed into beef.

* Santa Gertrudis Breeders International, Recorded Herds, Vol. I, 1953 (Kingsville, 1954), pp. 40-41.

Recent research at many experiment stations has shown that rate-of-gain in meat animals is inherited to a high degree. Because good rate-of-gain has been a major factor in selection of Santa Gertrudis cows and bulls from the very start, its rate-of-gain has become as characteristic of the breed as its color and its hardiness.

The creation of the Santa Gertrudis breed was the product of the ingenuity and skill of an experienced rancher as a solution to a difficult practical problem. Science, *a posteriori,* came to play an important part by proving the correctness of the procedures used and by explaining their success in the light of modern genetic concepts.

In 1951 the type-standard used by the King Ranch in developing the Santa Gertrudis was itemized in a "Standard of Excellence"* for the Santa Gertrudis Breeders International, and it is used by the breed association as the type basis on which it classifies Santa Gertrudis cattle in member herds outside the King Ranch.

The creation of the Santa Gertrudis breed has a definite significance to the livestock industry: Ranchers in the Southwest and in many other unfavorable environments of the world, confronted with problems of deterioration of their cattle because of difficult environments, now have an improved beef breed of predominately European origin adapted to harsh conditions—a beef breed that can be used in a simple grading-up program to increase productiveness without loss of hardiness.

Horses

BREEDING SYSTEMS used with horses are basically no different from those used with beef cattle; however, there is a great difference in the emphasis given to the various mating systems. For example, in this country, the grading-up system has disappeared as draft and carriage horses have passed from the scene. Crossbreeding has likewise disappeared with the passing of the remount stations and the gradual elimination of the mule. Horse breeding is now very largely confined to purebreeding with breeder interest centered on the development of families within the pure breeds and of superior individuals within families. Because of this situation, great emphasis is placed on pedigree selection with mass selection largely out of the picture.

Type in horses also receives particular attention because of the close relationship between conformation and function. Type, to some extent, is also related to performance. However, performance in horses, unlike any other class of livestock, is a reflection of their temperament, endurance and action. Temperament, the ability to learn the tasks for which they are trained and their desire or will to accomplish the tasks asked of them; endurance, the power to withstand the physical stresses of performance and action—are exceedingly important in horse breeding, yet difficult of definition. Because temperament and endurance are not fully discernible in the exterior and, along with action, are not recorded in pedigrees, clear decisions as to a horse's worth rest ultimately upon tests of performance. This complicates breeding because the mode of inheritance of temperament, endurance and action is not clearly defined and, also because performance is greatly influenced by good or bad training.

From its beginning the King Ranch has maintained large bands of horses for its own use and for sale. The Southwest is a naturally excellent breeding country for horses;

the ranch is located on part of what was formerly referred to as the Great Wild Horse Desert. No question of adaptability to local conditions is involved in horse breeding on the King Ranch.

At the present time the King Ranch uses approximately two thousand Quarter Horses, distributed over the ranch in breeding bands and working remudas. In 1935 the ranch established a breeding stud and a stable of Thoroughbred race horses. It is now one of the largest Thoroughbred breeding and racing establishments in this country. The King Ranch has been successful with both Quarter Horses and Thoroughbreds. It has developed a superior and popular family in the former and outstanding winners, even several great horses, in the latter.

The Quarter Horse is the last remaining utility horse in America. Other breeds are for pleasure and for sport, but the Quarter Horse has a definite and important place in ranch operations. It has special work to do and its type, temperament, intelligence, stamina, and maneuverability are hereditary characteristics that have given it a well-merited and permanent place as the cow horse of the rancher.

On the King Ranch all Quarter Horses are trained and performance-tested under actual working conditions before any, including stallions, are placed in breeding herds. Each stallion has a band of mares selected on quality of performance, trueness to breed type and on pedigree relationship to the sire. Stallions are on pasture with their bands of mares during the four- to five-month breeding season, after which they are brought into headquarters.

With the exception of about twenty mares, all Quarter Horses are descendants of Old Sorrel, the foundation sire of the King Ranch strain. Linebreeding to Old Sorrel is maintained and controlled through pedigree selection. In establishing the Old Sorrel family, Robert J. Kleberg, Jr., used inbreeding but not as intensively as he did in the case of Monkey, the foundation sire of the Santa Gertrudis. In maintaining a relationship to Old Sorrel it is now the practice to skip a generation, mating no closer than uncle to niece, or no closer than half first cousins of the same generation. Outcrosses to other families are made through females. This has been a general practice on the ranch when outcrosses are made.

In summary, the breeding objective with Quarter Horses is to maintain a superb performing strain by holding a continuous relationship between individuals within the Old Sorrel family. Concurrently some first generation outcrosses are kept on hand as a source of breeding stock to offset or correct any deleterious effects that may show up as the result of continuous linebreeding.

Linebreeding, used successfully by the King Ranch with both cattle and horses, is, as breeders are aware, a two-edged mating system. It can be destructive as readily as it can be constructive; the process by which it conserves or concentrates the desirable gene combinations of some favored ancestor simultaneously conserves or concentrates undesirable gene combinations. Independent of the possible presence of undesirable gene combinations there is also inherent in the system a gradual lowering of stamina and fertility if the matings between relatives, especially close relatives, are carried on continuously for some generations. Although the King Ranch has linebred to outstanding individuals in establishing its superior cattle and horses, it has

been cautious in the use of linebreeding. For instance, it follows the practice of having in its herds and studs some first generation outcross females to serve as genetic brakes on any adverse trends that continuous linebreeding may provoke.

With the Thoroughbreds the breeding objectives and problems are quite distinct from those of Quarter Horse breeding, although the emphasis on performance and pedigree is much the same. Type in the two breeds is very different but the same qualities of good temperament, endurance and action are required of both. The latter are even more accentuated in the Thoroughbred, and performance is more closely studied in setting up mating plans.

This is necessary because the margin which determines success with Thoroughbreds is much narrower than with any other class of livestock. This narrow margin is clearly visualized when one considers that for the breed as a whole, only forty-five per cent of all foals born reach the races and place "in the money." They get "in the money" only thirty-seven per cent of the times they start. Also, the difference in average time between a winner and a second-place horse, in the mile race, is less than one-fifth of a second, and between second- and third-place horses a shade more than one-fifth of a second. Against time, therefore, the margin for success is reduced to about a half a second as measured in average distances between first and third horses in the mile race. To breed winners consistently under these circumstances is not a matter of luck but of close study of pedigrees with matings, effected on the basis of performance supported with a knowledge of the individuality of each horse in the pedigree.

There are no sharply defined families in the modern Thoroughbred. Some two hundred years ago when the breed was in its formative stage there were well-defined families, but through many generations of matings, largely based on performance, family lines have virtually disappeared. A recent genetic analysis of the breed (1941) has shown a 16.8 per cent average, *inter se* relationship. This means that, as of 1941, Thoroughbreds had received, through the interlacing of their pedigrees over many generations, a percentage of genes from common ancestors equivalent to the percentage possessed by first cousins. Thoroughbred breeders are, therefore, working with a rather homogeneous, closed population. This fact contributes to the emphasis that breeders place on individuality aside from performance *per se*, whether it concerns a horse close up or several generations back in the pedigree. To go back several generations and breed to an outstanding individual is possible with horses, because of their long reproductive life. It is not uncommon for mares to be with granddaughters in the same band of brood mares. It is also possible to mate some worthy great-granddaughter of an outstanding sire to an outstanding son of the same sire. Furthermore, with Thoroughbreds reaching back three or four generations in the pedigree for exceptional qualities of some individual is not genetically retrogressive as would be the case in many other breeds because the Thoroughbred, according to several authorities, has for some generations reached its physiological limit of performance. While studious breeders justifiably place considerable importance on the performances and individualities of horses several generations removed, they do not lose sight of the fact that the performance and qualities of the immediate parents have the greater influence on the hereditary qualities sought for in the planned offspring.

The King Ranch breeding objectives and program feature the use of contemporary top sires and mares that trace back in some degree to the great American horse, Domino. This horse was foaled in 1891. The King Ranch foundation sire Bold Venture, foaled in 1933 and still active, traces back to Domino through his maternal grandsire Ultimus, an inbred son of Commando and Running Stream both by Domino. Bold Venture won the Kentucky Derby in 1936 and has sired two other Derby winners, Assault in 1946 and Middleground in 1950, a sire record unequaled to date.* Both Assault and Middleground were bred and raced by the King Ranch. Other King Ranch sires currently in use—Beau Max, Better Self, Bimelech, Brazado, Curandero, Depth Charge, Middleground, On the Mark, Prophet's Thumb and Poised — trace back to Domino one or more times, mostly through his son Commando but also through his son Disguise and his daughters Pink Domino, Noonday and Dominoes. Other names prominent in this line are the grandsons Peter Pan, Colin and Superman all by Commando and High Time, Hippodrome and Noontide; all, like Ultimus, inbred second-generation offspring out of daughters by Domino.

Of the ninety-two brood mares currently in the King Ranch breeding band, eighty-five trace back to Domino, thirty of these on one side and fifty-five trace through both sides of their pedigree. One mare traces back seven times to Domino. This mare, although a great-granddaughter of Man o' War on her sire's side, her linebreeding to Domino, six, seven and eight generations

[729]

* As of 1955.

removed, has concentrated his genes in such a manner that Domino genetically is moved up to the same generation as Man o' War in her pedigree. Almost thirty years separated Domino and Man o' War as active sires, but skillful matings brought them together as genetically contemporary sires in this mare's pedigree.

Man o' War, America's most famous race horse of recent times, is also featured in the King Ranch program. Of the eleven King Ranch sires in current use, five—Beau Max, Better Self, On the Mark, Prophet's Thumb and Poised—trace to Man o' War as well as Domino. Of the ninety-two mares, forty-one trace to Man o' War breeding; thirty-one to Man o' War directly; two to Masda, a full sister; and seven to Fair Play, the sire of Man o' War. Of these forty-one mares, thirty-seven also trace to Domino. Of these, thirty-three are of King Ranch breeding.

The major objective of Thoroughbred breeding on the King Ranch becomes evident from the above. It may be stated as, to conserve and combine the qualities of American Thoroughbreds through two of its most famous performers, Domino and Man o' War. This objective is realized by bringing these two lines together in the pedigrees of the stallions and in the pedigrees of the mares. In mating these stallions and mares, each tracing to Domino and Man o' War, additional linebreeding to these two horses results. The objective, however, is to concentrate the combination of the lines rather than to intensify the linebreeding specifically to one or the other horse.

As mentioned in the opening paragraph, the diversity and scale of the breeding operations on the King Ranch have required of its manager and his staff wide knowledge and experience in livestock improvement in order to have attained the success the ranch enjoys at the close of its first century.

Each generation of managers has had major problems related to the improvement of the stock. Emphasis has changed with changing conditions. Captain King developed a sizeable flock of sheep, but with changing conditions this part of the breeding operation was reduced. At present only a flock of light-colored and a flock of dark-colored sheep remain. They are maintained as a source of wool for the ranch's homespun saddle blankets. In 1912 Robert J. Kleberg, Sr., and his son Richard established a fine herd of Jersey cattle. This herd was maintained for many years at from 300 to 350 head. It was largely based on imported or out of stock imported from the Island of Jersey. Of the sires, Imported Combination Premier 150,715; You'll Do's Victor 163,146; The Imported Cid 199,361; and Worthy Light's Hustler 220,434 were the most noted. For many years this herd was a source of purebred breeding stock for the local dairy industry that was developing with the establishment of farms in the vicinity. After this industry was well established, the King Ranch Jersey herd continued as a source of milk for the ranch personnel. Robert J. Kleberg, Sr., was a noted purebred breeder. He established the largest purebred herds of Herefords and Shorthorns in the nation. He sold large consignments locally as well as to South America and Africa.

Some of the notable accomplishments in breeding cattle and horses which mark the present ranch administration had their inception under the administration of Robert J. Kleberg, Sr. Although manager of the ranch until 1926, Robert, Sr., had, for some years previous, his sons Richard and

Robert, Jr., and his nephew Caesar Kleberg as able assistant managers. The crossbreeding of Brahman with Shorthorn started under the administration of Robert, Sr., but as he had spent all of his managerial life grading-up Longhorns with Herefords and Shorthorns, he was not enthusiastic for the crossbreeding program, at least at its start. It was his young assistant managers who fostered the crossbreeding program.

His son Richard bred the bull Monkey while Robert, Jr., expanded the entire crossbreeding program and built the Santa Gertrudis breed around Monkey and his descendants. Essentially the same occurred with the Old Sorrel horse. He was discovered on a neighbor's ranch by Caesar Kleberg in 1915 while still nursing its dam and was purchased by authorization of Robert, Jr., the same year. Robert, Sr., lived to see many of the produce of both Monkey and Old Sorrel and had the satisfaction of watching the progress in the early developmental stages of the Santa Gertrudis breed and the Old Sorrel family.

It was during this period—in 1918—when J. K. Northway, DVM, joined the King Ranch staff as veterinarian. Dr. Northway ably assisted the management in the breed development program.

Although 1926 marked the beginning of the present administration, from the breed improvement point of view, it had started some years before. As early as 1916, shortly after returning from college, Robert, Jr., was given considerable responsibilities in the general management of the ranch. His influence soon became the determining factor in shaping the policies and plans of the major breeding operations. In May, 1926, he became *de facto* general manager of the ranch. Following the death of his father in 1932 and the incorporation of the ranch in 1935, Robert, Jr., became President and Manager of the King Ranch Corporation.

This period, covering thirty-eight years to date, has given continuity, with supervision by one person, to the planning and execution of the breeding operations. Continuity of purpose, although not a part of breeding techniques as such, is an extremely important factor in constructive cattle and horse breeding. Because of the long generation intervals (4-5 years with cattle and 11-12 years with horses) and low rate of increase, breeding plans covering twenty, thirty or more years are necessary even to approach the goals when the breeding objectives are as fundamental as the establishment of superior new breeds and families.

For success in undertakings of this scope one must add, therefore, to the breeding techniques as such the contributing factors of continuity of purpose, singleness of administration and, as mentioned before, adequate numbers. The King Ranch in its breeding efforts has been fortunate in possessing this combination of factors.

BIBLIOGRAPHY

KLEBERG, ROBERT J., JR., *The Santa Gertrudis Breed of Beef Cattle* (Kingsville, 1952).

RHOAD, ALBERT O., "The Santa Gertrudis Breed: The Genesis and the Genetics of a New Breed of Beef Cattle," *Journal of Heredity*, XL (May, 1949), pp. 115-126.

RHOAD, ALBERT O., "Procedures Used in Developing the Santa Gertrudis Breed," *Breeding Beef Cattle for Unfavorable Environments* (Austin, 1955), pp. 203-210.

RHOAD, ALBERT O. and KLEBERG, ROBERT J., JR., "The Development of a Superior Family in the Modern Quarter Horse," *The Journal of Heredity*, XXXVII (August, 1946), pp. 228-233.

THE DEVELOPMENT OF A QUARTER HORSE FAMILY

by J. K. NORTHWAY

FROM THE VERY beginning of his ranching venture, Captain King recognized the importance of good horses in ranching. This is attested to by early records showing that he paid $600 for a stallion during the time when he was first putting his ranch together. In 1868 he went to Kentucky to purchase "blood-stallions to improve my horse stock. . . . I paid as high as from three hundred to one thousand dollars."[*]

One of his earliest attempts to improve the breed of horses on his property was the selection of horses of good conformation and size for his *manada,* or band of mares. He went still further: In at least one pasture he divided his *manada* as to color. He increased the size of the Spanish horses on his properties from their normal size of 14½ hands to more than 15 hands. Naturally, since horses of good conformation and size were scarce they immediately attracted attention and, consequently, a higher price. They also attracted thieves. Captain King testified that 978 were stolen during a three-year period from 1869 to 1872.

In addition to developing horse stock for riding, Captain King made every effort to improve his driving and draft horses and mules by bringing in good blood wherever he could find it. He found a good market for his horse stock, many going to the United States and Mexican armies.

During the span of years after Captain King's death, Robert J. Kleberg, Sr., Sam Ragland and Caesar Kleberg continued this improvement program. They tried out different breeds of horses for highly specialized uses. The principal stallions were either Thoroughbred or Standardbred, although some Arabian, Morgan and Kentucky saddle-bred blood was tried. No attempt was made to perpetuate the old Spanish horse developed by Captain King, although the principle of adding the best available blood was carried on by his successors.

The Standardbred horses produced at that time did very well in their environment and provided outstanding teams much in demand by the carriage trade in general, particularly doctors and lawyers whose livelihood made it necessary for them to travel as rapidly as possible over the country.

Thoroughbreds were widely utilized in grading-up. The first and second crosses on the Spanish mares developed by Captain King were especially good cow ponies. Many of the larger ones were valuable as light horses for driving. Although they did not have quite as much speed for short distances as the Standardbred, their endurance was great in the hot climate. In solving its own need for good horses, the King Ranch soon had surpluses for sale, and during a number of years the sale of horse stock

[*] Testimony before U. S. Commissioners, Aug. 28, 1872, "Deposition No.107," *Memorial No.230,* pp. 157-158.

from the ranch exceeded that of cattle.

Before the advent of motor transportation, work horses and mules played an important part in the ranch's breeding program. After much trial and error, the selection narrowed down to Percherons for the slow heavy work and mules for lighter work throughout the ranch. For instance, until quite recently a six-mule team hauled the chuck wagons for the cow outfits; today the same chuck wagons are hooked to the rear of trucks or jeeps.

A good many well-bred Thoroughbred mares whose conformation left something to be desired as riding horses were bred to Kentucky jacks and produced very useful mules for work through the South because they stood the climate well and were more active than offspring from Percheron mares. Once this was known there was much demand for this type of mule.

In spite of all the selection by two generations of good livestock managers, the crossbreeding program of crossing Standardbred and Thoroughbred horses on the good Spanish mares which Captain King had developed did not, on the average, improve the horses as cow horses. The contrary was true. Many were too big and leggy for ranch work, although they were still in demand by the army remount service and as carriage horses.

About this time Richard M. Kleberg, Sr., and Robert J. Kleberg, Jr., entered into an intensive effort to select the best riding mares and breed them to the best Thoroughbred stallions in the hopes of developing a superior cow pony. Some good results were obtained, particularly in the use of stallions descended from a Thoroughbred known as "Old Tom." This indicated the possibility of developing a useful horse for ranch work,

but the over-all results were still disappointing.

This was the status of the horse breeding program at the time when Robert J. Kleberg, Jr., was becoming more active as manager of the ranch. He determined to direct the ranch's efforts toward producing a superior type horse for ranch work and general utility. He once defined the horse he wished to produce as "a horse that one would love to ride." Having really good horses has played an important part in keeping good men in the saddle, not only on the King Ranch but on other ranches.

Despite the mechanization of pasture improvement methods and cattle transportation during the last few years, handling cattle on the King Ranch is still fundamentally a horseback operation, involving the use of good cowhands mounted on good horses. The need for good horses has never abated.

In 1916, at the urging of young Robert J. Kleberg, Jr., Caesar Kleberg acquired the famous Quarter Horse foundation sire lovingly known as "Old Sorrel" as a colt from George Clegg, of Alice.

When he was broken and tried for cattle work, Old Sorrel proved to be outstandingly the best cow horse we had ever had on King Ranch. He was exceptional as to beauty, disposition, conformation, smoothness of action and fine handling qualities. Having seen other stallions, even after they had proven their merits for breeding, carry on for only one generation, we determined, if possible, to perpetuate the wonderful qualities of this stallion.

The first constructive effort in this direction was to breed Old Sorrel to fifty of the best handling and best riding mares on the ranch. These mares were in most instances of pure Thoroughbred or grade Thoroughbred breeding. The first important effort toward concentrating and preserving his blood was made when Solis, one of Old Sorrel's sons out of a Thoroughbred mare, was mated to his daughters from this same band of mares. In the course of a very short time, this band of mares was built up to 35 or 40 in number and in this way Solis was mated to forty of his half-sisters mostly from Thoroughbred mares. The results of this mating were very gratifying and it was clear that a long stride toward a fixed type had been made in this first mating.

During this same period, six other sons of Old Sorrel were bred to selected bands of mares which were thought best suited to them, and in this way quite a large population of grandsons and granddaughters of Old Sorrel was produced. In all instances the stallions and mares above referred to were broken to ride and were sufficiently tried out so that our permanent records regarding them were based on an intimate knowledge of their characteristics under the saddle as well as on their appearance. Fairly good results were obtained from those first matings, but the best results were obtained from the close breeding employed in the case of Solis.

As soon as it was possible to do so, selections were made from the related offspring above mentioned. In all cases the plan was to employ only such matings as would complement each other as to disposition, conformation and the great variety of characteristics which make up any living creature. . . . Through the years, as especially desirable individuals were produced, attention was given constantly to concentrating those traits which would actually improve the breed and this method has been used throughout the plan.

The ideal type and the superb performance of Old Sorrel under the saddle led his owners to use him extensively in their breeding plans. The manner in which he transmitted his good qualities to his descendants, showing his great prepotency, made it seem advisable to perpetuate these qualities through a carefully planned and controlled experiment in linebreeding and inbreeding. They were fully aware that not every exceptional sire has a balance of genetic qualities which will stand the test of close inbreeding without disaster. The only way in which this could be determined was by actual trial. He was mated on a few occasions to his best daughters and the results, while encouraging, were not exceptional. But when his son Solis was mated on Old Sorrel's daughters the results were so good that the management decided to try to perpetuate Old Sorrel through linebreeding and inbreeding.*

---

*A. O. Rhoad and R. J. Kleberg, Jr., "The Development of a Superior Family in the Modern Quarter Horse," *The Journal of Heredity*, Vol. 37 (August, 1946), pp. 228-233.

In 1940, after the King Ranch had been working on its Quarter Horse breeding plan for about twenty years, the American Quarter Horse Association was organized by a group of progressive Quarter Horse breeders. This association has accomplished much in the tabulation of bloodlines, maintenance of records, research, registration of transfers and the dissemination of information through its journal. It also writes rules for shows, racing events and rodeos.

To be entitled to Tentative Registry with the association a horse is required to qualify on three cardinal points: Pedigree, conformation and performance. Horses are not eligible for registration until two years from the date of foaling. Horses are advanced from the Tentative Registry to the Permanent Registry by siring twelve get or foaling three colts which have been awarded registry in the Tentative Registry.

The first meeting of the American Quarter Horse Association was held during the 1940 Southwestern Exposition and Fat Stock Show in Fort Worth. During that meeting it was decided to issue the first registration number in the association's first stud book to the stallion winning the stock show the following year. In 1941 the King Ranch's Wimpy, a double grandson of Old Sorrel, won this honor.

In writing on "The Mission and Place of the Quarter Horse in America" for the association's first stud book, Robert J. Kleberg, Jr., said:

If the range live stock men of America were asked to select the horse that is the most useful for their purpose and that had contributed the most pleasure and satisfaction to their lives, I believe that they would select the Quarter Horse, or the cross of the Quarter Horse on the Thoroughbred that has retained Quarter Horse conformation. If asked to give their reasons for this choice they would say, "Our horses have to live on the range and rely on the native shrubs and grasses for their food. The Quarter Horse takes on and carries enough flesh and muscle to stand the hard work that is required of him. He has a good, quiet disposition, is easy to gentle and train, has extreme early speed and the strength and sure footedness to carry heavy weight over any kind of country. He stops and turns easily and does not become leg weary or lazy even when asked to stop and start quickly many times in the course of the day's roping, cutting or other work."

On the average the Quarter Horse has the most symmetrical and muscular conformation coupled with the most perfect balance of any of the breeds. Good representatives of this breed are among the most beautiful of horses. Since these are the qualities desired in any type of riding horse the Quarter Horse makes an ideal foundation on which to cross the Thoroughbred or any other breed of horses used for riding.

Top cow horses are scarce and closely held. The ranchman is so jealous of these mounts that he is reluctant to see anyone but himself ride them and in only a few instances have they been allowed to leave the home ranch. For this reason their virtues are little known to the average horseman. Quarter Horses furnish the best of these and in order to preserve, increase and give the riding public a better understanding of this wonderful breed, the American Quarter Horse Association has been formed.

PRINCIPAL SHOW WINNINGS OF KING RANCH QUARTER HORSES
Compiled by the American Quarter Horse Association

WIMPY P-1, *by Solis*

1941 — *Grand Champion Stallion:* Fort Worth.

BILL CODY P-3244
by Wimpy

1950 — *Grand Champion Stallion:* Cisco, Sonora, Dallas, Uvalde, Beeville.

1951 — *Grand Champion Stallion:* Fort Worth; Santa Barbara, California; Dallas; Beeville.
First Place, Get of Sire: Waco.

1952 — *Grand Champion Stallion:* Odessa; Amarillo; Vernon; Albuquerque, New Mexico; Stamford; Olney; Enid, Oklahoma; Post; Fort Worth.
First Place, Get of Sire: Gladewater.

1952 — *Reserve Champion Stallion:* Lubbock, Amarillo.

1953 — *Grand Champion Stallion:* Houston, Amarillo.

1953 — *Reserve Champion Stallion:* Denver, Colorado.

1954 — *Grand Champion Stallion:* San Angelo.

1954 — *Reserve Champion Stallion:* Denver, Colorado.

1955 — *Grand Champion Stallion:* San Antonio.

MISS BEA* #16,060
by Bill Cody

1948 — *Reserve Champion Mare:* Stephenville.

1949 — *Reserve Champion Mare:* Pampa; Killeen; Kansas City, Missouri.
Grand Champion Mare: Breckenridge; Pomona, California; Weatherford; Bridgeport; Fort Worth Horseshoe Club; Wharton; Beeville.

1950 — *Grand Champion Mare:* San Antonio.

*Purchased by the King Ranch and later shown under King Ranch colors.

[735]

Miss V. O. H. #41,989 *by Bill Cody*	1950 — *Grand Champion Mare:* Killeen, Stephenville. 1951 — *Grand Champion Mare:* Raton, New Mexico. 1952 — *Grand Champion Mare:* Denver, Colorado.
Lee Cody #31,328 *by Bill Cody*	1952 — *Grand Champion Stallion:* Lubbock, Dallas. 1953 — *Reserve Champion Stallion:* Waco. *Grand Champion Stallion:* Temple, Gladewater. 1954 — *Grand Champion Stallion:* Wharton, Waco, Beeville.
King Cody p-43,801 *by Bill Cody*	1954 — *Grand Champion Stallion:* Angleton.
J. B. Cody p-28,102 *by Bill Cody*	1953 — *Grand Champion Stallion:* Marksville, Louisiana.
Joe Cody p-42,543 *by Bill Cody*	1954 — *Reserve Champion Stallion:* Gladewater.

Town Crier p-37,463
by Bill Cody
	1953 — *Reserve Champion Stallion:* Olney, Weatherford.
	    Grand Champion Stallion: Valley Mills.
	1954 — *Reserve Champion Stallion:* Post, Stamford.
	    Grand Champion Stallion: Temple, Haskell, Fort Worth.
	1955 — *Reserve Champion Stallion:* Houston, Amarillo, San Antonio.
	    Grand Champion Stallion: McKinney.

King Ranch Squaw #15,914 *by Wimpy*	1949 — *Reserve Champion Mare:* Houston; Pacific Coast Quarter Horse Assn. Show. *Grand Champion Mare:* Kleberg County, Johnson County.
Little Wimpy p-2412 *by Wimpy*	1949 — *First Place, Get of Sire:* El Paso.
Candy K. p-17,300 *by Wimpy*	1950 — *Grand Champion Horse:* San Angelo.
Chipper Wimpy p-29,926 *by Wimpy*	1951 — *Reserve Champion Stallion:* Saginaw, Michigan.
Showdown p-33,178 *by Wimpy*	1954 — *Grand Champion Stallion:* Clovis and Albuquerque, New Mexico.
Wimpy's Redman p-27,244 *by Wimpy*	1954 — *Reserve Champion Gelding:* Dallas, Fort Worth.
Escalera p-37,035 *by Wimpy*	1954 — *First in Class:* Valley Mills.
Dawson's Surprise p-32,296 *by Wimpy II* *by Wimpy*	1954 — *Grand Champion Mare:* Huxley.

REY DEL RANCHO P-7340   1951 — *First Place, Get of Sire:* Olney, Stamford, Dallas,
   by Ranchero   Bridgeport.
   by Solis

DALENE #29,156   1951 — *Reserve Champion Mare:* Odessa, Fort Worth.
   by Rey del Rancho   *Grand Champion Mare:* Vineyard, Amarillo.
                       1952 — *Reserve Champion Mare:* Fort Worth.

REY DEL POBLANO P-31,740   1951 — *Reserve Champion Stallion:* Chicago, Illinois.
   (CUBAN BROWN)   *Grand Champion Stallion:* Dallas, Bridgeport.
   by Rey del Rancho   1952 — *Grand Champion Stallion:* Fort Worth.

HIJO DEL REY P-28,909   1951 — *Reserve Champion Stallion:* Dallas, Amarillo.
   (CUBAN RED)
   by Rey del Rancho

CANADA'S KING P-28,908   1953 — *Grand Champion Stallion:* Liberty.
   by Rey del Rancho

TEE BAR HITONE #41,147   1954 — *Reserve Champion Stallion:* Havre, Montana.
   by Rey del Rancho

HIRED HAND P-2495   1948 — *Grand Champion Stallion:* Dallas.
   by Old Sorrel   1949 — *Reserve Champion Stallion:* Beeville.
                       Grand Champion Stallion: Houston, Kingsville.

LITTLE HIRED HAND P-15,790 1951 — *Grand Champion Stallion:* Portland, Oregon.
   by Hired Hand

STRAWBOSS T. P-19,874   1950 — *Reserve Champion Stallion:* Dallas; Omaha,
   by Hired Hand   Nebraska.

HIRED HAND'S CARDINAL   1953 — *Grand Champion Stallion:* Keller.
   P-38,194
   by Hired Hand

SILVER KING P-183   1950 — *First Place, Get of Sire:* Reno, Nevada; Fresno, Calif.
   by Old Sorrel   1951 — *First Place, Get of Sire:* Reno, Nevada.
                       1952 — *First Place, Get of Sire:* Reno, Nevada.

SCOOTER S. P-5000   1950 — *Reserve Champion Stallion:* San Angelo, Ozona.
   by Silver King

DOUBLE DIAMOND P-13,335   1951 — *Grand Champion Stallion:* Bozeman, Montana.
   by Silver King

DIAMOND GINGER MAY   1951 — *Reserve Champion Mare:* Pendleton, Oregon.
   P-20,740   *Grand Champion Mare:* Reno, Nevada.
   by Silver King   1952 — *Grand Champion Mare:* Reno, Nevada; Los Angeles,
                       California; Eureka, California.

DIAMOND SPARKLE P-20,619
    by Silver King

1950 — *Grand Champion Mare:* Pendleton, Oregon.

SILVER PRINCE P-9805
    by Silver King

1950 — *Reserve Champion Stallion:* Amarillo.

DIAMOND PEPPER P-32,741
    by Silver King

1952 — *Reserve Champion Mare:* Portland, Oregon.

LITTLE MAN P-1438
    by Old Sorrel

1948 — *Reserve Champion Stallion:* Dallas.

STRAWBERRY K. P-15,915
    by Little Man

1949 — *Reserve Champion Mare:* Breckenridge, Pacific Coast Quarter Horse Assn. Show, Stamford, Wise County, Fort Worth Horseshoe Club, Johnson County, Kingsville, Beeville.
1950 — *Grand Champion Mare:* Fort Worth.

MACANUDO P-211
    by Old Sorrel

1940 — *Grand Champion Stallion:* Kingsville.

BABE MAC C. P-13,014
    by Macanudo

1947 — *Grand Champion Stallion:* Odessa.
1949 — *Grand Champion Stallion:* Fort Worth, Odessa, El Paso.
1950 — *Grand Champion Stallion:* El Paso, Fort Worth.
    Reserve Champion Stallion: Odessa, Houston.
1951 — *Grand Champion Stallion:* Odessa, Amarillo.
1952 — *Grand Champion Stallion:* Monahans.
1953 — *Grand Champion Stallion:* Waco.
    Reserve Champion Stallion: Vineyard.
1954 — *Grand Champion Stallion:* Ozona, Pecos, Post.
    Reserve Champion Stallion: Monahans.

NEVA MAC #48,940
    by Babe Mac C.

1954 — *Reserve Champion Mare:* Post.

SNIP COLE #37,289
    by Babe Mac C.

1954 — *Grand Champion Gelding:* Fort Worth.
    Reserve Champion Gelding: Waco, Dallas.
1955 — *Grand Champion Gelding:* Fort Worth.

HICKORY RED P-2988
    by Macanudo

1948 — *Reserve Champion Stallion:* Amarillo.
1949 — *Grand Champion Stallion:* Amarillo, Paducah, Plainview, Floydada.
    Reserve Champion Stallion: Vernon.
1950 — *Grand Champion Stallion:* Amarillo.
1951 — *Reserve Champion Stallion:* Denver, Colorado.

[738]

MACANUDO MAN P-45,159 *by Macanudo*	1954 — *Grand Champion Gelding:* Wharton. *First in Roping:* Wharton.
LA FLOR K. #6450 *by Macanudo*	1951 — *First Place, Produce of Dam:* Bridgeport.
FLYING ANGEL #21,845 *by Kingwood*	1953 — *Reserve Champion Mare:* Amarillo.
BIG RED BARTON P-14,600 *by Chamaco*	1949 — *Grand Champion Stallion:* Killeen. 1952 — *Grand Champion Stallion:* Waco.
SUSIE BABE K. P-7701 *by Babe Grande*	1948 — *Grand Champion Mare:* Jacksboro. 1949 — *Grand Champion Mare:* Kansas City, Missouri; Erath County. *Reserve Champion Mare:* Wharton. 1950 — *Reserve Champion Mare:* San Antonio.
PEPPY P-212 *by Little Richard*	1941 — *Champion Cow Horse:* Tucson, Arizona. *Grand Champion Stallion:* Tucson, Arizona. *Best Horse in Show:* Tucson, Arizona.
SIR PEPPY #4000 *by Peppy*	1948 — *Reserve Champion Stallion:* Woodward, Oklahoma.
PEPPY'S POKEY P-13,691 *by Peppy*	1948 — *Grand Champion Stallion:* Denver, Colorado. 1950 — *Grand Champion Stallion:* Denver, Colorado; Amarillo.
RED BEAVER #12,721 *by Red Ryder*	1951 — *Grand Champion Stallion:* Lubbock, Cisco. *Reserve Champion Stallion:* Olney, Stamford, San Angelo, Coleman. 1952 — *Grand Champion Stallion:* Kansas City, Missouri; Fort Worth. *Reserve Champion Stallion:* Santa Barbara, Calif. 1953 — *Reserve Champion Stallion:* Tucson, Arizona. 1954 — *Grand Champion Stallion:* Emmett, Idaho.
COWBOY H. P-1544 *by Peppy*	1949 — *First Place, Get of Sire:* Fort Worth, Vernon. 1950 — *First Place, Get of Sire:* Fort Worth.
HOT SHOT B. P-4066 *by Cowboy H.*	1950 — *Reserve Champion Stallion:* Fort Worth. *Grand Champion Stallion:* Paducah. 1953 — *Grand Champion Stallion:* Vernon. 1954 — *Grand Champion Stallion:* Paducah.
LITTLE PEGGY H. P-12,765 *by Cowboy H.*	1949 — *Grand Champion Mare:* Vernon, Pampa, Stamford, Amarillo, Fort Worth.

RANCH THOROUGHBREDS AND THEIR WINNINGS

FOLLOWING IS A LIST of the best horses bred or owned by the King Ranch, the principal stake races or handicaps they have won, and their total winnings. Horses winning less than a total of $20,000 have not been included.

Horse	Total Winnings
STYMIE	$918,485

ASSAULT 672,500

1945 — Flash Stakes

1946 — Experimental Free Handicap
Wood Memorial
Kentucky Derby
Preakness Stakes
Belmont Stakes
Dwyer Stakes
Pimlico Special
Westchester Handicap

1947 — Grey Lag Handicap
Dixie Handicap
Brooklyn Handicap
Butler Handicap

1949 — Brooklyn Handicap

REJECTED 544,000

1953 — Westerner Stakes
Oakland Handicap

1954 — Santa Anita Handicap
American Handicap
Hawthorne Gold Cup

1955 — San Pasqual Handicap
Hollywood Gold Cup

HIGH GUN 486,025

1954 — Peter Pan Handicap
Belmont Stakes
Dwyer Stakes
Sysonby Stakes
Manhattan Handicap
Jockey Club Gold Cup

1955 — Metropolitan Handicap
Brooklyn Handicap
Sysonby Stakes

TO MARKET 387,325

1950 — Arlington Futurity
Washington Park Futurity

1952 — Arlington Handicap
Hawthorne Gold Cup
Massachusetts Handicap

BETTER SELF 383,925

1947 — East View Stakes
Saratoga Special

1948 — Discovery Handicap
Paumonok Handicap
Westchester Handicap
Yankee Handicap

1949 — All-American Handicap
Carter Handicap

1950 — Gallant Fox Handicap
Saratoga Handicap

Horse	Total Winnings	Horse	Total Winnings

BUT WHY NOT 295,155
    1947 — Acorn Stakes
        Alabama Stakes
        Beldame Handicap (2nd Div.)
        Arlington Classic Stakes
        Arlington Matron Handicap
        Pimlico Oaks
    1949 — Firenze Handicap
        Top Flight Handicap

CURANDERO 238,725
    1951 — Equipoise Mile Handicap

MIDDLEGROUND 237,725
    1949 — Hopeful Stakes
    1950 — Kentucky Derby
        Belmont Stakes

BRIDAL FLOWER 222,055
    1947 — Lady Baltimore Handicap
        Regret Handicap
        Westchester Handicap

HIGH SCUD 167,450
    1952 — Kent Stakes
    1954 — Inglewood Handicap

FLASHBURN 124,060
    1946 — Diamond State Stakes
    1947 — Gittings Handicap
    1948 — Omnibus Handicap

MARCADOR 110,425
    1952 — Butler Handicap
        Golden Gate Derby
        Oakland Handicap

FLYING MISSEL 97,687
    1949 — Daingerfield Handicap
        Sussex Handicap

OCEAN BRIEF 93,700
    1949 — Camden Handicap
        Colonial Handicap
        Correction Handicap

RENEW 91,005
    1951 — Firenze Handicap
    1952 — Top Flight Handicap

SONIC 81,737

SCATTERED 80,275
    1948 — Coaching Club American Oaks
        Pimlico Oaks

KINSMAN 80,187

INCLINE 73,630

SAFE ARRIVAL 71,085

TASK 65,430

ON YOUR OWN 60,725
    1954 — Betsy Ross Stakes
        Gazelle Stakes

CONTRADICTION 57,000

DISPOSE 56,500
    1941 — Flamingo Stakes
        Bahamas Handicap

CIENCIA 54,505
    1939 — Santa Anita Derby

TUZADO 53,200

DAWN PLAY 50,800
    1937 — Acorn Stakes
        American Derby
        Coaching Club American Oaks

BEE ANN MAC 46,480
    1946 — Selima Stakes

BEE MAC 44,900

RIVERINA 44,750

DONITA'S FIRST 43,656

PROPHET'S THUMB . . . 43,200

CONTEST 39,575

INSCOELDA 38,970

FREE PRESS 37,100

DINNER DATE 35,900

Horse	Total Winnings	Horse	Total Winnings
SALVO	35,135	ISLAY MIST	24,110
SUN LADY	32,485	TOP BRASS	23,636
MARKET LEVEL	32,380	MAC	23,175
MAC BEA	29,675	CLEAN SLATE . . .	22,950
HAUNTED	27,975	ON THE MARK	22,725
TASAJILLO	26,405	SUFIE	22,375
TILLY ROSE	25,017	BLACKIE II (Argentina) Pesos 190,367	

In the above list are two Kentucky Derby* winners, one of which was Assault who won the Triple Crown consisting of the Kentucky Derby, the Preakness and the Belmont Stakes. Among the winnings of King Ranch Thoroughbreds are:

3 Belmont Stakes
3 Brooklyn Handicaps
3 Coaching Club
   American Oaks
2 Butler Handicaps
2 Dwyer Stakes
2 Kentucky Derbies

2 Sysonby Stakes
1 Alabama Stakes
1 American Derby
1 Arlington Classic
1 Hopeful Stakes
1 Jockey Club Gold Cup
1 Manhattan Handicap

1 Pimlico Special
1 Preakness Stakes
1 Santa Anita Derby
1 Santa Anita Handicap
1 Selima Stakes
1 Suburban Handicap
1 Wood Memorial

King Ranch Standing on List of Leading Money-Winning Owners†

Year	Place on List	NUMBER OF WINS			Total Winnings
		1st	2nd	3rd	
1946	2	32	19	18	$504,820
1947	2	56	46	29	729,200
1948	2	51	50	46	490,832
1949	3	68	43	48	516,785
1950	4	47	34	47	464,994
1951	6	44	32	28	342,532
1952	3	56	41	55	563,555
1953	11	54	39	38	327,360
1954	1	31	52	29	837,615
1955	5	32	36	24	474,330

* The King Ranch owns Bold Venture, the only horse to win the Kentucky Derby and sire two sons who won it, Assault and Middleground.

† Compiled by *The Blood-Horse*, Lexington, Kentucky.

THE GRASS PROGRAM

by ROBERT J. KLEBERG *and* NICO DÍAZ

As told to FRANCIS L. FUGATE

BEEF CATTLE RANCHING, reduced to its essence, can be thought of in terms of producing the most grass possible—of acceptable quality—in a given area, then harvesting this grass with livestock which are adapted to the climate and which will show the highest efficiency both in rate of gain and quality of carcass.

No rancher can escape the importance of grass in making beef. The problem of finding grasses which would thrive under the adverse climatic conditions of the area was equal or greater in urgency to the problem of developing a breed of cattle to fit the country. Until the advent of the Santa Gertrudis breed, the ranch's cattle improvement program used already existing breeds of beef cattle. Of course, it was necessary to develop hardy animals of these breeds and to establish them in their new environment on the King Ranch.

It is significant that grass experimentation on the King Ranch started many years before the development of its new breed of cattle. The grass problem cannot be solved by a single solution or approached from a single direction; it must be attacked vigorously from several directions, each of which evolves into new and separate problems.

The land must be plowed with a root plow in order to rid it of mesquite and underbrush. The root plow breaks up the packed soil to a depth of twenty inches, but does not turn under the topsoil or existing grasses. After plowing, spreader dams and terraces are put in where indicated. Grasses must be found or developed which have the hardiness to spread and invade existing species under natural grazing conditions, and the grasses should have high nutritive value. This search involves the conducting of scientific experiments in the hope of providing improved species. One example is the changing, through scientific techniques, of the chromosome counts in order to permit the crossbreeding of certain species that otherwise could not be crossed because of different chromosome numbers. Fertilizer policies must be determined, which raises such questions as whether to use fertilizer and trace minerals on existing grasses or to add them at the time of sowing seed from introduced grass species.

At no point in the grass program are these separate problems, distinct from one another; they are entwined to the point that the whole problem becomes increasingly complex simply because of the many possible combinations of the problem's parts. Then, in the final analysis, no matter how much research and how much experimentation, the only real test of a range forage is practical trial under ranching conditions.

Prior to the turn of the century, Robert J. Kleberg, Sr., began testing grass. During the period from 1900 to 1925 an "introductory garden, trying new grasses and legumes," was maintained. The first really important step in range improvement was accomplished by the introduction of Rhodes grass (*Chloris gayana*). This was undoubtedly the most spectacular experiment, the most successful—and eventually the most troublesome.

Rhodes grass, well known as a native of South Africa, was cultivated by Cecil Rhodes in 1895. It was introduced into the United States by the Department of Agriculture in 1902. About 1912 Mr. Kleberg saw demonstration plantings of Rhodes grass— lush, waist-high stands of leafy, running grass that would capture the immediate attention of any cattleman.

Rhodes grass is a multipurpose grass suitable for pasture, hay, silage or seed. It seeds freely, producing clusters of from ten to twenty spikes, three to four inches long, at the top of the stem. It is a perennial with slender, erect stems, three to four feet tall with long blades. Numerous runners, often six to eight feet in length, take root at every joint which rests on the ground. These runners soon cover bare spots of considerable size, even when the original stand is thin, establishing a constant succession of vigorous, productive new plants.

Plantings of Rhodes grass were made on the King Ranch as a result of its having been brought to Mr. Kleberg's attention. But since little knowledge existed of just how to plant this new grass, uniform stands were not produced from the first planting. However, sufficient grass was available to test its grazing value, and it was given an extremely severe test on survival grazing. The grass had only been established about two years when it was subjected to the drought conditions of 1916-1918, the severest drought on the ranch up to this time. The grass came back more rapidly and more luxuriantly when the drought was broken than any of the native grasses. Consequently the ranch

was immediately interested in giving Rhodes grass a serious trial. Careful study developed a program for planting which turned out to be highly successful. Robert J. Kleberg, Jr., and Worth Wright, the ranch's farm manager, prepared planting instructions which were widely circulated.

The first plantings were made progressively on 17,000 acres of land around the headquarters division. At the time these plantings were started, these pastures were the most highly improved pastures of the entire ranch. The improvements had been made by hand-grubbing the land, allowing native grass species to establish themselves, and then exercising care to determine the proper stocking rate. The progressive improvement is illustrated by the land's increasing carrying capacity.

The native brush land would carry approximately one head to twenty-five acres. When cleared by hand and properly grazed, this land's capacity was increased to one animal to six acres. When planted to Rhodes grass, these same pastures would carry one animal to three acres. The dramatic potentiality of the new grass—not for the King Ranch alone but for the entire area—can be seen by application of the theory that ranching land is worth twice as much as the cattle it will carry.*

* This theory applies the following formula to determine the current value of ranching land:

$$2 \times \frac{\text{market value of cattle per head}}{\text{acreage required to carry a head}} = \frac{\text{per-acre}}{\text{land value}}$$

For example, if a given piece of ranching land will carry one head to fifteen acres, and the current price of beef is 8¢ to 10¢ per pound on the hoof, a 900-pound animal would bring from $72 to $90. Therefore, the land would be worth from $9.60 to $12 per acre.

$$2 \times \frac{\$72}{15} = \$9.60 \qquad 2 \times \frac{\$90}{15} = \$12$$

Such stands of grass were a living, producing fact, there for everyone to see. So far as is known this was the first large-scale pasture improvement effort under ranching conditions in the Southwest. Rhodes grass became popular in short order, perhaps the most popular grass ever planted on South Texas ranges. It seemed to be the answer to a rancher's prayer; it was cited as "the wonder grass" of South Texas.

Once the King Ranch had developed all of its cleared lands with Rhodes grass the management was so encouraged with the results that efforts on land clearing, erosion control, deep root plowing for retention of water and other pasture improvement activities were greatly intensified with the idea of properly preparing more land in order to expand the Rhodes grass pasture development program.

At the height of this program the King Ranch had more than 75,000 acres of Rhodes grass. The ranch was fattening its own steers and spayed heifers on its own properties, whereas it had formerly been necessary during many seasons to ship stocker cattle to pastures in West Texas or the fattening areas of Oklahoma and Kansas. Rhodes grass caused the ranch to make one of its major operational changes: conversion from producing stocker cattle for others to fattening all of its own cattle at the ranch.

Rhodes grass was used effectively from about 1915 to the fall of 1942, more than twenty-five years. It was well on its way to making it possible for South Texas to compare favorably with any of the best developed grazing areas in the world. As a grass that flourished under the severest climatic conditions and under all rigors of grazing conditions, Rhodes grass was a proven answer. But ranching and most range improvement programs are bound to have a great many disappointments. The King Ranch was soon to suffer the most severe reversal in its pasture improvement program.

The first hint of trouble developed in 1940. Normally Rhodes grass plantings had lasted indefinitely, but by 1940 it was noticeable that pastures were not lasting well. The difficulty persisted and increased. In 1942 the reason was pinpointed. On November 26 and 27, Nico Díaz, an agronomist with the Soil Conservation Service, was making an evaluation survey of research plantings near the Texas College of Arts and Industries in Kingsville. He found that Rhodes grass and perennial sudan were badly infested with a minute parasitic insect, a grass scale which was attacking the basal crown and nodes of the host grasses.

Specimens were supplied to the Bureau of Entomology and Plant Quarantine, United States Department of Agriculture, and on December 17 the scale was identified by Dr. Harold M. Morrison, Division of Insect Identification, as *Antonina graminis*. This was the first discovery of this species of scale on the North or South American continents. *Antonina graminis* was first identified in China in 1897. How it got to South Texas was never definitely established. One supposition was that the scale came to this country in packing material used to protect chinaware during shipment from Japan to the United States.

Within the space of two short years this parasitic scale had virtually wiped out all of the King Ranch's long standing and vast areas of Rhodes grass. Areas that had been lush pastures were reduced to barren stretches containing a few yellowing patches. In other words, the King Ranch was back again to native grasses and with an added danger—in fact, with visible evidence of that danger—that the scale was attacking a good many species of native grasses. *Antonina graminis* was eventually found in sixty-three Texas counties and on seventy-four species of grass, although Rhodes grass was by far the most susceptible host. The immediate question was not how the scale got to South Texas but how to get rid of it.

The King Ranch made a grant of $10,000 to the Texas Agricultural Experiment Station at Texas A. & M. College for the purpose of carrying on an intensive research program to find means of controlling or eradicating the scale which, having taken such a heavy toll of Rhodes grass pastures, was now moving on to other species at an alarming pace. Biological control studies of the scale were started in 1949 at the Lower Rio Grande Valley Experiment Station at Weslaco. Dr. Paul T. Riherd, a hard-working entomologist, was in charge of the work. He was joined by Dr. H. L. Chada, an entomologist from the Bureau of Entomology and Plant Quarantine, United States Department of Agriculture.

Everything in Nature's jungle has its enemy; the devastating scale was no exception. A small wasp-like parasite, known to scientists as *Anagyrus antoninae*, had been discovered some years before and was used in Hawaii in controlling this same scale on sugar cane plantations. The life cycle of the parasite which was to be enlisted against the Rhodes grass scale is about twenty days, and a female will lay approximately fifty eggs during that period. The problem was to prepare a vast army. Dr. Riherd was soon propagating 20,000 a month in the Weslaco laboratories.

Drought interfered with initial experiments, but enough host plants were grown in irrigated areas to indicate that during a period of normal rainfall the imported parasites would probably make it possible to use Rhodes grass in dryland pastures once more. In addition attempts are under way to cross Rhodes grass with a scale resistant species of native grass.

In spite of the disaster which overtook this first large scale improvement of rangeland by grass farming, there was a large dividend: The King Ranch's Rhodes grass program aroused a continuing interest in ranchland improvement which has spread over the entire South Texas area. With the clearing of land and the planting of Rhodes grass, ranching broke away from the old tradition of letting Nature take care of the range and hoping for rain.

As the difficulties with Rhodes grass developed, the King Ranch entered into its program of improving range grasses with new vigor. Not long before, the Department of Agriculture had started some grass nursery work at the Texas College of Arts and Industries in Kingsville, and a great many species of grass were being tried. Knowing that it is impossible to make an adequate evaluation of range grasses under nursery conditions—that the only real test is actual trial under grazing conditions—the King Ranch employed Nico Díaz in 1943. He was an outstanding authority on grasses and range management with sixteen years of previous experience with the Bureau of Plant Industry and the Soil Conservation Service.

The King Ranch, the Department of Agriculture, and Texas College of Arts and Industries then entered into an agreement. Under the terms of this agreement, the ranch would provide two hundred acres of land and plant grass seeds which had been collected from the college's nursery plots. Seeds from these plantings were to be harvested by the college and the Department of Agriculture for their use. After a period of two years the experimental plantings became the property of the ranch so that they could be subjected to grazing in order to determine which species of grass were best under normal grazing usage.

It was planned to add to these plantings at the rate of two hundred acres per year as long as the plan was successful. However, the United States became involved in World War II, and the plantings could not be kept up. Out of the initial trials, only two grasses were found which would stand the grazing test: Slender grama (*Bouteloua filiformis*) and Kleberg bluestem (*Andropogon annulatus*).

Graphic and drastic lessons had taught that a definite line of research is necessary to discover proper grasses for South Texas conditions. It was about this time, 1944, that the King Ranch management definitely gave up the idea of protecting delicate grasses which would not stand grazing and committed the ranch to roughly the same course which had been followed in its cattle improvement program. The grass program would be directed toward finding grasses more suitable to the severe climate and to other conditions unique to the area, and toward attempting various crossbreeding experiments with grasses. The ranch would enlist the aid of available scientific groups in the effort to find a grass as good or better than Rhodes grass which would be suited to the exact environment.

Mr. Díaz intensified his studies of grasses which he thought could be useful in this area. In 1944 he discovered the grass which is called "Kleberg bluestem." It was found growing on the ranch along the roadside near an abandoned grass nursery. At first it was thought to be Angleton grass (*Andropogon nodosus*); however, close study revealed differences between the two species, and it was eventually given the official scientific name *Andropogon annulatus*, Kleberg bluestem. Kleberg County seemed to be the only place in the United States where the species was to be found. Out of cultivated plantings other plantings were made and seed was harvested. Kleberg bluestem seemed to be invading other native grasses without any help; it was free of the scale that had destroyed Rhodes grass; it was standing up well under severe grazing. It has since proved itself to be one of the best-adapted forage grasses in South Texas. Thousands of acres of the King Ranch have been seeded with it.

In 1939, while with the Soil Conservation Service, Mr. Díaz had discovered another strain of grass on the ranch which would become known as King Ranch bluestem (*Andropogon ischaemum*), commonly called "KR bluestem." This grass was found growing on the Santa Gertrudis Division. Ranch employees reported that they had known the grass to be on the ranch for at least thirty-five years, and that it possibly started from a plot of introduced grasses which had been planted many years before near the ranch dairy barn.

The Soil Conservation Service conducted a ten-year period of tests and then summed up the qualities and advantages of KR bluestem:

A deep-rooted perennial, mid-tall, semi-prostrate tufted grass; drought resistant, cold resistant, quick to respond to moisture; erosion resisting and adapted to wide extremes of rainfall; well suited to soils ranging from acid to alkaline and from deep sand to tight clays; palatable and nutritious to livestock and suitable for hay; capable of surviving severe burning in droughty periods; a continuous seed producer from late spring through early summer, and throughout the fall to killing frost; well suited to seeding areas that cannot be planted by machine, because the seed germinates well without being covered; capable of producing good stands in one season on good soils when properly handled; capable of making good cover the second year if stand is thin or weed competition severe the first year; capable of spreading rapidly against stiff competition.

The report hastened to add that though KR bluestem is useful in many locations it is not a "cure-all" grass. It is susceptible, at intervals, to rust at low altitudes. A rust resistant strain is needed for the King Ranch area.

Work which has been carried on with KR bluestem illustrates the nature of the problems which face a grass management program. Various aspects of KR bluestem have been studied in the hope that this important imported species could be crossed with a native bluestem to combine its high nutritive value with the desirable characteristics of a native grass. So far, however, attempts at hybridization have been unsuccessful because KR bluestem is apparently apomictic —it is asexual. In addition, the species with which it would be most desirable to make the cross, Bristle-joint bluestem (*A. barbinodis*), is cleistogamous, that is, its flowers do not open.

Several important grasses have been found suitable to the King Ranch area. Besides Kleberg bluestem and KR bluestem, these include Coastal and Giant Bermuda. Two strains of another new grass, Caesar grass (*Urochloa tricophus*), are undergoing tests and offer promise.

Grasses on the ranch are divided into two general classes, imported (or improved) and native. In the first class are such grasses

as Rhodes grass, Kleberg bluestem, KR bluestem, Bermuda (*Cynodon dactylon*) and Coastal Bermuda (*Cynodon* species). In the second group are Seacoast bluestem (*Andropogon littoralis*), Sandhill grass (*Brachiaria ciliatissima*) and Sacahuiste (*Spartina spartinae*) on sandy soils, while on mixed and black soils are Curly mesquite (*Hilaria belangeri*), Buffalo grass (*Buchloe dactyloides*), Plains bristle (*Setaria macrostachya*), Texas grama (*Bouteloua rigidiseta*), Hooded finger (*Chloris cucullata*) False Rhodes (*Trichloris mendocina*) and others.

At the present time the King Ranch grass program follows a general procedure of first properly preparing the land by clearing away the brush, simultaneously plowing with the root plow and sowing grasses that have proven their ability to survive and produce large quantities of forage under prevailing conditions and that tend to invade the natural pastures. The deep plowing of the land increases its water holding capacity. In addition, spreader dams and large terraces are used. These must be substantial enough that cattle trails will not destroy them. Finally, the program includes the appeal to science and research to determine, among other things, just what fertilizers and trace minerals can be profitably used.

The ranch carries on extensive plantings of grass mixtures on land that is being cleared of brush. As the clearing machines knock down brush on the pasture, a mixture, for example, of Buffel grass (*Pennisetum ciliare*), Blue panic (*Panicum antidotale*), Rhodes grass, KR bluestem and Kleberg bluestem is sown behind the tractors at the rate of two pounds per acre. It is hoped that out of these widespread experimental plantings of mixtures will come a successful combination of grasses which, along with native grasses, will provide an abundance of grazing.

Grass is of use to a rancher in direct ratio to its ability to grow and its nutritive value. In an area such as South Texas it must be drought resistant. In order to produce beef profitably it must have a high nutritive value, largely a matter of its chemical composition. The ranch has participated in a great deal of research to determine the chemical compositions of various grasses and how a chemical composition differs in relationship to soil type, as well as how the grass responds to the application of fertilizers.

In its pasture improvement program, the ranch has applied fertilizers to large areas. Superphosphate has been applied to rangelands using both ground equipment and airplanes. A twenty per cent superphosphate is generally applied with ground equipment; a forty-five per cent has been applied by planes. Application of phosphorus to rangelands has produced evident improvement in grasses and forbs,* especially on sandy areas of the ranch. At the same time, cattle show a preference for grazing on fertilized ranges; their condition improves and the size of the calf crop increases.†

A new line of thinking has been developed on the ranch in regard to trace minerals, principally by Mr. Díaz, as a result of the long period of experimentation. In introducing new plants, especially legumes that should be adapted to the climatic conditions of the area, it is often necessary to accompany test plantings with fertilizers and trace minerals. Then when any plants, particularly legumes, are tried again and do not do well without added fertilizers and trace minerals, indications are that the application of molybdenum, zinc and copper will make it possible for them to grow and make seed. However, in general, it has been found that when fertilizers and trace minerals are used on native plantings many of them show little response. Native plants have already demonstrated their ability to survive and do well under existing soil fertility conditions.

The ranch has worked out a "checkerboard" test plot. Over this plot various combinations of "minor minerals" have been applied in squares; then the entire area has been seeded with a mixture of grass and legume seed. When the tests are completed the results will show what mineral or what combination of minerals will produce the greatest and most vigorous growth or adaptation.

The ranch's grass program is closely coordinated with the brush-clearing operation‡ and the game conservation and management program.§ The effect of brush clearing is showing encouraging results, although the abnormally dry weather during the past several years has made final appraisal impossible. On land that had been cleared and root plowed prior to the big rains which fell in September, 1951, native grasses have recovered to a better stand than prior to brush control.

The stocking rate on ranges is carefully regulated as part of the ranch's range improvement program. Although the stocking rate will necessarily vary with rainfall, generally it is twenty acres per animal unit on brush pastures and fifteen acres on prairie

* Forbs are range plants other than those which are classifiable as grasses.

† See Appendix XVII, "Experiments in Supplying Phosphorus Deficiency."

‡ See Appendix XI, "Defense Against Brush Encroachment."

§ See Appendix XVIII, 'Game Conservation and Management."

[749]

pastures. During normal seasons the rate on improved grasses is one animal on from three to four acres.

The ranch management has sponsored grass studies and associated research through grants to such institutions as the University of Texas, the Texas Research Foundation at Renner, Texas A. & M. College, and Texas College of Arts and Industries. Mr. Díaz has worked closely with the institutions and organizations involved in these studies, as well as with other scientists and grass specialists from all parts of the world.

Projects at the University of Texas, under the direction of Dr. W. Gordon Whaley, included distribution studies: an inventory and characterization of Texas grasses, which divided the state according to vegetational areas, correlated the distribution of grasses with soil and climate factors, and listed native grasses in order of abundance and relative value for grazing. The results of the study were published in *Texas Range Grasses,* by Benjamin C. Tharp.

A grass collection was made by the University of Texas. It is maintained in an experimental garden at Austin to provide materials for various aspects of grass research. Reproduction studies were made with particular attention to chromosome counts and cytological and reproductive patterns to lay the groundwork for hydridization experiments. Nutrition studies have been conducted on selected species with attention to correlation of nutrient levels of grasses and soil composition and climatic background.

The King Ranch has collaborated with the Texas Research Foundation at Renner since the establishment of the organization in 1944. The Texas Research Foundation started as a department of Southern Methodist University; two years later it was chartered by the state as a nonprofit institution. The foundation is the only agricultural experiment station in the nation supported entirely by private funds. Businessmen, bankers, farmers and ranchers in the Southwest subscribed more than $1,250,000 to a five-year operating fund for the foundation.

The King Ranch became one of the major financial supporters and cooperated in research projects, with the scientific staffs of the ranch and the foundation working side by side during investigations of soil, water and plant problems of interest to ranchers in general and to the King Ranch in particular. It is the policy of the ranch to release findings from such projects as public information.

Projects on which the two institutions have collaborated include establishment and maintenance of grass nurseries at the ranch and at Renner to seek new forage plants that are more adaptable to the rangelands of South Texas; survey of the King Ranch's Cuban properties for the same purpose; analyses of soil, water, forage and other plants for the ranch's livestock programs in South Texas and in Cuba, and for the ranch's wildlife program; evaluation of fertilizers; and exploration of the plant resources of the King Ranch.

In addition to these specific projects, Dr. C. L. Lundell, Director of the Texas Research Foundation, consults periodically with Robert J. Kleberg, Jr., and members of his staff on rangeland problems in the endless search for more practical and effective ranching methods.

The King Ranch has found that—while the Department of Agriculture has done wonderful work in introducing a tremendous variety of new grasses and legumes—

unless introductions are initially made in the areas where their use is intended, some of the most important subspecies are destroyed before they reach the environments where they would have done best. For this reason the foundation at Renner, as a plant introduction area, has started over again with many of the tried species plus a variety of new ones in the hope of still further expanding the grass improvement program on the King Ranch.

As a result of planning initiated in 1949, grass nurseries were established on the ranch by the Texas Research Foundation in 1953. Their purpose is to evaluate grasses and legumes from every quarter of the globe to find species or strains adaptable to the rangeland soils of South Texas and to the profitable production of livestock. Need for such nurseries resulted from the decreasing stands of the principal forage grasses because of disease, insects and drought, plus the ever-present need for new grasses which will attain new high levels of growth and nutrition.

Planted in March, 1953, in the Caesar and Escondida pastures, the nurseries were established on two of the ranch's major soil types—heavy blackland and sandy loam—in accordance with plans drawn by Dr. Lundell and the staff of the foundation. There have been 1712 test plantings on these two soil types under both dryland and irrigated conditions.

Hundreds of grasses and legumes have gone into these nursery tests, as well as into similar trial plots at Renner. In the forage crop introduction program, the cooperation of Dr. J. Clunies Ross, Chairman of the Commonwealth Scientific and Industrial Research Organization of East Melbourne, Australia, has been an outstanding example of unselfish collaboration on an international basis.

The scientific survey of the Cuban properties began in March, 1953, when Dr. Lundell visited the island. The foundation had sent grass seed to Cuba in July, 1952. After Dr. Lundell's visit, the foundation made specific recommendations on grasses and other forage crops, and on fertilizers. By January, 1954, the foundation's analytical laboratories had completed 772 soil and forage analyses for the Cuban project.

Analyses of soils, water, feed and plants have been made to further livestock management and, in some instances, game management programs on the King Ranch. By May, 1955, the foundation had completed a total of 4498 such analyses, including those for Cuba. Plants analyzed from the viewpoint of desirability as livestock and wildlife feed have included mesquite beans and cactus, both problem plants of the Southwest. A seasonal program of prickly pear tests, involving 310 laboratory analyses, was completed during 1953.

Dr. Lundell's botanical exploration of the plant resources of the King Ranch resulted in some notable discoveries of new species of grasses and other plants. Among the grasses are *Leptoloma arenicola,* the second species of that genus, and two undescribed species of *Eragrostis.*

Droughty times have made prickly pear experimentation and research an integral part of the King Ranch's range improvement program. There was a time when this homely plant was looked upon with considerable disfavor by stockmen; it was placed in the category of undesirable vegetation and marked for eradication. However, the prickly pear has the ability to withstand the periodic droughts to which South Texas is subject, and the result has given the lowly cactus an economic position on the ranch that would be difficult to appraise.

Feeding prickly pear to cattle is not an innovation on the King Ranch. In the correspondence file is a letter written by Luther Burbank to Robert J. Kleberg, Sr., on March 9, 1918. The letter reveals that Luther Burbank was then working at the behest of Mr. Kleberg "to make a better cactus for Texas." It was during a severe drought. Mr. Burbank wrote, "You certainly ought to know something about cactus if you feed one hundred fifty tons a day." In actuality, during the height of this drought the ranch fed more than a thousand tons of cactus per day.

Prickly pear again came into its own in South Texas during the 1951 drought. The toll of grass and forbs on the range was so great that pear-burning was launched on a big scale. The pear provided supplementary feed for thousands of head of cattle on all parts of the ranch with the herds streaming behind the burners waiting for them to sear the spines from the succulent green pads.

There has been a revolutionary development in pear-burning equipment within the past few years. Formerly the work was done by small, individual burners, operated by one man. The operation now involves crews working with modern, labor-saving equipment. Butane and propane are used instead of the old-style back-borne burners which operated on gasoline or kerosene. Long rubber hoses lead from the gas storage tank, permitting mobility on the part of the several operators who work from a single piece of equipment.

Prickly pear is found on all divisions of the King Ranch. It has special importance on the blackland areas where continued drought will take an early toll of grasses and forbs, and range forage is not as quick to recover as on lighter soils.

The King Ranch now plants prickly pear along all of its fences. This has a dual purpose: In the first place, it keeps livestock away from fences; in the second place, it gives added support to fences. In addition, the growth of prickly pear along fences provides cover for birds and other forms of wildlife. It also tends to prevent cattle from getting to a portion of the range, allowing new grass to mature undisturbed.

Although prickly pear is far from ideal as a livestock feed, it nevertheless provides life-saving sustenance when other types of forage are no longer available on the range. It is a reserve supply which can be tapped when other sources have dried up.

An average beef animal consumes at least fifty pounds of green or succulent forage daily in humid locations and probably half of that quantity in drier areas. The importance of grass—and lots of it—becomes vividly apparent. The rancher's battle for grass is a never-ending struggle, but the rewards for success are sufficiently great to make continued experimentation and improvement of the ranch's grass program a vital daily project.

It is doubtful if anyone has expressed the importance of grass with more ringing eloquence than John J. Ingalls in 1872:

Grass is the forgiveness of nature—her constant benediction. Fields trampled with battle, saturated with blood, torn with the ruts of cannon, grow green again with grass, and carnage is forgotten. Streets abandoned by traffic become grass-grown like rural lanes, and are obliterated. Forests decay, harvests perish, flowers vanish, but grass is immortal. Beleaguered by the sullen hosts of winter, it withdraws into the impregnable fortress of its subterranean vitality, and emerges upon the first solicitation of spring. Sown by the winds, by wandering birds, propagated by the subtle horticulture of the elements which are its ministers and servants, it softens the rude outline of the world. Its tenacious fibres hold the earth in its place, and prevent its soluble components from washing into the wasting sea. It invades the solitudes of deserts, climbs the inaccessible slopes and forbidding pinnacles of mountains, modifies climates, and determines the history, character, and destiny of nations. Unobtrusive and patient, it has immortal vigor and aggression. Banished from the thoroughfare and the field, it abides its time to return, and when vigilance is relaxed, or the dynasty has perished, it silently resumes the throne from which it has been expelled, but which it never abdicates. It bears no blazonry of bloom to charm the senses with fragrance or splendor, but its homely hue is more enchanting than the lily or the rose. It yields no fruit in earth or air, and yet should its harvest fail for a single year, famine would depopulate the world.

BIBLIOGRAPHY

C. L. LUNDELL and W. DERBY LAWS, "Soil Fertility in Relation to Production," *Breeding Beef Cattle for Unfavorable Environments* (Austin, 1955), pp. 68-88.

PAUL T. RIHERD and H. L. CHADA, *Some Scale Insects Attacking Grasses In Texas*, Texas Agricultural Experiment Station P. R. 1461 (College Station, May 10, 1952).

BENJAMIN CARROLL THARP, *Texas Range Grasses* (Austin, 1952).

C. B. WEBSTER and DAVID H. FOSTER, *King Ranch Bluestem*, United States Department of Agriculture Soil Conservation Service (Fort Worth, July, 1949).

W. GORDON WHALEY, "Breeding Range Grasses for a Difficult Environment," *Breeding Beef Cattle for Unfavorable Environments*, pp. 89-105.

EXPERIMENTS IN SUPPLYING PHOSPHORUS DEFICIENCY

by WILLIAM J. McBRIDE

(The following is a nontechnical account of mineral feeding experiments on the King Ranch. Mr. McBride has charge of the experiments which are being conducted on the Encino Division. This account was originally written as a letter to Richard Lappin of Woodstock, Illinois.)

Dear Dick:

I received your letter of inquiry about the phosphorus experiments here on the King Ranch, and I'll try to give you a picture of what has transpired since this type of work was begun. I'll give it to you as I have seen it develop. If you want to get the details of the experiment and data that has been collected, you can get the technical bulletins which have been published about it.* The Texas Agricultural Experiment Station, College Station, Texas, has copies of these various reports for the asking.

Some of the early history of what we now know to be phosphorus deficiency is interesting and should be recorded so that you'll know just how long it takes to find out some of these things, and the amount of trial and error involved in trying to find an answer to the problem. It is also interesting to note how much time and money was spent by individual ranchers in trying to find a way to help their cattle. They hadn't realized that what they were trying to combat was a common denominator for all of this South Texas area, the coastal region of the United States, and other similar areas of the world and not a problem peculiar to each indi-

vidual's ranch. Let me give you an example of one case of trial and error that occurred.

I can remember that one of the first things we did here on the King Ranch was to feed bone meal, free choice, to the cattle. We built feed troughs at each watering place and loaded them with bone meal. The cattle ate it in large quantities, and we thought we must have satisfied their craving. The idea of bone meal was hit upon because we noted cattle chewing bones and sticks, licking around old lakes (they are quite salty and brackish), taking bites of salt grass (zacahuiste), and in general showing a tendency to try to get something additional in their diet. This was noted by all of the people here, and it was finally concluded that bone or bone meal must be what they were craving and what they needed. So we gave them bone meal and plenty of it. They ate it with gusto.

Since the cattle were eating the bone meal so ravenously we then became alarmed that they might be eating too much of it, and in order to control their consumption of the stuff we started adding salt. You know, of course, that salt is an inhibitor to appetite

* See bibliography, page 759.

and this controls the amount of added material that is eaten. I was old enough, at this time, to be detailed to the salt truck and the back-breaking labor of keeping those troughs supplied. That work keeps my memories of those days quite vivid.

After a time we observed that the cattle most persistent at eating sticks et cetera were usually thin, showed poor condition and from slight to extreme lameness, had bone changes, and were stiff-jointed and sometimes sore-footed. Also, the cows with the biggest calves always seemed to be hardest hit with the strange malady. In a few extreme cases I have seen cattle actually walking on their knees because their feet and joints hurt so badly. You know how a foot that has been injured can pain when you try to walk. These cattle really had it. This condition was called "creeps." That name was probably given because it seemed to take them forever to get where they were going. The cattle just crept along and hence my interpretation of the origin of the word "creeps."

One of the earliest clues as to what our trouble might be was picked up by W. H. Black over in South Africa in 1929. Mr. Black, now deceased, was with the Bureau of Animal Industry in the USDA, and worked out of Washington. He had visited this South Texas area many times, had seen our troubles and knew of the persistence of the King Ranch to study this problem and find a practical and applicable answer to it. Mr. Black went to South Africa to bring some of the cattle from that area back to this country, Afrikanders which were ultimately received by the King Ranch. While he was in Africa he noted the similarity of that country to this area and that creeps prevailed there under the same cir-

cumstances and conditions. Also, he found out that some people were hand feeding their cattle and had no creeps where that was being done. I don't know what the African people were feeding to their cattle, but whatever it was, it contained phosphorus; I'll hazard a guess and say they were feeding bone meal. Mr. Black remembered this and when he delivered the cattle to the ranch, he mentioned this fact to Mr. Kleberg.

They immediately began talking over the problem and, after much conversation and correspondence, got a man assigned from the Bureau of Animal Industry to study this country, its grasses and general characteristics, and to report back to them on what he found. Understand that this was not the first man to give the problem scientific thought, but as far as I know he was the first man to tackle the problem full time.

He was Lowell H. Tash, now operating a ranch in Cuba for the King Ranch and Compañia Ganadera Becerra, S. A. Mr. Tash was the actual discoverer of phosphorus deficiency in the area. He went all over the coastal area of Texas and gathered grass samples, received copies of grass analyses from other states with areas comparable to this, and gathered data on grasses. He spent quite a bit of time in this South Texas area where creeps was heaviest, and the grasses were analyzed for mineral content as well as other qualities.

From the thousands of samples of grass that were taken, Mr. Tash noted from the data that phosphorus seemed to be low in comparison with the other minerals in the plants. This observation was given to Mr. Kleberg and Mr. Black. From these preliminary efforts, the first concrete evidence was obtained that phosphorus was deficient and might be the cause of creeps in this country. Out of this evidence the experimental area or station at Encino was born.

It might be well to mention another man who contributed a great deal of time, thought and assistance to Mr. Tash during the experiment. He was J. M. Jones, from the Texas Agricultural Experiment Station, a meticulous worker, and a very practical thinker on this and other of the state's ranching problems.

All of this early history that I've given you has been without dates, and with few names and places in most cases. It covers a period of time from when this country was stocked with cattle up until about 1936. Many other ranchers and related business concerns spent many hours discussing the problem and what it meant to them. No doubt many solutions were hatched up over coffee cups, but none of them had yet been put into practice at this time. People were thinking about the problem, but no real answer had come up. This history I have given is the basis and the groundwork which was laid for one trial that paid off in the end.

The historical data just mentioned was the first phase of the experiment—the groundwork, the collecting of loose ends toward something concrete. The questions that had been raised during the first phase all had to be answered and could be answered only by a well-programed experiment. The King Ranch made such a test possible by providing the necessary cattle and equipment on a part of the ranch that the grass analysis had indicated to be one of the areas most deficient in phosphorus. The ranch also provided much of the practical direction for the experiment. You know that in experimental work you can go off the deep end and wind up with a bunch of data that has no practical application, but sure looks good on paper. We wanted to make sure that this didn't happen, although there was no indication that it would in this particular experiment.

One hundred heifers, eighteen months of age, were divided into four groups of twenty-five each, number branded and placed in the pasture provided for them. These cattle were brought to the pen each day and hand fed. By hand fed, I mean that we actually opened each one's mouth and put the feed into its mouth. This was the only way that we could *know* that the animal was getting exactly what it was supposed to get.

The first group received no feed and were the check group, the second group received bone meal, the third group got disodium phosphate, and the fourth group got bone meal and a mixture of trace minerals.

It was a curious sight to watch those cows come through the chute. Most of the cows soon got the idea of opening their mouths and seeking the feed. They would come in with their noses pointing toward the sky and their tongues licking their lips. Incidentally, the disodium group were indebted to the brewing industry. Since the disodium was in powdered form it had to be washed down in some manner. We used beer bottles full of water to do this with.

The whole bunch became known by pet names such as La Manchada, La Gotcha, La Llorona, et cetera. I especially remember La Llorona. She would start a groaning noise as soon as she came into the chute and would keep it up until she got out. Nothing was hurting her or bothering her that we knew of; it was just a habit of hers. We knew she was coming into the chute as soon as we could hear her.

Blood samples were taken every fourteen days and phosphorus and trace mineral tests were run on them. The animals were also weighed and measured for height periodically. Calving data was recorded and the herd checked daily for any unusual developments. As the experiment progressed it was fairly obvious that the three groups receiving phosphorus were doing better than the check group. Later the cows with calves in the check group began to show signs of developing creeps, especially as the calves grew older. None of the fed groups showed any signs of creeps throughout the experiment.

"Creeps" now gave way to a more descriptive word for the deficiency: "Aphosphorosis," a six-bit word meaning shortage or lack of phosphorus in the animal structure, but I won't burden you with it any more. It is still "creeps" to me.

What happens in the cow's body is interesting. Perhaps you have already wondered why a calf and creeps are mentioned together. The cow's milk is the principal diet of the calf until it is weaned. Naturally, as the calf gets bigger he demands more and more milk. The cow's milk is complete in all the minerals and her only way of receiving them is through her feed. If, in the case of phosphorus and calcium, she cannot supply that demand from the feed, then in a complicated way, she supplies it from the bone in her body. Since calcium was being supplied by the feed in great quantities and phosphorus was lacking, she was taking only that from her bones, thereby causing an improper balance of phosphorus and calcium of the bone. The greater the disparity in the ratio of the balance, the greater the tendency for creeps.

The results of this experiment showed that cows receiving a supplement in any form averaged about 150-200 pounds heavier, produced a higher percentage calf crop, had heavier calves at weaning time, showed a tendency to calve earlier each year, and all showed good healthy conditions and fine luster. The check group were having less calves each year and lower weights in the cows and the calves at weaning time; blood tests were consistently low and showed several cases of creeps, some of them extreme cases. None in this group showed a good healthy condition and all showed practically no luster.

The year 1938 was a dry year and we had many cases of creeps on the range. We rounded up one pasture of about 1,000 head and cut out 125 cows with extreme cases of creeps, and took them to a trap and hand fed them disodium for about one month. To show you how bad they were, it took us two days to drive them about five miles. Four or five head were walking on their knees. The surprising thing was that those cattle walking on their knees were up and around and showing great signs of relief after being hand fed for only a week. While this was not a part of the experiment, it did show what phosphorus would do for an animal. It was further proof that we were on the right track.

There were many incidents, amusing and otherwise, but the significant thing was that the experiment had developed and proved a fact that heretofore had been only a question mark in the minds of many people, thanks to Mr. Tash's diligent work.

The big hurdle had been crossed. There was proof that phosphorus was the missing element. Next was to find the most economical means of supplying it to the cattle. This involved another experiment, on a larger scale. In 1941 the experiment pastures were enlarged to approximately 640 acres in size; there were six in all. The first group was again the check group; the second group got the disodium phosphate in water; the third group was given bone meal in self-feeders, free choice; the fourth group was given disodium in self-feeders, free choice; for the fifth group triple superphosphate was applied on a pasture at the rate of three hundred pounds per acre; and the sixth group received more hand feeding. The cattle were blood sampled, weighed, and data about calving was recorded and tabulated for four years.

The results were about the same as from the previous experiment. The calculated gross profit (at $15 per 100 pounds of weaned calf weight) from the check group was a little over $13 per acre for the four years, whereas the profits from the other groups ran from $17 to nearly $21 per acre for the four years, disodium being the leader. The answer was that phosphorus supplied in any form was economical with not too great a difference in the amount of money made. Our situation and method of operation here on the ranch, very fortunately, made it possible to use the disodium in water to the greatest advantage. You see, we do not depend on ponds and lakes or streams for water for the livestock. All of our water comes from water wells, hence it can be controlled easily. The cattle had to drink at those places, and they got the mineral in that manner.

One thing is nearly always true in experimentation: the solution of one problem brings to light new problems. This was true to some extent in this experiment. When we fertilized the pasture in 1941 with triple superphosphate, that treatment apparently caused a change in our range grasses. It looked as if fertilization had a tendency to decrease the tall-growing grasses and bring out the shorter ones. The reason for this is that the fertilizer stays in the top few inches of soil and the grass roots must look for it there. The taller grasses have deeper root systems as a rule and, therefore, suffer while the short grasses get all the good out of the fertilization.

Since 1947 this grass and fertilization field of research has been followed up on an elaborate scale. We have set up complicated and involved studies and are still working on them. To hinder the process, we have been in a drought practically since we started the experiment, and while there are results none is conclusive to any great extent and therefore better left unsaid.

The Range and Forestry Department of the Texas Agricultural Experiment Station has been carrying on the grass studies and has done their best on them, but the drought has been hampering them and the results and conclusions are sketchy. We have found out a lot about grasses under drought conditions, but I'd much rather know about grasses under normal conditions. It makes for easier ranching. This is wishful thinking, however, because we will have other droughts. I hope though, because of what we know about this past one, we will be better able to get through the next one. All the work has not been completely lost.

Well, Dick, I've rambled on about this experiment until I'm sure you have had enough of it. There is much more here to be looked into and I'm sure that in time we will get around to doing it. I'm looking forward to it, because it is a fact that good research is progress and we would like to be there sitting in the front row when the results are passed out.

Regards to your family and look out for a few pheasants. I'll see if we can get up that way during the season.

Regards to all,

Bill.

(Following is the "Summary and Conclusions" section from Methods of Supplying Phosphorus to Range Cattle in South Texas, *Texas Agricultural Experiment Station Bulletin 773, published in 1953.)*

An experiment was conducted on the Encino Division of the King Ranch near Falfurrias from 1941 to 1946 to determine the most practical methods of supplying phosphorus to range cattle and to determine the effect of applications of different phosphates on the yield and chemical composition of pasture forage. Phosphorus was supplied to cattle by feeding bone meal in self-feeders, by adding disodium phosphate to a controlled water supply and by fertilizing pasture with triple superphosphate.

Supplying phosphorus by all three methods gave good results and prevented phosphorus deficiency in normal seasons. The specific application of these findings, however, may be somewhat different, depending on the circumstances. For example, some ranchmen will find it feasible to supply phosphorus in a controlled water system. Others may find it more practicable to supply phosphorus supplements in self-feeders. Still others may prefer to supply phosphorus through pasture fertilization. The results show conclusively that the cattle will get the necessary phosphorus where any of these methods is used.

Cows that were fed phosphorus supplements and cows on fertilized pasture produced larger calf crops and heavier calves at weaning time than cows that did not receive phosphorus supplements. The cows that did not receive phosphorus supplements produced 93 pounds of weaned calves per acre; cows that were fed bone meal, 116 pounds; cows that received disodium phosphate in drinking water, 143 pounds; and cows on fertilized pasture, 176 pounds.

Cows that did not receive a phosphorus supplement yielded a gross return of $13.91 per acre for the 4 years [using $15 per 100 pounds weaned calf weight as a base]. After deducting the cost of phos-phorus supplements or fertilizer, the cows that were fed bone meal gave a return of $16.91 per acre; cows that received disodium phosphate in water, $20.39; and cows on fertilized pasture, $19.97.

Feeding phosphorus supplements also greatly increased the amount of inorganic phosphorus in the blood stream. Supplying phosphorus in self-feeders and in a controlled water system, in general, maintained a slightly higher level of blood phosphorus than pasture fertilization. Pasture fertilization, however, maintained an adequate phosphorus level in the blood stream except during the prolonged drouth of 1945 and 1946.

If pasture fertilization is used, it probably will be necessary to reduce the rate of stocking and feed phosphorus supplements during drouth to supply adequate phosphorus to the cattle. This system of management will utilize all the advantages of pasture fertilization and, at the same time, provide sufficient phosphorus for cattle at all times.

Applications of triple superphosphate, calcium metaphosphate, potassium metaphosphate and fused tricalcium phosphate increased the yield and phosphoric acid content of pasture forage. The increases in yield ranged from 33 to 84 percent, depending on the rate of application. Pound for pound of phosphoric acid, all the phosphates used apparently had about the same fertilizing value.

In general, the phosphoric acid content of the grasses increased as the rate of phosphate application was increased. The heavier applications of triple superphosphate doubled the phosphoric acid content of the grasses and provided adequate phosphorus for range cattle in normal seasons.

The application of phosphates apparently did not affect the protein content of grasses.

The application of approximately 200 pounds of 48 percent triple superphosphate per acre in 1941 was effective in increasing the yield and phosphorus content of pasture forage for 4 or 5 years. This amount of phosphate was profitable and is recommended where ranchmen can use it to advantage.

BIBLIOGRAPHY

Black, W. H., Tash, L. H., Jones, J. M. and Kleberg, R. J., Jr., *Comparison of Methods of Supplying Phosphorus to Range Cattle*, USDA Technical Bulletin 981 (Washington, 1949).

Black, W. H., Tash, L. H., Jones, J. M. and Kleberg, R. J. Jr., *Effect of Phosphorus Supplements* on Cattle Grazing on Range Deficient in This Mineral, USAD Technical Bulletin 856 (Washington, 1943).

FRAPS, G. S. and FUDGE, J. F., Chemical Composition of Soils of Texas, Texas Agricultural Experiment Station Bulletin 549 (College Station, 1937).

FRAPS, G. S. and FUDGE, J. F., The Chemical Composition of Forage Grasses of the East Texas Timber Country, Texas Agricultural Experiment Station Bulletin 582 (College Station, 1940).

FRAPS, G. S., FUDGE, J. F. and REYNOLDS, E. B., "Effect of Fertilization of a Crowley Clay Loam on the Chemical Composition of Forage and Carpet Grass, Axonopus affinis," Journal, American Society of Agronomy, Vol. 35 (1943), pp. 560-566.

REYNOLDS, E. B., FUDGE, J. F. and JONES, J. M., Supplying Phosphorus to Range Cattle Through Fertilization of Range Land, Texas Agricultural Experiment Station P. R. 1341 (College Station, 1951).

REYNOLDS, E. B., JONES, J. M., JONES, J. H., FUDGE, J. F. and KLEBERG, R. J., JR., Methods of Supplying Phosphorus to Range Cattle in South Texas, Texas Agricultural Experiment Station Bulletin 773 (College Station, 1953).

REYNOLDS, E. B. and WYCHE, R. H., Effect of Fertilizers and Lime on Yield, Protein Content and Phosphoric Acid Content of Pasture Forage, Texas Agricultural Experiment Station P. R. 1039 (College Station, 1946).

SCHMIDT, H., Field and Laboratory Notes on a Fatal Disease of Cattle Occurring on the Coastal Plains of Texas, Texas Agricultural Experiment Station Bulletin 319 (College Station, 1924).

SCHMIDT, H., Feeding Bonemeal to Range Cattle on the Coastal Plains of Texas, Texas Agricultural Experiment Station Bulletin 344 (College Station, 1926).

STANSEL, R. H., REYNOLDS, E. B. and JONES, J. H., Pasture Improvement in the Gulf Coast Prairie of Texas, Texas Agricultural Experiment Station Bulletin 570 (College Station, 1939).

GAME CONSERVATION AND MANAGEMENT

by V. W. LEHMANN

WILD GAME has perhaps received more attention on the King Ranch than on any other private ownership in North America. Purposeful conservation started about 1912 when Caesar Kleberg suggested and the King Ranch applied a hunting code designed to increase sport and reduce crippling loss. The code's provisions included:

1. Deer *(Odocoileus texanus)* and turkey *(Meleagris gallopavo intermedia)* should be hunted with rifles only, and shot in the neck or head.
2. Bobwhites *(Colinus virginianus texanus)* should not be fired into on initial covey rise.
3. Deer hunting should end when rutting reached a peak (usually about December 15).
4. Game should not be hunted at waterings or other concentration places, and in times of drought or other emergency.

State game preserves were authorized by the Texas legislature in 1925; 414,314 acres of the King Ranch were closed to all hunting under the program. Ranch personnel cooperated closely with state game wardens in patrolling, and protection was the pillar of early conservation efforts.

Organized predator control began with the hiring of a trapper for the Norias Division about 1925; three men were working full time in that activity by 1945. Wild turkey were trapped and transplanted from Norias to re-establish the flocks of the Santa Gertrudis and Laureles divisions, and importations in the 1930's added Nilgai antelope and Cuban guinea *(Numida* sp.) to the fauna of Norias.

Habitat improvement also received attention. Observing that game, particularly wild turkey, were often most numerous near windmill storage tanks which leaked, thus providing water at ground level, Caesar Kleberg, Richard M. Kleberg, Sr. and Robert J. Kleberg, Jr., modified at least thirty-three wells to provide continuous drinking facilities. Caesar Kleberg was among the first in South Texas to build fenced areas and brush shelters for quail; more than a score of fenced shelter-belts, still useful to both livestock and game, were planted by Robert J. Kleberg, Jr., in the 1930's. Meanwhile the ranges of the King Ranch improved naturally for deer, javelina, and turkey as mesquite *(Prosopis* sp.), oak *(Quercus* sp.), granjeno *(Celtis pallida),* and other brush succeeded the original tall climax grasses.

Early efforts to increase game were successful. Although wild turkey were a rarity in 1912 and deer were practically nil, increased populations were apparent by 1920. By 1928, both deer and turkey were sufficient on Norias to provide good hunting and a surplus for restocking. In 1945, top densities were a turkey to approximately thirty acres and a deer to approximately twenty-two acres in the most heavily populated oak range. Bobwhites, on the other hand, exhibited no gradual build-up. High populations were phenomena of "wet" years and low populations occurred after dry breeding seasons; this was observed as early as 1916.

By the early 1940's, Robert J. Kleberg, Jr., was convinced that wildlife might be developed into a major auxiliary crop on much South Texas rangeland. In 1946 an intensified research-management program was begun under the direction of the writer to test that thesis.

The initial management technique was intensified coyote-bobcat control. A permanent control staff, increased to four men and periodically assisted by other wildlife workers, used poison baits, cyanide guns (coyote-getters),* and steel traps to take a minimum of 1,754 coyotes prior to game breeding in 1946. In 1946 and 1947 more than 2,000 bobcats and coyotes per year were removed from the King Ranch; these kills were four times heavier than in any previous year. They changed the faunal status of large predators to real scarcity. Subsequent annual harvests of approximately 1,000 animals per year maintained low populations.

Small predators—rattlesnakes, wild housecats, skunks, opossums, badgers and raccoons—also received attention, but only periodically and in local areas which provided exceptional nesting cover for wild turkeys and bobwhites. Annual reductions amounting to about 80 per cent of original populations were effected by systematic den poisoning with cyanide "A" dust administered with foot pumps, selective trapping, and night hunting with dogs.

The quality of woody cover for bobwhites was improved on about 250,000 acres of sandy semi-prairie by half-cutting† approximately 75,000 desert shrubs, principally mesquite, granjeno, and huisache (*Acacia farnesiana*).

On experimental areas aggregating approximately 15,000 acres, where shrubs suitable for half-cutting were scarce or absent, woody cover for bobwhites was improved in key situations by building approximately 500 brush shelters. Experimental plantings of approximately 10,000 shrubs and vines of twenty-one varieties were largely unsuccessful, but living fences of three varieties of cactus (*Opuntia lindheimeri, Opuntia leptocaulis,* and *Opuntia lindheimeri* spp.) were established on approximately sixty-five miles of inside cross fences.

Feed for bobwhite, mourning dove, and wild turkey was increased locally by strip plowing. From twenty to sixty miles of combination food strips and fire guards were disced annually on the Santa Gertrudis

---

* The "coyote-getter" was first employed in South Texas on the King Ranch. The device consists of three main parts: a metal tube about one inch in diameter and six inches long, a firing device, and a "top" containing a .38 caliber pistol cartridge loaded with cyanide salts. When set, only the top protrudes above the ground, about three inches; it is baited with a mixture of decayed meat, beaver castor, artificial musk and mineral oil. When the coyote grasps the top of the getter with its mouth and exerts an upward pull, the cartridge fires the charge of cyanide salts. Death is usually almost instantaneous. Because an upward pull is required for firing, coyote-getters can be used around livestock waterings, where traps would be impractical because of trampling.

† "Half-cutting" is the partial severing of trunks or lateral branches of trees or shrubs to provide low cover.

Division. On the other hand, extensive efforts to increase game feed by planting, cultivation, and fertilization were largely unsuccessful because rainfall was often limiting.

In the almost continuous drought of 1950-1955, turkeys and bobwhites were sometimes fed experimentally on the Santa Gertrudis Division with domestic grains supplied in oil drum feeders or scattered from moving vehicles in the "middles" of ranch roads.

Fifty-five inside windmills which did not already supply ground water for game were modified by piping water to nearby ponds about ten feet in diameter and sloping to about four feet in depth. Drinking ponds for game were fenced to exclude cattle, and seepage was reduced by Akwaseal or concrete. A herd of North American antelope (*Antilocapra americana*) was established by a transplant on the Laureles Division.

Simultaneous with management, appropriate census techniques were developed and game was periodically inventoried. The first year-long Texas studies based on crop and/or paunch examinations were completed for deer and bobwhites. Dennis Illege determined the breeding cycle of deer by laboratory studies of reproductive organs; Raymond L. Henry recorded the kinds and numbers of turkey parasites. Comprehensive studies were also made of bobwhite parasites through periods of population rise and decline; three new species and a new genera of helminth parasites were found. Long-term population studies of the bobwhite emphasized the importance of soils, rainfall, tall perennial grass and population pressure. The probable importance of Vitamin A and of general nutrition in the breeding effort of wild quail was established for the first

time. Don Luthy tested various fish census methods. Rough fish were periodically reduced by poisoning, and extensive turbidity reduction tests, all unsuccessful, were made on many artificial lakes. Predator stomachs were periodically collected and analyzed.

Johnston inventoried the flora of major soil types. Pad cacti (*Opuntia lindheimeri* and *Opuntia lindheimeri* spp.) were proven to be valuable living fence species for the Southwest. In plantations where yields of 74,770 pounds per acre were obtained after only two and a half years, three kinds of prickly pear were proven valuable emergency cattle feed,* which would allow pasture deferment and hence range improvement on a practical basis.

During the first five years of intensified research-management, from 1946 to 1950, basic land use did not change and rainfall over the King Ranch as a whole was about average, ranging from 25 to 32 inches per year. Records for the Kingsville area indicate precipitation 15 inches above the annual average. From mid-1950 through 1955 land use was changed to a degree affecting game populations in brush country; about 150,000 acres of brush land were largely cleared. Severe drought prevailed. Over the entire ranch, rainfall ranged from 7.9 to 20.6 inches below the annual averages, as much as 32 inches below in the Kingsville area. Therefore, during the ten-year period opportunities were especially favorable for determining wildlife production potentials of South Texas rangeland under extreme as well as mean conditions.

The production potentials of South Texas rangeland for deer and turkey and javelina

---

* 428.7 to 955.4 micrograms of Vitamin A per gram of green pad, according to J. M. Dendy, Texas Research Foundation.

[763]

were found to be high. Although substantial javelina populations were not inventoried with satisfying exactness, deer attained peak densities of one to about 4.6 acres in brushland range, predominately oak, and one per twelve acres in predominately mesquite brushland. Peak densities of wild turkey were one to four acres in oak brush land and one to about fifteen acres in mesquite range. These were significant populations.

On one study area of 140,000 acres of predominately oak range, for example, the 1949 population was approximately 30,000 deer, 35,000 turkey and an undetermined number of javelinas. Thus, considering the cattle population at about 8,000 head, the deer and turkey were more than eight times as abundant. With deer weighing an average of 100 pounds and turkeys averaging fifteen, their gross live weight was about 3,525,000 pounds — more than twenty-five pounds of game for each acre of land. Assuming that 17.5 acres of range should be allowed a cow, the calf crop would be 80 per cent and calves would average 500 pounds at weaning time — all generous assumptions for the territory under consideration — its theoretical annual production potential for veal was 3,200,000 pounds per year, or 22.9 pounds per acre. In 1949, a harvest of one half of the deer and two-thirds of the turkey would have produced about 1,879,980 pounds of game, or 13.4 pounds per acre — more than one half the theoretical production of veal. Game harvest of that magnitude would hardly have been excessive since it could have been directed principally at turkey gobblers, which out-

numbered hens one and one half to one, and at buck deer, which were approximately as numerous as does.

Because twelve deer, aggregating 1,200 pounds, were found to be the approximate range equivalent of one steer weighing 1,000 pounds and because oak range appeared to have a greater sustained carrying capacity for deer and turkey than for cattle, it was concluded that some sections of oak range might be managed for a higher average poundage yield of game than of cattle.[*] Big game presently has greater unit value than slaughter calves and probably greater future value as well.

The immediate productive potentials of southwestern rangeland appeared to be less for bobwhites than for deer, wild turkey, and javelina. True enough, densities which may be saturation for bobwhites as a species (i.e., four quail per acre in late summer and early fall, one quail per two acres in late fall and winter, and one bird per four acres in spring and early summer) were obtained over appreciable areas in all excepting extremely dry years. There were many quail numerically: A bird per four-acre density in a part of Canelo Pasture produced an all-time field trial record of more than 100 coveys raised per day during the National Amateur Field Trial Championship of February, 1949.

While protection from over-killing by man and large predators appeared as the key to higher average deer populations in brushy range under present usage, and protection plus water improvement and occasional emergency feeding were generally followed by turkey increase in both oak and tall mesquite brushland, quail management was not consistently productive. This was because rainfall and grazing pressure, individually

[*] Richard B. Davis, *A Study of Some Interrelationships of a Native South Texas Range, Its Cattle, and Its Deer* (Doctoral dissertation, Texas A & M College, 1952).

or in combination, were often limiting. The application of specific bobwhite management techniques such as strip plowing, half-cut trees, predator control, water improvement, et cetera, were considered economically worthwhile in sandy mesquite semi-prairie and in sandy prairie grazed to sustain a flora approximately 50 per cent tall perennial grasses. Although the amount of sandy semi-prairie rangeland in South Texas is large, that grazed to sustain high quality range flora is not large.

While the productive potentials of South Texas rangeland for game are appreciable, it must be remembered that all substantial wildlife populations exist under threat of rapid and severe reduction by severe drought. In the winter of 1950-1951, for example, it was estimated that fully 90 per cent of all the bobwhites and scaled quail (*Calipepia squamata castanogastris*) in South Texas died of nutritional deficiencies during a period of sixty days. Mortality was also severe in turkeys and javelina and deer; an estimated 12,000 deer were lost on the Santa Gertrudis Division of the King Ranch alone. Severe drought is a recurring feature of South Texas climate and has been for as long as man has written record.*

Although game increases naturally in those years when rainfall is favorable, and increase may be stimulated by management, there can be no avoidance of periodic wastage under present conditions. This is because existing game laws do not allow man to effect often necessary population control.

Specifically, existing game laws do allow quail harvest until December 1, or fully thirty days after peak fall populations in the best ranges are reduced about 75 per cent by a myriad of factors operating during and after the fall (usually October) "shuffle."†

Deer and turkey populations cannot be regulated by man because existing state law prohibits the harvest of females, thus insuring eventual overpopulation and die-off wherever natural limiting processes are effectively removed. Quail and turkey populations which are not harvested when at annual peaks are merely wasted. Unharvested deer populations not only destroy themselves, but render the range less productive for future generations of deer, other game, and livestock.

Recognition of the important difference between laws appropriate for the harvest of relatively low game populations produced accidentally and regulations appropriate for the harvest of high game populations produced purposefully has been slow in Texas, but it is developing. Authority to set seasons and bag limits on the basis of game populations and fluctuating habitats has been transferred to the Texas Game and Fish Commission by the state legislature in the instance of sixty-six counties; doe harvests on a carefully controlled permit basis have been successfully conducted in several counties of the Texas hill country for three seasons. Implementation of existing laws to allow universal population control wherever and whenever needed would stimulate game management by private landowners. That would benefit game and man as well.

---

* Note the translation of the Santa Gertrudis de la Garza land grant, Appendix II, Volume I, of this work.

† The period when intra-specific psychological tensions—outwardly evidenced by excessive nervousness, pugnaciousness, and general unrest—are strong to the extent of outweighing tangible habitat considerations, even including unlimited food.

BIBLIOGRAPHY

ALLEN, D. L., *Our Wildlife Legacy* (New York, 1954).

ANONYMOUS, *Review of Texas Wildlife and Conservation* (Austin: Texas Game, Fish and Oyster Commission, 1929).

———, *Full Text of the Game, Fish and Fur Laws of Texas* (Austin: Texas Game and Fish Commission, 1951).

BECK, J. R. and D. O., "A Method for Nutritional Evaluation of Wildlife Foods," *Journal Wildlife Management*, Vol. 19, No. 2, 1955, pp. 198-205.

BOGUSCH, E. R., "Brush Invasion of the Rio Grande Plain in Texas," *Texas Journal of Science*, Vol. 4, No. 1, pp. 85-92.

BRAY, W. L., *Distribution and Adaptation of the Vegetation of Texas*, Bul. No. 10 (Austin: University of Texas, 1906).

BURR, J. G.,"What the King Ranch Is Doing About Game," *Texas Game and Fish*, Vol. 5, No. 2, 1947.

DAVIS, R. B., *The Food Habits of White-Tailed Deer on the Cattle Stocked Liveoak-Mesquite Ranges of the King Ranch as Determined by Analysis of Deer Rumen Contents*, (Master's thesis, Texas A. & M. College, 1951).

———, *A Study of Some Interrelationships of a Native South Texas Range, Its Cattle, and Its Deer*, (Doctoral dissertation, Texas A. & M. College, 1952).

ILLEGE, D. J., "An Analysis of the Reproductive Pattern of White-Tailed Deer in South Texas," *Journal of Mammalogy*, Vol. 32, No. 4, 1951, pp. 411-421.

JAMESON, J. F., *Spanish Explorers in Southern United States, 1528-48* (New York, 1907).

JOHNSTON, M. C., *Vegetation of the Eolian Plain and Associated Coastal Features of Southern Texas* (Doctoral dissertation, University of Texas, 1955).

KENEDY, W., *The Rise, Progress and Prospects of the Republic of Texas* (Fort Worth, 1925).

LEHMANN, V. W., *Increase Quail by Improving Their Habitat* (Austin: Texas Game, Fish and Oyster Commission Bul., 1937).

———, "Restocking on King Ranch," *Transcription Thirteenth North American Wildlife Conference* (Washington, 1940), pp. 236-242.

———, "Bobwhite Quail Reproduction in Southwestern Texas," *Journal Wildlife Management*, Vol. 10, No. 2, 1946, pp. 111-123.

———, "Mobility of Bobwhite Quail in Southwestern Texas," *Journal Wildlife Management*, Vol. 10, No. 2, 1946, pp. 124-136.

———, "Time for Decision," *The American Field*, December 3, 1949.

———, "Bobwhite Population Fluctuations and Vitamin A," *Transcription Eighteenth North American Wildlife Conference* (Washington, 1953), pp. 199-246.

LEHMANN, V. W. and FULLER, W. G., *Experimental Wildlife Management in the Southwestern Chaparral*, Quar. Rpt., Fed. Aid Project 1-R, Unit C, Sec. 1, Texas Game and Fish Commission, 1943.

SMITH, J. G., *Grazing Problems of the Southwest and How to Meet Them*, USDA Bul. No. 16 (Washington, 1899).

WEBSTER, J. D., I. "Studies on the Life Cycle of Mesocestoides Latus Mueller." II. "Helminths of the Bobwhite Quail." (Doctoral thesis, Rice Institute, 1947).

———, "A New Acanthocephalan from the Bobwhite," *Journal of Parasitology*, Vol. 34, No. 2, 1947, pp. 84-86.

WEBSTER, J. D. and ADDIS, C. J., "Helminths from the Bobwhite Quail in Texas," *Journal of Parasitology*, Vol. 31, No. 4, 1945, pp. 286-287.

EXPANSION OUTSIDE OF TEXAS

THE KING RANCH'S expansion into other areas of the United States and into foreign countries has been a natural development to meet demands of the changing ranching and marketing conditions which have confronted the ranch during the past two decades.

Pennsylvania Division

FOR MANY YEARS the King Ranch had from time to time pastured large numbers of cattle in grazing areas in other parts of the country, principally Oklahoma and Kansas, as a grass conservation measure, lightening the loads on Texas pastures during the hot summer months and periods of severe drought.

Pennsylvania as the location of King Ranch operations in the North had its beginning in a close friendship between Robert J. Kleberg, Jr., and Plunket Stewart, who had substantial landholdings in western Chester County. The Stewart land was used primarily for fox hunting, although Mr. Stewart had also pastured numerous stocker steers in this area. He showed these properties to Mr. Kleberg, suggesting that he might like to try a few of his Texas cattle there: It would be a useful place to prepare them for market.

The reports on an inspection of the Pennsylvania lands by members of the ranch staff and the response of test herds were highly favorable. The rainfall in the area was uniform; it was believed that if the pastures were properly limed and phosphated they could be converted into one of the finest fattening areas in the United States. The location offered distinct marketing advantages: The opportunity to introduce beef from Santa Gertrudis cattle into the large eastern consumer centers. If cattle could be properly finished in that area a great deal could be saved by the prevention of shrinkage and bruising en route to the packers.

In 1946 the ranch purchased 4300 acres near Coatsville, in Chester County, and the Buck and Doe Run Valley Farms became a working unit of the King Ranch. The development in modern retail marketing methods for beef made it increasingly important to prepare cattle for market at an early age, at acceptable weight and with a higher finish, which involves some grain feeding. The Pennsylvania properties were well adapted to this purpose. Landholdings were increased and intensive pasture improvement measures were inaugurated.

At the present time the King Ranch is marketing about 5000 steers a year from this area. It started by finishing three-year-old cattle, but is now finishing cattle before they are two-year-olds, with the goal of having them ready for market at a weight of 1050 pounds and in condition to grade from good to choice.

The ranch owns about 9200 acres in Pennsylvania and leases an additional 2500 acres. The carrying capacity of the lush pastures on the Buck and Doe Run Valley Farms is phenomenal compared to the Texas divisions of the ranch, particularly during drought years.

Kentucky Division

THE 680-ACRE Bluegrass farm near Lexington, Kentucky, was purchased in November, 1946, to further the King Ranch's racing and horse breeding program, and to serve as a safe place to keep a nucleus breed herd of the ranch's new breed of cattle as insurance in the event the then current outbreak of hoof - and - mouth disease in Mexico should spread across the border into South Texas.

The ranch had been racing Thoroughbreds for some years on eastern tracks and found it was continually boarding mares in Kentucky for breeding to Kentucky stallions or boarding horses which were recovering from injury or unsoundness resulting from training. As the ranch's racing enterprise developed, it became obvious that it would be easier to fill the books of King Ranch-developed stallions in Kentucky than in Texas.

Not only did the Kentucky farm serve as a place of refuge for Santa Gertrudis cattle, as one of the great breeding centers of the world, Kentucky was a natural place to display the new breed. As an added dividend of the operation, the response of that Kentucky herd was the initial demonstration that in comparison with other breeds Santa Gertrudis cattle show excellent results under mild climatic conditions and on lush pastures, as well as in the hot, dry climate of Texas which prompted the breed.

At the present time the King Ranch runs about two hundred Santa Gertrudis cattle on the Kentucky farm. It stands six of its stallions and keeps about forty brood mares there. Most of the foals from these mares, after weaning, are sent to the headquarters division in Texas for development and training along with the foals born on the ranch.

Foreign Expansion

THE ACCEPTANCE of the Santa Gertrudis breed by cattlemen and breeders brought problems to the King Ranch as the demand for the breed jumped the borders of the United States. Experience proved that it prospered in such countries as Mexico, Peru, Cuba, Costa Rica, Colombia, the Virgin Islands, Guatemala, Puerto Rico, Venezuela, the Hawaiian Islands, Australia and Brazil. There was demand for the new breed from foreign cattlemen, as a means of increasing beef production in their respective countries.

It became apparent to the King Ranch that the cost of exporting bulls to some of the countries, particularly those as far away as Australia and Brazil, was materially interfering with the opportunity of doing a volume business in those countries. Often the transportation cost was as much as half the value of the animal involved. In addition, the King Ranch felt it important that in more vital beef producing areas the ranch should control the breeding of purebred herds so that the breed would have the maximum opportunity to show its true merit in these new environments.

During the course of foreign expansion the King Ranch's policy has been to participate in foreign projects through joint ventures, mutually financed with citizens and industries of the countries concerned.

Australia

THE FIRST STEP in expansion abroad was a long one, all the way across the Pacific and down under to Australia. In 1932 the King Ranch had shipped a Santa Gertrudis bull to the government of the Commonwealth of Australia to be used for experimental purposes. Results were encouraging. Interest grew over the potentialities of the new breed. Some Australian cattlemen and breeders thought the Santa Gertrudis breed might be the answer to some of Australia's beef production problems. The King Ranch was approached by some of the nation's leading breeders.

After much talk, many conferences and a visit to Australia by Mr. Kleberg in 1952, two Australian companies were formed: King Ranch (Australia) Proprietary Ltd. and Associated Stations Proprietary Ltd.

King Ranch (Australia) bought a property comprised of 7560 acres, known as "Risdon," approximately fifteen miles from Warwick, Queensland. This property was for the purebred Santa Gertrudis herd which was to be sent to Australia for stud cattle breeding. The stock in King Ranch (Australia) is owned by the King Ranch, Sir Rupert Clarke, Peter Baillieu, Samuel Hordern and W. S. Robinson. It was agreed that as part of its capital contribution to the company the King Ranch was to supply cattle and stand the expense of delivering them to the company in Australia.

After an exasperating period of vaccinating and untangling export red tape, 202 Santa Gertrudis heifers and 73 young bulls were loaded into cattle cars from the Caesar pens just outside of Kingsville in May, 1952. The shipment arrived in California in time to be tied up in the cars for fifty days because of a dock strike then in progress. The cars had to be washed and sprayed every day; the cattle suffered in close quarters. Feeding was a problem and King Ranch cowboys had to stay on hand night and day for the duration of the strike. Management representatives made flying trips to wrestle with the laws and shipping regulations of both the United States and Australia. Special stalls had to be built on the SS *Sierra* of the

Matson Lines. Finally the *Sierra* sailed at 10:30 on the morning of July 31, 1952, with the first shipment of purebred Santa Gertrudis cattle for Australia. Additional shipments were made of 12 heifers and 41 bulls.

At the first Australian auction sale of Santa Gertrudis bulls, held at Risdon on November 14, 1952, twelve bulls were sold at an average of $2595 per head which, according to the Queensland Primary Producers' Co-operative Association Ltd., constituted "Australian team record for any breed." At subsequent annual auctions the prices paid for Santa Gertrudis bulls equaled or surpassed the first year's bidding. Sixteen bulls were sold in 1953; the following year twelve went on the market, the first Australian-bred Santa Gertrudis bulls.

Associated Stations Proprietary Ltd. — 240,640 acres composed of "New Twin Hills" and "Elgin Downs," two properties located near Clermont, Queensland — was established for commercial cattle breeding. This is a joint venture between the King Ranch and Swift Australian Company Proprietary Ltd. The stock in Associated Stations is owned by the King Ranch, Swift Australian Co. Pty. Ltd., Sir Rupert Clarke, Samuel Hordern, Peter Baillieu, W. S. Robinson and W. S. Harris.

Sir Rupert Clarke is the chairman and managing director of both of the Australian companies. He is assisted by A. W. Talbot and C. W. Travers, both of the Swift Australian Co.

Robert J. Kleberg, Jr., summed up the hopes for the Australian operation at the King Ranch Centennial Conference in October, 1953:

. . . while the coastal fringes of Australia are seasonally lush and at times about as green as the British Isles, much of Australia is in the hot, dry tropics . . . While European breeds do very well indeed in the cooler and greener areas, they do not do so well in these tropics. In the hot summer months they run considerable sun temperatures. We believe that a breed like the Santa Gertrudis, which has a high heat tolerance and which runs little or no sun temperature, which fares well in the tropics, is tick resistant, carries a good beef carcass, matures at an earlier age, and under similar conditions where it has been tried has been 15 to 20 per cent heavier than the British breeds at the same age—when such a breed is crossed and used to grade up the fine Shorthorn cattle, which I saw in many areas of Australia, greater beef production for the Commonwealth should result.

Cuba

THE KING RANCH's second foreign enterprise was across the Florida Straits in Cuba, but it was already familiar ground so far as Santa Gertrudis cattle were concerned. Since before the turn of the century Colonel Harry Maud and E. J. Barker had been partners in a cattle operation at Moron, Camagüey, Cuba, on the Island of Turiguano. They had experienced indifferent success by the use of Brahman bulls and "a few Red Polls."

In 1936 Colonel Maud, who had known Robert J. Kleberg, Sr., in the early 1900's, renewed an old friendship with the King Ranch. He wrote Robert J. Kleberg, Jr., inquiring about the possibility of purchasing "half a dozen to a dozen of your young Santa Gertrudis bulls." Colonel Maud and Mr. Barker visited the ranch and completed negotiations for the purchase. On December 29, 1936, thirty-five yearling bulls were shipped to Cuba, the first lot of Santa Gertrudis cattle to be sold abroad.

Experience with this herd provided the first practical evidence that the Santa Gertrudis breed would do extremely well in a tropical area. Other Cuban breeders ob-

tained bulls from the Barker herd and from the King Ranch. It shortly became obvious that Santa Gertrudis blood was contributing much to improve the beef producing qualities of Cuban cattle.

On November 26, 1950, George A. Braga, whose family had been prominent in the Cuban sugar business for many years, sent one of his top executives, Michael J. P. Malone, to the King Ranch to discuss the possibility of a joint cattle venture on some of the properties owned by the various sugar businesses, particularly the Manatí Sugar Company.

As a result of this conference Robert J. Kleberg, Jr., Leroy G. Denman, Jr., and other ranch representatives made the first of several trips to Cuba with Mr. Braga and Mr. Malone to inspect the properties under consideration. Suggestions were made by Mr. Kleberg on the possibilities of working out a joint venture which, on March 12, 1952, developed into an agreement between the King Ranch and the Manatí Sugar Company. This agreement resulted in the formation of the Cuban corporation, Compañia Ganadera Becerra, S. A., on May 12. Initially the King Ranch held twenty-five per cent of the stock and the Manatí Sugar Company owned seventy-five per cent. In March, 1955, a supplemental agreement made ownership a fifty-fifty proposition.

In May, 1952, Compañia Ganadera Becerra employed Lowell H. Tash, who had been active in phosphorus feeding experiments on the King Ranch* and had a great deal of practical experience with the ranch's operation, as manager of the Cuban company, a capacity in which he has continued. Mr. Malone is president of the organization.

The initial area involved in May, 1952, at

---

* See Appendix XVII.

the start of operations was approximately 30,741 acres, located in both Oriente and Camagüey provinces. Subsequently, on March 10, 1955, an additional 5671 acres were purchased, and on June 29 approximately 2321 acres were added. At the present time the company has slightly more than 40,000 acres of which about 1600 acres are a sugar cane farm which was within the area of one of the purchases.

On April 11, 1952, the first shipment of bulls, heifers and horses, along with four D-8 tractors, fencing material, and other equipment left Houston on the SS *Nancy Lykes* for Manatí, Cuba. Cattle and horse stock were shipped as follows:

April 11, 1952: 79 yearling bulls
151 Santa Gertrudis heifers (commercial)
30 mares
18 Quarter Horses
2 stallions
May 17, 1952: 280 Santa Gertrudis heifers (commercial)
June 16, 1952: 270 Santa Gertrudis heifers (commercial)

On December 13, 1955, a purebred herd was flown down from the King Ranch: 49 heifers and 3 bulls. An additional 50 purebred Santa Gertrudis cows were purchased from E. J. Barker for the breeding herd. In February, 1956, the manager of the Cuban operation reported a population of approximately 4500 head of cattle, including calves, of which about 1500 are Santa Gertrudis.

After his appointment, Lowel Tash proceeded rapidly with the development of this area into a ranching enterprise which, except for differences imposed by climate, is quite similar in design and operation to the King Ranch in Texas. The headquarters ranch bears the name "Becerra." The Running W inverted with a bar under it ᴔ is used as a brand. It is anticipated that the venture will build to more than 10,000 cattle.

To date the most serious problem encountered in Cuba has been the control of an obnoxious brush known as *marabu*. Much work has been necessary, not only to control *marabu* but to eliminate other brush and weeds. The brush clearing machines developed by the King Ranch in Texas have proved exceedingly useful. In the spring of 1953, after a visit to Brazil, Robert J. Kleberg, Jr., suggested the importation of a Brazilian grass, *Colonião (Panicum maximum)*. A thousand kilos (2204.6 pounds) of seed were purchased. The South American grass has done very well at Becerra, as well as in other parts of the island where it has been tried.

It was after the conversion of jungle growth to first class grazing land and the fencing of pastures with wire net fence that the King Ranch began to move some of its high quality purebred Santa Gertrudis cattle into the country. In addition to cattle herds, the ranch has established a herd of King Ranch Quarter Horses, since they appear to be well suited to Cuban ranching needs.

The most recent development on the Cuban scene has been the production on the ranch of Sumner Pingree, at Ermita, of the first choice and prime steers—graded according to American standards—which, so far as is known, have been produced in the tropics. This was additional verification of the value of Santa Gertrudis blood under tropical conditions.

In addition to Mr. Barker and Mr. Pingree, among the earliest Cuban breeders to produce high quality Santa Gertrudis cattle, both for breeding and commercial purposes, were Federico Castellanos, Estanislao del Valle and Alvaro Sanchez.

One of the greatest attractions of the ranching development in Cuba has been the fact that the country produces barely enough beef for its own consumption. The sugar business has been curtailed in Cuba, and it appears that the land lends itself next best—if not best—to cattle production. From the pioneering experiences of Mr. Barker and other early breeders, the use of purebred Santa Gertrudis bulls on the Brahman and Brahman-type cattle of Cuba will increase both quality and quantity of beef. The hope is that volume introduction of Santa Gertrudis blood into Cuba will step up beef production to the point of benefit to the national economy.

In going into the Cuban enterprise, the King Ranch was aware of an additional attractive possibility. Cuba is to some extent a gateway into and out of South America; certainly it has served as a testing ground for the new breed of cattle under tropical conditions. It was felt that once purebred Santa Gertrudis become available in sufficient number and have been exposed to tropical diseases and the fever tick, the ranch can help supply the South American demand.

Brazil

IN 1953 ROBERT J. KLEBERG, JR., as president of the King Ranch corporation, was invited to Brazil by A. Thomas Taylor, of International Packers Ltd., to survey the cattle situation in Brazil. Together they made an extensive inspection trip through the states of São Paulo, Mato Grosso and Minas Gerais by private plane and auto-

mobile. International Packers' subsidiary, Companhia Swift do Brasil, S. A., had already developed a 54,000-acre operation near Rancheria, State of São Paulo, a fine ranching property with wonderful grazing on which they were fattening some 20,000 cattle, mostly steers.

This ranch had at one time been part of a ranching venture which had been stocked with Shorthorn cattle. The venture was a failure, and it is now known that the failure was because Shorthorn cattle were not adaptable to climatic and range conditions prevalent in the area.

As a result of the trip made by Mr. Kleberg and Mr. Taylor, the King Ranch organized a subsidiary Brazilian company known as King Ranch do Brasil, S. A., and this company entered into a joint agreement with Companhia Swift do Brasil, an agreement involving cattle land already owned by the Brazilian company and land to be purchased. King Ranch do Brasil acquired properties totaling about 70,000 acres: Mosquito, the southernmost, 34,469 acres; Formosa, 16,650 acres; and in joint ownership with Swift a 42,228-acre tract known as Brasilandia—all located in the southwest corner of the State of São Paulo on the Rio Paranapanema. These various purchases brought the total of all the lands included in the agreement to approximately 147,000 acres.

In addition to the land, the King Ranch and Swift do Brasil supplied either capital or cattle of equivalent value. Swift do Brasil was named to manage the operation and the King Ranch agreed to furnish a herd of purebred cattle from the King Ranch in Texas and give technical advice on breeding up the Brazilian cattle.

In January, 1954, thirty-four Santa Gertrudis bulls and 225 heifers were shipped from the King Ranch to Brazil. The following month an additional shipment was made of 113 bulls, 7 Quarter Horse mares and 1 stallion, Saltillo Jr. In March of 1955 there was another shipment of 125 bulls.

At the present time the joint ranching venture has something over 30,000 cattle on its 147,000 acres. The ultimate goal is to run in excess of 60,000 head on this land, approaching or even surpassing the productive capacity of the King Ranch's Texas lands.

NOTES

and

SOURCES

1 "What I Live For" was written by George Linnaeus Banks (1821-1881), an English editor, song writer, dramatist and social reformer. This poem is believed to have first appeared in a Liverpool newspaper. In 1865 it was included in a volume of poetry by Banks and his wife, *Daisies in the Grass;* it has also appeared under the title "My Aim." Its lines were frequently quoted by platform and pulpit orators of the late nineteenth century.

2 "Estate of Richard King, Deceased: Order Admitting Will to Probate," August 4, 1885, *Probate Minutes*, Nueces County, Vol. F, pp. 10-11.

3 Same, p. 11.

4 Same.

5 "Estate of Richard King, Deceased: Inventory and Appraisement." See Appendix X, Vol. I.

6 It is impossible at this late date to arrive at an exact total of Captain King's indebtedness. The *Wells Papers* contain numerous references to notes and debts, but existing records are far from sufficient to reconstruct anything like an exact accounting.

7 Quotations are from correspondence in the *Wells Papers*.

"Collins" referred to Collins Station, about five miles east of present-day Alice, the mailing address for the ranch. The ranch's letterhead of that day carried the inscription "King's Rancho, Santa Gertrudis, Collins, Nueces County, Texas."

8 *Wells Papers*.

9 He was christened Johann Christian Justus Robert Kleberg.

10 As quoted by Brown, *Indian Wars and Pioneers of Texas*, p. 289.

11 Biographical material on the Kleberg family was taken from Gilbert Giddings Benjamin, *The Germans in Texas, A Study in Immigration* (Philadelphia, 1909), pp. 14-17; Rudolph Leopold Biesele, *The History of the German Settlement in Texas, 1831-1861* (Austin, 1930); Don H. Biggers, *German Pioneers in Texas* (Fred-ericksburg, 1925), p. 11; Sam Houston Dixon and Louis Wiltz Kemp, *The Heroes of San Jacinto* (Houston, 1932), pp. 179, 194; Rosalie von Roeder Kleberg, "Some of My Early Experiences in Texas," *Quarterly of the Texas State Historical Association*, Vol. I (July, 1897), pp. 297-303; same, Vol. II (April, 1898), pp. 170-173; Rudolph Kleberg, "Biography of Rosalie von Roeder Kleberg," (apparently prepared for inclusion in a family history); Fulmore, pp. 162-164; Brown, *Indian Wars and Pioneers of Texas*, pp. 289-295; Frank W. Johnson, *A History of Texas and Texans* (Chicago, 1914), Vol. IV, pp. 1629-1630; and other standard sources of biographical data on Texas pioneers.

12 Literally "The Red Estate."

13 Prior to World War II the Sack family published a family history every ten years, *Das Silberne Buch (The Silver Book)*, so-called because the background of the family coat of arms was silver. The last edition was in 1936. Lilly Hohfeld Mooney, a member of the Sack family wrote:

This project is not the biography of an individual but of a family, a family unique in the world from the standpoint of family solidarity. It is the history of the famous Sack family which originated in Germany and is now spread over six continents, thirty-two countries, and six hundred and one cities. In our own country members of the family are to be found in twenty-four states, and in fourteen counties of Texas where they became pioneers and empire builders.

In addition to the family history, this old and far-flung family maintained contact by means of a semi-annual paper, *Die Taube (The Dove)*. The central figure of the family coat of arms was a dove with an olive branch. The motto on the Sack family coat of arms was *Hilft dir selbst, so hilft der Gott* — God helps him who helps himself.

14 Robert J. Kleberg, Jr., "Our One Hundred Years of Ranching — What's Next?" *Breeding Beef Cattle for Unfavorable Environments, A Symposium Presented at the King Ranch Centennial Conference*, ed. Albert O. Rhoad (Austin, 1955), p. 223.

15   Later E. B. Raymond organized the Raymond Town and Improvement Co., in 1904, and established Raymondville.

16   Alvarado, "Memoirs."

17   "Record of Cattle Business, Nueces County, Texas," courtesy of James Rowe, *Corpus Christi Caller-Times.*

All sales of stock in Nueces County were apparently subject to registration by hide and cattle inspectors and should, therefore, be included in the above-cited record. However, there is definite indication that all sales did not get into the record or some of the records have since been lost. For example, Alvarado's "Memoirs" report the sale of a lot of 2000 head which does not appear in the cattle inspectors' record.

18   The town which would become Alice was founded in 1888 as a depot for the San Antonio and Aransas Pass Railway Co. It was first called Bandana, then Kleberg after Alice Kleberg, and finally Alice. Between 1890 and 1895 it was an important shipping center for cattle.

19   *Kingsville Record,* July 3, 1929; Ralph W. Steen, *History of Texas* (Austin, 1939), p. 368.

20   "Dad" Stevens, as quoted by "When Wild Horses Were Trapped in City of Kingsville," *Kingsville Record,* July 3, 1929.

21   Alvarado, "Memoirs."
Alvarado's reference was to Rodolfo Gaona, the great *torero* of Mexico who developed a cape figure known as the *Gaonera.* Alvarado was obviously looking back with a knowledge of the present. Gaona was born in 1888, about the time of this roundup; he did not become a full-fledged *matador de toros* until May 21, 1908; he was at his height in the late teens and early twenties.

22   Stevens, as cited; Dobie, *The Longhorns,* p. 150; Robert J. Kleberg, Sr., to Robert J. Kleberg, Jr.

23   Frank Goodwyn, *Life on the King Ranch* (New York, 1951), p. 26.

24   Notes in the handwriting of Mrs. Alice Gertrudis King Kleberg, King Ranch vault.

25   Biographical data on Samuel G. Ragland comes from an obituary from an unidentified newspaper clipping and from personal interview with those who knew him.

26   Bass, p. 66; Ragland's obituary.
Jot Gunter operated the well-known T Anchor Ranch and engaged in numerous ranching and cattle enterprises. In 1901 he entered the real estate business in San Antonio, where the Gunter Hotel and the Gunter Office Building were named for him.

27   Robert J. Kleberg, Jr., and Ragland's obituary.

28   "Growth and Development of the King Ranch," *Kingsville Record,* July 3, 1929; *Prose and Poetry of the Live Stock Industry,* p. 84.

29   The disease was known but not the cause. The early outbreak in Pennsylvania followed the introduction of cattle from South Carolina. Virginia (in 1812) and North Carolina (in 1837) prohibited the entrance of cattle from Georgia and South Carolina between April 1 and November 1.—T. C. Richardson, p. 315.

30   Robert J. Kleberg, Sr., to Robert J. Kleberg, Jr.

31   Bass, pp. 65-70.

32   Doctor Curtice's investigations proved the culprit to be *Margaropus annulatus.* The findings were published in a government bulletin, *Prevention and Treatment of Diseases of Cattle.* Doctor Curtice's early recommendations were to immunize by allowing a tick from a diseased cow to bite another or by injecting with serum made from the blood of infected animals. The resulting fever was treated by injections of Trypan blue. Early experiments were reported to result in ten per cent loss for ninety per cent immunity.

33   Mary Whatley Clarke, "Scions of Great King Ranch Headed Association," *The Cattleman,* XXXVII (March, 1951), pp. 23ff.

34   Same.

35   Robert J. Kleberg, Jr., to Tom Lea.

36   Clarke, p. 66.

37   *Wells Papers.* See Appendix X, Vol. I.

38   Chatfield, p. 38.

39 Considerable information concerning the land transactions is found in the *Wells Papers,* but because of the lack of copies of outgoing correspondence, the story is often fragmentary and one-sided. However, correspondence pertaining to acquisitions in the San Juan de Carricitos area reveals that the entirety was being laboriously pieced together, scrap by scrap, with the consequent maze of legal technicalities. See Vol. I, Chap. XI, Nt. 18.

40 "Power of Attorney: Henrietta M. King to Robert J. Kleberg," *Bond and Mortgage Records,* Nueces County, Vol. H, p. 400.

41 The close relationship between James B. Wells and the Kleberg family is indicated by correspondence in the *Wells Papers.* Robert J. Kleberg addressed him as "Friend Jim," Mrs. Alice G. King Kleberg as "Kind Friend," from El Sauz E. B. Raymond wrote him as "Dear Compadre," and in later times Caesar Kleberg wrote "Dear Partner." Wells named his son Robert for Mr. Kleberg.

42 The changes in the law firm membership are indicated by letterheads found in the *Wells Papers.* See Vol. I, Chap. VII, Nt. 7.

43 Robert J. Kleberg, Jr., "Our One Hundred Years of Ranching," p. 224.

44 Mathew John Kivlin to Holland McCombs, June 16, 1952.

45 *Kingsville Record,* July 3, 1929.

46 *San Antonio Express,* August 13, 1933.

47 For an official government report on the rainmaking experiments see Sen. Ex. Doc. No. 45, 52nd Cong., 1st Sess., *A Report of the Special Agent of the Department of Agriculture for Making Experiments in the Production of Rainfall.*

48 *Corpus Christi Caller,* December 21, 1900, and July 28, 1929; Bass, pp. 88-93.

49 The *Corpus Christi Caller,* December 21, 1900, reported John G. Kenedy, Robert Driscoll and Edward C. Lasater among those who were successfully drilling wells.

50 Mathew John Kivlin to Holland McCombs, June 16, 1952.

CHAPTER XIV

1 Dr. Arthur E. Spohn married Sarah Josephine Kenedy in 1876.

2 Except as indicated by notes or in the text, details of fact and anecdote for this chapter have been obtained from living members of the family or have been taken from letters, notes, and similar material on file in the King Ranch vault.

3 In 1881 Captain King placed seventeen German carp in the Tranquitas.—McCampbell, *Saga of a Frontier Seaport,* p. 90.

4 Richard M. Kleberg, Sr., and J. T. Canales.

5 Goodwyn, pp. 137-141.

6 Robert J. Kleberg, Jr., and Mrs. Thomas R. Armstrong to Tom Lea. See Allhands, *Gringo Builders,* p. 17, for reproduction of a photograph.

7 Richard Harding Davis, "The West from a Car Window," *Harper's Weekly,* XXXVI (April 30, 1892), pp. 412-415.

8 Mrs. Jeff N. Miller to Holland McCombs, January 17, 1954.

9 In a letter written November 13, 1896, to Addie Gillette Chamberlain, wife of Mrs. King's youngest brother.—King Ranch vault.

10 *Corpus Christi Caller,* as quoted by McCampbell, *Saga of a Frontier Seaport,* p. 51.

11 From an unidentified newspaper clipping in the King Ranch vault.

12 McCampbell, *Saga of a Frontier Seaport,* pp. 150-151.

13 *Corpus Christi Caller,* March 15, 1895.

CHAPTER XV

1 For example, according to available records, in July, 1900, Mrs. King paid $14 per head for 1000 heifer calves from the "Texas Land and Cattle Company, Laureles Ranch."

2 *Wells Papers.*

3 Details of the transactions are from King Ranch records. However, it is not known if the sums cited were the total payments for land and

improvements alone, with purchases of stock being a separate transaction, or if a single agreement covered all. As noted above, there were earlier sales of cattle to Mrs. King by the Texas Land and Cattle Co. There were also other financial transactions. For example, there is a canceled check in the King Ranch vault dated October 28, 1901, for $166,856.50. The date indicates that it could have been a result of the Kleberg-Wells meeting with Captain Tod and Mr. Ogden. It might have been a "down payment," or it could have been a purchase of livestock as a separate transaction.

4 On September 12, 1901, James B. Wells had wired Charles Ogden that the King Ranch would not retain the Laurel Leaf brand but would return it to the Kenedys.—*Wells Papers.*

The Laurel Leaf brand is in use today on the Kenedy ranch by Mrs. Sarita K. East, the founder's granddaughter.

5 Bass, "Table I," pp. 249-250.

6 Charles Rogan, *Report of the Commissioner of the General Land Office, State of Texas, From August 31, 1900, to September 1, 1902* (Austin, 1902), p. 42.

7 *Wells Papers.*

8 The lease, dated April 23, 1901, was transferred to the King Oil Co. on May 4, 1901. Filed June 17, 1901, *Deed Records*, Nueces County, Vol. K, pp. 276-277.

9 *Houston Chronicle*, as quoted by *A Twentieth Century History of Southwest Texas* (Chicago, 1907), Vol. I, pp. 492-493:

Ten million dollars, spot cash, is the neat little sum that has been refused by heirs of the King estate for the great King ranch in Southeast Texas, . . .

Eastern parties, some of whom live in New York, and others in eastern and northern cities, desired to become possessors of the property. The *Chronicle* is not at liberty to reveal their names, . . .

The land was to be cut up into plantations, which were to be watered by artesian wells, as the experience at Kingsville has shown that artesian water may easily be obtained on the territory.

Street car systems were to connect the entire territory and form a network all over it, and more than the pur-

chase price — that is to say, a sum in excess of ten million dollars — was to be spent in making the land ready for the occupancy of the agriculturists who were to be invited to colonize it . . . but prospects are now not so good that a trade may be made.

10 A few forward-looking citizens continued the fight for railroads. The outstanding visionary outlook was that of Lieutenant W. H. Chatfield, who in 1892 started the first movement to provide the valley with a comprehensive irrigation system including a dam across the river and a reservoir north of Rio Grande City. In an open letter in the Brownsville *Cosmopolitan*, December 22, 1892, he said:

If the people of this section want railroads, as well as every other luxury which wealth will bring, let them rub their eyes and arouse themselves to the standing offer I have made to irrigate their lands. After their lands are provided with irrigation, let them parcel them out to the thousand of buyers who will eagerly purchase them at a fair price. Away with this lethargy. Arise to the situation, secure railroads — or flying machines if you prefer them. You would have money to buy both if you wished. —As quoted by Allhands, *Gringo Builders*, pp. 163-164.

This was in 1892, eleven years before the Wright brothers flew at Kitty Hawk.

11 The New York, Texas & Mexican Railway Co. was organized by Count Joseph Telfener, an Italian count. His dream was of a railroad to reach into Mexico, crossing the border by means of a drawbridge at Brownsville. It reached Wharton, revitalized a village and named it Hungerford after one of the builders, and created the town of Telfener. The road was generally known as "The Macaroni," because of the Italian workmen employed by Count Telfener.—Same, pp. 75-77.

12 Same, pp. 64-66, 77-78; McCampbell, *Saga of a Frontier Seaport*, pp. 41-45.

13 *Corpus Christi Caller*, June 13, 1902.

14 On October 20, 1891, the Pan-American Railway was granted authority to build a railroad between Victoria and Brownsville. Ten miles of track was all that materialized.—Same, pp. 78-79.

15 Same, pp. 115-116.

16 According to communications in the *Wells Papers,* Major Armstrong arranged for subscriptions from several people including Mrs. King, Captain Kenedy, James Stillman, Thomas Carson and Francisco Ytúrria.

17 Allhands, *Gringo Builders,* pp. 36-40.

18 As a result of his experimental farm, irrigated by artesian water, Mr. Kleberg reported a return of $300 per acre from cabbage and of from $350 to $500 per acre from onions.—F. C. Carter, "Santa Gertrudes Ranch," *Harper's Weekly,* L (August 18, 1906), pp. 1170-1171.

19 Chatfield, p. 38.

20 Bass, pp. 110-112; *Texas Stockman and Farmer,* July 5, 1905, as quoted by "First Year of Kingsville History Written in 1905," *Kingsville Record,* July 3, 1929; McCampbell, *Saga of a Frontier Seaport,* p. 91; Allhands, *Gringo Builders,* pp. 21-22.

21 "Growth and Development of the King Ranch," *Kingsville Record,* July 3, 1929.

22 Lott had employed Yoakum earlier, at the age of twenty-six, as chief clerk on the S. A. & A. P. Eventually Yoakum worked up to become vice president and general manager. When Lott lost control of the property they went their individual ways. Yoakum became general manager of the Gulf, Colorado & Santa Fe, and in 1896 moved on to the St. Louis & San Francisco Railway in the same capacity. In 1905 the Frisco and the Rock Island lines were combined into a seventeen-thousand-mile system with Yoakum as chairman of the executive committee.

23 "The Building of the Brownsville Railroad Told," *Kingsville Record,* July 3, 1929.

Later Yoakum wrote:

Without previous notice I received at St. Louis a telegram signed by Robert J. Kleberg, John Kenedy, Major John B. Armstrong and Robert Driscoll, asking for an appointment with me in St. Louis. These gentlemen outlined a proposition to build a railroad connection with the Texas Mexican Railroad from Robertson to Brownsville.—B. F. Yoakum, "Some of My Activities in the Upbuilding of Corpus Christi and Gulf Coast of Texas," *Corpus Christi Caller,* July 4, 1929.

24 "The Building of the Brownsville Railroad Told," as cited.

25 Allhands, *Gringo Builders,* p. 12.

26 The party was composed of the consulting engineer for the project, J. F. Hinckley, and B. F. Johnston, F. P. Read, J. H. Hedges and J. L. Allhands.—Same, p. 13.

27 Allhands, *Uriah Lott,* p. 29.

28 Allhands, *Gringo Builders,* p. 35.

29 Same, p. 85.

30 Same, p. 40.

31 *Brownsville Herald,* June 3, 1903, as quoted by Allhands, *Gringo Builders,* p. 37.

32 The estimates of construction costs on the Brownsville line were $12,250 per mile for 141.75 miles of main line and $11,500 per mile for 55.73 miles of branch lines. This did not include equipment costs, right of way and other expenses. It was estimated $3,000,000 would have to be raised by subscription.—Allhands, *Uriah Lott,* p. 107.

33 Allhands, *Gringo Builders,* p. 45.

34 Jeff N. Miller, "Historic Events in the Early Life of Kingsville," *Kingsville Record,* July 3, 1929.

35 Allhands, *Gringo Builders,* pp. 45-47.

36 B. F. Yoakum, as cited.

37 "Building of the Brownsville Railroad Told."

38 Same.

39 Allhands, *Gringo Builders,* p. 147.

40 Robert W. Stayton to Holland McCombs, October 18, 1951.

41 The deeds from Mrs. King to the Kleberg Town & Improvement Co. were not executed until August 20, 1904, because of legal entanglements. Land sales prior to this date were covered by options. The deed to the Kingsville area referred to the sites of the towns of Kingsville, Escondido, Richard, Tranquitas, Capitan, Venado and Uriah. The deed to the Raymondville area mentioned Raymondville, Lyford, Still-

man, Narcisso and Jose.—*Deed Records,* Nueces County, Vol. 12, p. 546; *Transcribed Records, Cameron to Willacy County,* Vol. 1, pp. 241-246.

42 *Wells Papers; Defendants' Brief, Equity No. 74, Edwin K. Atwood,* et al, v. *Robert J. Kleberg, Jr.,* et al, *in the United States District Court for the Southern District of Texas, Corpus Christi Division* (hereafter cited as *"Defendants' Brief"*), pp. 256-258.

43 Same.

44 *Wells Papers.*

45 "A Vision of Faith," *Kingsville Record,* July 3, 1929; Bass, pp. 121-127.

46 Harlingen, for example, had a particularly hectic development. On the first day of clearing land for the new railroad, sixteen rattlesnakes were killed. Naturally, the place was called "Rattlesnake Junction." A saloon was the first business establishment and the community quickly earned the sobriquet "Six-Shooter Junction." The name that stuck was applied by Lon C. Hill, a name which by a strange quirk of coincidence was an ancestral name of Uriah Lott, the railroad's builder:

"The railroad was going to establish a townsite near the present city of Harlingen, and they wanted me to select the name. The Arroyo Colorado some day, I think, will be the Intracoastal Canal, and besides, this being an irrigated country, I naturally wanted to select a name of some of the ship canals. I knew that in Holland there are a great many ship canals, and in looking over the map of Holland I found a town by the name of Van Harlingen. The post office directory showed no town in Texas by that name, so I decided to leave off the 'Van' and name this town Harlingen.

"At that time Col. Uriah Lott was president of the railroad, and when I told him of my intentions in regard to naming the town, he stated that was fine, and that his grandmother was named Van Harlingen, and that the town of Van Harlingen in Holland was named for her family."—Lon C. Hill, as quoted by "Harlingen Had Several Names in Old Days," *Corpus Christi Caller,* July 4, 1929.

47 Allhands, *Gringo Builders,* pp. 83-84.

48 Jeff N. Miller, "Historical Review of the Construction of the St. Louis, Brownsville & Mexico Ry.," *Corpus Christi Caller,* July 4, 1929.

49 Mathew John Kivlin to Holland McCombs, June 16, 1952. The restaurant was operated by Mr. and Mrs. O. S. Watson. Watson was also justice of the peace and pumper for the railroad.

50 Allhands, *Gringo Builders,* p. 84; *Uriah Lott,* p. 133; *Kingsville Record,* July 3, 1929.

51 Allhands, *Uriah Lott,* p. 132.

52 For a description of Kingsville and events which transpired in 1904 and the years following, see the various accounts by old-time residents in the *Kingsville Record,* July 3, 1929. This issue of the *Record* was published to commemorate the twenty-fifth anniversary of the completion of the railroad between Brownsville and Corpus Christi.

53 Roy Miller held the post of "Advertising and Immigration Agent" to the railroad. He later took over the *Corpus Christi Caller,* in which Mrs. King was the principal stockholder. The July 4, 1929, issue of the *Caller* was a "Silver Anniversary Issue," dedicated to Robert J. Kleberg and commemorating the anniversary of the completion of the railroad connection with Brownsville.

54 McCampbell, *Saga of a Frontier Seaport,* p. 91; Allhands, *Gringo Builders,* p. 86; Marcus Phillips, "Kingsville's First Postmaster Relates Early History," *Kingsville Record,* July 3, 1929.

55 Bass, p. 125; "First Year of Kingsville History . . .," as cited.

56 Bass, pp. 170-171; see also Marcus Phillips, as cited.

57 "Inventory and Appraisement of the Estate of Henrietta M. King, Deceased," *Minutes of the Probate Court,* Kleberg County, Vol. I, pp. 609 ff. (hereafter cited as "Inventory and Appraisement"); *Kingsville Record,* July 3, 1929.

58 Allhands, *Gringo Builders,* p. 85.

59 Bass, p. 171.

60 *Wells Papers.*

61 Bass, p. 22; Allhands, *Gringo Builders,* p. 88.

62 *Defendants' Brief,* pp. 245-256, 272-275.

63 Same, pp. 240-245, 256-265; *Kingsville Record*, July 3, 1929.

64 The first church services were conducted by Rev. A. S. McCurdy.—Marcus Phillips; Allhands, *Gringo Builders*, pp. 85-86.

65 *Kingsville Record*, July 3, 1929.

66 The lodge room was located in the upper story of the frame building which housed the Kingsville Lumber Co.

67 "History of Masonic Lodge in Kingsville," *Kingsville Record*, July 3, 1929; see also Marcus Phillips.

68 Same.

69 *Daily Corpus Christi Caller*, July 24, 1909; *The Texas Almanac and State Industrial Guide, 1925* (Dallas, 1925), p. 307.

70 *For God, America, and Mexico* (Kingsville, n.d.); *Corpus Christi Caller-Times*, July 12, 1953.

71 The railroad's time table listed the stations as Robstown, Coldris (Driscoll), Julia (Bishop), Caesar, Kingsville, Richard (Ricardo), Spohn (Riviera), Sarita, Mifflin, Turcotte, Katherine (Armstrong), Norias, Rudolph, Yturria, Raymondville, Lyford, Stillman (Sebastian), Harlingen, Combes, Bessie (San Benito), Fordyce, Olmito, Brownsville. Twelve were flag stops.—Allhands, *Gringo Builders*, p. 147.

72 There was competition between the various land companies which formed to exploit the new lands opened by irrigation and the coming of the railroad. Old-timers tell of how promoters who were selling the idea that irrigated land in the valley was best would attempt to keep their prospects from seeing that dry-farming was being successfully carried on. As the train approached Raymondville the land company agents would come through the coaches pulling down shades and announcing that it was time for prayers. Thus they kept their prospects occupied with prayers while the train was going past the nonirrigated farms.—Robert C. Wells.

73 Bishop was one of the more colorful promoters. A story is told that one day he had a prospect out showing him a stretch of land. While they were talking a messenger arrived from town with a telegram which had been arranged for previously. Bishop excused himself while he read the message; then he exclaimed "Why, there's old J. P. Morgan after me again!" He waved the telegram at the land across the road. "Old J. P.'s been trying to buy that land for a long time and he won't give me my price." Then, of course, he named a price in the vicinity of what he had been quoting his prospect.—Theodore F. Koch, Jr., to Robert C. Wells.

74 "Bishop Named After Native of Tennessee," *Corpus Christi Caller*, July 4, 1929; *Defendants' Brief*, pp. 440-441.

75 Thomas F. Koch, "Interesting Sidelights — Early History of Kleberg County," *Kingsville Record*, July 3, 1929.

The article which Koch read was "The Growth of Southwest Texas," *The American Monthly Review of Reviews*, XXXIII (February, 1906), pp. 206-211.

The article told of great profits to be made in Texas farming, but did not discount the possibility of failure. A warning was sounded against growers putting blind trust in northern commission merchants:

. . . . Several unscrupulous agents were detected and forced to refund, but the majority kept the money which rightfully belonged to the grower.

This disheartened many, and those who have been rushing to Kingsville, Brownsville, and Laredo in the past few months have met a few coming away. Organization and business methods will right all this. Southwest Texas, especially Corpus Christi, sends vegetables and fruits to the Northern markets from two to six weeks ahead of any other section of the South, and such an advantage is bound to prove permanently profitable.

76 Bass, pp. 182-184.

77 Allhands, *Gringo Builders*, p. 89.

78 Bass, pp. 206-209.

79 Allhands, *Gringo Builders*, p. 91.

80 Same, pp. 183-184.

81 J. T. Canales, "Personal Recollections," April 28, 1945, courtesy Harbert Davenport.

[82] Allhands, *Gringo Builders,* p. 176.

[83] Canales, "Personal Recollections."

[84] Same; Roy Miller, "The Realization of an Assured Future — Being the Story of Corpus Christi," *Corpus Christi Caller,* July 4, 1929.

[85] O. Douglas Weeks, "The Texas-Mexican and the Politics of South Texas," *American Political Science Review,* XIV (August, 1930), pp. 618-619.

[86] *Hebbronville News,* December 29, 1923.

In the spring Judge Wells' party lost the city election to the Republicans and Independents. —*Brownsville Herald,* April 9, 1910. This made the fall county elections doubly important and doubly difficult. For the month leading up to the event, the *Brownsville Herald* is replete with political news and political advertisements, charges and countercharges. The issue of November 10, 1910, contains the official returns.

[87] "Willacy County," *Handbook of Texas,* Vol. II, p. 911.

[88] "Kenedy County," same, Vol. I, p. 947.

[89] "Jim Wells County," same, Vol. I, p. 913.

[90] "Kleberg County," same, Vol. I, p. 969.

[91] Bass, pp. 237-238.

The King Ranch lost control of Kleberg County at the first election after the organization of the county. Judge Wells was then called in and it required all of his acumen to get the situation in hand.—Harbert Davenport to Holland McCombs, August 8, 1952.

[92] *Wells Papers.*

[93] Harbert Davenport to Holland McCombs, August 8, 1952.

[94] Mrs. Jeff N. Miller to Holland McCombs, January 17, 1954.

[95] The tutor was acquired while the family was vacationing in New York. Dick saved a Frenchman, "a little man in a derby hat, with a superbly curving mustache," from being involved in an accident. Dick took the Frenchman back to the hotel and introduced him to his father. Mr. Kleberg employed him as a tutor and took him back to the ranch where he remained for eight and a half years.—Richard M. Kleberg, Sr., to Holland McCombs.

[96] Goodwyn, pp. 278-279.

[97] For a biographical sketch of Judge Simkins see the *Dallas Morning News,* November 28, 1926.

[98] In the interval between graduation from college and marriage, Richard M. Kleberg, Sr., gained some practical legal experience during a short period of working in Brownsville in the office of James B. Wells and then in Austin.

[99] Later Mrs. Richard M. Kleberg, Sr.'s daughter Alice, Mrs. Richard Reynolds, would also graduate from the University of Texas with Phi Beta Kappa honors.

[100] The catalogue of the Running W Saddle Shop, "A Department of the Kingsville Lumber Co.," advertised a large line of saddles including several models of the "Dick Kleberg Special," featuring the "Kleberg Special Tree":

This tree was designed by a ranchman with the special purpose in mind to rid himself of sore back horses as well as to be comfortable to ride. After studying the faults and defects of other trees as well as the backs of the average ranch horse, this tree was designed, special attention being given to the shape of the bars which are the essential features of a tree not hurting, along with the leg cut under swell, make the saddle fit just right, easy to ride and stay where it is put and consequently it will not hurt and will not be found wanting in the most legitimate test of heavy ranch work.

[101] George Clegg to Holland McCombs.

[102] Villa died in 1929 on the Santa Gertrudis ranch, ending a life of activity which was of the nature from which traditions and myths evolve. Stories of Villa's exploits will linger throughout South Texas as long as the great ranching tradition endures and if the tales are magnified as the years pass it will be only because they are based on facts in an unusual life.

Known to have been approximately 21 years old in 1832 when Santa Anna first crossed into Texas, Villa was approximately 118 years old at the time of his death. He lived a life of the greatest activity until the day he was struck down by a fatal attack of double pneumonia.

In 1832 Faustino lived in Matamoros, near which city he was born. He was married when he was 46 and his son, Juan Villa, who is more than 70 years old now, lives in Corpus Christi.

Villa lived under five flags. He served under the Emperor Maximilian of Mexico and after Maximilian's overthrow, under General Miramon, also in Mexico. In 1851 he went to Matamoros and was employed by Capt. Richard King and Capt. M. Kenedy as a fireman on the "Corvette," which they operated on the Rio Grande river. In 1854 he left the company and accompanied Capt. King to the Santa Gertrudis ranch as a cowhand.

Villa was a man of the greatest daring and personal courage. . . In all of Texas it was said he had no equal as a swimmer and his reputation extended throughout the state.

A man of remarkable endurance, Villa rode horseback until two weeks before his death at which time he was still on the ranch payroll. He refused to accept a pension, declaring "When Faustino Villa gets so he can't earn grub he'll be ready to go." He survived an attack of double pneumonia in 1923 in spite of his advanced age, and later spent two days lost on the open range in bitter cold weather but returned to the ranch none the worse for his experience . . .

Villa knew Corpus Christi when there was only one white man living here. He made his first trip to this vicinity in 1834 and told the story that at that time the country was unbroken prairie from the Arroyo Colorado, south of Harlingen, to Corpus Christi with the exception of a few scattered mots or thickets. At that time deer ran over the land in herds of three and four hundred and Villa told that he once saw more than 1,000 to a herd, south of the Oso. . . —*Corpus Christi Caller,* March 17, 1931.

[103] President Taft's letter of appreciation for the gifts and a letter of thanks to his hostess are contained in a family scrapbook in the King Ranch vault.

[104] *San Antonio Light,* January 4 and 5, 1912.
Data for the account of the fire has been obtained from the memories of living participants.

[105] This house is at present the residence of Mr. and Mrs. Robert J. Kleberg, Jr.

[106] Carleton W. Adams of San Antonio was the architect. His memories of his experiences while building the house form a revealing picture of the family:

I have a rich and delightful memory of the whole family group at Santa Gertrudis.

Of course, my first contact was with Mr. Kleberg, a large, handsome gentleman, definitely of the German type, whose kindly, keen eyes and forceful mouth and chin at once bespoke of power and ability to carry the responsibilities of the empire he controlled. I don't remember ever seeing him so taxed as to overburden his abilities, or remember his losing his temper or self-control. He spoke with the even, measured voice of authority, and in a way that left no doubt as to the meaning of his words.

I will never forget the occasion when, after numerous conferences Mr. Kleberg told my partner [Carl Adams] and me that he had decided to assign us to the architectural and engineering contract for the design of the Santa Gertrudis Ranch House. In essence he said that he had a deep desire to help ambitious young men who appeared to be basically honest, and who appeared not only to have a sincere desire to render good service, but also appeared to have reasonable ability to do so, conditioned upon a will to remain steadfast to their task. At the same time Mr. Kleberg made us realize that failure on our part would hurt him as well as ourselves, because he was intentionally accepting on faith the services of young men whose actual business experience hardly warranted the decision he made in employing us rather than one of the widely recognized firms that were soliciting the work. My thought in mentioning this is not by way of endeavoring to compliment ourselves, but rather to illustrate Mr. Kleberg's able manner in making persons feel their individual responsibility whenever he delegated authority to them.

Mrs. Kleberg seemed to me to be an ideal mate for this husband-wife team. There appeared to be a fine balance in their individual abilities and acceptance of family responsibilities as applied to their sons and daughters and all affairs of mutual interest. Mrs. Kleberg seemed to have the management of the home well in hand. If there were conflict it was never apparent or displayed in public. The family bark appeared to be on an even keel and to sail serenely on in untroubled waters, but I doubt not that all the while unseen and able hands were pouring out oil to smooth the way.

Mrs. King was a little over 80 years of age at the time of which I write. I remember her as an able and kindly lady, of great religious faith (Presbyterian), keenly interested in both the family and business affairs that surrounded her. In quiet dignity she easily maintained her rightful position in the household.

. . . I would like to express appreciation for the privilege of knowing and having delightful fellowship with Richard (and his wife, Mamie), Robert, Henrietta, Alice and Sarah, and also Caesar (nephew of R. J.) and Sam Ragland, all of whom lived at the Ranch as one big family.

As a family I remember them as being interested in each other, and interested in the activities of the other, and all interested in life on the Ranch and in the things of the Ranch. They were all *able* ranch-folk, experienced in handling cattle and horses, and in hunting the various kinds of game to be secured in the extensive pastures of the Ranch . . .

Much of their social life consisted of activities within the family group and also with their guests and intimate friends. When they occasionally went to Kingsville or Corpus Christi to the picture show, or some other place of entertainment, some of the townspeople considered the Kleberg clan as being "exclusive," but this was because they enjoyed being with each other, and not because of "high-hat" personalities.

Many of the outstanding memories of my life consist of the busy but happy year and one-half that I was associated with the fine folks at Santa Gertrudis, and was also a participant in the wonderful way of life there. —Carleton W. Adams.

CHAPTER XVI

[1] Madero's book was published in 1908. The date in its title had reference to the coming election year.

[2] Parkes, p. 325.

[3] For a study of this turbulent period in Mexican history see Parkes, pp. 311-367.

[4] Pierce, p. 75.

[5] Following a revolt against Madero in Mexico City, the garrison of regulars in Matamoros renounced allegiance to Madero on February 16, 1913. Díaz partisans seized the city government. Major Ramos, troop commander, requested loans from both sides of the Rio Grande for payment of his troops, otherwise he would have to allow members of his force "to go uncontrolled" and "he feared . . . there might be some looting." The county judge and sheriff of Cameron County communicated with the governor of Texas. —Same, pp. 77-78.

[6] On February 26, 1913, the following companies of Texas militia arrived in Brownsville: Co. C, 3rd Texas Infantry from Corpus Christi; Co. A, 3rd Texas Infantry, and Co. A, Texas State Cavalry, both from Houston; and Co. C, Texas State Cavalry from Austin. They remained until July 28, 1913.—Same, pp. 78-79.

[7] Same, pp. 79-82.

[8] Parkes, pp. 343-346; Pierce, pp. 83-85

[9] Webb, *Texas Rangers*, pp. 474-475.

[10] Lon C. Hill, *Investigation of Mexican Affairs*, Sen. Doc. No. 285, 63rd Cong., 2nd Sess., pp. 1253 ff., as quoted by Webb, *Texas Rangers*, p. 482.

[11] Lon C. Hill brought out the source of the trouble as he quoted Mexican informants:

A. . . . they said, 'we have organized, and we have got some foreigners going to help us, and we are going to take all the land back that you Gringos stole from us before the constitution of 1857.'

Q. What term did they use to describe these foreigners?

A. Well, 'enrejeros'—something like that.

Q. Extranjeros?

A. . That is it; that is the name.

Q. Do the Mexicans . . . mean Mexican citizens?

A. No; they don't; them fellows didn't; they mean Alemans, to come out and tell you the right of it.

Q. Aleman means German?

A. Aleman means German. They would tell you they had instructions not to kill any Germans . . . there was a whole raft of Germans came down there and lived down there, and on both sides of the river, . . . they were going to take the country between the Rio Grande and the Nueces. . . .

Q. And they were going to take it back?

A. Yes, sir; and the Aleman was going to help them, furnish them ammunition, money, and everything. —Same.

[12] Webb, *Texas Rangers*, p. 484.

[13] Same, p. 485.

[14] D. P. Gay wrote an account of his experiences, "The Amazing Bare-Faced Facts of the Norias Fight."—Courtesy of Harbert Davenport. Gay was inspired to write his account some years later when he heard a Texas Ranger falsely claiming that he had participated in the extinction of Mexican bandits during the Norias raid.

[15] The old Norias headquarters was originally built by the railroad to serve as a hotel for prospective land purchasers and others with business in that part of the country. When Highway 77

was constructed the old house was torn down and the new Norias headquarters facilities were constructed.—*Corpus Christi Caller-Times*, July 12, 1953.

[16] There are several published accounts of the Norias raid, none complete in all details. For the most part the information for this account came from Lauro Cavazos, a participant.

[17] Gay, as cited.

[18] For a detailed enumeration of the various raids see Charles C. Cumberland, "Border Raids in the Lower Rio Grande Valley, 1915," *Southwestern Historical Quarterly*, LVII (January, 1954), pp. 285-311.

[19] Mrs. Thomas T. East to Holland McCombs.

[20] Webb, *Texas Rangers*, pp. 509-510.

[21] Mrs. Jeff N. Miller, Mrs. Albert Walter Reynolds and Richard M. Kleberg, Sr., to Holland McCombs.

[22] Pierce, pp. 100-102.

[23] The laconic language of official publications of the United States Weather Bureau for the period reveals the seriousness of the drought:

1916: The most noteworthy features of the weather were a severe dry period in February and March, which in the lower Rio Grande, lower coast and adjacent southwestern counties, continued until July; and a tropical storm, which moved inland over the lower Texas coast on August 18 caused much damage to property and crops by high winds and heavy rains.

FEBRUARY: The rainfall over the state was not only the least of record for February, but was also the least of record for any calendar month during the past 29 years. MARCH: In many lower coastal and southwestern counties stock suffered severely on account of the backward conditions of the ranges.

MAY: There was a decided deficiency of rainfall in the lower coast, lower Rio Grande, and adjoining southwestern counties, and cattlemen were compelled to sell or ship their cattle to other counties to prevent starvation.

JUNE: Rainfall was lightest in the lower coast sections and adjacent southwestern counties where much farmland remained idle for want of moisture to germinate seed.

JULY: The dry weather in lower coast and southwest counties was broken by numerous showers.

AUGUST: Tropical storm moved inland over lower coast on the 18th. Heavy showers occurred in coast and southwestern counties.

1917: In west and southwest Texas, ranges were poor throughout the year, stock water was scarce, and the movement of cattle out of the dry sections to prevent starvation began early in June and continued until the close of the year. Dry conditions prevailed over the lower coast and southwestern counties throughout the year.

1918: Extremely dry conditions continued throughout most of the year. Precipitation was badly distributed. —Courtesy of Richard D. W. Blood, Office of State Climatologist, United States Department of Commerce, Weather Bureau, Austin, Texas.

[24] Richard M. Kleberg's enlistment papers reveal that he officially took the oath of office as a private in the Texas Rangers on April 4, 1918. His commission was renewed in January of the following year.

[25] Profit and loss statements, King Ranch accounting records.

[26] For a discussion of events during this period see Webb, *Texas Rangers*, pp. 504-505.

[27] One result of the Canales investigation was to bring about the passage of a bill on March 31, 1919, reorganizing the Texas Ranger force, calling for pay raises and other reforms.—Same, pp. 513-516.

[28] A. B. Fall was chairman and leading spirit of the Senatorial investigating committee. The report of the investigation was published as *Investigation of Mexican Affairs*, Sen. Doc. No. 285, 66th Cong., 2nd Sess. For a discussion of the investigation see Webb, *Texas Rangers*, pp. 475-476.

[29] Weather bureau records reveal that rainfall was more than double that of normal years on parts of the ranch, the total greatly swollen by a tropical storm during September:

1919: Precipitation was excessive in most sections for most of the year. Ranges were good over the entire state. Floods occurred on several streams in late June and during July. On September 14 a tropical storm moved inland near Corpus Christi, where it destroyed much property and killed a large number of people. Heavy rains brought by this storm caused serious flood on streams from the Rio Grande to the Colorado.—Blood, as cited.

30 The cost of developing the land was no small item. It had to be grubbed; schools had to be built; roads had to be graded. One of the heirs of P. A. Chapman's estate later testified:

. . . the cost per acre of improving said land and putting same in cultivation, exclusive of interest, taxes, land lost by grading roads, and the general expense of improvements at the headquarters, known as Chapman Ranch, is not less than $48.00 per acre . . . in addition . . . the cost of building school houses, approximately $70,000.00, and maintenance of schools for tenants during time said land was being developed of approximately $25,000.00. —J. O. Chapman, June 7, 1927, Exhibit No. 16, "Estate of Henrietta M. King" (a protest against tax valuations assessed by the United States Treasury Department, hereafter cited as "Tax Protest").

31 At the time of the sale there was an oral agreement between Chapman and Mrs. King to split the cost of constructing a division fence and prorate taxes. The two costs being substantially equal, Mrs. King paid the taxes and Chapman built the fence.—*Defendants' Brief*, p. 547.

32 "Tax Protest," pp. 18-19.

33 *Defendants' Brief*, p. 168.

34 *Minutes of the Probate Court*, Kleberg County, Vol. I, pp. 609ff.

35 Filed January 22, 1919, *Deed Records*, Kleberg County, Vol. IX, pp. 527-540; *Defendants' Brief*, pp. 53-57.

36 *Deed Records*, Nueces County, Vol. 147, pp. 440-442; "Robert J. Kleberg, Trustee, Account Book."

37 "Warranty Deed: Chauncey Stillman et al. to Robert J. Kleberg, Jr., Trustee," *Deed Records*, Willacy County, Vol. II, pp. 418ff; "Warranty Deed: Ed. C. Lasater et al. to Robert J. Kleberg, Jr.," *Deed Records*, Brooks County, Vol. III, pp. 597-601; *Defendants' Brief*, pp. 53-54; "Robert J. Kleberg, Trustee, Account Book."

38 *Defendants' Brief*, pp. 53-57.

39 The document was filed April 25, 1919, recorded in *Power of Attorney Record*, Kleberg County, Vol. I, pp. 46-48.

40 *Defendants' Brief*, p. 692.

41 Same, pp. 367ff.

42 The files of the Corpus Christi newspapers contain the history of the long struggle to obtain the port, a listing of articles too vast to cite. As Roy Miller put it in his dedication address for the opening of the port, "Time does not permit the telling of the story."

43 *Corpus Christi Caller-Times*, July 12, 1953.

44 "Judge James B. Wells," *Hebbronville News*, December 29, 1923.

45 On November 21, 1952, on the occasion of the King Ranch's donation to honor the memory of James B. Wells in a proposed State Bar Administration Building.

46 From the "Prayer of the Aged Mrs. Moody," which Mrs. King copied into her Bible:

Let my last days be my best days. Help me to stay myself in the promises of Thy word, when earthly props are failing me; cheer me with a hope full of immortality as my change draws near and be my patron in time and Eternity through mercy in Thy dear Son.

CHAPTER XVII

1 "Application for Appointment of Temporary Administrators," *Minutes of Probate Court*, Kleberg County, Vol. I pp. 596-597.

2 *Corpus Christi Caller*, April 9, 1925.

3 "Inventory and Appraisement," as cited; *Minutes of the Probate Court*, Kleberg County, Vol. I, pp. 609 ff.

4 Same.

5 *Defendants' Brief*, pp. 35 ff.

6 Affidavit: J. M. Freeland, Secretary-Treasurer, Stock Yards Loan Co., Kansas City, Missouri, January 4, 1927, "Tax Protest," Exhibit No. 37.

7 The Shorthorn breed was originated in the British Isles during the last quarter of the eight-

eenth century by two brothers, Charles and Robert Colling, who started to improve the local cattle in the area of Durham known as the Teeswater district.

8   Robert J. Kleberg, Jr., "The Santa Gertrudis Breed of Beef Cattle," *Santa Gertrudis Breeders International, Recorded Herds*, Vol. I, (Kingsville, 1953), pp. 3-4. See also Jan C. Bonsma, "Degeneration of the British Beef Breeds in the Tropics and Subtropics," *Breeding Beef Cattle for Unfavorable Environments*, pp. 17-20, and Douglas H. K. Lee, "Heat Tolerance in Cattle," same, pp. 21-30.

9   "Tax Protest," p. 31.

10   There was a great deal of speculation in the press as to the extent of Mrs. King's estate and the inheritance taxes to be collected on the vast holdings. Such headlines appeared as "Texas Will Get Its Largest Inheritance Tax from King Estate." W. M. Woodall, chief of the inheritance tax division of the comptroller's department, was quoted as saying: "The tax may run into millions."—*Texarkana Texarkanian*, April 4, 1925.

11   For example, the appraisers of the estate valued 28,450 acres of brush land in the San Juan de Carricitos at $6 per acre; field agents of the internal revenue department raised the valuation to $10. There were similar cases all over the ranch. Appraisers of the estate valued cattle at $844,965; field agents raised the figure to $1,767,915. The valuation of horses was raised from $21,250 to $40,900 and of mules from $16,076 to $33,200.—"Tax Protest."

12   *Memorial No. 230*, as cited.

13   "Special Examination, Trust Estate Mrs. H. M. King, Kingsville, Texas, for the period from March 31, 1925, to December 31, 1928," a report by Ernst and Ernst, a Houston accounting firm; "Special Examination, Trust Estate Mrs. H. M. King, Kingsville, Texas, for the period from January 1, 1929, to December 31, 1934," a report by F. M. Lafrentz & Co., New Orleans, Louisiana.

14   "The World's Biggest Ranch," *Fortune*, VIII (December, 1933), p. 90.

15   The interest was later reduced from five per cent to three per cent.

16   Hereafter statistics and other data of obvious origin in recent or contemporary King Ranch accounting records will not be documented.

17   "Klebergs Led South Texans in Acceptance of Rhodes Grass," *Corpus Christi Caller-Times*, July 12, 1953; see also Appendix XVI.

18   "Statement of Plan of Operation and Management of the King Ranch Property," "Tax Protest," p. 7.

19   "Power of Attorney: Robert J. Kleberg, Sr., to Robert J. Kleberg, Jr.," filed July 8, 1926, *Power of Attorney Records*, Kleberg County, Vol. 1, pp. 208-209.

20   "Power of Attorney: Alice G. K. Kleberg, et vir., to Robert J. Kleberg, Jr.," filed July 31, 1928, *Power of Attorney Records*, Kleberg County, Vol. 2, pp. 14-15.

21   Clarke, pp. 23 ff.; *The Cattleman*, XLII (June, 1955), p. 79.

During his first term as president of the Texas and Southwestern Cattle Raisers' Association 404 new members joined the association and 390 joined the next year. On February 28, 1926, the association's financial report showed an overdraft of $604.62. Two years later a cash balance of $5,049.06 was reported.—*Corpus Christi Caller-Times*, July 12, 1953.

22   During subsequent court litigation over the question of Mr. Kleberg's health during the period of trusteeship, L. F. Cavazos, foreman of the Santa Gertrudis, testified that the speedometer of Robert J. Kleberg, Sr.'s car showed some 65,000 miles which had been put on the car on the ranch during a period of about three years.—*Defendants' Brief*, pp. 22-23.

23   Will Rogers, "He Stops Over to See Real Cowboys Doing Their Stuff," *Atlanta Journal*, December 6, 1931.

24   The event was described by Max H. Jacobs, managing editor of the *Houston Post*. Of all the stories and eulogies written of Robert J. Kleberg, Sr., following his death, this was the one most favored by his wife and sons:

As funeral services were being conducted for Robert J. Kleberg, a grizzled Mexican from the ranges walked slowly to his bier. He gazed long at the face of the man who built a vast cattle empire. Tears rolled down his wrinkled, brown cheeks, and, as he turned away, he half-sobbed, "Adios, amigo mio." . . . .

There are many to pay tribute to Robert J. Kleberg as a builder of a far-flung domain, many to sing praises for his constructive geinus. His character as a man, however, can not be better portrayed than by the sorrowing Mexican from the ranges, who wept as he murmured, "Adios, amigo mio."—As quoted, *Corpus Christi Caller-Times*, July 12, 1953.

25 Ownership of the corporation was divided among the Kleberg children in five equal parts: Richard M. Kleberg, Sr.; Robert J. Kleberg, Jr.; Henrietta Rosa (Mrs. John A.) Larkin; Alice Gertrudis (Mrs. T. T.) East; and Sarah Spohn (Mrs. J. H.) Shelton.

26 *Defendants' Brief*, p. 692.

27 *Edwin K. Atwood, et al, Plaintiffs, v. Robert J. Kleberg, Jr., Defendants*, Equity No. 74, in the United States District Court for the Southern District of Texas, Corpus Christi Division. The suit was filed on November 22, 1933.

28 Three suits were filed in behalf of the Atwoods. The first, in 1933, was primarily an accounting case against the trustees; two were filed in 1935, one contesting the correctness of the partition of the estate and the other contesting the validity of the Humble oil lease. The Supreme Court refused to review the latter. A series of hearings before Master in Chancery at Kingsville stretched from 1936 to 1939. In 1939 the hearing moved to Houston where there was a lengthy session before Judge Kennerly. The final day for the case in his court was still eleven years away.

29 News of the partition was featured by the press under such headlines as "King Ranch Lands Divided," *Corpus Christi Caller*, April 21, 1935, and *The Cattleman*, May, 1935, pp. 7-8. There was speculation as to the future of the ranch, and several papers were singularly inaccurate in their predictions that in view of the recent interest in oil the greatness of the empire as a cattle domain would soon fade. See the *Brownsville Herald*, April 21, 1935.

30 During the intervening years adjacent and outlying pieces of property were bought and sold by Robert J. Kleberg, Jr., acting as trustee for his brother, sisters, Caesar and himself. Consequently, the areas varied from time to time and did not at this date agree with the acreages of the two tracts at the time of their purchase.

31 While these acreage figures have been taken from the precise notations to be found in the many legal documents and abstracts in the King Ranch files and the total is in accordance with those records, the whole is subject to the hedging legal phrase "more or less," which is also found so often in the documents.

32 For an account of everyday life at Norias see Goodwyn, *Life on the King Ranch*, as cited. The author is the son of Francis Eppse Goodwyn.

33 Dr. J. K. Northway, "Horse Breeding Operations at the King Ranch, Kingsville, Texas," an address before members of the Horse Association of America, December, 1948.

34 The interested researcher will find innumerable columns of reading matter pertaining to the highway debate. During the long period of the controversy, newspapers in the counties concerned furnished their readers with bitter and voluminous coverage of the issue by way of both news and editorial comment, for the most part shedding more heat than light in accordance with each paper's stand on the issue.

35 Caesar Kleberg, at Norias, first put the ranch's hunting code into effect in 1912, providing that deer and turkey should be hunted with rifles only and shot in the neck or head, that bobwhites should not be fired into on initial covey rise, that deer hunting should end when rutting reached a peak, and that game should not be hunted at watering places or other concentration places.

36 The United Press broke the story under a San Perlita dateline, see *Houston Chronicle*, November 26, 1936. Press treatment of the affair swelled to nation-wide proportions. The December 7, 1936, issue of *Time* carried a more melodramatic than factual account.

CHAPTER XVIII

[1] Louisiana cattle breeders had imported Brahman cattle from India as early as 1885. The breed was introduced into Texas about 1895 in the Victoria-Refugio area. In 1906 A. P. Borden went to India to purchase Brahman cattle for the O'Connor and Pierce estates. Only thirty-three out of an original shipment of fifty-one head survived an outbreak of surra, a livestock disease causing serious bleeding and high fever. Because of this outbreak, the United States forbade further cattle importations from India. Subsequently Texas cattlemen imported Brahman blood by way of Mexico and South America.—"Brahman Cattle," *Handbook of Texas*, Vol. I, p. 205.

[2] Albert O. Rhoad, "The Santa Gertrudis Breed: The Genesis and the Genetics of a New Breed of Beef Cattle," *Journal of Heredity*, XL (May, 1949), pp. 115-126; Robert J. Kleberg, Jr., *The Santa Gertrudis Breed of Beef Cattle*, Rev. ed., (Kingsville, 1952).

[3] It was the King Ranch custom then, as it still is, to watch for exceptionally good milkers among the beef herds and cut out these cows to be retained at residential areas on the ranch so that their milk could be used.

[4] Albert O. Rhoad, "Procedures Used in Developing the Santa Gertrudis Breed," *Breeding Beef Cattle for Unfavorable Environments*, pp. 203-210.

[5] The ranching industry kept watch on the breeding experiments, particularly on potential dollars-and-cents results at the stockyards. For example, in June, 1930, *The Cattleman*, official publication of the Texas and Southwestern Cattle Raisers Association, reported that "Cross-Bred Cattle Produced on King Ranch" were attracting attention:

A load of 18 steers that averaged 1,394 pounds on the hoof in Fort Worth, and dressed 64.4 per cent in Swift's cooler, was part of the market receipts at Fort Worth the past month. They were sent in by the King Ranch of Kingsville, and a number of things about this load of cattle attracted an unusual amount of attention when they arrived on the yards. . . .

Men who knew nothing of the breeding experiment which produced this load of steers commented on their difference from the average load of cross-bred cattle. They had better backs and loins, deeper bodies and were smoother in flesh—a better beef type than the average cross-bred animal. . . .

This breeding experiment has been going on for some time. At the ranch they speak of it as the Santa Gertrudis breed, and feel they are making progress in developing a type of breed of animal that will do well in their section of the country.

In support of this belief they point to the following figures. This spring they sent out approximately 5,000 head of these double cross-bred two-year-old steers for shipment to Oklahoma grass. They averaged 830 pounds at the loading point. At the same time they shipped about 5,000 head of Hereford steers of approximately the same ages, and they averaged 675 pounds.—As cited, p. 25.

[6] Rhoad, "Santa Gertrudis Breed: Genesis and Genetics," p. 125.

[7] Animals with thick hides are more tick repellent than those with thin hides. Breeds of cattle developed in tropical regions have thick hides with greater vascularity of hide, an attribute which promotes the dissipation of heat.

Apart from sleekness of coat and thickness and mobility of hide, pigmentation of hide is of the utmost importance to the breeder of cattle in tropical and subtropical regions. Ultraviolet radiation sets up irritation in the hides of cattle which lack pigmentation, causing hyperkeratosis. Lack of pigment in and around the eye makes . . . animals vulnerable to conditions such as eye cancer.—Jan C. Bonsma, "Degeneration of the British Beef Breeds in the Tropics and Subtropics," *Breeding Beef Cattle for Unfavorable Environments*, p. 19.

[8] The results of recent tests by the University of Missouri Department of Dairy Husbandry indicate that the Santa Gertrudis breed not only inherits heat tolerance from the Brahman side of its ancestry but it may have some of the ability to resist cold which is characteristic of the British breeds:

The studies dealt with cattle of the European, Indian, and Santa Gertrudis breeds housed in climatic chambers of constant day and night temperature with the same wall, ceiling, and air temperatures and the same humidity and air movement. Under these conditions, the "comfort zone" of European cattle was found to be between about 30° and 60° F. and that of the Indian cattle 50° to 80° F. The higher heat tolerance of the

Indian cattle seemed to be due to lower heat production, greater surface area per unit weight, shorter hair, and other body-temperature regulating mechanisms not visually apparent. The larger the animal and the higher her productive level, the lower was the "comfort zone" temperature. The inner body temperature was shown to be constant at about 20° F. above the comfort zone by an S-shaped increase in evaporative cooling. At 105° F. environment the near-lethal temperature of 108° F. was reached in the Holsteins, 106° F. in the Jerseys, and 105° F. in the Indian cows of the same weight as the Jerseys. At environmental temperature of 105° to 107° F. the European cows were near collapse. The Santa Gertrudis were found to be near Brahmans in heat tolerance; they grew equally well and maintained the same rectal temperature at 80° F. as at 50° F. The Santa Gertrudis were more cold-tolerant than the Indian heifers. Their critical temperatures have not yet been determined.—Samuel Brody, "Climatic Physiology of Cattle," *Journal of Dairy Science*, XXXIX (June, 1956), pp. 715-725.

[9] Official recognition of Santa Gertrudis cattle as a distinct breed dates from August 12, 1940, when J. R. Mohler, Chief of the Bureau of Animal Industry, United States Department of Agriculture, wrote to Robert J. Kleberg, Jr.:

. . . I wish to inform you that a revised copy of Farmers' Bulletin 1779 has been sent to the printer with the word "breed" substituted for "strain" in the paragraph describing Santa Gertrudis cattle.

However, for a decade prior to recognition by the Department of Agriculture, the press had recognized and ranchers had accepted the new breed. In 1931 J. Evetts Haley, the historian of the Texas and Southwestern Cattle Raisers Association, cited Santa Gertrudis cattle as "a new breed of red Brahmas."—"Committee Visits King Ranch," *The Cattleman*, (April, 1931).

In 1933 *Fortune* magazine announced the creation of the first new breed of cattle in the United States with something of a flourish:

"The United States has evolved three or four breeds of hogs, one of sheep and two of horses," reads the latest *Encyclopaedia Britannica*, "but has originated no breed of cattle." The Klebergs are knocking that statement into a cocked hat at this very moment with their "Santa Gertrudis" breed.—"The World's Biggest Ranch," *Fortune*, VIII (December, 1933), p. 53.

In 1936 the King Ranch exhibited Santa Gertrudis cattle at the Texas Centennial. Wayne Gard reported in the *Dallas Morning News*, May 24, 1936:

The famous brand of the Running W will thrill thousands of Texas Centennial visitors who pause in the cattle pavilion to see the superb specimens with which the new American cattle breed, the Santa Gertrudis, makes its bow to the livestock world.

The following year a writer for the *American Magazine* was taking the new breed as an established fact:

I think Bob Kleberg's most important contribution to modern ranching . . . is the production of the new American bovine breed. . . . I was thrilled when I saw for the first time one of the ranch's finest specimens of this new creature, something that never walked the earth before—a gigantic bull, dark cherry-red in color, a full ton of beef drifting easily through the tall gray-green African grass on tiny feet, tipped with white. This gigantic animal, almost rectangular in shape, with a huge head like a buffalo, was feeding in the heat of the day while the gentler, pure-blooded cattle panted in the creeks or lay in the shade.—Hubert Kelley, "America's Forbidden Kingdom," *American Magazine*, CXXIV (October, 1937), p. 74.

[10] The King Ranch's first sale of bulls within the United States was to J. T. Maltsberger of Cotulla, Texas. The Maltsberger Ranch's advertisements of Santa Gertrudis cattle usually carry the notation "Maltsberger Ranch bought first Santa Gertrudis bulls ever sold off the King Ranch in 1934." The first sale abroad was made to E. J. Barker, Moron, Cuba (see Appendix XIII). After these initial sales the ranch marketed its crop of surplus bulls at from $350 to $400 per head, and a waiting list of more than three thousand accumulated.

[11] Initially the plan was to offer only Quarter Horses at the auction. However, the King Ranch was interested in determining how other ranchers would value the breed; so it was decided to offer some bulls at the auction. As advertisements in *The Cattleman* and the auction catalog put it:

The King Ranch has up to now booked and filled orders for Santa Gertrudis bulls in the sequence which they were received, but the demand has far exceeded its ability to supply them. For that reason we are now offering, for the first time, approximately 25 head of yearling bulls, so that our friends may have a chance to evaluate them and acquire one immediately rather than await their turn on our long booking list.

Results exceeded expectations: Bidders paid a whopping $99,000 for twenty-nine bulls, an average of $3,413.79. Edgar W. Brown of Orange, Texas, was highbidder at $10,000.

At the following year's auction, 1951, twenty-five bulls brought $212,550, an average of $8,502 a head. Mr. and Mrs. Garvin Tankersley of Washington, D. C., paid $27,200 for the highest price of the auction. Powell Crosley of Cincinnati, Ohio, paid $23,000. In 1952, twenty-one bulls sold for $280,250. The top bid was $40,000 by the Briggs Syndicate, a group of breeders from the San Antonio area. Searching for a name to give the bull just purchased, after due consideration the syndicate discarded the name Golden Rod in favor of El Torazo.

At the Centennial Year auction the average for twenty-four bulls was $8,439.54, with the top price of $31,000 paid by Winthrop Rockefeller.

[12] This first meeting of Santa Gertrudis breeders in the schoolhouse was attended by some forty or fifty cattlemen. A committee was appointed, and the committee decided on a meeting in San Antonio in March, 1951, for the purpose of organizing a "breed association."

That meeting was held at the Gunter Hotel on March 5; ninety-eight applications for charter membership had been received by the corresponding secretary. Organizational committees went into action and the association filed its charter in the office of the Secretary of the State of Texas on April 9, 1951.

[13] As of January, 1956.

[14] The ranch's practical experience in Kentucky and Pennsylvania, as well as early results from a scientific testing program (see Brody, as cited), tend to indicate that in addition to top performance under the conditions for which it was bred, the Santa Gertrudis breed will equal the British breeds' performance in temperature zone climates.

[15] Sam Lazarus was so disgusted at the closing of Texas race tracks that he sold out. He offered

to sell his band of breeding mares to Robert J. Kleberg, Sr., who sent Caesar Kleberg to look at them. Caesar was impressed. But there was no interest in racing at the ranch. He told Lazarus that Mr. Kleberg would not want to buy because the price would surely be too high. Lazarus said he would sell for $100 a head, plus the promise that none of them would ever be raced. Caesar telephoned Mr. Kleberg for approval and bought. It was an important purchase. The blood of "the Lazarus mares" is still present on the ranch in some of the best King Ranch Quarter Horses. —Dr. J. K. Northway.

[16] The King Ranch's most spectacular horse on the quarter track was Miss Princess, a chestnut mare sired by Bold Venture and registered with the Jockey Club as Woven Web. Though Miss Princess was foaled in 1943, her racing career actually started the year before.

In 1942 the King Ranch's great short-horse stallion, Nobodies Friend, was defeated by Shue Fly at Tucson in the "World's Champion Quarter." Immediately Bob Kleberg began looking over the crop of King Ranch foals for something which could even the score. In 1945 he found Miss Princess; she was turned over to the management of Ernest Lane. On May 3, 1947, the meeting with Shue Fly came off.

Though Assault was running that day in the Grey Lag Stakes at Jamaica—and winning—Bob Kleberg was at Del Rio for the event which was billed as a "Special Match Race." The King Ranch sorrel picked up the $15,000 side bet by a length and a half.

In October, 1947, again in Del Rio, Miss Princess defeated Barbra B, the short-horse sensation of the year, by more than a length— :18.0 for the first mark and :22.2 for the quarter. In a single race she set new world's records for both 350 yards and the quarter mile. Later, she would skim the quarter track in twenty-two seconds flat.—Nelson C. Nye, *Champions of the Quarter Tracks* (New York, 1950), pp. 62-66.

[17] Step by step illustration of the King Ranch's horse training procedure was the principal feature of the booklet *Training Riding Horses,*

which was published in 1941 by the Horse and Mule Association of America. See also The American Quarter Horse Association, *Ride A Quarter Horse: A Compilation of Standards, Characteristics and General Information Pertaining to the Famous Quarter Horse Breed* (Amarillo, n.d.).

[18] At the King Ranch's first sale of Quarter Horses, in 1950, fifty-one head sold for $33,440, an average of $655 a head. The top price of $3,200 was paid by Louis P. Reed of Meridian, Texas. The following year fifty-seven head sold at an average of $895. The highest bid was $3,775 by Sumner Pingree, Sr., of Cuba. In 1952, twenty-five head averaged $966. Again Mr. Pingree was high bidder at $3,000. At the 1953 sale, bidders purchased twenty-five head at an average of $723.40 with Bill Reynal of Argentina paying a top of $1,450.

[19] *Corpus Christi Caller-Times*, July 12, 1953.
Ada Jones was by Little Joe out of Mamie Crowder, bred by Ott Adams, veteran Quarter Horse breeder of Alfred, Texas. Ada Jones was the maternal great-grandmother of Miss Princess.—Nye, pp. 14-15, 62.

[20] As a two-year-old Boojum set the world's record for 6½ furlongs on August 31, 1929, in the Hopeful Stakes at Saratoga, carrying 117 pounds in a time of 1:17.

[21] Twenty Grand's Kentucky Derby time of 2:01-4/5 was the fastest to that date. It was bested in 1942 by Whirlaway with 2:01-2/5.

[22] The Triple Crown, consisting of the Kentucky Derby, the Preakness and Belmont Stakes, is turfdom's most coveted honor. Triple Crown winners are

    1919 – Sir Barton
    1930 – Gallant Fox
    1935 – Omaha
    1937 – War Admiral
    1941 – Whirlaway
    1943 – Count Fleet
    1946 – Assault
    1948 – Citation

[23] In Thoroughbred racing the Coaching Club American Oaks at Belmont is considered to be the equivalent for three-year-old fillies of the Kentucky Derby for colts of the same age.

The King Ranch retired the Coaching Club American Oaks trophy in 1948 after winning it three times: 1937, Dawn Play; 1943, Too Timely; 1948, Scattered.

[24] In 1946, Assault won more purse money than any other horse in Thoroughbred racing had ever won in a single year, $424,195.

[25] The machine was built by the William K. Holt Machinery Co., Caterpillar dealers, San Antonio, and is marketed under the name Twin "Cat" D8 Tractor. See Appendix XI for details of its development and operation.

[26] Control of brush by "cabling" or "chaining" is the process of attaching each end of a 300- to 360-foot length of heavy battleship chain to a piece of heavy equipment and then dragging the chain through the brush. Chaining is a rapid and economical method for large scale clearance. As many as one to two hundred acres per day can be knocked down. However, the process leaves many stumps and roots, and an area so cleared is subject to heavy regrowth.

[27] The well for the purpose of returning surface water to subterranean sands was drilled for the ranch by the Humble Oil Company under the direction of Dr. Frank H. Dotterweich of Texas A. & I. College.

[28] The metering device, known as the "Fos-Feeder," was developed in conjunction with the Mineral Supplement Company of Houston.

[29] A "Christmas tree" is that portion of an oil well's controls which protrudes above the ground, a complicated array of valves which make up roughly into the shape of a small Christmas tree.

[30] The ranch's garage and machinery maintenance department is under the management of Foreman Robert C. Dear. The garage at the ranch headquarters is staffed by three mechanics, a paint and body man, a parts man who also serves as bookkeeper, a wash man who also helps the mechanics, a grease man, two men in the

blacksmith and machine shop, and two men who dispense oil and gasoline and repair flat tires.

The headquarters garage maintains ninety-four automotive units operating on the Santa Gertrudis Division and nineteen units from the Laureles Division. The Norias Division operates fifteen units and the Encino Division nine. Because of the distance involved, it is not practical for the garage to make all repairs on the Norias and Encino vehicles.

[31] The fence is manufactured by the Keystone Steel & Wire Company, Peoria, Illinois, under the trade name, Special Super Galvanneald King Ranch Fence.

[32] The Argentine cattle chute, located on the headquarters division, is a highly efficient and highly complicated piece of ranching equipment. It is used for branding, vaccinating, doctoring and many other operations involved in working cattle. A dipping vat was added to the original chute which was brought from Argentina. The chute has a four-way cut for working cattle, two cuts before cattle reach the scales and two cuts after.

The Argentine chute has been duplicated in oak in the King Ranch carpenter and machine shop.

[33] Two foremen's wives, Mrs. Tom Tate and Mrs. Charlie Burwell, are schoolteachers on the ranch—Mrs. Tate at Norias and Mrs. Burwell at Laureles.

[34] Robert C. Wells to Tom Lea.

[35] During no year prior to Mrs. King's death did the proceeds of cattle sales exceed $650,000; the average was about $400,000. During the period of trusteeship and the development of the Santa Gertrudis breed, the income from this source reached a total of more than a million dollars a year.—*Defendants' Brief*, pp. 565, 569.

[36] During the time since 1935 there have been noticeable improvements in both the ranges and forage: Brush clearing has made more land available for pasture; prosphorus and improved grasses have provided more nutritious forage. In spite of these improvements, the pastures have not

been able to keep abreast of increasing drought conditions to maintain their former carrying capacity.

[37] Previously the ranch had paid from $25,000 to $40,000 annually for handling cattle for a few months while pastured in Oklahoma on the way to market.—*Defendants' Brief*, p. 40.

[38] Robert J. Kleberg, Jr., "Continuous Testing Resulted in King Ranch's Own Cattle," *Corpus Christi Caller-Times*, July 12, 1953.

[39] Feedlot experiments with Hereford and Santa Gertrudis steers were conducted by the King Ranch in 1950 and 1951 to determine which breed was superior in feeding demonstrations.

. . . the ranch obtained some of the best eight-month-old Hereford calves . . . they were placed on feed Nov. 29, 1950. A comparable weight group of Santa Gertrudis calves was put into the feed lot 43 days later. In order to keep within a comparable weight bracket, the ranch had to use younger Santa Gertrudis calves, . . .

The two groups were placed in the same feed lots, and initial weights were recorded at the start of the feeding demonstration . . .

During the first 150-day feeding period, the Hereford steers showed a slight gain in weight over the Santa Gertrudis calves. In the next weight period, however, the Santa Gertrudis steers outweighed the Herefords by 53 pounds each.

When the Santa Gertrudis steers had been on feed for 202 days and the Herefords on feed 245 days, three of the best calves were selected from each breed group. . . .

On the killing floor, the Santa Gertrudis steers outweighed the Herefords by 202 pounds, and outdressed them 2.68 per cent.—"Santa Gertrudis Steers Top Herefords in Tests," *Corpus Christi Caller-Times*, July 12, 1953.

In addition to numerous and continuous tests by the ranch, Santa Gertrudis cattle have been put on official rate-of-gain tests at several experiment stations, and the results obtained have spoken well for the breed.

In a beef cattle evaluation test conducted in 1953 at Bluebonnet Farms, Texas Agricultural Experiment Station, McGregor, Santa Gertrudis steers outgained all other groups on a per-day-age basis (from birth to finish of test). The breed also proved the most uniform gainers. Of the group tested, the Santa Gertrudis heifers and steers had the shortest range of gain between the low and high gainers.

In a rate-of-gain feeding trial at the Balmorhea sub-station of the Texas Experiment Station over a 138-day period, November 15, 1951, to April 1, 1952, a group of twenty-two Santa Gertrudis yearling bull calves made an average daily gain of 2.51 pounds. All other breeds made an average daily gain of 2.09 pounds.

40 During the 1950 Texas State Fair at Dallas three five-year-old Santa Gertrudis steers were exhibited by the King Ranch. They were slaughtered at the close of the fair and dressed out a record 71.9 per cent. Anything over sixty per cent is considered good.

The live weights of the steers were 2400, 2395 and 2300 pounds; on the packing house hook they weighed 1727, 1683 and 1629 pounds respectively. The percentage was figured on the live weights less three per cent shrinkage.

It is not the general practice to feed to these weights. However, the ranch customarily feeds a few head to maximum weights in order to determine the upper limits of growth.

CHAPTER XIX

1 "Foreword," *Breeding Beef Cattle for Unfavorable Environments*, p. vi. See Appendix B, pp. 239-242, for a roster of guests.
2 Richard M. Kleberg, Sr., "Modern Point Men: An Address of Welcome," same, p. xii.
3 Robert J. Kleberg, Jr., "Our One Hundred Years of Ranching—What Next?" same, p. 227.
4 Robert J. Kleberg, Jr., to Tom Lea.

A NOTE OF THANKS

A NOTE OF THANKS

THE TASK of gathering the material for this account of a hundred years of ranching in South Texas could not have been accomplished without help from many sources. The basic body of information of course came from the King Ranch itself, from the cordial cooperation of all the people there, employers and employees alike, and from unlimited access to all papers, letters and memorabilia now preserved at the ranch. Yet the earlier records there, partially destroyed by fire in 1863 and in 1912, were haphazard and incomplete. To establish many salient points in the ranch's own history, and to view it in its proper perspective as a chapter in a larger history, it was imperative to search far afield for important portions of the information desired. Consequently, facts for this study were assembled from sources as varied and as far apart as a maritime museum in New England and a governmental archives in Tamaulipas.

Acknowledgement of a very great indebtedness must be made to Harbert Davenport, veteran lawyer of Brownsville, whose fund of information concerning South Texas and whose probings into the history of that area elaborated the pattern and enlarged the scope of this study. Material he supplied, and good counsel he supplied with it, were of inestimable value in chronicling earlier lives and times along the troubled lower Rio Grande.

It is a pleasant duty to record indebtedness to other contributors: to Mrs. Lennie Stubblefield for her kind permission to use the unpublished John Fitch papers in her possession; to Mrs. Benjamin H. Carr for her skilled sleuthing in the National Archives at Washington; to Walter Prescott Webb and his publisher, Houghton Mifflin, for gracious permission to quote extensively from *The Texas Rangers;* and to J. Frank Dobie not only for quotations from his work and additions to this text but for friendly encouragement while writing was in progress.

Grateful acknowledgement is also made to LeRoy P. Graf whose doctoral dissertation, *The Economic History of the Lower Rio Grande Valley 1820-1875,* is frequently quoted and cited; to the University of Oklahoma Press for permission to quote from the late Carl Coke Rister's *Robert E. Lee in Texas.*

Gratitude of a special kind is here expressed to Robert C. Wells for the rôle he has played in bringing the present work to completion. He has examined the manuscript for error, he has made contributions and suggestions which have improved the text, and he has acted as coordinator between researcher, author, annotator and copy editor during the long preparation of the work for the press.

Particular thanks are rendered to Winnie Allen at the Eugene C. Barker Texas History Center, University of Texas, for valuable aid; to staff members of the El Paso Public Library, Houston Public Library, Library of Texas College of Arts and Industries at Kingsville, Library of Texas Western College at El Paso, Orange County Historical Society, Goshen, New York, Retama Library of Corpus Christi, Robert J. Kleberg Historical Society, San Antonio Public Library, St. Louis Public Library, University of Texas Library, and the Witte Memorial Museum of San Antonio, for many courtesies; to William H. Tripp, Old Dartmouth Historical Society and Whaling Museum, New Bedford, Massachusetts; F. Arnicar, Centre College, Danville, Kentucky, for helpful replies to queries; and to John M. Sharp for translating the de la Garza Santa Gertrudis land grant.

Much pertinent material has been brought to this work by the generosity of numerous individuals who delved into their own special knowledge or personal memories; their names are gratefully recorded: Carleton Adams, Thomas

R. Armstrong, the late Dr. John Ashton, Stirling W. Bass, Raymond Bell, Jr., Mrs. John M. Bennett, Sr., John M. Bennett, Jr., the late Walter Billingsley, J. T. Canales, Owen Combe, Fidel G. Chamberlain, Jr., J. E. Connor, Mrs. H. C. Cowan, Mrs. Harbert Davenport, Leroy G. Denman, Jr., Judge C. D. Duncan, Lamar Gill, Victoriano Ochoa Gonzalez, Ben R. Howell, Bishop Everett Holland Jones, W. W. Johnson, Richard King III, W. H. Kittrell, Jr., Jack Kivlin, Edward Kleberg, the late Lula Kleberg, Tillie Kleberg, Theodore W. Koch, Robert McCracken, Mrs. Jeff Miller, William Miller, Dr. Merton Minter, Tad Moses, Dr. Pat I. Nixon, Dr. J. K. Northway, Lieutenant General and Mrs. Joseph D. Patch, George Sessions Perry, Carolyn Pfeiffer, Albert O. Rhoad, James Rowe, Jane Scholl, Dr. Z. T. Scott, Henderson Shuffler, Robert L. Stayton, W. W. Sterling, Mrs. Andrew Stewart, Mrs. K. A. Votaw, Hortense Warner Ward, Mrs. Joseph K. Wells, Mrs. Ruth Wilson, Edgar E. Witt, and Frank Ytúrria.

To all of these, and to all not recorded here by name, who in large measure or small helped add substance to this book, warmhearted thanks are here warmly given.

El Paso
Fourth of February, 1957

Tom Lea

INDEX

PAGES numbered 1 through 467 are in Volume I, pages 469 through 801 are in this volume. Subject matter in notes has been indexed by page and note number, with chapter designations added only when two notes of the same number appear on a page. The map designated in the index as "vol. 2, viii-ix" is the frontispiece of this volume. The following abbreviations have been used to identify animal breeds: [Jer] for *Jersey;* [QH], *Quarter Horse;* [Th], *Thoroughbred.*

A

Austin County: 475-476
Australia: King Ranch operations in, 693-694, 768-770
ÁVALOS, FRANCISCO: 85-86, 91

B

Baffin Bay, Texas: 554
Baffin's Bay: map, 102
Baffin's Bay & Western Ry.: 554
Bagdad, Texas: 10, 49, 80, 183, 201, 230, 233; cotton trade at during Civil War, 186-187, 192, 212-213, 445—nt 44; economic conditions at, 244; hurricane damaged in 1844, 22; map, 27, 78; during Mexican War, 424-425—nt 21; stolen cattle loaded at, 280
BAILLIEU, PETER: 769
BAKER, MOSELY: Robert Justus Kleberg I under, 475
BALDWIN, ELIZABETH ATWOOD: sold interest in Mrs. King's estate, 630, 631, 635-636
BALERIO, CAPT. ———: 223
Ball Ranch: leased by King Ranch, 636; map, vol. 2, viii-ix
BALLÍ, FRANCISCO: received La Barreta grant, 380
BALLÍ, GUADALUPE: 132; quoted, 438—nt 30
BALLÍ, JOSÉ MARÍA: awarded La Feria and San Salvador del Tule grants, 380
BALLÍ, PADRE NICOLÁS: 132, 380
Bandana, Texas (see also Alice, Texas): 778—nt 18
BANKS, GEORGE LINNAEUS: 777—nt 1; quoted, 470
BANKS, NATHANIEL P.: 202; quoted, 210
Barbra B [QH]: 793—nt 16
BARKER, E. J.: 770, 771, 792—nt 10
Barranco Blanco brand: 270
Barranco Blanco grant: map, 378-379
BARRERA, MANUEL: 104-105
BARRETT, T. H.: 235
BARROUM, JAMES L.: 615
BASS, STIRLING W.: 800
BASSE, ELISHA: 410
Basse & Herd: 410
Baxter Springs, Kansas: as cattle shipping point, 461—nt 10
Bea Ann Mac [Th]: 667, 741
BEAN, J. H.: 42
BEARD, LOUIE: 661
Beau Max [Th]: 729-730
BEE, HAMILTON P.: 199; attorney for Lewis estate, 137; commanded Confederate troops during Union capture of Brownsville, 201-212; ordered to defend Rio Grande, 194; quoted, 201, 205, 211

BEE, MRS. HAMILTON P.: 197
Bee County: 632
Bee Mac [Th]: 741
BELANGEL, ANTONIO: 275
BELDEN, SAMUEL A.: bought, steamboats, 44-45; built home in Brownsville, 68; entered Mexican trade venture with Kenedy, 55-56; promoted Brownsville, 430—nt 16; promoted railroad, 453—nt 28
BELL, PETER H.: 141
BELL, RAYMOND, JR.: 801
Belmont Stakes: 667, 670, 742, 794—nts 22, 23
BENAVIDES, SANTOS: 178, 202, 212-214, 221, 225, 263, 449—nt 102, 451—nt 147; quoted, 212
BENJAMIN, JUDAH P.: 188
BENNETT, JAMES GORDON: quoted, 525
BENNETT, JOHN M., JR.: 801
BENNETT, MRS. JOHN M., SR.: 801
Bennie M. [Th]: 662
Bermuda grass: 748
Bessie, Texas: 783—nt 71
Bessie: 252, 454—nt 39
Better Beef Association: 619
Better Self [Th]: 667, 729-730, 740
BEYNON, THOMAS: 270, 458-459—nt 48; appraiser for Richard King's estate, 417, 419, 471; trail boss for King Ranch, 307
Bexar County: 623
"Big Drift, The": 222-223, 261-262, 450—nt 121
Big Hatchee: 427-428—nt 36
Big Santa Gertrudis grant: see Santa Gertrudis grant
BILLINGSLEY, WALTER: 801; quoted, 370; on trail drive, 363
Bimelech [Th]: 729
BISHOP, F. Z.: 553, 783—nt 73
Bishop, Texas (see also Julia, Texas): 546, 553, 598, 783—nt 71; King Ranch farmed near, 595; map, vol. 2, viii-ix
Bishop's Castle: 33
BLACK, JOHN C.: 214
BLACK, W. H.: 755
Blackie II [Th]: 742
BLANTON, JOHN: disappearance of, 644-646
BLANTON, LUTHER: disappearance of, 644-646
BLANTON, MRS. LUTHER: 644
BLUCHER, CHARLES: 496
BLUCHER, FELIX A.: 155, 239, 496; biographical data on, 440—nt 37; as surveyor, 105, 435—nt 19; during Union attack on Corpus Christi, 446—nt 47
Blue Panic grass: 748

early rail shipment of cattle, 337, 484; economic reverses in 1920-1925, 608; effect of boom on, 351-353, 354; effect of drought of 1880's on, 474, 484-485, 497-498; effect of 1873 panic on, 300; effect of Rhodes grass on, 745; hide and tallow business, 258-259, 297, 301, 304, 458—nt 27; land valuation formula, 745; mustangs of little value, 486-487; northern markets, 298-299; Texas Fever conquered, 490-495; trail drives, 296-297, 305-321, 461—nt 10, 462—nt 28

Cattleman, The: quoted, 600

CAVAZOS, JOSÉ MARÍA: 461—nt 18

CAVAZOS, JOSÉ NARCISO: 380, 461—nt 18, 497, 638

CAVAZOS, JUAN ANTONIO BALLÍ: awarded El Paistle grant, 410

CAVAZOS, LAURO F.: 638, 789—nt 22; in Norias raid, 584-587

CELAYA, SIMÓN: 250

Centre College: 169, 355; Hiram Chamberlain, Jr., attended, 324, 442—nt 70; Richard King II attended, 325

Cerralvo, Mexico: 85

CHACE, W. B.: 170-171

CHAMBERLAIN, ADDIE GILLETTE: 526

CHAMBERLAIN, ADELIA: 323

CHAMBERLAIN, ANNA ADELIA GRISWOLD: 65

CHAMBERLAIN, EDWIN: 323, 526

CHAMBERLAIN, FIDEL G., JR.: 801

CHAMBERLAIN, HENRIETTA MARIA MORSE: *see* King, Henrietta M. Chamberlain

CHAMBERLAIN, REV. HIRAM: 63-65, 79, 126-127, 143; as Confederate chaplain, 210-211; death of, 323; during attack on King Ranch, 217-219; Kingsville lodge in memory of, 551-552; quoted, 63, 65, 66, 174, 431—nt 45, 437—nt 21; reaction to Richard King, 437—nt 21; went to Texas, 67

CHAMBERLAIN, HIRAM, JR.: 65, 323; schooling, 169, 324, 442--nt 70

CHAMBERLAIN, MILTON: 65

CHAMBERLAIN, PETER BLAND: 65, 67; death of, 353; quoted, 351; worked for Richard King, 323, 457 —nt 20

CHAMBERLAIN, WILLIAM: 323; saved by Pasteur, 525

Chamberlain Lodge No. 913: 551-552

Champion: 8-9

CHANDLER, REV. S. E.: 603

CHAPA, VICTORIANO: 119

CHAPA, YLAIRO: 120

CHAPMAN, MRS. HELEN B.: 137, 334

CHAPMAN, P. A.: purchased land from King Ranch, 594, 595-596; quoted, 788—nt 30

CHAPMAN, W. W.: 43-45, 87, 125, 148, 439—nt 24; bought land for Richard King, 136-137; in partnership with King, 333-334

Chapman & Barnard: 615

Chapman Ranch, Texas: 377, development of, 594, 788—nt 30

Chapultepec, Mexico: 38

Charles Stillman & Bro.: 37

CHARNOCK, HENRY: 473

CHASE, C. B.: 543-544

CHASSIGNET, BROUGNOIR E.: 49

CHATFIELD, W. H.: quoted, 432—nt 5, 454—nt 39, 780—nt 10

Chemera: 648, 650

CHESSHIRE, SAM: 639

Chester County, Pennsylvania: 691, 767

Chicago, Illinois: cattle market at in 1850's, 153; and in 1870, 297

Chicaro [Th]: 660-661, 662, 663-664

Chicle [Th]: 661, 662

Chihuahua, State of: 112

Chocalula [Th]: 662

CHURCH, W. I.: 543

Churubusco, Mexico: 38

Ciencia [Th]: 665, 741

Citation [Th]: 794—nt 22

Civil War: Brownsville captured by Union forces, 201-209; cattle business during, 179-180; Confederate currency, 446—nt 60; Confederate supply troubles during, 197-201; Corpus Christi attacked by Union forces, 193; Cortina's activities during, 178-179, 203-204, 209-210, 230-232; cotton trade during, 182-193, 195-196, 200-201, 206-207, 210-215, 224-225, 228, 232-235, 444—nts 24, 25, 29, 31; 445—nts 38, 39, 44; 445-446—nt 46; 446—nt 55; 446-447—nt 61; 447—nt 64; Ford established courier service, 451—nt 141; Ford recaptured Brownsville, 220-221, 223-228, 451—nt 147; Galveston surrendered to Union, 193-194; King Ranch attacked by Union force, 215-219; last battle of, 235; M. Kenedy & Co. got Confederate supply contract, 197-199, 404-407; Mexican politics during, 181-182; 184, 210-211, 230-233; postwar conditions, *see* Reconstruction; railroad built during, 226; Rio Grande defenses organized by Ford, 177-178; steamboat operations during, 75, 177-178, 179, 185-186, 210, 214, 220-221,

Civil War *(cont.)*:
 229, 443—nts 9, 10; 444—nts 28, 29; Texas' seces-
 sion, 176, 179; truce negotiations, 234; Twiggs'
 surrender of U. S. troops, 176
CLARK, JASPER "Jap": 357, 422
CLARKE, SIR RUPERT: 769
Clarksville, Texas: *see also* Boca del Rio; damaged
 by hurricane, 251; named, 230
Clean Slate [Th]: 742
CLEGG, GEORGE: 660, 733; King Ranch bought
 horses from, 655-656
CLEMENT, IDA LARKIN: 689
CLEMENT, JAMES H.: 688-689, 697
CLENDENIN, D. R.: 284
Clydesdale horses: 490
Coaching Club American Oaks: King Ranch horse
 won, 665; trophy retired by King Ranch, 794—
 nt 23
Coahuila, State of: 13, 230
Coahuila-Texas, State of: 13, 220; seized by
 Madero, 577
Coastal Bermuda grass: 748
Coatsville, Pennsylvania: 691, 767
COBB, MAJOR——: 348
Cobb's Rancho: 185
COBOS, JOSÉ MARÍA: executed, 209
COCKE, J. J.: 472
CODY, PAT: 567
COKE, RICHARD: 278
Coldris, Texas (*see also* Driscoll, Texas): 783—nt 71
Colin [Th]: 729
COLLING, CHARLES: 788-789—nt 7
COLLING, ROBERT: 788-789—nt 7
Collins Station, Texas (*see also* Alice, Texas): 337,
 368, 479, 536, 777—nt 9
Colonel Cross: 40, 57; bill of sale for, 44; bought by
 Richard King, 43-45; cost of, 45, 427—nt 29;
 Richard King piloted, 19; and became captain of,
 39; and owned, 53-54, 60-61; record run by, 36;
 General Taylor on, 39; Faustino Villa worked on,
 567
Colonel Holcomb: 75
Colonel Hunt: 43, 45; sale of, 428-429—nt 2
Colonel J. Stephens: 43
Colorado [oil] Field: 680
COLT, SAMUEL: 33
Columbus, New Mexico: raided by Pancho
 Villa, 588
Comanche: 76, 87, 89; delivery of, 71; operation of,

72-75, 432—nt 3; specifications for, 59, 430—nt 36
Comanche Indians: 13, 95, 98, 106, 117
COMBE, DR. CHARLES BERTHOUD: arrival in Browns-
 ville, 432—nt 56; met Richard King, 69-70
COMBE, OWEN: 801
Combes, Texas: 783—nt 71
Commando [Th]: 664, 729
Como Se Llama, Texas: 225
Companhia Swift do Brasil, S. A.: 694, 772
Compañia Ganadera Becerra, S. A.: 755, 770
Concepción de Carricitos grant: awarded to Eugé-
 nio and Bartolomé Fernandez, 380; map, 378-379
Concrete, Texas: 312
Concrete College: R. J. Kleberg, Sr., attended, 477
Congregación del Refugio (*see also* Matamoros,
 Mexico): 429—nt 9
CONKLING, ROSCOE: 190
CONNOR, J. E.: 801
Contest [Th]: 741
Contradiction [Th]: 741
Contreras, Mexico: 38
CONVERSE, WILLIAM P.: promoted railroad,
 453—nt 28
COOPER, JOSEPH: 247
Cora: 75
Cornsilk [Th]: 661-662, 663-664
Cornwall-on-the-Hudson, New York: 247
Corpus Christi, Texas: 104-105, 131, 148, 170, 215,
 257, 277, 409, 557, 600, 620; development as a
 port, 601-602; early history of, 96-97, 154-156;
 early law firms at, 498-499; First Presbyterian
 Church of, 523; first state fair at, 90-92, 93;
 Kenedy moved to, 354; Richard King's first visit
 to, 94, 100; King supported development as port,
 335; Mrs. King built home at, 523; King family
 lived at, 507-508; Kinney at, 434—nt 3, 435—nt
 15; Kleberg family at, 523-527; R. M. Kleberg,
 Sr., lived at, 618; land promoted near, 783—nt 75;
 G. K. Lewis at, 101; map, 11, 102, 378-379, vol.
 2, viii-ix; Mexican depredations near, 278; President Taft at, 567-568; railroad connection with,
 336, 536-538, 544-545; railroad development
 in vicinity of, 536-538, 543, 545; rivalry with
 Brownsville, 156-157; "the Ropes Boom," 537;
 smuggler's post at, 13; Spohn Sanitarium built in,
 525; Union invasion repelled at, 193, 446—nt 47;
 wool trade at, 301, 461—nt 20
Corpus Christi Advertiser: 270
Corpus Christi Bay: 380

E

Edinburg, Texas: 283, 459—nt 60; map, vol. 2,
viii-ix
Edwards County: 633
EGAN, WILLIAM F. "Bill": 668
EKIN, JAMES A.: 454—nt 37
El Alazán grant: map, 378-379
El Charco de los Sauces grant: map, 378-379
El Chiltipín grant: 377; Mrs. King purchased land
in, 533; map, 378-379
El Convoy, Battle of: 245, 453—nt 19
El Infernillo grant: map, 378-379; purchased by
Mrs. King, 533
El Lucero grant: map, 378-379
El Paisano grant: map, 378-379
El Paistle grant: awarded Juan Antonio Ballí Cava-
zos, 409; owned by R. King & Co., 454-455—nt
40; map, 378-379
El Palmito grant: map, 378-379
El Pasadizo grant: 332; map, 378-379
El Paso, Texas, 577
El Peñascal grant: map, 378-379
El Perdido grant: map, 378-379
El Primero: 75, 244, 251, 452—nt 16
El Sauz Rancho: 94, 409, 411; owned by R. King &
Co., 454-455—nt 40
El Torazo: 792-793—nt 11
El Tule grant: map, 378-379
Elf [Th]: 661
Elgin Downs: 769
ELISONDO, MANUEL RAMÍREZ: 108-109, 137-138
ELLIOTT, BISHOP ROBERT W. B.: 329; quoted,
463—nt 48
Ellis & Lane: 317
Encantadora [Th]: 667
Encino, Texas: map, vol. 2, viii-ix
Encino Division: 636, 638, 686, 687, 795—nt 30;
experiment station on, 756; land acquired for,
599; map, vol. 2, viii-ix; soil experiments on, 675-
676
England: 81; as Mexican War cause, 13, 425—nt 1
English Propeller: 185
Enterprise: 75, 244, 251, 452—nt 16; exploded, 427
—nt 32
Equestrian [Th]: 667
Ere Flecha: 402; first King Ranch brand, 150, 152;
registration of, 403
ESCAMILLA, DOMINGO: surveyed Rincón de Santa
Gertrudis, 435—nt 19
ESCANDÓN, DON JOSÉ DE: colonial activities of, 376-

377; founded Reynosa, 23; and Camargo, 24; and
Mier, 24
Escondido, Texas: 781-782—nt 41
ESTILL, MARY KING: 632
Eugenia: sold to Imperialist forces, 244, 452—nt 14
EVANS, GEORGE: 273
EVANS, GEORGE F.: backed South Texas railroad,
541
Exchange: 427-428—nt 36

F

Fair Play [Th]: 664, 730
FALCÓN, BLAS: 122, 124
FALCÓN, BLAS MARÍA DE LA GARZA: 124, 377, 441—
nt 47
FALCÓN, JOSÉ SALVADOR DE LA GARZA: 380; award-
ed Potrero del Espíritu grant, 441—nt 47
FALCÓN, MARÍA GERTRUDIS DE LA GARZA: 159, 377,
380, 441—nt 47
Falfurrias, Texas: map, vol. 2, viii-ix
FALL, ALBERT B.: 787—nt 28
False Rhodes grass: 748
FARRAGUTT, DAVID G.: 444—nt 29
Fayette County, Kentucky: 667-668
FENN, F. F.: 442—nt 76
FERNÁNDEZ, BARTOLOMÉ: awarded Concepción
de Carricitos grant, 380
FERNÁNDEZ, EUGÉNIO: awarded Concepción de
Carricitos grant, 380
FILLMORE, MILLARD: 139
FINNEGAN, JOHN D.: managed King Ranch office,
640; trustee for Mrs. King's estate, 605, 634;
worked for King-Kleberg interests, 551, 556;
worked for railroad, 543, 551
First Cortina War: 160-170
First Presbyterian Church [Brownsville]: 67, 126-
127; R. E. Lee at, 143
First Presbyterian Church [Corpus Christi]: 523
FISHER, J. B. "Bud": 640, 688
FISHER, THOMAS HART: 634-635
FITCH, HOMER: represented Charles Stillman,
453—nt 20
FITCH, JOHN: 348; made contract for trail drive,
413-416; quoted, 316; trail boss for King Ranch,
307, 308-321
FITZSIMMONS, JOSEPH: 257, 403
Flashburn [Th]: 741
FLATO, CHARLES, JR.: 547
Flatonia, Texas: 313
FLORES, ANSELMO: 119, 121

KLEBERG, ROBERT JUSTUS, SR.: 368, 469, 482, 515, 594, 689, 709, 793—nt 15; active in raising horses, 655-656; activities in bringing railroad to South Texas, 539-545, 781—nt 23; activities in promotion of Kingsville, 541-542, 545, 547-551; admitted to the bar, 478; ancestry of, 474-477; appointed ranch manager, 470, 474, 479; appointed trustee of Mrs. King's estate, 605, 624; character of, 478-479, 536, 785—nt 106; continued Richard King's land purchase policy, 497-498; courtship of, 360-361, 466—nt 41; death of, 627, 630, 789-790—nt 24; drilled water wells, 502; envisioned development of South Texas, 506; experimented with prickly pear as cattle feed, 752; farming experiments by, 538-539, 781—nt 18; family of, 618; in family life, 507, 509-510, 521-523, 524, 527; found artesian water on King Ranch, 503-504, 532; graded up Longhorns with Herefords and Shorthorns, 647-648; health broke, 592, 601, 609, 624-626, 789—nt 22; hired by Richard King, 339-340; imposed hunting regulations on ranch, 678; in law partnership, 438—nt 7, 478; led fight to control anthrax, 495; led fight to control Texas Fever, 490-495; marriage of, 479-481; met Alice G. King, 341; negotiated early oil exploration leases on ranch, 600; negotiated purchase of Laureles ranch, 533-534; organized Kleberg Town & Improvement Co., 545-546; planted Rhodes grass, 614, 743-744; planned for his children, 564, 574-575; planned new ranch house, 571-572; played large part in developing Corpus Christi as a port, 601-602; political activities of, 558-559, 620; portrait of, 519, 628; as president of Texas & Southwestern Cattle Raisers' Association, 619; quoted, 479, 481, 492; 504, 549; ranching methods of, 482-490; relationship with Mrs. King, 479, 513-514; schooling of, 477-478, 490; in settlement of Richard King's estate, 472-473; showed ranching aptitude, 360-361; stock breeding by, 730-731; supported rainmaking experiment, 502-503; talked out of selling ranch land by R. J. Kleberg, Jr., 595; wrote testimonial for water well drilling equipment, 504-505

KLEBERG, ROSALIE VON ROEDER [Mrs. Robert Justus I]: 508; death of, 510; early life in Texas, 476; at Santa Gertrudis, 509-510; *see also* von Roeder, Rosalie

KLEBERG, RUDOLPH: 476, 478, 509, 510

KLEBERG, SARAH SPOHN: birth of, 508, 524; childhood of, 560, 561-562; death of, 618; family life

of, 617-618, 626; marriage of, 618

KLEBERG, TILLIE: 801

Kleberg Bank: 547, 548

Kleberg bluestem grass: 674-675, 747, 748

Kleberg County: 600, 623; controversy over highway through, 643; effect upon King Ranch, 558-559; formation of, 558; map, vol. 2, viii-ix; politics in, 784—nt 91

Kleberg County Standard Dairy & Livestock Association: 619

Kleberg First National Bank: 689

Kleberg First National Bank Building: 688

Kleberg Town & Improvement Co.: 781-782—nt 41; organized, 545-546; promoted Kingsville, 547-548, 550-551; promoted Raymondville and Lyford, 552

KLEIBER, PAULINE J.: 338

KOCH, THEODORE F., JR.: quoted, 783—nt 73

KOCH, THEODORE F., SR.: promoted Riviera and other towns in area, 553-554

KOCH, THEODORE W.: 801

L

LK connected: 150-152; registration of, 403

LKV connected: 152; registration of, 403

La Alameda grant: map, 378-379

La Anima grant: map, 378-379

La Bahía del Espíritu Santo mission: 377

La Barreta grant: 124; awarded to Francisco Ballí, 380; John B. Armstrong owned property in, 538; map, 378-379

La Blanca grant: map, 378-379

La Bolsa, battle of: 166, 167-169

La Bóveda grant: 119, 332; land in bought by Koch, 553; map, 378-379

La Burrita: 48; map, 27

La Ebronal: 163-164

La Encantada grant: map, 378-379

La Feria grant: granted to José María Ballí, 380; map, 378-379

La Noria de Tío Ayala grant: map, 378-379

La Parra grant: 354, 527; map, 378-379

La Puerta ranch: 600

La República de la Sierra Madre: 82

La Rucia grant: map, 378-379

La Sal del Rey: Mrs. King owned interest in, 596; owned by Stillman, 453—nt 20; map, 378-379

La Tinaja de Lara grant: map, 378-379

La Trinidad grant: map, 378-379

La Vaca grant: map, 378-379

La Villa de Matamoros: *see* Matamoros, Mexico
La Villa de Santa Ana de Camargo: *see* Camargo, Mexico
LaFitte, Jean: 46, 49
Lafon, Ramón: 47-48, 429—nt 8
Lafon, Ramón, Jr.: 429—nt 8
Laguna Madre: 20, 103, 377, 380; map, 27, 78, 102
Lake Charles, Louisiana: 692
Lake Tampaquas: 91
Lama: 428—nt 37
Lamar, Mirabeau: 476
Lane, Ernest: 793—nt 16
Lappin, Richard: 754
Laredo, Texas: 170, 211, 212-213, 215, 335; first railroad to, 336-337; land promotion near, 783 —nt 75
Larkin, Henrietta A.: 618
Larkin, Henrietta Rosa Kleberg [Mrs. John A.]: 696; children of, 618; owned one-fifth of King Ranch corporation, 790—nt 25; *see also* Kleberg, Henrietta Rosa
Larkin, Ida L. [Mrs. James H. Clement]: *see also* Clement, Ida Larkin
Larkin, John Adrian: 574, 696; children of, 618
Larkin, John Adrian, Jr.: 618, 696
Larkin, Peter A.: 618
Las Animas, Texas: 215
Las Barrosas grant: map, 378-379
Las Comitas grant: map, 378-379; purchased by Mrs. King, 533
Las Cuevas: Texas Rangers raid, 283-291
Las Mesteñas Petitas y la Abra grant: Kenedy sold land in, 442—nt 78; map, 378-379
Lasater, Edward C.: 779—nt 49; R. J. Kleberg, Jr., purchased land from, 598; quoted, 649
Laurel: 38, 428—nt 37
Laurel Leaf brand: 257; returned to Kenedy Ranch, 534, 780—nt 4
Laureles Division: 380, 631, 635, 650, 679, 686, 687, 723, 795—nts 30, 33; Charlie Burwell foreman at, 638; game conservation and management on, 763; oil found on, 680; map, vol. 2, viii-ix; size of, 636
Lazarus, Sam: 655, 793—nt 15
Lazo, Carlos: 47-48
Leary, Tom: 504-505
Lee, Robert E.: 439—nt 17; advised Richard King, 144, 145; against Cortina, 167; left Rio Grande, 146, 439—nt 11; met Richard King, 142-143; in Mexican War, 142; quoted, 143, 144, 145, 167,

176; at Santa Gertrudis, 167, 439—nt 15; selected site for King's ranch house, 439—nt 19; visited the Kings', 143, 144; visited by the Kings, 323-324
Lehmann, V. W.: 679
Leo: 75
León, Fernando de: *see* de León, Fernando
León, Martín de: *see* de León, Martín
Lerdo de Tejada, Sebastián: *see* Tejada, Sebastián de
LeTourneau Manufacturing Co.: 711
Levy, John: 409
Lewis, Gideon K. "Legs": 120, 128, 150, 438—nt 30, 601; death of, 132-134; estate of, 135-137, 435—nt 15, 438—nt 1; met Richard King, 91, 99-100; partnership with King, 100-102, 103-105, 108-109, 110, 131-132, 333; in Texas Mounted Volunteers, 101; ranching activities, 116-124
Lindell Hotel [St. Louis, Missouri]: 345
Lipan Indians: 13, 95, 98, 106
Llano Grande grant: awarded to Juan José Hinojosa, 386; map, 378-379
Loma Alto Rancho: 303
Loma Blanca grant: map, 378-379
Lone Star Fair: *see* Texas State Fair
Longhorn cattle: 148-149, 297, 305, 306; did not produce choice meat, 299; graded up, 608, 648, 731
Longoria, Agipito: 270
López, Rafael: 212
Los Algodones: 183; *see also* Cotton trade during Civil War
Los Cerros de Santa Gertrudis: 377
Los Finados grant: map, 378-379
Los Jaboncillos grant: map, 378-379
Los Laureles grant: 124, 181; fenced by Kenedy, 254-255; map, 378-379; owned by Rey, 107; owned by Stillman, 444—nt 20, 533; purchased by Kenedy, 253-254; purchased by Mrs. King, 533-534; sold by Kenedy, 354
Los Olmos Creek: map, 102
Los Preseños de Abajo grant: map, 378-379
Los Preseños grant: 332; map, 378-379
Los Sauces grant: 332; map, 378-379
Los Toritos grant: map, 378-379
Lott, Ed: 313
Lott, Uriah: 481, 781—nt 22, 783—nt 46; activities in building St. Louis, Brownsville & Mexico Ry., 540-543; backed by Mifflin Kenedy, 529; built first railroad to Laredo, 336-337; collected Richard King's subscription to railroad, 464—nt 67;

quoted, 540-541; testified on cattle depredations, 458—nt 42; witnessed Richard King's will, 369
LOUGHRIDGE, COLONEL ——: 166
Luby [oil] Field: 680
LUCIO, SEVERO: 590
LUNDELL, DR. C. L.: 750-751
LUTHY, DON: 763
Lyford, Texas: 552-553, 781-782—nt 41, 783—nt 71
LYLE, JOHN E.: 623

M

M. Kenedy & Co.: 86, 91, 118, 120, 124, 125-126, 141-142, 152, 155, 173, 452—nt 10; Army had contracts with, 400-401; boat of attacked by Cortina, 167-169; boats under Mexican flag, 444—nts 28, 29; boats operated by Union army, 210, 214, 220-221; claims for damage by, 170-171; Confederate supply contract negotiated by, 197-201, 224, 404-407; office of burned, 208; operation of, 71-78, 80-82, 84, 87-89; organization of, 58-59, 430—nt 34; preparation of for Civil War, 171-172; reorganization of after Civil War, 242-245, 247-248; steamboat operation by during Civil War, 177-178, 179, 185-186, 196, 229, 443—nt 9; Francisco Ytúrria in, 452—nt 17
Mabry & Bulkley: 318
Mac [Th]: 742
Mac Bea [Th]: 742
McAllen, Texas: map, vol. 2, viii-ix
McBRIDE, BILLY: 638
McBRIDE, JIM: 638
McCAMPBELL, JOHN S.: 277; quoted, 277; testified on cattle depredations, 458—nt 45
McCLANE, JOHN: 280, 321; quoted, 316
McCRACKEN, ROBERT: 801
McCULLOUGH, BENJAMIN "Ben": 33, 176
McCURDY, REV. A. S.: 783—nt 64
McGILL, J. C.: appraiser for Mrs. King's estate, 606
McGUIRE, MRS. ——: 323
McKENZIE, D.: 316
McLEOD, HUGH: 98
McMILLAN, R. J.: 543
McMURRAY, BILL: 646
McNELLY, LEANDER H.: 316; appointed Texas Ranger, 278-280; Richard King erected monument to, 293; operations of against Mexican cattle thieves, 280-292; quoted, 281-282, 295, 460—nt 73

MADERO, FRANCISCO: 577-578
MAGRUDER, JOHN BANKHEAD: 194, 221, 224; ordered Confederates to withdraw from Rio Grande, 201; quoted, 198-199, 212
Major Brown: 426—nt 17; cost of, 427—nt 29
MALLETT, LEWIS: 122
MALONE, MICHAEL J. P.: 770
MALONEY, ——: 185
MALTBY, HENRY: 155; biographical data on, 440—nt 39
MALTBY, WILLIAM: established *Corpus Christi Free Press,* 464—nt 61
MALTSBERGER, JOHN T.: 792—nt 10; quoted on King Ranch trail drives, 462—nt 25
Man o' War [Th]: King Ranch used ancestry of in breeding Thoroughbreds, 664, 667, 729-730
Manatí Sugar Co.: 770
Manhattan Handicap: 742
MANN, ESTHER S.: 409
MANN, WILLIAM B.: 155, 181, 258; biographical data on, 440—nt 36; brands of, 444—nt 21
Marcador [Th]: 741
Market House [Brownsville, Texas]: 68
Market Level [Th]: 742
MARTIN, CAPTAIN ——: 168
MARTIN, FRANK: in Norias raid, 584-587
Martin Bank [Kansas City, Missouri]: 319
Mary Emma: 18
Masonic Lodge: 84; in Kingsville, 783—nt 66
Masda [Th]: King Ranch used ancestry of in breeding, 730
Massachusetts: 142
MATAMOROS, MARIANO: 48
Matamoros, Mexico: 22, 36, 38, 56, 155, 230, 288, 426—nt 12; *American Flag* published at, 18; captured by Constitutionalist forces, 580, 786—nt 5; captured by Díaz, 292; during Civil War, 181-182, 207, 209-210, 228, 448—nt 87; cotton trade at during Civil War, 184-187, 189-190, 191-192, 213, 232-233, 445—nt 38; early history of, 48-49, 429—nt 10, 430—nt 16; economic status, 237, 244; map, 11, 27, 78, 378-379, vol. 2, viii-ix; merchants of asked for loan by Mejía, 245; merchants of finance Ford's forces during Civil War, 220-221, 225, 450-451—nt 134; during Mexican War, 23, 27-28; occupied by U. S. troops, 9, 15; railroads bring trade to, 555-556; siege of, 85-86; as a smugglers' paradise, 440-441—nt 44; spelling of, 445—nt 36; Stillman arrived in, 52-53; stolen cat-

Matamoros, Mexico *(cont.)*:
tle sold at, 267-268, 269; General Taylor relieved
at, 39; toured by Union occupation officers, 239;
trade at, 49-52, 198, 200
Matamoros: 75, 171, 177, 185, 210, 229, 243
Matamoros II: 75
Matson Lines: 769
MAUD, HARRY: 770
MAXAN, NESTOR: death of, 337; law partnership of,
438—nt 7
MAXIMILIAN: 230, 236-238
MEAD, J. J.: investigated cattle stealing, 272,
273-275
Mechanics Bank [St. Louis, Missouri]: 313,
318-319, 344
Media luna: 265
MEJÍA, TOMÁS: 231-233, 238; denounced invasion
of Mexico, 31; final defeat and death of, 245
MENDIOLA, JUAN: 103-106, 333, 408
Menger Hotel [San Antonio, Texas]: 371; Richard
King at, 345, 346; King died at, 368, 369
Mentoria: 75; cost of, 427—nt 29
Mercedes, Texas: 556; map, vol. 2, viii-ix
MERRIMAN, ELI T.: published *Corpus Christi Free
Press*, 464—nt 61
Mesquite: elimination of on King Ranch, 499-501,
709-712, 743-752
Mexican land grants: 330, 417; map, 378-379; oil
discoveries cause re-examination of, 534-535; ti-
tles of confirmed, 100-101
Mexican National Ry.: 336
Mexican War: 91; Battle of Buena Vista, 17-18; be-
ginning of, 14, 425—nt 2; causes of, 12-14, 49;
character of Mexican soldiers in, 30-31; character
of U. S. soldiers in, 31; Cortina in, 158-159; H. L.
Kinney in, 96-97; Matamoros during, 27, 28;
Monterrey fell, 15; Scott's campaign, 38; steamboats used in, 9-10, 427—nts 29, 32; 427-428—nt
36; 428—nt 37; General Taylor arrived on Rio
Grande, 26; Taylor relieved of duty, 39; Texan
volunteers in, 32-33; treaty of peace, 39-40; U. S.
Army life during, 29-30, 34; U. S. politics during,
16; U. S. troops leave Rio Grande, 40
Mexico: brands in, 257-258; cattle smuggling to,
435-436—nt 22; claim against for cattle theft, 411-
412; control of siezed by Díaz, 292; depredations
on U. S. from, 117, 261-295, 456—nt 1, 456-457
—nt 5, 457—nt 24, 458—nts 33, 42; 459—nt 58;
under Díaz, 576-577, 579-580; early ranching in,
112-113, 115; effect of World War I on, 581;

government of investigated cattle depredations,
275; import duty policy of, 440-441—nt 44; land
grants of confirmed, 100-101; land grants made
in Texas by, 381; under Madero, 577-578; occupied by U. S. forces, 581; political upheaval in
1910-1913, 576-581; politics in, 80-89, 106; politics of during Civil War, 181-182, 184, 210-211,
230-233, 448—nt 87; post-Civil War politics in,
236-238, 245-247, 453—nt 19; racial cleavage
with U. S., 157-158, 579-591; railroads into, 780
—nt 11; settled Richard King's claim for depredations, 610-611; steamboats fly flag of during Civil
War, 75, 201, 444—nts 28, 29; trade with, 48-52,
55-56; U. S. Army against rustlers from, 269; U. S.
and Texas troops sent to border of, 580; U. S.
troops cross border in pursuit of raiders, 588, 590-
591; vaqueros of described, 436—nt 4
Mexico: 75, 177
Mexico City: 14, 16
Meyersville, Texas: 475, 478, 509
Middlebury College [Middlebury, Vermont]: 63
Middleground [Th]: 665-667, 729, 741
Mier, Mexico: 15, 21, 33, 39, 80, 90, 123; founding
of, 376; head of navigation on Rio Grande, 22;
history of, 24-25; map, 11, 26; occupied by U. S.
troops, 9
Mier Expedition: 25, 33, 131, 134
Mifflin, Texas: 783—nt 71
Miguel Gutiérrez Santa Gertrudis grant: 332; map,
378-379
MILLER, —— "Heaven Bent": 432—nt 56
MILLER, —— "Hell Bent": 432—nt 56
MILLER, HENRY: 68-70, 409, 432—nt 54
MILLER, JEFF N.: 543, 545, 547, 560, 569-570
MILLER, MRS. JEFF N.: 569-571, 801
MILLER, ROY: 782—nt 53; promoted King Ranch
area, 548, 553; quoted, 788—nt 42; worked for
port at Corpus Christi, 601
MILLER, WILLIAM: 801
Miller Hotel [Brownsville, Texas]: 68-70, 267, 409,
432—nt 54
Mineral Supplement Co.: 794—nt 28
MINTER, DR. MERTON: 801
Mirasoles grant: map, 378-379
Miss Princess [QH]: 793—nt 16; 794—nt 19
Mission, Texas: map, vol. 2, viii-ix
Missouri, University of: Richard King III attended,
568; tested Santa Gertrudis cattle, 791-792—nt 8
Missouri Pacific Railroad: 461—nt 12, 555; map, vol.
2, viii-ix

Pretat & Co.: 49

PRICE, JOHN T.: 33

Prickly pear: *see* cactus

PRIETO, PEDRO LÓPEZ: 429—nt 10

Princeton Theological Seminary: 63

Prophet's Thumb [Th]: 729-730, 741

PROUT, P. H.: 42

Puebla, Mexico: 18

Puenticitos grant: map, 378-379

Puerta de Agua Dulce: 173, 411; origin of name, 442—nt 80; granted to Raphael García, 408-409; owned by R. King & Co., 454-455—nt 40; *see also* Agua Dulce grant

Puerto del Refugio: *see* Matamoros, Mexico

Q

Quanah, Texas: 540

Quarter Horse breed: auction of on King Ranch, 792-793—nt 1, 794—nt 18; bought by King Ranch, 793—nt 15; breeding history of on King Ranch, 732-734; breeding techniques of on King Ranch, 726-728; breeding up of with Thoroughbreds, 660-661; King Ranch created strain, 656; R. J. Kleberg, Jr., on, 734-735; picture of, 658; qualifications of, 656-657, 734; raced by R. J. Kleberg, Jr., 793—nt 16; show winnings of, 735-739; training methods of on King Ranch, 657-659

Queensland Primary Producers' Co-operative Association Ltd.: quoted, 769

Querétaro, Mexico: 40, 376

QUINTANILLA, AUGUSTÍN: 483, 567

QUITMAN, JOHN A.: quoted, 30

R

R. King & Co.: 179, 242, 243, 266, 333-334; cattle losses by theft, 295; cattle sales by, 297, 456—nt 54; during Civil War, 179-181; dissolution of, 252-257, 408-410, 452—nt 10; name of used by heirs of Richard King II, 632; organization of, 173, 442—nt 80; property owned by, 454-455—nt 40

RAGLAND, JOHN B.: 548

RAGLAND, SAMUEL G.: 513-514, 516, 522, 570, 593, 638, 710; on cattle drive, 489; effect on R. J. Kleberg, Jr., 562, 563-564; employed by King Ranch, 488-489; R. J. Kleberg, Jr., on, 489; met Caesar Kleberg, 510-511; quoted, 564; as ranching manager, 565-566; as trustee of Mrs. King's estate, 605

Ragland's: 689

Railroads in South Texas: backed by Richard King, 464—nt 67; Baffins Bay & Western Ry., 554; Brazos Santiago-White Ranch military road, 226, 230; citizens support of, 781—nts 16, 23; coming of opposed by King and Kenedy, 248-251; competition of with steamboats, 248-249; Corpus Christi & Rio Grande Railroad, 537; Corpus Christi, San Diego & Rio Grande Narrow Gauge Railroad Co., 336-337; Corpus Christi & South American Ry., 537; early development of, 335-337; first to Laredo, 336-337, 464-465—nt 69; Gulf Coast Line, 555; Gulf, Colorado & Santa Fe, 781—nt 22; Indianola Railroad, 453—nt 27, 555; International Railroad Co., 335-336, 461—nt 12; R. J. Kleberg, Sr.'s activities in promotions of, 539-545; led to economic development, 555-556; map, vol. 2, viii-ix; Missouri Pacific, 461—nt 12; New York, Texas & Mexican Ry. Co., 780—nt 11; Pan-American Ry., 537, 780—nt 14; refrigeration on in 1873, 335; regulated cattle shipments for control of Texas Fever, 352, 465—nt 21; Rio Grande Railroad Co., 250-251, 453—nt 28; Rock Island Lines, 781—nt 22; St. Louis, Brownsville & Mexico Ry., 539-546, 555, 781—nt 32; St. Louis & San Francisco, 781—nt 22; San Antonio & Aransas Pass Ry., 529, 536, 778—nt 18; Southern Pacific, 529; Texas Mexican Ry., 336-337, 536, 781—nt 23

RAMOS, BASILIO [*alias* B. R. García]: 582-583

Ranchero: 75, 76, 170; attacked by Cortina, 167-169; cost of, 59; R. E. Lee on, 142, 146

Rancho Davis: *see* Davis Landing

Rancho Las Rucias: 225-226

Rancho Puerta de Agua Dulce: given to Richard King II, 358

Rancho Ramireño: 204-205

Rancho Santa Gertrudis: *see* King Ranch

Rancho Real de Santa Petronila: 124, 377, 380; founded by Blas María Falcón, 441—nt 47

Rancho Santa Cruz: 411, 417

Rancho Viejo: 125

Randado: 80, 437—nt 8; map, vol. 2, viii-ix

RANDLETT, JAMES F.: 286-287

RANKIN, JOHN: 334

RANSOM, HENRY: 586-587

RAWLINSON, WILLIE: 347

RAYMOND, E. B.: 482, 559, 778—nt 15, 779—nt 41

Raymond Town & Improvement Co.: 778—nt 15

Raymondville, Texas: 546, 552-553, 557, 559, 643, 644, 781-782—nt 41, 783—nt 71; land promotion in vicinity of, 783—nt 72; map, vol 2, viii-ix; establishment of, 778—nt 15

Reconstruction: amnesty conditions during, 240; cattle prices during, 259; Confederate soldiers joined Mexican cause, 236-238; economic conditions in South Texas during, 237, 244-245, 250-251, 259; Mexican politics during, 236-238, 245-247; occupation of Brownsville, 238, 239; Sheridan as U. S. troop commander during, 237-238, 248-249

REED, JAMES: 313

REED, LOUIS P.: 794—nt 18

Rejected [Th]: 667, 740

Remembrance [Th]: 661

Renew [Th]: 741

RENTFRO, ROBERT B.: as a lawyer, 438—nt 7

Resaca de la Palma, battle of: 9, 14, 27, 158, 425—nt 3

REUSS, AUGUST: 409

Review of Reviews, The American Monthly: 553; quoted, 783—nt 75

REY, EUGÉNIA: 108

REY, JOSÉ PÉREZ: 108; bought Santa Gertrudis land grant, 107; established Rincón de los Laureles, 380

REYNAL, BILL: 794—nt 18

REYNOLDS, MRS. RICHARD W.: 784—nt 99

Reynosa, Mexico: 22, 85-86, 115, 380, 426—nt 14, 555; founding of, 23, 376; map, 11, 26, 378-379, vol. 2, viii-ix; taken by Constitutionalist forces, 580

RHOAD, ALBERT O.: 690, 700-701, 801

RHODES, CECIL: 744

Rhodes grass: 748; attacked by scale, 674, 745-746; cultivated on ranch, 614, 674, 743-745

Rhodes grass scale: 674, 745-746

Rhyne Bros.: 188-189

Ricardo [Richard], Texas: 554, 781-782—nt 41, 783 —nt 71; map, vol. 2, viii-ix

RICHARDSON, JAMES: 117-118, 120, 125, 128, 216, 218-219, 223, 266, 458-459—nt 48

RICHEY, JOHN A.: death of, 425—nt 7

RIHERD, DR. PAUL T.: 746

Rincón de Corpus Christi grant: awarded to Ramón de Hinojosa, 380; map, 378-379; purchased by Mrs. King, 534

Rincón de Santa Gertrudis grant: 173, 303, 330, 332, 408, 411; bought by King and Lewis, 103-105; King purchased, 135-137, 333-334, 653-655; in litigation, 464—nt 59; map, 102, 378-379; owned by R. King & Co., 454-455—nt 40; survey of, 435 —nt 19; title of quoted, 103-104

Rincón del Grullo grant: 332; map, 378-379

Rincón del Oso grant: map, 378-379

Ringgold Barracks: 78, 87-88, 195, 283-284, 288, 431—nt 41; Ford's headquarters at, 225; R. E. Lee at, 142, 146; Union troops evacuated, 177

Ringling Brothers Circus: 657

Rio Grande: 9-10, 13, 33-34, 100, 109; became U. S. boundary, 39-40; cattle depredations across, 261-295; crookedness of, 426—nt 13; defense of abandoned by Confederates, 193; development along, 780—nt 10; economic conditions along, 44-45, 49-55; R. E. Lee on, 142-146; map, 11, 26-27, 378-379, vol. 2, viii-ix; Mexicans raid across, 581-591; navigation of, 19-26, 426—nts 12, 17; post-Civil War economic conditions along, 237, 244-245, 250-251; railroad to, 543; General Scott at, 16; shipping attacked on, 167-169; Spanish colonization along, 376-381; steamboating on during Civil War, 177-178, 185-186, 210, 220-221, 229 (*see also* Steamboating on the Rio Grande); strife and violence along, 157-171, 580-581, 587; General Taylor arrived at, 26-27; Taylor crossed, 15; as Texas boundary, 14; Texas Rangers crossed after cattle thieves, 283-291; trade on, 18-19, 46-48, 156-157; trade diverted from, 170; U. S. troops crossed in pursuit of Mexican raiders, 588, 590-591

Rio Grande, Republic of the: 25, 426—nt 14

Rio Grande City, Texas: 37, 40, 84, 168, 170, 196, 211-212, 214, 288-289, 780—nt 10; Ford's headquarters at, 225; founding of, 25; looted by Cortina, 164-165; map, 26, 78, 104, vol. 2, viii-ix; raided, 117

Rio Grande Female Institute [Brownsville]: 126, 437—nt 22

Rio Grande Railroad Co.: 250-251, 453—nt 28

Risdon Stud [Australia]: 693, 769

RISTER, CARL COKE: 800; quoted, 163, 439—nt 17

Riviera, Texas: 557, 643, 783—nt 71; beginning of, 553; development of, 554; map, vol. 2, viii-ix

Riviera Beach, Texas: 554; map, vol. 2, viii-ix

Riverina [Th]: 667, 741

ROBB, THOMAS P.: 272; investigated cattle stealing, 273-275

ROBERTS, ORAN M.: quoted on Ford, 443—nt 5, 446—nt 51

ROBINSON, W. S.: 769

ROBLES, LUIS: 482

Robstown, Texas: 544, 547, 552, 623, 783—nt 71; map, vol. 2, viii-ix

Rock Island Lines: 781—nt 22

ROCKEFELLER, WINTHROP: 792-793—nt 11

Rocket Gun [Th]: 667

ROGERS, WILL: quoted, 625-626; visited King Ranch, 624-626

Roma, Texas: 78, 141, 212; map, 26; promotion of, 42-43; raided, 117

ROOSEVELT, FRANKLIN DELANO: 623

ROPES, E. H.: 537

Ross, DR. J. CLUNIES: 751

Rough and Ready: cost of, 427—nt 29

ROUSE, HOWARD: 667

ROWE, E. D.: 456—nt 54

ROWE, JAMES: 801

RUDD, W. L.: 290-291

Rudolph, Texas: 783—nt 71

RUIZ, MANUEL: 203, 209-210, 222

RUNNELS, HARDIN RICHARD: 163, 164-165

Running Stream [Th]: 729

Running W.: 152, 455—nt 50, 455-456—nt 52, 771; nationally known, 363-364; origin of, 257-258, 444—nt 21; registration of, 257, 403

RUSK, J. M.: 495; R. J. Kleberg, Sr., discussed Texas Fever with, 492

RUSK, THOMAS J.: 107, 139, 141

RUSSELL, CHARLES: 201, 404-407; quoted, 199

RUSSELL, JOHN C.: 418

S

Sacahuiste grass: 501, 748

SACK, CAROLINE LOUISE: 478

SACK, PHILIPP WILHELM: 477-478

SACK, SIMON HEINRICH: 447-448

Safe Arrival [Th]: 741

Saltillo, Mexico: 42, 52, 55; map, 11

Saltillo Jr [QH]: 773

Salvo [Th]: 742

Sam Fordyce, Texas: map, vol. 2, viii-ix

St. Louis, Missouri: 319; as cattle shipping point, 306; Richard King at, 298

St. Louis, Brownsville & Mexico Ry.: 548, 551; construction of, 539-546, 547; construction costs of, 781—nt 32; map, vol. 2, viii-ix; pass on in facsimile, 545; schedule of, 545; stockholders and board of directors, 541; taken over by Frisco, 555

St. Louis & San Francisco Ry.: 781—nt 22

St. Mary's Church [Brownsville]: 434—nt 29

San Agustín de Agua Dulce grant: awarded to Benito López de Jaen, 380

San Antonio, Texas: 148, 193, 212, 215, 219, 221, 223, 335, 478, 778—nt 26; Civil War cotton scandal at, 189; map, 11; politics in, 620, 623; surrender of Union troops at, 176

San Antonio de Agua Dulce grant: 332; map, 378-379

San Antonio del Alamo grant: map, 378-379

San Antonio del Encinal grant: map, 378-379

San Antonio Academy: attended by Richard King III, 568

San Antonio & Aransas Pass Ry.: 536, 778—nt 18; bought by Southern Pacific system, 538; Mifflin Kenedy backed, 529

San Antonio Express: quoted, 241-242

San Antonio Herald: quoted, 132-133, 134

San Antonio Loan & Trust Co.: 598, 637

San Antonio National Bank: 637

San Antonio River: 376, 377

San Antonio Viejo Ranch: 573-574, 635-636; map, vol. 2, viii-ix; Mrs. King acquired, 596; King Ranch received title to, 632; oil found on, 680; raided by Mexicans, 588-589

San Benito, Texas: 783—nt 71; map, vol. 2, viii-ix

San Diego, Texas: 336, map, vol. 2, viii-ix; rainmaking experiment at, 502-503

San Diego de Abajo grant: map, 378-379

San Diego de Arriba grant: map, 378-379

San Fernando Creek: 103, 273, 408; map, 102

San Fernando grant: map, 378-379

San Francisco grant: map, 378-379

San Jacinto, battle of: 12-13; Robert J. Kleberg I in, 475

San Juan, Texas: map, vol. 2, viii-ix

San Juan: 75, 458—nt 33

San Juan de los Esteros grant (*see also* Matamoros, Mexico): purchased by Lorenzo de la Garza, 429 —nt 10

San Juan de los Lagos, Mexico: 55

San Juan River: 24, 25; map, 26

Starr County: 104, 376, 600; map, vol. 2, viii-ix

STAYTON, JOHN W.: 498; R. J. Kleberg, Sr., read law under, 477

STAYTON, ROBERT W.: 801; was law partner of R. J. Kleberg, Sr., 438—nt 7, 498-499

Stayton & Kleberg: 471, 498-499

Steamboating on the Rio Grande: 35-38, 72-73, 74-78, 80, 115-116, 141-142; boat specifications, 57-60; boats idle during First Cortina War, 170; Charles Stillman in, 52-54; cited as monopoly, 156; cost of boats, 59-60, 427—nt 29; difficulties of, 54, 427—nt 32, 428—nt 37; during Civil War, 75, 177-178, 185-186, 210, 220-221, 229, 443—nts 9, 10; 444—nts 28, 29; during Mexican War, 9-10, 427-428—nt 36, 428—nt 37; early attempts at, 426—nt 12; economic reverses in, 250-251, 452-453—nt 18, 454—nt 39; end of, 251-252; freight rates, 87-88, 433-434—nt 25, 454—nt 37; M. Kenedy & Co. plans for, 57-58; post-Civil War reorganization, 242-245, 247-248; profits from, 75-76; railroad competition to, 248-250; record runs in, 36-37; Richard King into, 52; ships at Bagdad during Civil War, 445—nt 44; wages in, 19; war surplus boats sold, 41, 43-45

STEELE, FREDERICK: occupied Brownsville, 239-240, 241; quoted, 240

STERLING, W. W.: 801

STEVENS, J. C.: 484

STEVENS, JAMES H.: as Richard King's livestock agent, 308, 312-320; quoted, 313, 315, 317, 318-319

STEVENS, WESLEY: 467—nt 52; quoted, 485, 487

STEWART, MRS. ANDREW: 801

STEWART, PLUNKET: 767

STEWART, WILLIAM: 428—nt 37

STILES, HARVEY C.: 539

STILLMAN, CHARLES: 37, 159; backed Carvajal revolution, 86-87; bought steamboats, 45; built house in Brownsville, 68; during Civil War, 179, 185-187, 224-225, 450—nt 130; in cotton trade, 199-201, 224-225, 404-407; early ranching, 124, 437—nt 19; employed Ytúrria, 429—nt 11; escaped capture by Mexicans, 53; interests of in South Texas, 453—nt 20; left border, 247; marriage of, 432—nt 55; to Matamoros, 53; moved from Matamoros, 28; owned Laureles ranch, 444—nt 20; portrait of, 246; promoted Brownsville, 52, 430—nt 16; promoted railroad, 453—nt 28; into steam-

boat business, 53-54, 56-58, 72-77; withdrew from M. Kenedy & Co., 242-243; quoted, 185-186, 187

STILLMAN, CORNELIUS: 598; sold Laureles ranch, 253-254

STILLMAN, FRANCIS: 53

STILLMAN, JAMES: backed South Texas railroads, 781—nt 16

Stillman, Texas: 781-782—nt 41, 783—nt 71; see also Sebastian, Texas

Stillman & Belden: 55

Stillman Building [Brownsville]: 72, 76

Stock Raisers' Association of Western Texas: 268-269, 277; supplied funds to Texas Rangers, 282

STONEMAN, GEORGE: against Cortina, 165, 169

Stratton [oil] Field: 680

STUBBLEFIELD, MRS. LENNIE E.: 413, 799

Stymie [Th]: sold by King Ranch, 665; winnings of, 665, 740

Suburban Handicap: 742

Sufie [Th]: 742

Sun Lady [Th]: 742

Sunset Gun [Th]: 662

Superman [Th]: 729

Swan: 74, 75

Swenson, Perkins & Co.: 313, 315, 317, 326

Swift Australian Co. Pty. Ltd.: 768

Swift & Co.: 692

Sysonby Stakes: 742

T

T Anchor Ranch: 778—nt 26

TAFT, WILLIAM HOWARD: sent troops to Mexican border, 580; visited Mrs. King, 567-568

TALBOT, A. W.: 769

TALLEY, GEORGE: went to work for Richard King, 294, 460—nt 71

Tamaulipas, State of: 13, 157-158, 220, 230, 376, 580

Tamaulipas: 75, 244

Tamaulipas II: 75

TAMBREÑO, AUGUST: 457—nt 20

Tampico, Mexico: 46, 376

TANKERSLEY, GARVIN: 792-793—nt 11

TANKERSLEY, MRS. GARVIN: 792-793—nt 11

Tasajillo [Th]: 742

TASH, LOWELL H.: experimented on phosphorus deficiency in cattle, 755-756; manager of Cuban operation, 770-771

Task [Th]: 741
TATE, TOM: 583, 586, 639
TATE, MRS. TOM: 795—nt 33
TAYLOR, A. THOMAS: 772
TAYLOR, JOE: in Norias raid, 584-587
TAYLOR, ZACHARY: 91, 93, 97, 139, 158; arrival of at Rio Grande, 26-27, 31, 425—nt 2; defeated Santa Anna, 17-18; established Fort Brown, 28, 426—nt 16; left Mexico, 39; in Mexican War, 9, 425—nts 2, 3; to Nueces River, 14; quoted, 425—nt 3; route to Rio Grande, 434—nt 2; in Seminole War, 15-16; to Texas, 12; took Monterrey, 15, 18; troops of depleted, 16; as war hero, 15-16; war mission of, 15
TEJADA, SEBASTIÁN LERDO DE: 276, 292
Telegraph: cost of, 427—nt 29
TELFENER, COUNT JOSEPH: 537, 780—nt 11
Templeton, Brooks, Napier & Ogden [of San Antonio]: 533
Texas, State of: ceded by Mexico, 39-40; Civil War in, 175-235; 443—nts 5, 7, 8, 9, 10, 12; 444—nts 24, 25, 28, 29, 31; 445—nts 38, 39, 44; 445-446—nt 46; 446—nts 47, 51; 447—nts 61, 64, 67; 448—nts 75, 82; 449—nt 101; 450—nts 113, 115; 450-451—nt 134; 451—nts 141, 147; colonization of by Spain, 376-381; confirmation of Spanish land grants by Texas legislature, 100-101, 381; secession from Union by, 176, 179, 443—nt 1; see also Cattle Industry in South Texas and Railroads in South Texas
——, early ranching in: 106-108, 113-114, 124-125, 150-154, 437—nt 19; "The Big Drift," 222-223, 261-262, 450—nt 121; brands, 150-152, 173, 257-258; cattle markets and prices, 152-153, 462—nt 26; cattle theft, 261-295, 411-412, 456—nt 1, 456-457—nt 5, 457—nt 24, 458—nt 33, 459—nt 58; during Civil War, 179-180; cost of fencing, 267, 455—nt 47; first brand recording, 436—nt 5; first fencing by King and Kenedy, 254-255, 302-303, 455—nt 47; hide-peeling, 265, 457—nt 16; hide and tallow business, 153, 258-259, 304, 440—nt 31, 462—nt 27; meat curing experiment by Richard King, 153-154; picture of early cowboy, 151; post-Civil War economics in, 258-260; Tick Fever, 352, 465—nt 20; type of stock, 152
——, Reconstruction government in: 236-242, 269-271; Texas Rangers disbanded by, 262; voted out, 278
Texas, General Land Office of: 376, 381

Texas, Republic of: 13-14, 109, 475-476; cattle stealing in, 435-436—nt 22; flag of used in Civil War, 443—nt 8; land certificates of, 331
Texas, University of: 750, 784—nt 99; R. M. Kleberg, Sr., at, 564-565
Texas A. & M. College: 676, 746, 750
Texas College of Arts & Industries: 746-747, 750
Texas Democrat: established by Ford, 429-430—nt 12
Texas Fever: 352, 465—nt 20, 778—nt 26; early treatment of, 778—nt 26; fight to control, 490-495; South Texas declared free of, 613
Texas Game and Fish Commission: 679, 765
Texas grama grass: 748
Texas Land & Cattle Co., Ltd.: 354; sold Laureles ranch to Mrs. King, 533-534; 779, ch XV, nt 1; 779-780, ch XV nt 3
Texas Livestock Sanitary Commission: R. J. Kleberg, Sr., first head of, 494
Texas-Mexican Industrial Institute: 552
Texas Mexican Ry.: 336-337, 536, 781—nt 23; map, vol. 2, viii-ix
Texas Mounted Volunteers: Ford in, 429-430—nt 12; G. K. Lewis in, 101
Texas Rangers: 91, 117; against cattle thieves, 280-292, 294; against Cortina, 163-169; Charlie Burwell in, 638; Sam Chesshire in, 639; cooperated with King Ranch, 294; disbanded by Reconstruction government, 262; Ford commissioned in, 164-165; R. M. Kleberg, Sr., member of, 592, 787—nt 24; during Norias raid, 583; raided Las Cuevas, 283-291; re-established, 278-280; reorganized, 787—nt 27; returned stolen King Ranch cattle, 290-291; in service at Sauz Ranch, 645-646; Tom Tate in, 639; during World War I, 583, 593-594
Texas Research Foundation: King Ranch works with, 750-751
Texas and Southwestern Cattle Raisers' Association: R. J. Kleberg, Sr., and R. M. Kleberg, Sr., presidents of, 619; R. M. Kleberg, Sr.'s activities in, 789—nt 21; publication of quoted, 791—nt 5
Texas State Fair: 90-92, 98-99; King Ranch exhibited at, 796—nt 40
Texas State Police: 269-271; abolished, 278
Texas Stockman & Farmer: quoted, 549
THARP, BENJAMIN C.: 750
Theodore F. Koch Land Co.: 554
THOMAS, WILLIAM D.: quoted, 262, 269
THOMPKINS, COLONEL ——: 44

Virginia: 18
VON PAPEN, FRANZ: 592
VON ROEDER, ANTON SIGISMUND: 478
VON ROEDER, ROSALIE: ancestry, 477-478; came to
  Texas, 474-475; marriage, 475
VOTAW, MRS. K. A.: 801

W

Waco, Texas: 312
WAELDER, JACOB: witnessed Richard King's
  will, 369
WALKER, SAM: 33, 85
WALLACE, LEW: 234-235, 451—nt 3
WALLACE, WILLIAM A. "Big Foot": 33
WALWORTH, JAMES: 150, 438—nt 4, 452—nt 10;
  brand of registered, 403; during Civil War, 443—
  nt 12; death of, 243, 443—nt 12; estate of, 409;
  invested in ranch with Richard King, 138-139,
  333, 403; in Mexican trade venture with Kenedy,
  55-56, 138; partnership with King and Kenedy,
  173; Secession Convention delegate, 173, 179;
  witnessed Army contract with R. King, 400-401
WALWORTH, JANE M. [Mrs. James]: 243, 333,
  452—nt 10
War Admiral [Th]: 794—nt 22
WARD, HORTENSE WARNER: 801
WARREN, FRED: surveyed Kingsville, 547; surveyed
  Raymondville and Lyford, 552
Warren: 427-428—nt 36
WATSON, O. S.: 782—nt 49
WEBB, WALTER PRESCOTT: 799; quoted, 456—nt 3
Weekly Ranchero [Brownsville]: 464—nt 62
WELDER, JOHN J.: backed South Texas railroad, 541
WELLS, JAMES B.: 351, 464—nt 59, 478, 689, 779—
  nt 41; advised King Ranch against selling land,
  595; as attorney for railroad, 543, 554; backed
  South Texas railroad, 541; brought R. J. Kle-
  berg, Sr., and Ragland together, 488-489; death
  of, 602; handled land litigation for King Ranch,
  535; hired by Richard King, 338-339; honored by
  Texas bar association, 788—nt 45; negotiated for
  purchase of Laureles ranch, 533; in partnership
  with Stephen Powers, 337-338, 438—nt 7; played
  major rôle in growth of King Ranch, 498-499; prepared Mrs. King's will, 596; purchased land for
  Richard King, 338, 366; purchased and sold land
  for King Ranch, 496-499; in settlement of Richard
  King's estate, 472; trustee of Mrs. King's estate,
  605-606; as South Texas political boss, 557, 559,
  784—nts 86, 91

WELLS, JOSEPH K.: 453—nt 20, 557; law partnership
  of, 438—nt 7; represented King Ranch, 637
WELLS, MRS. JOSEPH K.: 801
WELLS, ROBERT C.: 376, 689, 779—nt 41, 800;
  quoted, 442—nt 80, 690
WELTON, ELLA KING: 470, 526, 568, 604, 631; *see
  also* King, Ella Morse
WELTON, HENRIETTA MARY: 568
WELTON, LOUIS M.: married Ella King, 343
Wendy [Th]: 661
WERBISKI, ALEXANDER: testimony of on Mexican
  cattle depredations, 456-457—nt 5
Weslaco, Texas: 746; map, vol. 2, viii-ix
WEST, DUVAL: 543
West & Chenery: 248-249
West Stratton [oil] Field: 680
WHALEY, DR. W. GORDON: 750
Wharton, Texas: 477, 780—nt 11
Whirlaway [Th]: 794—nts 21, 22
Whirlpool: 653
White & Gardner: 122
White Ranch: 58, 72, 78, 143, 248-249; railroad
  built to, 226
Whiteville: 43-44, 54, 60-61, 67, 430—nt 22; cost of,
  427—nt 29; General Taylor on, 427—nt 30
WHITNEY, JOHN HAY "Jock": 664
Wichita, Kansas: 318
Wild Horse Desert: 12-13, 14, 22, 92, 95, 276;
  described by Grant, 434—nt 2; map, 11
Wildlife on King Ranch: 678, 761-765; in 1874, 302;
  poachers on, 643-646; *see also* Game conservation
  and management
WILKINSON, L. F. "Red": 683
WILKINSON, WILLIAM: 42
WILLACY, JOHN G.: 557
Willacy County: 380, 431-432—nt 53, 600, 645;
  formation of, 557; map, vol. 2, viii-ix
Willamar [oil] Field: 680
WILLETT, JOHN: 131, 435—nt 15
William K. Holt Machinery Co.: 711, 794—nt 25
William R. McKee: 43
WILLIAMS, EZEKIEL: brand of, 436—nt 5
WILSON, MRS. RUTH: 801
WILSON, WOODROW: 581, 588
Wimpy [QH]: awarded first studbook registration,
  734, 735; picture of, 658
Winchester Quarantines: 490-491
Wisconsin, University of: R. J. Kleberg, Jr.,
  attended, 575, 589, 592

THIS BOOK

was designed, printed and bound in Texas
by the photo-offset process; plates and
presswork by Guynes Printing Company.

The type for the text is 16 point *Centaur*
Roman with *Arrighi* Italic, composed on
the Monotype and reworked by hand;
chapter titles and initials handset in larger
sizes of the same types. Appendices and
Notes are in *Caledonia,* composed on the
Linotype. Bold titles are in *Hadriano.*
Typography by Carl Hertzog of El Paso,
chapter titles designed by the author.

Binding by Universal of San Antonio.

EL PASO
TEXAS